Dr John Lattimer

D1552360

Kennedy and Lincoln

KENNEDY

AND

LINCOLN

Medical and Ballistic Comparisons of Their Assassinations

BY JOHN K. LATTIMER

M.D., Sc.D., F.A.C.S.

 HARCOURT BRACE JOVANOVICH

NEW YORK AND LONDON

Library of Congress Cataloging in Publication Data

Lattimer, John K.
  Kennedy and Lincoln.

  Includes index.
  1. Kennedy, John Fitzgerald, Pres. U.S., 1917-1963
—Assassination. 2. Lincoln, Abraham, Pres. U.S.,
1809-1865—Assassination.   I. Title.
E842.9.L35   364.1′524′0922   80-7936
ISBN 0-15-152281-2

DESIGNED BY PHILIP GRUSHKIN

Printed in the United States of America

First edition

B C D E

DEDICATION

This book is dedicated to my family: my illustrator wife, Jamie; my daughter, Evan; my sons, Jon and Gary, one now a surgeon and the other a pathologist; and my late father and mother, who have borne up under hundreds of deafening rifle reports during vacations, have tripped over piles of Carcano carbines, and have seen their household dust bins spirited away to become bullet traps.

They have eaten the institutional chicken of the National Press Club and the Dutch Treat Club and have attended a hundred meetings of Civil War and Lincoln groups from Boston to Los Angeles, uncomplainingly. They have gingerly eaten bullet-riddled fresh ham, commenting only occasionally about the bullet fragments they encountered in their dinners.

My mother was delighted to see me shift from working on tuberculosis of the kidney, as it melted away under new medications (Thank God for streptomycin, she would say). She looked askance at the stacks of slides of cancer viruses. But she was surprisingly tolerant of our enthusiastic gatherings around each Kennedy or Lincoln simulation, where we discussed the outcome of our latest experiments. Her big complaint about the assassination experiments was that we never finished them. There was always some new question to investigate. Indeed, this has been an impressive characteristic of this project: people cannot resist the idea of a conspiracy; they always have one more question that must be examined.

CONTENTS

LINCOLN

KENNEDY

ACKNOWLEDGMENTS

The Lincoln chapters reflect the help and the eye for detail of a dozen experts on the assassination and on the activities of Booth and his fellow conspirators. Dr. Richard Sloan, who is the voice of the New York Lincoln enthusiasts through his publication, *The Lincoln Log,* was the gadfly and synthesizer who provoked a new burst of activity on Lincoln.

Arthur Loux provided me with accurate details and dates of Booth's theatrical activities.

The dedicated Lincoln scholars of the Washington and Maryland areas James O. Hall and John Brennan checked this manuscript for accuracy at every turn; along with young Mike Kauffman, they have researched this subject in depth without a moment's hesitation. I am grateful for their help. They made me prove every item that I mentioned. This book would be twice as long, but only half as accurate, if all my thoughts about Lincoln had not been subjected to their scrutiny.

The Surratt Society members, headed now by their president, Mrs. Joan Chaconas, worked with dedicated zeal and with expert knowledge of how to penetrate the bastions of neglected and almost unopened government vaults to bring forth treasures for reference and exhibition. Involved in restoring the Surratt Tavern and conducting tours of Dr. Samuel Mudd's house, group members create such enthusiasm in their listeners that one cannot spend ten minutes with them without wanting to pitch in with whatever one can contribute. Their Booth's-escape-route tours are most intriguing, with a wealth of material about this episode in our history. If it had not been for their chemistry, I would never have gathered the steam to do this book.

My secretary, Edna Di Paolo, and her assistants, Dorsey Gorst, Maria Alameda, Jo-Ann Perez, Lilly Ortiz, and Dominick De Curtis have put up with the months of clutter and off-and-on distractions that writing a book produces and have steered the work to completion in an easy and relaxed way. Without Edna it could not have been done.

Our medical artists and photographers, Harriet Phillips, Robert Demarest, Eric Grave, Alfred Lamme, the Morris Camera Shop, and, particularly, medical student Michael Macfarlane, produced the excellent illustrations. Our expert pathologist, Dr. Myron Tannenbaum, stepped in repeatedly to solve technical problems.

I had available to me the advice and help of top specialists at the Columbia-Presbyterian Medical Center: neurologist H. Houston Merritt, neurosurgeon Edward Schlesinger, orthopedists Frank Stinchfield and Keith McElroy, roentgenologists William Seaman, Gerhardt Schwartz, Joshua Becker, David Follett, David Habif, Jr., Kent Ellis, and their staffs. Anatomist Edward Dempsey, pathologists Donald King and Myron Tannenbaum, and Drs. James J. Humes and J. Thornton Boswell helped me whenever I needed it.

I was able to confer frequently with the mentor who interested me in forensic pathology in the first place, Dr. Milton Helpern. I had the advice and assistance of navy photographer John H. Stringer, navy artist H. A. Rydberg, Civil War arms experts John Rountree and Val Forgett, and the members of the New Jersey Arms Collectors Association, as well as the advice and counsel of the Grand Master of the Meat Department at the Fort Lee A & P. National Archives expert Marion Johnson, National Park Service expert Harold Peterson, and Aberdeen Proving Grounds expert Dr. Alfred J. Olivier provided me with superior technical advice. Dr. Paul Peters and Dr. John Denman showed me Dallas.

Authors Priscilla Johnson McMillan and Joan Blair have been generous in trading information, as have biographers David Keiser and Charles Hamilton, and illustrator Lloyd Ostendorf.

Without all of these people this book would never have been initiated.

INTRODUCTION

In World War II, I was a military surgeon in the European Theater. My patients were the soldiers of Generals Ridgway, Taylor, Patton, and Patch. The bullets with which the Germans and Italians were wounding and killing my men were the very type of heavy bullet with which President Kennedy and Governor Connally were shot. I was thoroughly familiar with the type of wounds they caused. Those bullets were different from today's smaller, higher-velocity military missiles.

I was quite startled, therefore, when the Warren Commission report came out showing the only illustration of the head wound of President Kennedy to be one that was not nearly severe enough to match my expectations of the great damage such a bullet would cause and what it should have done to the President's skull. In addition, the path of the neck bullet through the President was depicted as practically parallel to the ground, whereas Oswald had been high above the President. There were other discrepancies that caught my eye. It was obvious to me that something was wrong. Even the ballistic experiments done at the Aberdeen Proving Grounds did not quite match the President's wounds. This seemed to me to be very odd.

Maybe the assassination buffs and raucous critics were right. Maybe there was something peculiar going on. I thought someone ought to repeat those experiments, someone with access to laboratory facilities, X-ray facilities, firing-range facilities, the correct firearms and ammunition and appropriate anatomical test materials, plus plenty of help. It slowly dawned on me that *I* had all those facilities, and a couple of interested young sons to help.

Long ago, I had done wounding experiments during my tour of duty in the army, so I was familiar with the techniques. I was also familiar with the routes of access to the National Archives vaults, thanks to an earlier interest in the Lincoln assassination, but that is another story.

I am often asked way I, a urologist, was the first "outsider" to be permitted access to the restricted Kennedy autopsy materials and why I was interested in ballistics at all. Even in the war, it is true that my surgical specialty was urology, but in wartime all army doctors do what is needed at the moment, not just what their specialty is. Besides, all urologists are trained in general surgery, and I did plenty of it. In fact, at times I was chief of all surgery in some of the units I was with, such as field hospitals.

Between battles, our healthy young troops did not require much medical care, and during those intervals doctors were used for many non-medical duties. While we were waiting for the Normandy invasion, for instance, I became a firing-range officer, I taught snipers, I did studies of the relative wounding capabilities of various missiles on human tissues, and I drilled troops. At one time, I had a battalion of 800 army nurses who were so good at close-order drill that they rivaled the Rockettes. They were so good that even Winston Churchill came to watch them, and they made the front page of the Sunday *New York Times*. The alumni of some of these army units remained close and were very helpful, particularly the paratroopers.

I have been asked how I came to assemble all of the experimental work described in this book and still had time to run the huge Department of Urology of the College of Physicians & Surgeons of Columbia University, with its research laboratories, its hundreds of students, and its six New York hospitals, along with the Squier Urological Clinic, and a demanding surgical practice. During this period, I was also busy as president of the American Urological Association, the International Society of Urologists, and the Society of University Urologists. It is true that many of these activities interfered with each other, and that is why the experiments detailed in this book were spread over seventeen years. For a teacher of medical students, the utilization of historical materials and real-life examples livens academic presentations of medical matters. I work Presidents Kennedy and Lincoln and their assassins in and out of my presentations on various occasions, to pique the interest of students.

I hasten to point out that several of the country's best forensic pathologists had reviewed the Kennedy material before I did, but always under government auspices. I was the first *non-government* person to be allowed to review it: a second opinion, you might call it, by an unobligated observer.

The fact that my organization has its own Surgical Pathology Section, large enough and sophisticated enough to own and operate three electron microscopes, plus all manner of tissue-analyzing facilities, is an indication of its depth and capabilities.

And the fact that I have firing facilities available on a family farm in Michigan as well as on ranges in New Jersey made the ballistic experiments easier. My sons and I could conduct detailed experiments in an unhurried manner.

As we completed each experimental series, we would publish a small article in one of the medical or scientific publications, of which we distributed reprints liberally to any who was interested.

During these seventeen years, we accumulated a substantial private archive of original materials pertaining to both the Lincoln and the Kennedy assassinations. Included are Oswald's rifle scorebook from the Marine Corps and a substantial number of the letters and exhibits from the Lincoln and Kennedy investigations. For these we did not have to depend on hearsay about the contents, and could be sure that they are not modified or tampered with.

While serving as a visiting professor at the Southwestern Medical School in Dallas, shortly after the assassination, I was permitted to sit on a box in the actual window from which Oswald fired. I could see immediately from this experience and from the very low window sill how relatively easy a shot it was. This firsthand view was invaluable.

The storm of criticism against the Warren Commission report raised many points that were still open for experimentation. This surprised me and stimulated me to investigate some myself. For example, when the ammunition was said to be unreliable, I gradually procured and tested some 700 rounds of the exact lots used by Oswald. (The FBI had tested 100 rounds.) When the rifle was said to be inaccurate or incapable of a higher rate of fire, I tested several myself and published the results.

A representative of the Kennedy family had turned the pictures and X-rays of the President's body over to the National Archives, with strict stipulations that they be made available only to qualified reviewers after 1971, eight years after the assassination. Because I still had doubts about some of the contentions of the Warren Commission, as brought out in the report, I sent a request to review the actual autopsy photographs and X-rays when they were made available to qualified reviewers. When I was told that my request would be submitted to the adjudicator of these matters, I sent along a set of the reprints showing the results of our experimentation with the firearms, the only experiments done since the Warren Commission had been disbanded, so far as I knew.

In December of 1971, I received an onion-skin carbon copy of a very brief letter to the National Archivist from Burke Marshall, indicating that I had been granted permission to review the restricted Kennedy autopsy materials. Hesitant to go to Washington, with no more than an unsigned onion-skin carbon copy, and try to see the restricted forensic exhibits from the crime of the century, I waited. In January, the *New York Times* Washington Bureau called me to ask if I was going to take advantage of this permission or not. They indicated that the permission was carte blanche, and that they would verify this for me. On January 6, 1972, I received a notice from the National Archivist that I had been granted permission by Marshall, who was then Deputy Dean of Yale Law School and the adjudicator for the Kennedy family. I made the first of several reviews of the restricted materials on January 7, 1972, under the strict security conditions stipulated in the agreement with the National Archives, which forbade photographing or tracing of the materials, but otherwise imposed no restriction.

I was startled by the reception my comments got on the front pages of the *New York Times* and many other papers throughout the world. Since that time, my experimental studies have been quoted by the Rockefeller Commission on the CIA, the House of Representatives Select Committee on Assassinations, *Time* and many other publications in articles dealing with the death of President Kennedy. Recent books, including *Marina and Lee* and *The Search for JFK*, have drawn on my reports.

My review of the restricted materials verified some gross differences with the Warren Commission findings, including the fact that the bullet hole in the back of President Kennedy's head was four inches higher than on the diagrams in the official report. I quickly deduced that the first bullet must have struck Kennedy's spinal column and that it was this that caused the President's elbows to pull up in a reflex spasm described by a London neurologist a century before and identified for me by an associate, Dr. Edward Schlesinger, when I queried him about it. I was also able to demonstrate that the bullet that left Kennedy's neck tumbled in midair and struck Governor Connally going almost sideways. It continued to tumble as it penetrated his wrist and then the skin of his thigh. These new concepts were published in 1974, but were ignored until the 1978 congressional inquiry adopted them.

I went to great pains personally to interview Dr. James J. Humes and Dr. J. Thornton Boswell, who did the autopsy, and corresponded with roentgenologist Dr. John Ebersole. I was able to discover by talking with Navy Medical Center photographer John H. Stringer and Navy Medical Center illustrator H. A. Rydberg, who made the official drawings in the Warren Commission report, that the drawings had been made from hearsay and the artist had not been allowed to see either the body or the photographs. This explained discrepancies in the angle of entry of the neck bullet. The fact that the X-rays and photographs had been denied to the men who did the autopsy accounted for other discrepancies between the diagrams and the X-rays.

Following leads suggested by Professor Luis Alvarez and his associates Don Olson and Paul Hoch, at the Berkeley Radiation Laboratories in California, I verified the fact that a bullet from the front was not necessary to cause the President's head to jerk backward, as it could be seen to do, since this movement could also be induced by the jet-recoil phenomenon when the exact type of wound of the back of the head was reproduced. A neurological reflex also added to the backward jerk.

I had earlier become interested in the Lincoln assassination indirectly. It started when I was at the Argosy Galleries in New York, looking for a print of Henry Knox to go with his sword, which, with the swords of several of my ancestors from American Revolutionary times, including that of Ethan Allen, I own. The man at the next booth asked if I was a print collector, and I said, "No. You might say I'm a sword collector." He then commented that I should be interested in a knife he owned, which was used to stab Secretary of State William Seward on the night Lincoln was shot. At that time, I did not even know Seward had been stabbed. On a trip to Washington, I checked with Dr. Harold Peterson, Chief Curator of the National Park Service. I found out that the knife in question was indeed bona fide. In doing research on the knife, I discovered the beautifully handwritten testimony taken at the trial of the Lincoln conspirators. I also learned about all the controversies and the confusion concerning President Lincoln's autopsy findings. It was apparent that there had been debate about whether Booth had shot himself and what weapon he was shot with, and exactly where Seward's wounds were. Each of these made a project to investigate.

I was in the process of writing an article for the *Journal of the American Medical Association*, concerning Lincoln's wounds, when Kennedy was shot. As that story developed, much in it seemed to be the same as in the Lincoln assassination. The questions raised—such as from which direction the bullet came and whether there was a second assassin—were so reminiscent of the questions raised when Lincoln was shot that my interest was stirred to compare these impressive similarities.

The "cluster of capabilities" concept—my laboratory and weapons facilities and my previous experience with wounding experiments—made it relatively easy to put together this analysis of exactly what happened to both Lincoln and Kennedy, a century apart. The most striking finding in my study of the two events has been the similarity of so many medical aspects of the two cases. Separating the wheat from the chaff in the vast array of rumor and counter-rumor has been fascinating and fun. I hope you enjoy the book as much as I did in doing the work that went into it.

1.

WHY LINCOLN WAS SHOT

When the Civil War first started, everyone who knew anything about military matters was convinced that the Confederate Army would run roughshod over the Northern Army, permitting the South to secede and the cotton trade to boom once again.

The reasons for this were quite obvious. The vast majority of the U.S. Army officers were Southerners. Many were highly skilled, dashing commanders who immediately resigned their commissions in the U.S. Army and joined the Confederate forces. The army was considered an honorable career for the flower of the young manhood of the Southern states, whose accomplishments and capabilities were legendary. Until 1864, it had not mattered that the more numerous and densely populated Northern states had more men than the Confederate states. Anytime the Confederate Armies began to run low on manpower, it was easy to arrange an exchange of prisoners. This would bring the Confederate units back up to strength and the war would continue. In addition, the quality of the Confederate military units was so well known, and the legends of their prowess so pervasive, that the Northern soldiers were at a substantial psychological disadvantage until late in the war.

The astute British, for example, who were the large cotton consumers of the day, were so impressed with the probability of a quick victory for the South that they threw in with the Confederates early in the war, providing them with vast amounts of modern arms, industrial products, and even warships built to their specifications to prey on the overseas commerce of the North.

In fact, the war started out very favorably for the South, exactly as predicted. The Southern Armies overran the Northern Armies the way professionals overrun amateurs. It was a matter of sheer luck for the Northerners that the Southerners did not continue right on in to capture Washington, congressmen and all, after their initial victory at Bull Run, just outside the city.

Fig. 1

JOHN WILKES BOOTH

Booth was a handsome, truculent, daring, but short (five feet eight inches), dramatic actor who was also a vigorous enemy (Confederate) sympathizer. Hungry for fame, he murdered the President before a packed audience and leaped to the stage to proclaim himself the assassin.

Booth was himself gunned down by Boston Corbett twelve days later. Restricted by his broken leg and surrounded by his captors, he was shot through the spinal cord with a Colt revolver in the glare of light from the fires set by his captors, and died after about two hours.

A century later, Lee Harvey Oswald was shot down in a similar situation and also lived only two hours. (*J. K. Lattimer*)

Lincoln Halts Prisoner Exchange

After three years of frustrating impasse, Mr. Lincoln and General Grant finally got their heads together and figured out the remedy for this problem. They merely halted the exchange of prisoners, and from that point onward the Southern Armies began to crumble. At the same time, the Northern Armies were slowly replacing their unsuccessful officers with battle-tested men, and Grant decided to adopt techniques of grinding down the manpower of the South through campaigns of bulldog tenacity. ("We will fight it out on this line, if it takes all summer.") These new tactics began taking their inexorable toll of the Southern Armies. It was gradually becoming apparent to everyone that unless the prisoner-exchange mechanism could be revived, the Southern Armies were on a course toward annihilation. Once that process got going, moreover, it would escalate rapidly.

Booth's Grand Plan to Kidnap Lincoln

FIG. 1
page 4

John Wilkes Booth, a brooding, truculent, dramatic actor, hungry for fame, was a dedicated enemy sympathizer with daring and a flair for violence. A member of a famous acting family, he found his reputation overshadowed by those of his father and two older brothers, Edwin and Junius Brutus Booth, Jr. His father, a famous tragedian, died when John was ten, depriving John of the tutelage he had provided the older brothers.

In some of his early performances, Booth had himself billed simply as J. Wilkes so that the family name would not be tarnished if he did badly. As J. Wilkes, he had been embarrassed by disdainful critics during his early appearances, and he was straining for a shortcut to greatness. While he had actually done quite well as a rising young actor, his voice was giving him problems and there was concern that this would limit his future as a dramatic actor.

When the War of the Rebellion got underway, Booth's violently secessionist speeches were suppressed at the insistence of his managers. But he then undertook, on his own, to position himself where he could render covert help to the South while residing among the unsuspecting Union civilians in Washington, Baltimore, and New York. He thus could watch and wait for an opportunity to serve the Confederacy in some dramatic role in which he could demonstrate that his contribution might exceed that of anyone else. In these subversive characteristics we find a parallel, a century later, in the personality and actions of another assassin, Lee Harvey Oswald, a dedicated enemy sympathizer with a craving for fame, who was named Lee, coincidentally, after Robert E. Lee, Booth's commander-in-chief.

Booth had kept a relatively low profile throughout the war, with his theatrical activities permitting him fluidity of movement from city to

Fig. 2
page 7

city. He skillfully maintained the easy access to the best social circles which is afforded popular actors in our open society. And he had even performed for Lincoln, who loved the theater, in *The Marble Heart* at Ford's Theater, on November 9, 1863, according to Lincoln's secretary, John Hay, ten days before the President delivered the Gettysburg Address. He was thoroughly familiar with the Maryland Confederate spy corridor between Richmond and Washington, including Surrattsville and Bryantown, where Dr. Samuel A. Mudd lived. There were some rumors that Booth had been a double agent, being paid indirectly by federal Secret Service Chief Lafayette Baker through a dummy corporation in New York, but actual evidence for this charge is lacking.

In the fall of 1864, Booth elected to make a spectacular effort to salvage the crumbling Confederate Armies of General Lee. His grand idea was to kidnap Mr. Lincoln, carry him off through the well-known spy corridor in Prince Georges and Charles counties in Maryland and across the Potomac and Rappahannock rivers into northern Virginia. This route ran through an area which was studded with well-organized Confederate spy stations, including the Surrattsville Tavern, which were maintained by an interwoven network of Southern sympathizers capable of abetting his daring scheme.

The objective of the kidnapping—bizarre as this must sound today—was to use Lincoln as a pawn who would be released only if the North would agree to a status quo armistice or, at the very least, to resume the exchange of prisoners. No sooner had Booth conceived this plan than he began to hear of other groups that had similar ideas. Not wanting to be upstaged, he was impatient to get on with his plotting. The word went out and fast horses and low-silhouette rowboats were placed "at the ready" for Booth's escapade.

Kidnap Team Assembled

By September of 1864, Booth had already begun to recruit his assistants to help kidnap President Lincoln. Within a six-month period, he was able to sign up Lewis Thornton Powell, a large, handsome ex-Confederate soldier who had adopted the name of Lewis Payne. Payne had been wounded and captured at Gettysburg, escaped from a hospital in Baltimore, and joined John Singleton Mosby's Confederate guerrilla rangers. In January 1865, he deserted Mosby and went back to Baltimore, where he was arrested for assault on March 12. He was released after signing an oath of allegiance and a statement that he would not engage in activities against the North. While he used his own name, L. T. Powell, when signing a receipt for clothing issued to him as a member of Mosby's Rangers, he signed the oath of allegiance as L. Paine. (Because of identification problems, he was referred to as Payne throughout the 1865 conspiracy trial.) Payne (Powell) was the son of a Baptist minister in Florida. He was a clean-cut, well-coordinated, fearless young man who

ABRAHAM LINCOLN

A photograph by Alexander Gardner made in Washington, D.C., on November 15, 1863, just four days before Lincoln delivered his immortal Gettysburg Address. Gardner was an assistant to Mathew Brady, the well-known Civil War photographer.

This is universally accepted as the greatest of the Lincoln presidential photographs, portraying the President in his prime. The responsibilities and anxieties of his office had begun to show in his face, but it was not as weary and sad as the photographs taken a little over a year later, just before his death. The Civil War was far from over, but the victory at Gettysburg and the emergence of General Ulysses S. Grant gave signs of the ultimate successful end of the terrible war.

This is the Lincoln who had reached the zenith of his popularity and success, both in the military field and in holding together the Union. The South was guaranteed a fair peace, and Lincoln would defend this thesis against the segment of the population who would exploit the South. This is the man John Wilkes Booth chose to kill, ignoring his good qualities, on the outside chance that Lee might reconsider his surrender if the President, the Vice President, and the Secretary of State were all killed at once and the government thrown into panic. His assassination made Lincoln immortal, at the height of his popularity. (*National Archives*)

Fig. 2

made an excellent impression upon all who saw him. Even the hangman who knew him in the prison and on the gallows commented that this young fellow conducted himself with dignity and admirable composure. Payne had the intelligence and savoir-faire to carry out the convincing deception necessary to penetrate to the very side of Secretary of State William H. Seward in an attempt to kill him, as we shall see later.

Booth also recruited George Atzerodt, a rather brutish carriage painter and blockade runner, who provided another pair of willing hands, at least for the attempt to kidnap Lincoln. When Booth changed his plan from kidnapping to murder, a protesting Atzerodt was the man he assigned to kill Vice President Andrew Johnson. Atzerodt's value lay in his familiarity with the countryside and with the river crossings in the Port Tobacco area.

Also part of Booth's group was a young drug clerk named David Herold, who guided Payne to Seward's house and then followed Booth out of town across the Navy Yard Bridge, accompanying him on his escape ride and acting as a guide and personal servant. Booth and others of his group frequented the Washington rooming house of widow Mary E. Surratt. Mrs. Surratt owned and had formerly lived at a tavern at Surrattsville, ten miles below Washington, along the way to Richmond. It was here that the kidnappers secreted two Spencer carbines, ammunition, and liquor. Mrs. Surratt herself brought Booth's field glasses to the tavern on the day of the assassination to be picked up that night by the conspirators. Unable to manage her farm and tavern after her husband died, Mrs. Surratt had rented out the tavern and farm at Surrattsville to a man named Lloyd and had moved into Washington, about six months previously, where she had established a boardinghouse at 541 H Street. One of Mrs. Surratt's first customers, living at the boardinghouse at the time but apparently not a plotter, was a college classmate of her son, John Surratt, one Louis J. Weichmann, who was then a government employee in the office of the commissary general of prisoners. Weichmann said that he had reported his suspicions of this subversive group to one of his co-workers in his office. His report was apparently taken no further at that time, but when Booth was recognized and identified as the assassin who had fired the shot at Ford's Theater, the authorities had information enough to go directly to Mrs. Surratt's house that night, looking for her son, who was not there. A second search of the house was ordered on the night of April 17, and while this search was in progress, Lewis Powell, alias Payne, walked in, carrying a pickax over his shoulder and claiming to be a ditch digger hired by Mrs. Surratt. Mrs. Surratt's story and Payne's did not match, however, and Payne was quickly identified as the person who had attempted to assassinate Secretary Seward and as one of Booth's group of conspirators. The capture of Payne at her house helped to incriminate Mrs. Surratt, in the eyes of the authorities.

Mrs. Surratt's son, John Surratt, a Confederate courier, was intro-

ANNOUNCEMENT OF WAR'S END

Front page of *The New York Herald* announces Lee's surrender on April 9. When Booth saw the headlines he was alleged to have said, "My God, I no longer have a country!" With Lee surrendered, there was no longer any purpose in kidnapping President Lincoln, and Booth's kidnap group was left without a mission or a chance to become heroes. Booth apparently thereupon made the decision on short notice to kill Lincoln, the Vice President, and the Secretary of State, hoping to panic the government so Lee could reconsider his surrender. This might seem ridiculous, except that Napoleon did something of this sort when he "unsurrendered" and returned from Elba. *(J. K. Lattimer)*

Fig. 3

duced to Booth by a mutual friend, Dr. Samuel Mudd. He became an enthusiastic member of the group who planned to kidnap Lincoln. Luckily for him, he was out of town when Booth changed his plan and tried to kill the top officers of the government. In spite of his absence from Washington, Surratt's name was carried on the reward posters; he was pursued all over the world in a dramatic chase, extending even into the Vatican, where he had worked as a papal guard. He escaped from Rome and several other cities before extradition could be arranged and kept up his flight for over a year (much like the more recent flight of James Earl Ray) before being apprehended and brought back to the United States to stand trial in 1867. His trial brought about a reopening and review of the 1865 assassination inquiry (reminiscent of the 1978 reopening of the Kennedy inquiry) but ended with his being released, not only because, being out of town, he had not participated in the murder, but also because the intense rage against the conspirators had subsided. The actual murderer had been shot and four of the participants hanged.

John Surratt's trial in 1867 was conducted under civilian auspices, moreover, rather than by the 1865 military commission, which might have handed down a quicker and harsher verdict had he been included in the original group of those tried. Indeed, his own mother had been hanged despite the common expectations (including those of the hangman, Capt. Christian Rath, and the prison commandant, General Hartranft, who delayed the hanging as long as he could in the event she were pardoned at the last minute). There was much recrimination over her hanging, which may also have helped to save her son, John. A difference between plotting to kidnap and plotting to murder, which had not been considered at the 1865 trial, had been more clearly established by that time. John Surratt was tried for murder.

In addition to Payne, as he will be referred to hereafter, and David Herold, Booth also recruited ex-Confederate soldiers Samuel Arnold and Michael O'Laughlin, boyhood friends of his, and Edward Spangler, a stagehand at Ford's Theater. Spangler had worked for Booth's father on his farm and was accustomed to taking orders from Booth.

Kidnap Plan Perfected

On March 15, the entire group was assembled for its first and last general meeting. Posing as a Baptist preacher, Payne arrived at Mrs. Surratt's boardinghouse and looked over their arsenal of revolvers and knives with young Surratt. That night he and Surratt accompanied two of the young lady boarders to Ford's Theater and, thanks to Booth's efforts, sat in the presidential box to reconnoiter it.

After the theater the entire group met in a private dining room at Gautier's Restaurant.

Booth, in true theatrical style, proposed that they seize Mr. Lincoln at a theatrical performance, tie him up in the theater box, and lower his trussed-up body over the edge of the box. Arnold and O'Laughlin objected, and strove to convince Booth that this was a bit *too* theatrical, and that other opportunities would be more practical. Booth was irritated and he muttered something about killing as the meeting ended.

The plotters then waited for an opportunity, knowing that Lincoln frequently drove out to the Convalescent Soldiers' Home on the outskirts of Washington to enjoy a cooler evening away from the heat and flies of the city.

On March 17, Booth heard from a producer friend that the President hoped to attend a matinee performance at the Campbell Hospital just outside the city. He assembled his group and they lay in wait for the presidential carriage. But when they surrounded the vehicle, ready to ride off with Lincoln, they discovered to their intense disappointment that he was not in the carriage. Booth ascertained that Lincoln had not arrived at all, and the conspirators then scattered, realizing that they might now be tracked down by the Secret Service. But the final hopeful events indicating the end of the war were beginning to accelerate so rapidly that the attention of the authorities was diverted elsewhere.

Surratt and Atzerodt then rode out to Surrattsville the next day to recall Herold, who had been sent on ahead in Booth's buggy with the two deadly Spencer carbines, ammunition, and supplies. He had waited in vain for the kidnap party. Surratt and Lloyd then hid the carbines by entering a small attic over the kitchen of Mrs. Surratt's tavern, from which they could push the weapons between the joists supporting the floor of the adjacent bedroom. There the carbines stayed like evil eggs, incubating until the night of Lincoln's murder, when Mrs. Surratt's doom was sealed by her tenant Lloyd's testimony that she told him on the afternoon of April 14 to have "the shooting irons" ready to be called for that night, as indeed they were.

After the abortive kidnap attempt on March 14, the conspiracy began to break up. While Surratt, Herold, Weichmann, and Atzerodt did attend Booth's last performance at Ford's Theater on March 18, O'Laughlin and Arnold returned to Baltimore, Surratt then went to Richmond, and Booth and Payne went to New York. Herold and Atzerodt hung around Washington. But Booth was not ready to abandon further action, and when he and Payne returned to Washington on March 25 he sought to put new life into the plot. Finding that O'Laughlin and Arnold were not interested, Booth went back to New York and on to Boston, probably to raise money. He returned to Washington on April 8. Further plans were

Fig. 3
page 9 being discussed when, on April 9, a calamitous development occurred. General Lee surrendered.

2.

LEE SURRENDERS;
BOOTH DECIDES TO KILL

On April 9, 1865, at Appomattox, to Booth's dismay and disbelief, General Lee surrendered the entire Army of Northern Virginia to General Grant, unconditionally. Booth was disgusted. Here he was with his plotters all ready to go, and his plan was destroyed.

When he heard the news, Booth is alleged to have remarked, "My God! I no longer have a country!"

After brooding briefly over Lee's disappointing capitulation, Booth decided that the few remaining stalwart conspirators of his group might still make a desperate attempt at a contribution to the Southern cause. His plan escalated; he proposed that by killing President Lincoln, Vice President Andrew Johnson, and Secretary of State Seward, thereby destroying the Northern leadership, he might throw the government into a panic and Lee could "unsurrender." While this notion seems ludicrous today, we must remember that Booth was the head of a group of loyal fanatics eager for the hero status they had anticipated, who were willing to lay their lives on the line for a moment of glory. They had been swept up in a wave of emotional activity, they had an exceptional opportunity for access to the President through Lincoln's enjoyment of the theater, and they were well organized and tired of failed opportunities. Suddenly deprived of one chance to become top heroes of the Confederacy, they needed to find another way. They were not discouraged; they had had some minor successes. They had conducted a highly encouraging dry run by infiltrating the crowd around the President during his second inauguration on March 4, five weeks earlier, when each had achieved a position in the crowd within easy pistol range of Lincoln. Booth had commented, after that occasion, that he could easily have killed the President, if that had been his objective. Now, that objective became a reality.

Lincoln had returned to Washington from his triumphal entry into Richmond. On April 14, General Grant, having concluded the formalities and technical details of Lee's surrender, also returned to Washington to receive the hero's welcome he deserved as the conquering lion of his day. Washington was ablaze with lights and a happy delirium gripped the city, released from the continuous state of dreadful tension it had suffered throughout the four years of the war. Always there had been the fear of a lightning strike by the Confederate cavalry, intent on burning the capital city to the ground and killing or capturing its leaders. Now everyone was filled with joy; the frightful carnage was over.

Theater Party Announced

When it was announced that General Grant would appear in Washington, the city went even wilder. The General spent most of April 14 at the War Department in Washington, attending to formalities. He and Mrs. Grant were invited, by the Lincolns, to attend a gala performance at Ford's Theater that evening. The play was to be a popular comedy — unsophisticated and contrived but appealing to Civil War audiences— called *Our American Cousin*, starring Miss Laura Keene and her company. When it was printed in the newspapers that General and Mrs.

Figs. 4, 5
page 14

Grant would accompany President and Mrs. Lincoln to the theater, the demand for tickets became heavy.

When Booth heard the news, he was electrified. He realized that his perfect opportunity had arrived. Ford's Theater was his home base. He assembled his cohorts, hastily laid and rehearsed the plan, and began to consider the minor details of his forthcoming act. (And here we have another striking similarity between the Lincoln assassination and the Kennedy assassination 100 years later, in that both assassins were elated to read in the newspapers that the President was about to come to them at their place of work. Booth and Oswald each quickly looked for the very best arrangement for surprising and shooting his presidential victim. As we shall see, each man made some physical changes in the furnishings of the area so he could not be observed as he prepared to do his murderous act and so that no one could reach him to interfere.)

Booth wanted to kill his three intended victims simultaneously. There were rumors, later, that he had also wanted to kill the Secretary of War, Stanton, but there is no real evidence that this was part of his plan. At any rate, he assembled those members of the group who were still in town at Martha Murray's boardinghouse for a final planning session. Payne was assigned the task of killing the Secretary of State; Atzerodt was to kill the Vice President; Booth would kill Lincoln; and Herold was first to guide Payne to Seward's house and then to follow Booth out of town, accompanying him on his escape route as guide and personal servant. As already stated, two Spencer carbines and possibly two Colt revolvers had been hidden at the Surrattsville Tavern, and Booth had arranged to

LIEUT. GENERAL GRANT, PRESIDENT and Mrs. Lincoln have secured the State Box at Ford's Theater TO-NIGHT, to witness Miss Laura Keene's American Cousin. 1t

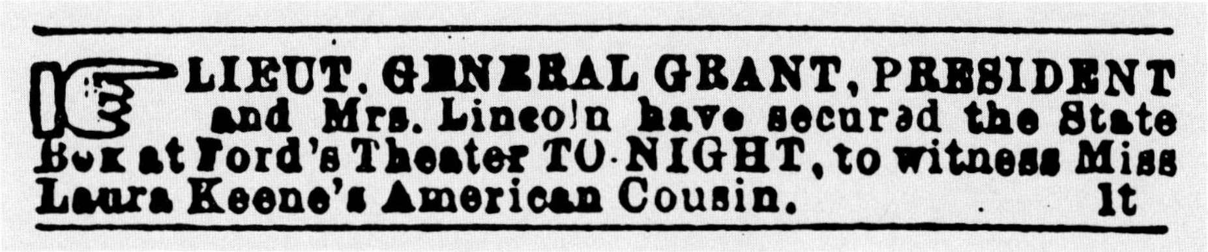

NEWSPAPER NOTICE OF LINCOLN'S VISIT TO FORD'S THEATER

The Washington newspaper announcements spread the word that President and Mrs. Lincoln would be hosts to the hero General Ulysses Grant and Mrs. Grant, at the final gala performance of the comedy *Our American Cousin,* which Miss Laura Keene and her company had made so popular in recent years. Ford's Theater was Booth's "home base" in Washington. Having heard the news the morning of the 14th, Booth was able to go to the theater and not only survey the scene for the shooting of Lincoln but also prepare the area by drilling a peephole through the door that would be behind Lincoln's head and hiding a wooden bar behind the outer door with which he could jam it shut once he was inside, so that no one could follow and disturb him.

Here again is an analogy with President Kennedy, whose assassin discovered by reading the newpapers that the President would pass before him at his place of employment. *(J. K. Lattimer)*

Fig. 4

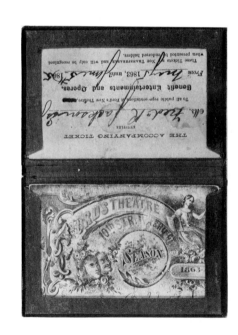

TICKET TO FORD'S THEATER

It was good for the fatal night. *(J. K. Lattimer)*

Fig. 5

have his field glasses brought by Mrs. Surratt herself to the tavern, since she was driving down there anyway, on the day of the assassination. Booth could then pick them up that evening to help him in his escape flight. This additional evidence of conspiracy helped to turn the military commission which tried the conspirators against Mrs. Surratt. The fact that the plot was "hatched in her nest" was not considered by many as a sufficient reason to hang her.

Many things were in Booth's favor. Not only was Ford's Theater his headquarters; he received his mail there, and he knew every inch of the building. He knew, for example, that when the President came to the theater, the partition between the two boxes on the balcony at the right side of the theater would be removed (by Spangler), making one large presidential box. He knew, also, that the President's favorite rocking chair would be brought and placed in a special position on the side of the box nearest the audience and that Mrs. Lincoln would be seated in another chair immediately to the President's right. Booth knew that the lock to the outer door of the box was broken, so that the box could not be firmly locked; the door would yield to a push.

FIG. 6
page 16

Booth Prepares the Theater Box

Booth acted fast. He hid a sturdy stick of wood behind the door of the box and dug a hole in the plaster behind the door so that he could wedge this stick (it was apparently part of the foot of a music stand) into the hole in the plaster in such a way that the door could not be opened by pressure from the outside until the stick was removed. He then drilled a hole through the door of the little anteroom of the box so that, once he was safely inside the anteroom, he would be able to peer through his peephole and make sure exactly where the President was seated. Once he was through the other door and into the main part of the box, he would know where to move among the occupants. He realized that he would have to act almost instantaneously, before anybody saw him. It was therefore to his advantage to know exactly where, in the darkened box, the President would be sitting.

(Here again we have a surprising similarity to the actions of Oswald 100 years later. Oswald piled up boxes to form a wall so no one could see him as he prepared to shoot, and brought the elevator up to the sixth floor, where he left the safety gate open so the elevator could not be used to come up to the floor from which he would be shooting.)

Unfortunately for Lincoln, the Grants did not attend the theater that night. Mrs. Grant, who disliked Mrs. Lincoln intensely, persuaded her husband to renege on his acceptance of the invitation and to leave with her that afternoon for a visit to their children in New Jersey. The General was embarrassed but Mrs. Grant was insistent; they left Washington by train, accompanied by General Grant's highly competent bodyguard. The author has heard Grant's grandson state that General Grant always

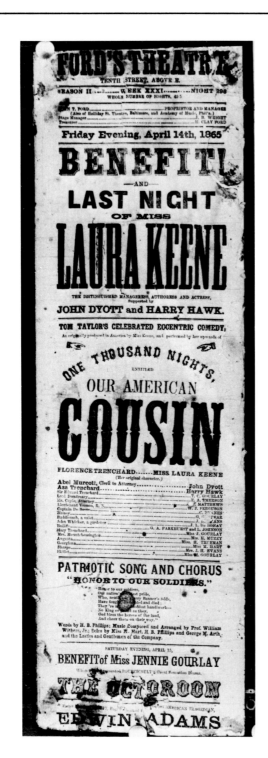

Fig. 6

PLAYBILL FOR THE FATAL PERFORMANCE AT FORD'S THEATER

The Lincolns invited the Grants to attend this performance of a popular rough-hewn comedy that had been immensely enjoyed by Civil war audiences in Washington. *(National Park Service)*

regretted not going to the theater that night. Had he gone, his bodyguard would never have permitted anyone to get into the presidential box. Thus a seemingly minor friction led to a mammoth change in history. It must be remembered that, in wartime, assassinating enemy commanders is a perfectly legitimate act of war, and that resourceful militarists know this and work at it. Successful generals, like Grant, take all possible precautions. Even though the war was over, there was a sense of awareness on the part of the federal soldiery that some disgruntled Southern sympathizer might seize any opportunity for retribution, especially during the emotion-ridden period immediately after the surrender. In fact, there had been great apprehension about the possibility of danger when Lincoln visited Richmond just after its fall ten days previously.

The Lincolns Arrive Late at Ford's Theater

Thus the Lincolns were left with an announced theater appearance and no guests. The President invited some of the visitors who were in his office, but they could not go. He invited Senator and Mrs. Ira Harris of New York, but found that they too had a previous engagement and could not accompany the Lincolns. Neither could their older daughter. However, their younger daughter, Miss Clara Harris, would love to come but had no transportation. The Lincolns agreed to pick her up along with her fiancé (and stepbrother), Maj. Henry R. Rathbone, at 15th and H streets. The party arrived at the theater well after the performance had started.

Fig. 7
page 18

The presidential carriage drew up to the front of Ford's and the presidential party entered after the crowd that had assembled to see them and the Grants had dispersed, thinking that the presidential party had decided not to attend. The Lincolns and their guests walked up the stairs and around the back of the dress circle to the door of the presidential

Fig. 10
page 22

box. As they entered, the orchestra leader spotted them, stopped the show, and the orchestra played "Hail to the Chief." Lincoln bowed, the party took their seats, and the play resumed.

It was time for Booth's hastily arranged drama to begin. The three simultaneous attacks had been scheduled for 10:15. About 9:00 P.M., he rode his horse slowly down the alley at the back of Ford's Theater and called Spangler to hold his horse. Spangler (luckily for him) had to shift scenery and gave the reins to a young man, Joseph "Peanuts John" Burroughs, to hold in readiness for the moment of Booth's escape. Booth then entered the back of the theater, went into a passageway underneath it, and came up on 10th Street, where he entered Taltavul's Tavern, immediately next door to the theater. Booth ordered a drink and made cryptic remarks to the effect that, by tomorrow, everyone would know who *he* was. There was no doubting the implication that he was going to do something so momentous that his name would be well known.

Then, glancing at his watch, he went out into the street, up to the same door of Ford's Theater through which the Lincolns had entered, ban-

FORD'S THEATER

The Lincolns had invited Mrs. Grant and the General, who was the conquering lion of the day, to accompany them to the final benefit performance there of Laura Keene's company, in the play she had made popular with Civil War audiences called *Our American Cousin*. The Lincolns were late because, when the Grants could not go, they had to pick up Miss Harris and her fiancé. By the time they arrived in front of the theater, after the show had started, the crowd that had gathered to watch them and the Grants arrive had dispersed. They were ushered into the theater by the ticket taker, made their way around the back of the dress circle to the presidential box. When the orchestra leader saw them come in, he stopped the show and played "Hail to the Chief." Lincoln bowed, the party sat down in the presidential box, to the right of the stage, and the play resumed.

In this picture, on the right is Taltavul's Tavern, where Booth took his final drink, glanced at his watch, and made a cryptic remark to the effect that everybody present would certainly know who "he" was the next day. He then sauntered out to follow the Lincolns' route, chatted with the ticket taker, who knew him well, and walked up and around the dress circle to the door of the presidential box. *(National Park Service)*

Fig. 7

tered with the theater doorkeeper, Mr. Buckingham, who knew him well, and followed the route of the Lincolns up the stairs and around the back of the dress circle toward the door of the presidential box.

Booth Enters Presidential Box, Unchallenged

Fig. 8
page 20

Just after the second intermission, at about ten o'clock, Booth was noticed by some of the audience who were sitting in the back rows as he came up the stairs to the back of the dress circle. There he paused for a moment, where he was observed to be selecting a letter or visiting card from among several in his pocket, showing it to the President's messenger, Charles Forbes, who had a seat near the entrance to the box. The card undoubtedly verified that he was a legitimate member of the theater staff. The messenger then permitted him to advance toward the door of the presidential box, which was built partly out onto the stage.

Booth did not encounter any professional guard at the door of the box because John Parker, the White House policeman ostensibly charged with protecting the President, was not present at the presidential box door at that moment. He reportedly had left his post on at least one occasion to get a drink and on another occasion to move to a position where he could see the stage more clearly. It is entirely possible that the President had told Parker to find himself a seat and to enjoy the play, as would have been quite in character for Lincoln to have done. Lincoln, like Kennedy, was known for his fatalistic attitude toward the possibility of danger.

It has been noted as strange that testimony was never taken from Parker, either during the initial trial of the conspirators or during the trial of John Surratt two years later. On May 1, 1865, however, Supt. of Police A. C. Richards filed a formal complaint against Parker, charging that he allowed an assassin to shoot at the President. The case was dismissed, indicating that Parker's defense must have been a reasonable one. It is known that he had worked at the White House as a policeman and guard for only a month or less and that Mrs. Lincoln had signed a letter on his behalf to the draft board eleven days before the shooting, having him excused from the draft. There have been some suggestions that Mrs. Lincoln acted improperly, and there have even been intimations that she accepted money from him for this favor. A careful and perceptive review of the draft-exemption matter has been made by the noted historian James O. Hall, who concluded that what Mrs. Lincoln did was merely her way of "defending her turf" by seeing to it that her household staff was not stripped away just as she had gotten it organized to her liking for her second term in the White House.

It should be noted here that Lincoln allegedly requested that Maj. Thomas T. Eckert, who was one of the mainstays of the War Department telegraph office staff, accompany the Lincolns to the theater that night, presumably as a combination guest and bodyguard. Major Eckert was a

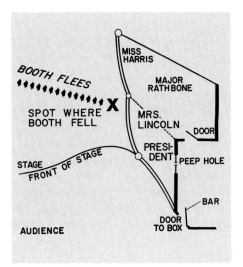

FORD'S THEATER FLOOR PLAN

The edge of the stage is across the middle of the drawing, the audience at the bottom, and the door to the presidential box far over to the right side of the theater. Booth had previously determined that the door lock was broken and would yield to the gentlest pressure. He had hidden a wooden bar behind the door earlier in the day and had dug a hole in the plaster so that he could jam this bar behind the door to keep anyone from opening it once he was inside. He had drilled a peephole through the door on the left-hand side of the small anteroom so that he could peer through and determine that his victim, the President, was seated exactly where he expected him to be, with Mrs. Lincoln at his side but not in the way.

At exactly 10:15 P.M. he stepped through the door at the top end of the anteroom, pointed his pistol toward the right side of the back of the President's head, and pulled the trigger. Major Rathbone, who was seated with Miss Harris on a settee at the far end of the box, jumped to his feet and tried to grapple with the dark figure. Booth then threw down his single-shot pistol, which was now useless, pulled out his hunting knife, which was razor-sharp, and stabbed Rathbone severely on his upper arm for a distance of eight inches. Rathbone staggered back, bleeding heavily.

Booth went to the edge of the box in front of Mrs. Lincoln and climbed backward over the edge, leaping outward so that he would fly down to the stage with his black clothes billowing and his glittering dagger, his boots, and his flashing spurs giving him a dramatic appearance. Unfortunately, one of his spurs caught in a flag on the edge of the box and turned him so that he landed on one foot at the point indicated by the X and fractured the fibula, the small bone of the leg just above the ankle. Although he could still hobble with this painful but not totally disabling injury, it slowed him down enough so that he was caught and killed some twelve days later. He hobbled across the stage, waving his knife and shouting "Sic semper tyrannis," the motto of Virginia, then out the back of the theater to where his horse was waiting.

It might seem that the twelve feet down to the stage would be too far for safety, but this was the type of athletic entrance on which Booth prided himself and was entirely in keeping with his dashing and vigorous style of acting.
(*J. K. Lattimer*)

Fig. 8

man of enormous physical strength, sometimes demonstrating this by bending heavy iron bars with his hands, to the astonishment of everyone who saw him do it. Peculiarly, Secretary of War Stanton would not permit him to go with the Lincolns, saying that he (Stanton) had something important that he wanted Eckert to do at the War Department office. A perusal of the records, reported by Eisenschiml, indicated that no important duty was done by Eckert that evening, and Eisenschiml raised the question, by innuendo, as to whether or not Stanton knew an attempt on Lincoln's life might be made that night and did not want the President to be guarded in any special way. There is no proof for this allegation, of course, but implied bits of circumstantial evidence do seem to place Stanton in a peculiar light in this regard. In a recent analysis of Eisenschiml's innuendoes made by Dr. William Hanchett, history professor at the San Diego Community College, the conclusion was reached that the implied charges against Stanton are not justified and have no real merit as indicators of Stanton's involvement.

FIG. 9
page 22

Once inside the box—the broken lock had not been fixed, and the door did indeed yield to the pressure of his hand—Booth wedged the door tightly shut with the wooden bar he had secreted behind the door so that no one could follow him inside. He then peered through the peephole toward the back of President Lincoln's head. Lincoln was sitting in his favorite high-backed rocking chair with satin cushions at the end of the box nearest the audience, with Mrs. Lincoln at his right side. (Mrs. Kennedy was similarly seated beside President Kennedy when he was mortally wounded, although on his left.)

Booth Fires

Booth verified that Major Rathbone and Miss Harris were together on a settee far over toward the right against the wall nearest the stage. At 10:15 P.M.—right on schedule—Booth stepped quickly through the door in the end of the little anteroom, turned sharply to his left behind Mrs. Lincoln's chair, pointed his single-shot derringer pistol at the right side of the back of President Lincoln's head, and pulled the trigger. There was a flash and a loud report, and the half-inch Britannia metal ball crashed into Lincoln's skull.

FIGS. 11, 12
page 23

The last words heard by Lincoln before the bullet crashed into that unique brain to silence it forever were those shown in figure 9 uttered by Harry Hawk, one of the comical characters in *Our American Cousin*. Lincoln was fond of comedies and was prone to slap his thigh to express his enjoyment of even rough humor.

The noise of the shot startled not only those in the box but also the audience and the players. All looked toward the box in bewilderment, not knowing whether this was part of the action or an unexpected event.

Booth threw down his empty pistol and pulled out his hunting knife as Major Rathbone leaped to his feet and began to grapple with the in-

LINCOLN'S ROCKING CHAIR

The chair in which President Lincoln was sitting when he was shot. The dark spot where his head was resting was the subject of an interesting link with President Kennedy, as we shall see. *(National Park Service)*

Fig. 9

THE SCARF MRS. LINCOLN WORE TO THE THEATER

This is the black scarf Mrs. Lincoln was wearing on the fatal night at Ford's Theater. She gave it to Mrs. Keckley, her seamstress, from whose descendants it was purchased by the famous Lincoln Collectors Oldroyd and then Townsend. It was acquired from that collection by the author. *(J. K. Lattimer)*

Fig. 10

biling over with affections, which I'm ready to pour out all over you like apple sass, over roast pork.

Mrs M   Mr. Trenchard, you will please recollect you are addressing my daughter, and in my presence.

Asa   Yes, I'm offering her my heart and hand just as she wants them, with nothing in 'em.

Mrs M   Augusta, dear, to your room.

Aug   Yes, ma, the nasty beast.   [*Exit*, R.

Mrs M   I am aware, Mr. Trenchard, you are not used to the manners of good society, and that, alone, will excuse the impertinence of which you have been guilty.

Asa   Don't know the manners of good society, eh?   Well, I guess I know enough to turn you inside out, old gal—you sockdologizing old man-trap.   Wal, now, when I think what I've thrown away in hard cash to-day I'm apt to call myself some awful hard names, 400,000 dollars is a big pile for a man to light his cigar with.   If that gal had only given me herself in exchange, it would'nt have been a bad bargain,   But I dare no more ask that gal to be my wife, than I dare ask Queen Victoria to dance a Cape Cod reel.

LAST WORDS HEARD BY LINCOLN

Underlined are the last words heard by Lincoln before his life was snuffed out by Booth's bullet, fired into his brain. They were uttered by actor Harry Hawk. (*From* The Mad Booths of Maryland *by Stanley Kimmel*)

Fig. 11

ACTOR HARRY HAWK

This is the man who uttered the last words heard by President Lincoln before the fatal shot was fired into his head. His words are underlined in the accompanying script of the play. (*National Archives*)

Fig. 12

BOOTH'S KNIFE

This is the hunting knife with a razor-sharp blade used by Booth to stab Major Rathbone, who tried to grapple with him in the theater box, and which he was waving as he hobbled off across the stage. It was still on him when he was shot down and killed in Garrett's barn twelve days later.

Seeing this knife in Booth's hand prompted Dr. Leale, giving first aid to the unconscious President, to look first for a knife wound, and he cut Lincoln's collar and shirt away quickly with a borrowed penknife, searching for a stab wound of the chest. He found no knife wound, but noting blood on the shoulder and that the pupil of one eye was smaller than the other, he quickly ran his fingers through the hair on the back of Lincoln's head, until one finger fell into the bullet hole, to the left of the midline. *(National Park Service)*

Fig. 13

BOOTH'S FATAL SPUR

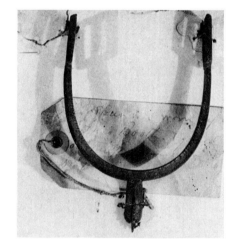

This is the actual spur from Booth's boot which caught on the flag on the margin of the presidential box as Booth vaulted over the edge to make his last dramatic appearance, flying down to the stage twelve feet below. In the brilliant glare of the footlights, with his black clothing flying, and waving his glittering knife, he was dramatic indeed. Unfortunately, when this spur caught in the flag, it turned him so that he landed heavily on one foot, breaking the small bone in his leg just above the ankle. This slowed his flight enough so that he was captured and killed. *(National Park Service)*

Fig. 14

FORD'S THEATER SHORTLY AFTER THE ASSASSINATION

This photograph, taken by Brady, is actually a composite of two pictures, with the line of junction seen down the center.

The flag is pulled away from the edge of the presidential box at right center (A), where Booth's spur caught on it to turn him so that he landed heavily on one foot at the point indicated by the light spot on the stage immediately below the presidential box (B). After making this dramatic leaping entrance, Booth hobbled off across the stage, completely over to the left side of this picture, and then out a smaller door to the rear of the theater where his horse was being held for him by a young man named "Peanuts John" Burroughs. One member of the audience got up over the footlights quickly enough to reach him as he was getting on his horse rather laboriously because of his broken leg, and barely missed pulling him down before he rode off along his planned escape route. *(National Park Service)*

Fig. 15

FIG. 13
page 24

truder. In the darkness of the box, Booth shouted something that Rathbone heard as "Freedom!" as Booth slashed at his opponent. Rathbone parried the blow upward with his left forearm. The knife, which had a 7¼-inch blade and was razor-sharp, caused a deep laceration in Rathbone's arm, despite the protection of the thick fabric of his jacket. The wound began to bleed profusely, and the Major staggered back. Booth evaded him, pushed forward around Mrs. Lincoln to the edge of the box, placed his left hand on the edge, and climbed backward over the edge of the box. Then, leaping the twelve feet to the stage, he made what might have been his most dramatic entrance ever—black clothing flying, boots, spurs, and hunting knife glittering in the bright stage lights.

FIG. 14
page 24

Unfortunately for Booth, fate intervened. As he vaulted from the rim of the flag-draped box, his toe struck the frame of a large engraving of George Washington that hung on the front of the box, and one of his spurs caught in the flag draped over the margin of the box. This threw him off balance, and he landed with all his weight on one foot, snapping the smaller bone just above his ankle.

FIG. 15
page 25

Limping across the stage, waving his flashing knife, Booth scattered the performers before him, exited by a passageway at the left side of the stage, and went out into the alley where "Peanuts John" Burroughs stood, holding his horse. He struggled onto the horse and rode off down the alley on his planned escape route. At least one member of the audience climbed up the wall of the deep orchestra pit and over the footlights and gave chase, very nearly dragging Booth off his horse as he got underway. Booth evaded his pursuer, turned right into F Street and right again to continue his flight, which probably went down 5th Street, to Pennsylvania Avenue, around the base of the Capitol Building, and down the road toward the Navy Yard Bridge over the Anacostia River.

3.

THE STRUGGLE FOR LIFE

Lincoln's head slumped forward on his chest. Mrs. Lincoln began to scream and took the President's head in her hands (just as Mrs. Kennedy would hold her husband's bullet-torn head 100 years later). Major Rathbone staggered toward the door of the box, gripping his bleeding arm, and tried to pull away the wooden bar wedging the door. He could not budge it while people were pushing on the door from the other side, and the uproar was so loud that he could not make himself heard for some time. When he was finally able to stop the pushing and could dislodge the bar, one of the first people to come into the box was Dr. Charles Leale, a young surgeon from New York who was working at the Army General Hospital at Armory Square. A Lincoln admirer, he had come to the theater primarily to see the President and General Grant and had taken pains to secure a seat in the balcony as close to the presidential box as possible.

Dr. Leale's examination told him that his President was mortally wounded. The bullet had crashed into the back of his head, traversing his brain, coming to rest against the front of his skull, and inflicting a fatal wound on the brain. The ball remained inside his skull and was later recovered at autopsy.

Others crowded around, and there was great pressure to move the President out of the theater. When someone realized that it was Good Friday, the pressure to get the President out of the theater mounted. There had always been a good deal of public criticism of Lincoln's open enjoyment of the theater. Dr. Leale tried to prevail over these protestations, insisting that if the President were carried the many blocks over rough roads to the White House, he would surely die in transit. More time went by as still others insisted that it was absolutely unthinkable for a president to die in a theater on Good Friday. Finally a compromise was reached: it was decided that Lincoln would be moved across the street to Petersen's rooming house.

Fig. 16
page 29

Dr. Leale accompanied the wounded President on the harrowing trip down the theater stairs and across the street to Petersen's rooming house, and remained with him until he was pronounced dead nine hours later. His account of the tragedy—which he wrote many years later, in 1909—tells the story with vividness and immediacy.

As I looked at the President, he appeared to be dead. His eyes were closed and his head had fallen forward. He was being held upright in his chair by Mrs. Lincoln, who was weeping bitterly.

I placed my finger on the President's right radial pulse but could perceive no movement of the artery. For the purpose of reviving him, if possible, we removed him from his chair to a recumbent position on the floor of the box, as I held his head and shoulders while doing this, my hand came in contact with a clot of blood near his left shoulder. Remembering the flashing dagger in the hand of the assassin, and the severely bleeding wound of Major Rathbone, I supposed the President had been stabbed, and while kneeling on the floor over his head, with my eyes continuously watching the President's face, I asked a gentleman [William T. Kent] to cut the coat and shirt open from the neck to the elbow to enable me, if possible, to check the hemorrhage that I thought might take place from the subclavian artery or some other blood vessel. This was done with a dirk knife, but no wound was found there. I lifted his eyelids and saw evidence of a brain injury. I quickly passed the separated fingers of both hands through his blood matted hair to examine his head, and I discovered his mortal wound. The President had been shot in the back of the head, behind the left ear. I easily removed the obstructing clot of blood from the wound, and this relieved the pressure on the brain.

As the President did not then revive, I thought of the other mode of death, apnoea, and assumed my preferred position to revive by artificial respiration. I knelt on the floor over the President, with a knee on each side of his pelvis and facing him. I leaned forward, opened his mouth and introduced two extended fingers of my right hand as far back as possible, and by pressing the base of the paralyzed tongue downward and outward, opened his larynx and made a free passage for air to enter his lungs. I placed an assistant at each of his arms to manipulate them in order to expand his thorax, then slowly to press the arms down by the side of the body, while I pressed the diaphragm upward: methods which caused air to be drawn in and forced out of his lungs.

During the intermissions I also with the strong thumb and fingers of my right hand by intermittent sliding pressure under and beneath the ribs, stimulated the apex of the heart [a crude form of closed chest cardiac massage], and resorted to several other physiological methods. [Perhaps he used anal dilation, a popular method.] We repeated these motions a number of times before signs of recovery from the profound shock were attained; then a feeble action of the heart and irregular breathing followed.

The effects of the shock were still manifest by such great prostration, that I was fearful of any extra agitation of the President's body, and became convinced that something more must be done to retain life. I leaned forcibly forward directly over his body, thorax to thorax, face to face, and several times drew in a long breath, then forcibly breathed directly into his mouth and nostrils, which expanded his lungs and improved his respiration [mouth-to-mouth artificial respiration]. After waiting a moment I placed my ear over his

DR. CHARLES A. LEALE, WHO RESUSCITATED THE PRESIDENT

Dr. Leale was an Army physician who had come to the theater to see President Lincoln and General Grant and had obtained a seat in the dress circle near the door of the presidential box. After the shot was fired and Booth leaped down to the stage, Leale was among the first to reach the door of the box, pressing upon it so hard that the injured Major Rathbone, inside, could not pull away the bar with which Booth had wedged it shut. When Rathbone finally made himself heard and the pushers stopped pushing, the door was opened, and Leale was among the first to reach the President's side. He found him without pulse or respiration and laid him down immediately beside the chair, to give him mouth-to-mouth artificial respiration and closed-chest cardiac massage. These actions restored his breathing and his pulse once again, and he lasted nine more hours, until 7:20 the next morning. Leale accompanied the President across the street to Petersen's rooming house and would not permit him to be moved to the White House, because he felt it was so far that he could die en route. He pronounced the wound to be fatal.

The doctor later became a successful physician in New York City and president of the New York County Medical Society. (*National Archives*)

Fig. 16

thorax and found the action of the heart improving. I rose to the erect kneeling position, then watched for a short time, and saw that the President could continue independent breathing and that instant death would not occur.

I then pronounced my diagnosis and prognosis: "His wound is mortal; it is impossible for him to recover."

When brandy and water arrived, I very slowly poured a small quantity into the President's mouth, this was swallowed and retained.

We decided that the President could now be moved from the possibility of danger in the theater to a house where we might place him on a bed in safety. To assist in this duty I assigned Dr. Taft to carry his right shoulder, Dr. King to carry his left shoulder and detailed a sufficient number of others, whose names I have never discovered, to assist in carrying the body, while I carried his head, going first. We reached the door of the box and saw the long passage leading to the exit crowded with people. I called out twice: "Guards, clear the passage! Guards, clear the passage!" A free space was quickly cleared by an officer and protected by a line of soldiers in the position of present arms with swords, pistols and bayonets. When we reached the stairs, I turned so that those holding the President's feet would descend first. At the door of the theatre, I was again asked if the President could be taken to the White House. I answered: "No, the President would die on the way."

It was necessary to stop several times to give me the opportunity to remove the clot of blood from the opening of the wound.

The great difficulty of retaining life during this brief time occupied in moving the President from the theater to Mr. Petersen's home conclusively proved that the President would have died in the street if I had granted the request to take him such a long distance to the White House. I asked for the best room and we soon had the President placed in bed. He was lifted to the longitudinal center of the bed and placed on his back, while holding his face upward and keeping his head from rolling to either side, I looked at his elevated knees caused by his great height. This uncomfortable position grieved me and I ordered the foot of the bed removed. Dr. Taft and Dr. King reported that it was a fixture. Then I requested that it be broken off. As I found this could not satisfactorily be done, I had the President placed diagonally on the bed and called for extra pillows, and with them formed a gentle incline plane on which to rest his head and shoulders.

I examined the President's entire body from his head to his feet and found no other injury. His lower extremities were very cold and I sent the hospital steward, who had been of great assistance to us in removing the President from the theater, to produce bottles of hot water and hot blankets, which were applied. I also sent for a large sinapism and in a short time one very nicely made was brought. This I applied over the solar plexus and to the anterior surface of his body.

As the symptoms indicated renewed brain compression, I again cleared the opening of clotted blood and pushed forward the button of bone, which acted as a valve, permitted an oozing of blood and relieved pressure on the brain. I again saw good results from this action.

Then I sent the hospital steward for a Nelaton probe. No drug or medicine in any form was administered to the President, but the artificial heat and mustard plaster that I had applied warmed his cold body and stimulated his nerves.

The hospital steward arrived with the Nelaton probe and an examination was made by the surgeon general and myself, who introduced the probe to a

Fig. 17
page 31

30

THE REAR BEDROOM OF PETERSEN'S ROOMING HOUSE
WHERE PRESIDENT LINCOLN DIED

Lincoln was so tall that he had to be laid cater-cornered on the bed, with several pillows propping him up so that his feet could also be on the bed. Attempts to break off the foot piece of the bed were unsuccessful because of its construction. The blood-soaked bed coverings were torn up and dispensed to many people as souvenirs. Mrs. Woodrow Wilson is said to have crocheted the bedspread in this picture. The National Park Service has installed this bed in the position of the one in which Lincoln died. *(National Park Service)*

Fig. 17

distance of about two and a half inches, where it came in contact with a foreign substance (possibly a fragment of bone), which lay across the track of the ball; this was easily passed and the probe was introduced several inches further where it again touched a hard substance at first supposed to be the ball, but as the white porcelain bulb of the probe on its withdrawal did not indicate the mark of lead it was generally thought to be another piece of loose bone. The probe was introduced the second time and the ball was supposed to be distinctly felt. After this second exploration nothing further was done with the wound except to keep the opening free of coagula, which, if allowed to form and remain for a short time, produced signs of increased brain compression, the breathing becoming profoundly stertorous and intermittent, the pulse more feeble and irregular.

During the night Mrs. Lincoln came frequently from the adjoining room accompanied by a lady friend. At one time Mrs. Lincoln exclaimed, sobbing bitterly: "Oh, that my little Taddy might see his father before he died!" This was decided not advisable. As Mrs. Lincoln sat on a chair by the side of the bed with her face to her husband's, his breathing became very stertorous and the loud, unnatural noise frightened her in her exhausted, agonized condition. She sprang up suddenly with a piercing cry and fell fainting to the floor. Secretary Stanton, hearing her cry, came in from the adjoining room and with raised arms called out loudly: "Take that woman out and do not let her in again." Mrs. Lincoln was helped up kindly and assisted in a fainting condition from the room. Secretary Stanton's order was obeyed and Mrs. Lincoln did not see her husband again before he died.

As morning dawned it became quite evident that the President was sinking, and at several times his pulse could not be counted. Two or three feeble pulsations being noticed, followed by an intermission when not the slightest movements of the artery could be felt. The inspirations became very prolonged and labored, accompanied by a guttural sound. The respiration ceased for some time and several anxiously looked at their watches until the profound silence was disturbed by a prolonged inspiration, which was followed by a sonorous expiration.

President Lincoln Dies

The protracted struggle ceased at twenty minutes past seven o'clock on the morning of April 15, 1865, and I announced that the President was dead.

Immediately after the death the few remaining in the room knelt around the bed while the Rev. Dr. Gurley delivered one of the most impressive prayers ever uttered.

Then I gently smoothed the President's contracted facial muscles, took two coins from my pocket, placed them over his eyelids and drew a white sheet over the martyr's face. I had been the means, in God's hand, of prolonging the life of President Abraham Lincoln for nine hours.

Dr. Charles S. Taft, acting assistant surgeon, U.S. Army, who was boosted up over the edge of the presidential box by people on the stage, thus to become the second doctor on the scene, gave his own description of "The Last Hours of Abraham Lincoln," in an article written on April

32

22, 1865, for *The Philadelphia Medical and Surgical Reporter*. His account bears out the essentials of Dr. Leale's statement but contains a series of conflicting descriptions of the pupillary and other findings. His account does add some interesting details, and it is as follows:

The President was removed to a house opposite, and laid upon a bed in 15 minutes from the time the shot was fired.

The wound was there examined, the finger being used as a probe, and the ball found to have passed beyond the reach of the finger into the brain. The respiration now became labored; pulse 44, feeble, eyes entirely closed, the left pupil much contracted, the right widely dilated; total insensibility to light in both. The left upper eyelid was swollen and dark from effused blood; this was observed a few minutes after his removal from the theatre. About 30 minutes after he was placed upon the bed, discoloration from the effusion began in the internal canthus of the right eye, which became discolored and swollen with great protrusion of the eye.

About 11:30 P.M., twitching of the facial muscles of the left side set in and continued some 15 or 20 minutes, and the mouth was drawn slightly to the same side. Sinapisms over the entire anterior surface of the body were ordered, together with artificial heat to the extremities.

The wound began to ooze very soon after the patient was placed upon the bed, and continued to discharge blood and brain tissue until 5:30 A.M., when it ceased entirely; the head, in the meantime, being supported in such a position as to facilitate the discharge of the wound, and in keeping the orifice free from coagulum while the wound was discharging freely, the respiration was easy; but the moment the discharge was arrested from any cause, it became at once labored.

It was also remarkable to observe the great difference in character of the pulse whenever the orifice of the wound was freed from coagulum, and discharged freely; thus relieving, in a measure, the compression. This fact will account for the fluctuation in the pulse, as given in the subjoined notes.

About 2 A.M., an ordinary silver probe was introduced into the wound by the surgeon general. It met an obstruction about three inches from the external orifice, which was decided to be the plug of bone driven in from the skull and lodged in the track of the ball. The probe passed by this obstruction, but was too short to follow the track the whole length. A Nelaton probe was then procured and passed into the track of the wound for a distance of 2 inches beyond the plug of bone, when the ball was distinctly felt, passing beyond this, the fragments of the orbital plate of the left orbit were felt. The ball made no mark upon the porcelain tip, and was afterwards found to be of exceedingly hard lead.

Some difference of opinion existed as to the exact position of the ball, but the autopsy confirmed the correctness of the diagnosis upon first exploration. No further attempt was made to explore the wound.

After cessation of the bleeding from the wound, the respiration was stertorous up to the last breath, which was drawn at 21 minutes and 55 seconds past 7; the heart did not cease to beat until 22 minutes and 10 seconds past 7.

The wonderful vitality exhibited by the late President was one of the most interesting and remarkable circumstances connected with the case. It was the opinions of the surgeons in charge that most patients would have died in 2 hours; Lincoln lived from 10:30 P.M. until 7:22 A.M.

About 1 A.M., spasmodic contractions of the muscles came on, causing pronation of the forearms; the pectoral muscles seemed to be fixed, the breath was held during the spasm, and a sudden and forcible expiration immediately succeeded it.

At about the same time both pupils became widely dilated and remained so until death.

During the night Drs. Hall, May, Liebermann and nearly all the leading men of the profession in the city tendered their services.

It was at this time, as Dr. Leale placed silver coins on the eyelids, that Secretary of War Stanton is said to have uttered the immortal words: "Now he belongs to the ages."

FIG. 17
page 31

Lincoln's body was moved from Petersen's to the White House and permission for an autopsy—the one referred to in Taft's article—was obtained by Dr. Robert King Stone, Lincoln's family physician. At about noon, some five hours after death, a partial postmortem examination—of the brain only—was made in the President's bedroom.

The Autopsy

The man who actually did the autopsy was an army doctor who was on duty at the Army Medical Museum, Asst. Surgeon J. Janvier Woodward. He was assisted by another army doctor, Asst. Surgeon Edward Curtis. Dr. Woodward's brief report—which was handwritten—is as follows:

Surgeon General's Office
Washington City D.C.
April 15, 1865
Brigadier General J. K. Barnes
Surgeon General U. S. A.

General:
I have the honor to report that in obedience to your orders and aided by Assistant Surgeon E. Curtis, U. S. A., I made in your presence at 12 o'clock this morning an autopsy on the body of President Abraham Lincoln, with the following results: The eyelids and surrounding parts of the face were greatly ecchymosed and the eyes somewhat protuberant from effusion of blood into the orbits.

There was a gunshot wound of the head around which the scalp was greatly thickened by hemorrhage into its tissue. The ball entered through the occipital bone about one inch to the left of the median line and just above the left lateral sinus, which it opened. It then penetrated the dura mater, passed through the left posterior lobe of the cerebrum, entered the left lateral ventricle and lodged in the white matter of the cerebrum just above the anterior portion of the left corpus striatum, where it was found.

The wound in the occipital bone was quite smooth, circular in shape, with bevelled edges. The opening through the internal table being larger than that through the external table. The track of the ball was full of clotted blood and contained several little fragments of bone with a small piece of the ball near its external orifice. The brain around the track was pultaceous and livid from capillary hemorrhage into its substance. The ventricles of the brain were full of clotted blood. A thick clot beneath the dura mater coated the right cerebral lobe.

There was a smaller clot under the dura mater of the left side. But little blood was found at the base of the brain. Both the orbital plates of the frontal bone were fractured and the fragments pushed upwards toward the brain. The dura mater over these fractures was uninjured. The orbits were gorged with blood. I have the honor of being very respectfully your obedient servant.

J. J. Woodward
Assistant Surgeon
U. S. A.

A True Copy, George A. Otis, Assistant Surgeon U.S.A.

Partial Nature of the Autopsy

Here again we have an analogy with President Kennedy, on whom also only a partial autopsy was done. Although in the Kennedy case the report did encompass the body cavities and was a great deal more complete than in the Lincoln one, its incompleteness in certain details was seized upon as the basis for vigorous criticism of the official investigation by the Warren Commission.

One might think that if photographs were taken of an assassinated President's wounds and X-rays made of the body, it would be easy to avoid the pitfalls of memory which confused the testimony as to the findings in the Lincoln autopsy. However, as we shall see, 100 years later in the Kennedy case, even photographs and X-rays are not infallible evidence—especially when the men who were working up the autopsy report were not permitted, because of the family's wishes, to see the extremely revealing color photographs they had taken of the body and were permitted only a hasty glance at the X-rays. As a result, even with President Kennedy's rather well-documented autopsy, there was at least as much confusion and recrimination as in Lincoln's case.

True Lodgment of Bullet Left in Doubt

Dr. Taft was also present when Dr. Woodward did the autopsy, but he did not participate in it. Before writing his article about Lincoln's last hours, he made statements to the newspapers at various times concerning the final location of the bullet within the brain. On the very day of the autopsy, he made a statement to one newspaper indicating that the bullet was on the right side, which was contrary to the reports of Dr. Woodward and later reports by other doctors. His description of the actual autopsy—which is included in "The Last Hours"—states his opinions in a manner calculated to establish his authority:

The following brief report of the circumstances attending the assassination, last hours and autopsy of the late President will doubtless prove of much interest to the profession and may be relied upon as correct in all particulars, the notes from which it is written having been submitted to comparisons with others taken, and corrected by the highest authority. . . .

The calvarium was removed, the brain exposed, and sliced down to the track of the ball, which was plainly indicated by a line of coagulated blood extending from the external wound in the occipital bone, obliquely across from the left to right through the brain to the anterior lobe of the cerebrum, immediately behind the right orbit. The surface of the right hemisphere was covered with coagulated blood. After removing the brain from the cranium the ball dropped from its lodgement in the anterior lobe. The small piece of ball, evidently cut off in its passage through the occipital bone, was previously taken out of the track of the ball, about 4 inches from the external wound. The hole made through the occipital bone was as cleanly cut as if done with a punch.

The point of entrance is one inch to the left of the longitudinal sinus and opening into the lateral sinus. The ball is flattened, convex on both sides, and evidently moulded by hand in a derringer pistol mould as indicated by the ridged surface left by the nippers in clipping off the neck. The orbital plates of both orbits were the seats of comminuted fractures, the fragments being forced inward, and the dura mater covering them remaining uninjured. The double fracture was decided to have been caused by contre-coup. The plug of bone driven in from the occipital bone was found in the track of the ball about three inches from the external wound, proving the correctness of the opinion advanced by the surgeon general and Dr. Stone as to its nature, at the exploration of the wound before death.

One of the most surprising features of a study of the records of this case is the repeated disagreement and contradiction of the various authors who described the autopsy findings, particularly concerning above which eye the bullet came to rest. Dr. Woodward, when he performed the autopsy, described the bullet's lodging place as above the left eye, as did Dr. Stone, Lincoln's family physician. Testifying at the trial of the conspirators, Dr. Stone stated:

The next day, previous to the process of embalmment, an examination was made in the presence of surgeon general Joseph K. Barnes, Assistant Surgeon Edward Curtis, and Assistant Surgeon J. Janvier Woodward, of the Army. We traced the wound through the brain and the ball was found in the anterior part of the same side of the brain, the left side; it was a large ball, resembling those which are shot from the pistol known as the derringer; an unusually large ball— that is, larger than those used in the ordinary pocket revolvers. It was a leaden handmade ball, and was flattened in its passage through the skull, and a portion had been cut off in going through the bone I marked the ball "A. L.," the initials of the late president, and in the presence of the Secretary of War, in his office, enclosed it in an envelope, sealed it with my private seal and endorsed it with my name.

FIG. 18
page 37

Both Surgeon General Barnes and Dr. Taft stated that it was lodged above the right eye, while Taft in another of his descriptions stated that it was above the left. Taft also contradicted himself by stating that the

THE BALL THAT KILLED LINCOLN

This is the .44-caliber Britannia-metal ball that was removed from Lincoln's brain. Note that a slice was sheared off by the sharp edge of the wound of entrance in the back part of the skull, just as a large fragment of Oswald's bullet was sheared off by the skull of President Kennedy 100 years later. *(National Archives)*

Fig. 18

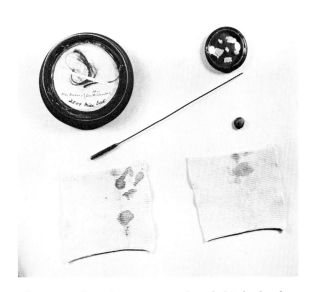

MEMENTOS OF THE AUTOPSY ON LINCOLN

Dr. Curtis, one of the physicians who assisted at the autopsy, placed this lock of Lincoln's hair, these chips of his skull, the probe used to follow the track of the bullet, the actual bullet, and the bloodstained (from Lincoln's blood) cuffs of his autopsy gown in the Army Medical Museum. *(National Archives)*

Fig. 19

Nelaton probe, following the track of the ball, struck the bones of the left orbit, whereas in describing the autopsy he stated that the ball came to rest behind the right orbit. On still another occasion Dr. Taft stated that the point of the Nelaton probe struck the orbital plate of the right eye.

Dr. Joseph K. Barnes, the surgeon general of the U.S. Army, appeared two years later as a witness in the trial of John H. Surratt and said, "The ball entered the skull to the left of the middle line, and below the line with the ear. It ranged forward and upward toward the right eye, lodging within a half inch of that orbit." Thus the true location of the resting place of the bullet is left in doubt by the conflicting accounts of four men who attended the autopsy.

FIG. 20
page 39

Dr. Edward Curtis, after assisting at the autopsy, wrote a letter to his mother in which he stated, "I was surprised to find that the great man's brain weighed no more than that of an ordinary mortal." He also wrote, "I was simply astonished at the showing of the nude remains, where well-rounded muscles built upon strong bones told the powerful athlete. Now did I understand the deeds of prowess recorded of the President's early days."

Dr. Curtis spoke reverently of the examination that was done: "There is laid bare what a few short hours hence was the foundation of a wit and wisdom that could save a nation. The part is lifted from its seat, when suddenly from out a cruel vent that traverses it from end to end through these very fingers, a something hard slips and falls with a metal's mocking clatter into a basin set beneath. The search is satisfied; a little pellet of lead."

FIG. 19
page 37

Dr. Curtis's bloodstained cuffs, with splinters of bone and bits of hair cut from Lincoln's head at the time of the autopsy, were presented to the National Park Service and by them to the Army Institute of Pathology and are on display in their museum in Washington along with the fatal bullet and the probe used at the autopsy.

Lincoln's Physique

Curtis's description of Lincoln's general state of health and other evidence from photographs and physical descriptions of Lincoln's appearance and muscularity clearly negate the speculations that have been made that he might have been suffering from Marfan's syndrome, a rare disease whose symptoms include excessively slender, spidery fingers, dislocation of the lenses of the eye, and heart trouble. Not only were these symptoms missing in Lincoln, but there was also evidence to the contrary: his great physical strength, his muscular development, and his ability to lock his joints and foil the strongest opponent in wrestling. These physical signs completely rule out the possibility of Marfan's syndrome.

No mention was made of any adhesions or residuals from a previous head injury sustained by Lincoln in his early teens when he was kicked in

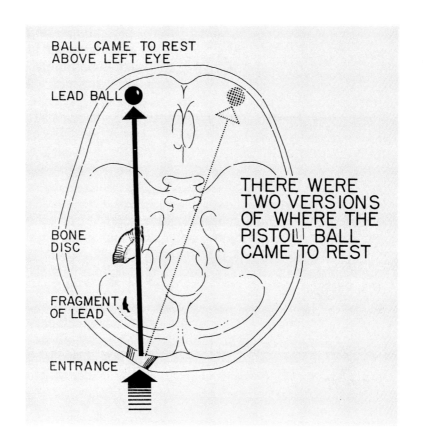

BALL CAME TO REST
ABOVE LEFT EYE

LEAD BALL

THERE WERE
TWO VERSIONS
OF WHERE THE
PISTOL BALL
CAME TO REST

BONE
DISC

FRAGMENT
OF LEAD

ENTRANCE

VERSIONS OF WHERE THE BALL ENDED UP IN LINCOLN'S BRAIN

Dr. Woodward, who did the autopsy, and Dr. Curtis, who assisted, stated that the ball traversed the open space in the left side of the brain and came to rest over the left eye. However, Dr. Barnes, the Surgeon General, and Dr. Taft, who was the second doctor to reach Lincoln (having been boosted upward from the stage over the edge of the box), both stated positively at the trial of the conspirators, and later, that it ended up over the right eye. Moreover, there were conflicting statements, by two different observers, as to which pupil was large and which pupil was small. Even Dr. Leale got the side of the wound entry mixed up in writing to a friend shortly after the assassination (see fig. 21). It might be thought that photographs and X-rays could prevent this kind of dilemma. One hundred years later, however, in the case of President Kennedy and with modern technology available, the photographs and X-rays were taken away from the autopsy surgeons before they could consult them at length or in detail, and again there was confusion about autopsy findings. (*J. K. Lattimer*)

Fig. 20

the forehead by a balky horse he was using to turn a gristmill. He had been unconscious for "most of a day," and "came to" continuing the same remarks he had been addressing to the horse when he lost consciousness. This was one of Lincoln's favorite stories about himself.

Data gleaned from other sources indicate that Lincoln was six feet four inches tall, weighed about 180 pounds (having lost weight since he left Springfield), wore a hat size 7⅛ and boots that measured about size 12B. (It may be that his boots were slightly larger when new, since leather shrinks with a century of aging.) Life masks measure 6 and $^{11}/_{12}$ inches from ear to ear and an estimated 8 inches from front to back of the brain case. His fingers were long but sturdy and his arms and legs were long for his body. Herndon described him as wiry, sinewy, raw-boned, thin through the chest from front to back, and narrow across the shoulders. While his left pupil was closer to his upper lid, it seems unlikely that this represented a muscular imbalance since he was unable to reproduce the one or two episodes of double image which he had experienced even though he strove to do so. His athletic prowess as a rail-splitter and champion wrestler was well documented, and only a few months before his death he had put on a demonstration of woodchopping, making chips fly in all directions, and finishing by holding the heavy ax out at arm's length, much to the awe of the wounded soldiers he was visiting.

He was known to have had recurrent malaria, smallpox, frostbitten feet, lifelong constipation, and probably scarlet fever. The fact that his son Tad later died of a disease suspected of being tuberculosis is also of interest.

Certainly he was a tall, wiry, asthenic, moody type, from Old American stock, who might have lived to a ripe old age had he not become president.

All my own attempts to deduce, indirectly, which side of the brain was the final lodgment of the bullet have also proved frustrating and fruitless, because the two available statements as to which pupil was dilated and which was contracted are completely contradictory. These doctors had been continuously awake for over thirty hours and were under great stress, so that some confusion is understandable. Even Dr. Leale reversed himself inadvertently in a letter to a friend (author's collection) where he described the wound of entry as on Lincoln's right.

Fig. 21
page 41

The statement that there was twitching of the face on the left side at about 11:30 P.M. (seventy-seven minutes after the shooting), with the mouth drawn slightly to the left during the twitching, is unchallenged in the descriptions of the symptoms and may have reflected irritation of the "facial" area of the surface of the brain on the right lateral surface of the brain from the "thick clot" found at the autopsy, "coating the right cerebral lobe." Perhaps this clot was indeed caused by contre-coup where the brain, set in motion by a blow, strikes the opposite side of the skull so hard as to injure it against the far side of the skull. Whether the mouth was drawn to the left by the twitching on the left or because of the

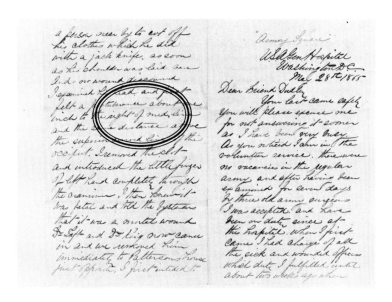

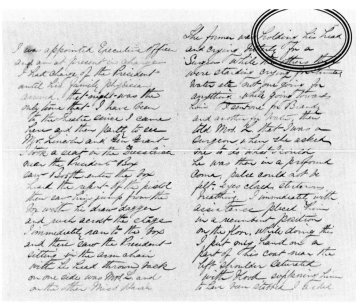

ERROR IN DR. LEALE'S LETTER

Two pages from a letter written by Dr. Leale (who resuscitated Lincoln in the theater box) to a friend, shortly after the event. In it he mistakenly writes that the President's head wound was in the right side of the back of his head (top). Elsewhere (bottom) he states that Mrs. Lincoln was holding President Lincoln's bullet-torn head in her hands, just as Mrs. Kennedy did a century later. *(J. K. Lattimer)*

Fig. 21

transitory paralysis of the right side of the face is not known. It seems as though the mouth was pulled to the left by the twitching facial muscles. Large, destructive, soft-tissue cavities have been shown by modern ballistic studies to form in the brain when bullets enter the skull, and it is possible that some brain surface areas such as this one, opposite the wound of entrance, might be damaged by this mechanism. The spasmodic contractions of the muscles with pronation (inward twisting) of both forearms, at 1:00 A.M., almost three hours after the shooting, may have reflected either severe brain stem damage from the progressive swelling and a state of decerebration, or a convulsive "seizure" from the cortical irritation of the surface of the brain. The fact that the President's condition then worsened progressively without further convulsions is more in keeping with a "decerebrate" status.

On the other hand, it is surprising that, if the bullet had indeed traversed the central part of the brain (stem) damaging it directly as it would if it crossed the midline, respirations could be maintained at all. Inequality of pupils is a frequent initial finding in many brain injuries with unequal brain damage on the two sides. Possibly the right and the left third cranial nerves were irritated to different degrees as the inevitable swelling to the brain occurred, from both the cavity formation at the time of the bullet wound and the resultant swelling. Whether the forces involved were sufficient to drive the brain downward into the opening at the base of the skull, compressing the side lobes over the free margins of the partitions in the skull with the resultant ominous signs of the "incisural syndrome," is not known, although this is possible. If it were possible to be sure which pupil was contracted and which one dilated shortly after the passage of the bullet, some better conjecture as to the final resting place of the bullet might have been possible. But since the testimony was conflicting, accurate deductions are impossible. The wide dilation of both pupils at 1:00 A.M., less than three hours after injury, certainly marked a progression of swelling of the brain as the President's condition worsened steadily. The cessation of bleeding and oozing at 5:30 A.M., seven hours after the shooting, was another ominous sign of terminal blood pressure fall from both blood loss and nervous system damage.

The fact that a small piece of metal had separated from the pistol ball and was found partway through the brain, along the track of the ball, is slightly more suggestive of a tangential entrance of the ball into the skull (toward the left eye), since the edges of the skull frequently shave fragments from bullets when the angle of entry is tangential. On the other hand, the skull edges can shave off fragments even from bullets fired squarely into the skull (toward the right eye), so this differential point is of little value. The clear, punched-out edges of the wound in the bone sound more typical of a course directly into the skull, which might be considered to favor a course toward the right eye. Here again, one can only speculate.

Why Were the Roofs of the Eye Sockets Fractured?

During the past century, a number of authors have written pages of puzzled speculation as to why the orbital plates (roofs of the eye sockets) should have been fractured by a gunshot wound at the opposite end of the head. Several different theories have been advanced to explain the fractures. Some favored the theory of transmission of intracranial pressure from the semifluid contents of the brain, fracturing the orbital plates down into the orbits with their subsequent elevation by the accumulation of blood within the orbits. Others speculated about contre-coup, while still another thought that the President's head must have fallen forward and struck the edge of the box or some other hard object in order to fracture the orbital plates. One Englishman decided the ball must have struck the orbital plates and bounced back into the brain. This seems unlikely. Only one author quoted a similar case where a bullet, creasing the top of the skull, brought about a similar fracture of one orbital plate, but not both. Still another author suggested that the conductor of the autopsy might have been completely mistaken and that blood vessels over the roofs of the orbits, torn by the prosecutor, might have resembled fractures where none existed. Dr. Ashhurst, in his review of medical and surgical history of the War of the Rebellion, quotes Saucerote et al. and suggests that a blow on the back of the head might distort the ovoid shape of the brain case, making it round momentarily, thus drawing the front positions toward the center with any fragments displaced inward, as in this case. The thin, delicate bone of the orbital roofs would certainly fracture easily under these conditions.

Many, many questions probably always will remain unanswered. But it is gratifying to have even these sparse and somewhat contradictory records to study in an effort to find out what really happened to one of the greatest men of modern times.

A great many people feel that in the case of presidential assassination or the mysterious death of any well-beloved person, the subject—like the body itself—should be laid to rest. Nevertheless, since 100 years of research and theory had failed to come up with a definitive explanation of the details of Lincoln's assassination, I decided to do some research of my own to investigate this point.

It seemed logical, at the outset, to consult an experienced modern medical examiner on the question of the displaced orbital fractures, so I consulted the then chief medical examiner of the city of New York, my early mentor, the late, great Dr. Milton Helpern.

First, I described the wound of entry into the occipital bone, one inch to the left of midline, and laid the facts and the theories about the shooting systematically before the doctor. When the detailed description of the wound of entrance was completed, Dr. Helpern commented that the bullet had entered through one of the thickest areas of the skull, and that it obviously required most of the force of the missile to penetrate the bone, causing the skull to absorb a tremendous amount of energy in that instant. The elasticity of the skull would have permitted it to be noticeably distorted at the moment of impact. Dr. Helpern's next remark was, "I presume that the roofs of the orbits were found to be broken." He went on to relate that this finding was well known to medical examiners and that it accounted for the eye sockets being gorged with blood in many other shooting victims. In persons shot through the front portions of the skull, for example, the roofs of the orbits (eye sockets) sometimes open so widely as to catch herniations of dura (bulging bits of skull lining) as they snap back into place after the shot. Upward displacement of the fragments of the eye socket roofs was not uncommon in his experience. Dr. Helpern asked if the dura mater (lining of the skull) had been stripped up from the floor of the brain case, speculating that additional fracture lines might have been present there, running from the wound of entry to the eye sockets. According to the record, the dura had not been stripped from the floor of the brain case.

In an effort to find out what really does happen when a skull is struck on its thick back portion, I next conducted an experiment with models of skulls which I had sawed into narrow strips so each strip looked like a side view of the skull as might be seen in an X-ray film of the region of the skull in question. I took several of these oval outlines of the brain case (main part) of the skull and hit each one on the back-of-the-head area where Booth's bullet had struck. The resulting distortion of each oval outline of the skull indicated that the displacement of fragments from fractures of the roofs of the eye sockets, resulting from the distortion of such a blow on the back of the head, might well be upward toward the brain, as the ovoid shape of the skull became more rounded from the

FIG. 22
page 45

force of the blow. These experiments led me to agree with the opinion expressed by Dr. Saucerote and associates in the late 1700s that upward displacement of the fragments would not be surprising.

Thus our experimentation confirmed what Dr. Helpern had predicted from his years of experience in the medical examiner's office *of New York City.*

Did the Bullet Come from the Wrong Direction?

Still another puzzling fact now came to light.

Since the assassin approached from the President's right side, according to the testimony of the only two witnesses, it was puzzling that the wound of entrance should be on the rear-left side of the head. This dilemma mystified some of those concerned with the assassination. There were cries that it could not have been Booth, that the shot must have come from the opposite direction, and that therefore it must have been a different shooter. This is amazingly similar to the cries of the Kennedy generation of critics 100 years later, that the shot must have come from the opposite direction from a different shooter.

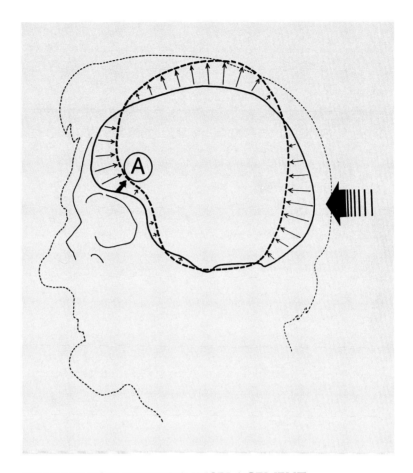

REASON FOR UPWARD DISPLACEMENT
OF ROOFS OF EYE SOCKETS

One of the mysteries following the Lincoln autopsy was the fact that the thin bone layers that formed the roofs of his eye sockets were fractured upward into the brain case. There was much speculation about the reason for this. When an experimental model of the brain case was made, in the form of an oval, and it was deformed by a blow on the back on its sturdiest portion, the templet tended to distort into a more circular configuration (dotted line). This made the area where the roofs of the eye sockets (A) would be move upward and inward, and probably explains the reason for the upward displacement of the fragments. Dr. Milton Helpern has pointed out that this phenomenon of fracturing of the roofs of the eye sockets is frequent after bullet wounds of the head, and that sometimes the fragments separate so widely that folds of soft tissue are caught by them as the distortion is relieved and the fracture lines snap back into place. *(J. K. Lattimer)*

Fig. 22

As with the Kennedy assassination, when all of the facts were in, the case seemed much less mysterious. It happened that a Mr. James P. Ferguson, who was sitting on the opposite side of the theater, had come there to see his old idol, General Grant. Mr. Ford had told him that "his favorite, General Grant, would be attending that night." Mr. Ferguson was watching the presidential box intently a moment before the pistol flash, wondering whether the person who had just entered the box was Grant. He was aware that Grant was a modest man who might have delayed arriving until after the show had started in order to avoid the uproar of hysterical admiration that would have greeted his appearance. While peering intently, Ferguson noted that President Lincoln turned his head sharply to the left just before the shot was fired. The President twisted his head so far around toward his left side that the back of the *left* side of his head was presented to the pistol, rather than the back of the *right* side of his head.

Other people who noted the turning of President Lincoln's head thought he was looking at something out in the audience. It seems most likely of all, to me, that out of the corner of his eye the President saw the pistol being pointed at the back of the right side of his head and flinched away from it, twisting his head far around to the left just as the shot was fired. This might better explain the extreme twist of the head needed to permit the bullet to cross the brain, from left to right, if indeed it did. In any case, the shot was fired into the back of Lincoln's head at the moment when the head was twisted sharply away from the assassin, presenting the left-rear portion of the head toward the pistol. This fact does not help in deciding near which eye the ball would lodge, since one does not know how far around the head was turned at the moment the shot was fired. It is certainly a fact that a ball fired solidly into the head would be more likely to go across the brain into the right hemisphere than to travel, more tangentially, completely within the left side of the brain.

It is all very well to speculate on the path the fatal bullet may have taken, but it leads to another, more diffi*cult question, to more speculation, and to further unanswered and unanswerable questions. It is inevitable that we, in our perusal of the evidence and our search for the truth, must ask whether or not, with modern neurosurgical techniques, blood transfusion, supportive and anti-bacterial therapy, it might have been possible for Lincoln to have survived had he been shot in 1980 instead of 1865.*

Could Lincoln Have Been Saved?

Many competent authorities have expressed their opinions that Lincoln could not possibly have survived, even today. The large projectile, striking the head with the force of a sledge hammer, had driven a disc of bone almost one inch in diameter ahead of it, through the lateral venous sinus, across the meninges, and into the brain to a depth of three inches. A fragment of metal the size of a modern dime had torn off and was left in the track and the balance of the projectile had traveled a distance of 7½ inches through the brain to lodge almost at the front side of the skull. Bits of Lincoln's long, heavy hair must necessarily have been driven into the brain by the bullet, and there is a question as to whether bits of grease, patch, or paper wadding, which may have accompanied the bullet, might still have clung to it during the passage of only a few inches before striking Lincoln's head. This combination of foreign materials scattered in a track through the entire length of the brain would have been impossible to locate and clean out completely, as any experienced wartime surgeon knows.

In addition, in an attempt to locate the ball, the brain had been probed to the full length of the unsterile fingers of at least two of the doctors who attended him, and with two unsterile probes, a silver one approximately 6 inches long and a porcelain-tipped rubber Nelaton probe, which reached to a depth of 7½ inches. The principles of aseptic techniques and the concept of germs as the cause of wound infections were unknown in Lincoln's day; while occasional Civil War soldiers were reported to have recovered from bullet wounds of the brain, these were rare exceptions.

The autopsy report that the track of the bullet could be easily distinguished because of the extensive destruction and the presence of "pultaceous" brain material along the track points up the tremendous local damage, but does not take into account the further damage which is now known to result from the momentary creation of a large cavity in the brain when it is traversed by a missile traveling at the speed of a bullet. There seems to be no reason to disagree with those who have stated that Lincoln could not possibly have survived this wound, even in modern times, and that, indeed, it is remarkable that he survived for nine hours, as he did, after the shooting. Even if he had survived, he most certainly would have been a decerebrate "vegetable"; a cruel transformation from the sensitive, compassionate, and thoughtful chief of state which he had been. Death probably also spared him a vicious campaign of character assassination and defamation which would have accompanied his avowed attempts to curb postwar profiteering, exploitation, and vengeance directed at the prostrate South. As it was, assassination, at the very peak of his popularity, enshrined him forever in the history of the world.

While Lincoln often spoke and dreamed about being assassinated, his fatalistic attitude led him to deprecate all attempts to guard his life, despite the fact that his hat had once been shot from his head in an unsuccessful assassination attempt.

The Assassination Weapon

It is always fascinating to know exactly what sort of weapon an assassin chooses, how he carries and conceals it, and how the weapon is studied, by experts, after the crime—provided that it is recovered.

Fig. 23
page 49

Lincoln was shot with a small pistol only 6 inches long, of a type popular among gamblers and adventurers because it could be easily concealed on the person. It was a type known as a derringer, a name taken from a pioneer manufacturer of such pistols, Henry Deringer of Philadelphia. It is now always misspelled, with a double r as the standard spelling. Indeed, the words Deringer and Philadelphia appear on the lock and barrel of the murder pistol. To the gunsmith's trade, a derringer was a short-barreled pistol of large caliber, with a rifled barrel to spin the ball in an effort to give it greater stability in its flight. While Booth's murder weapon had a barrel length of only 2½ inches, it fired a large ball almost ½ inch in diameter (.44 caliber) and Booth had elected to have it loaded on that night with a handmade ball of Britannia metal, which is harder than lead and may have required something wrapped around the hard bullet in order to seat it well among the grooves of the rifled barrel. Heavy grease, or a greased paper wad, or a thin leather or cloth patch was sometimes used for this, and to prevent grains of powder from trickling out around the ball. Certainly some grease, a paper wad, or a patch were in the charge fired into Lincoln's head from close range. One can only guess at the charge of powder used, but ten grains of black powder were used in the first cartridge pistols of the same caliber, which came into being a few years later and displaced the percussion-cap ignition system of Booth's pistol. The barrel of the pistol was of iron, but the trigger and mountings were of German silver with a slightly brassy glint, probably accounting for the many erroneous references to the pistol as a small brass derringer. There was a tiny box in the butt of the pistol for a spare percussion cap.

The pistol was found later the same night when William T. Kent, one of the first men into the box after the shooting, returned to look for his latchkey, which he realized must have fallen from his pocket when he lent surgeon Leale his knife to cut open Lincoln's coat, vest, and shirt. While searching on the floor of the box for his latchkey, his foot struck an object which turned out to be the murderer's derringer. Mr. Kent's friend Private Ferree, who accompanied him to Ford's, also found on the floor of the theater box the bloodstained collar which had been cut from Lincoln's neck in the search for the wound.

Fig. 24
page 49

While the pistol was small, it fired a large heavy projectile which must have struck the back of the head with tremendous force even at its relatively low velocity.

Today Booth's pistols and knife can be seen in the museum on the basement floor of Ford's Theater.

And while Lincoln lay dying at Petersen's boardinghouse, long before all the complicated and conflicting reports about his death and his autopsy were written, Booth, injured in his fall, was trying to get away.

.44-CALIBER DERRINGER

This is the type of .44-caliber single-shot percussion pistol Booth used to kill Lincoln. Its half-inch Britannia-metal ball was held in place by a wad of grease or a patch of greased cloth or thin leather, the debris from which was fired into Lincoln's brain along with the ball, adding to the contamination. A Derringer by definition is a short-barreled pistol in which the barrel is rifled. The type was devised by Henry Deringer, a Philadelphia pistol maker whose name appears on Booth's pistol. Its mountings are of German silver, which has a slightly brassy glint, leading to the erroneous characterization of this pistol as a brass Derringer, which it was not. There was a tiny pocket for an extra percussion cap in the butt of the pistol. *(J. K. Lattimer)*

Fig. 23

LINCOLN'S BLOODSTAINED COLLAR

This collar was cut from Lincoln's neck by Dr. Leale, who, having seen Booth go across the stage waving his knife, feared a stab wound of the chest. The collar was found later by Kent and Ferree, who were searching for Kent's latchkey, which had fallen out of his pocket when he gave Dr. Leale his pocketknife to cut open Lincoln's shirt. *(J. K. Lattimer)*

Fig. 24

4.

BOOTH'S ESCAPE AND DEATH

Booth galloped on. His broken leg pained him at every stride, but at least he was not encumbered by the living, resisting, trussed-up body of President Lincoln, as he would have been if the plan to kidnap, not murder, Lincoln had been put into effect. He was able to flee safely over his well-studied escape course, down onto Pennsylvania Avenue, around the Capitol Building, and then on to the Navy Yard Bridge over the Anacostia River. At the bridge, the armed sentry brought him to an abrupt halt. Booth gave his own name to the guard at the bridge, which ordinarily had been closed to civilians after 9:00 P.M. The alarm was not yet out, however; both Booth and Herold (who arrived at the bridge a short time later) were permitted to cross without serious challenge. Both claimed to be legitimate residents of the area on the other side of the bridge, and their knowledgeable replies satisfied the extensive questions of the sentry posted at the bridge. Booth's detention and release during his escape were very similar to the experience of Oswald a century later. After he had shot President Kennedy, Oswald was detained at gunpoint and then released (because the alarm for him was not yet out) to continue his escape, until he also, in the long run, was fatally wounded by a single gunshot. The sentry at the bridge was accustomed to challenging young officers, some in mufti, who were making a last-minute rush to get back to their bases at the forts around Washington before their curfew hour of midnight, after an evening on the town. Besides, the war was more or less over and regulations were being gradually relaxed.

Across the river, Booth and Herold rode unchallenged and unseen between two of the rings of forts guarding the capital. Herold caught up with Booth after about eight miles. They stopped at the Surrattsville Tavern long enough to pick up one of the two Spencer carbines that had been hidden there, Booth's field glasses, and possibly the two Colt percussion-cap revolvers (one an army pattern and one a navy pattern). It seems unlikely that Booth would have had both these very large revolvers on him at the time he made his prodigious leap downward from the theater box onto the stage. One has to be familiar with the weight and large size of these huge pistols to appreciate the difficulty of concealing and retaining them if one were to jump that distance without their falling out of a belt or even a holster. They are so long that they would make it even harder to mount a horse unassisted when favoring a freshly broken leg. It seems to me much more likely that the pistols were either picked up at the Surrattsville Tavern or brought along by Herold.

The two late-model Spencer repeating carbines, plus cartridges, had been somehow procured by the conspirators and taken to the Surrattsville Tavern at the time of the abortive attempt to capture Lincoln in his carriage the month previously. They were hidden between the joists above the ceiling of the main building. Lloyd, the tavern keeper, later hid the carbine that Booth and Herold did *not* take with them by suspending it on a cord in the space between the wall studs and the laths in one of the rooms. These spaces could be reached because of a difference in the levels of the floors of the main part of the tavern and a supplementary attic storeroom over the small kitchen, which had been built on at the rear. Booth's expensive field glasses were alleged to have been in a package Booth gave to Mrs. Surratt to deliver to the tavern for him on the day of the shooting, when she was driving down there anyway to try to collect some money. It was a description by Lloyd and Weichmann of this alleged act which hurt Mrs. Surratt's credibility at the trial of the conspirators, since it implied more complicity than merely running a rooming house where the conspirators happened to do their plotting. The tavern keeper, John M. Lloyd, anxious to save himself (as was the Surratt house boarder, Louis J. Weichmann, who acted as her driver that day), testified that she told Lloyd to have the "shooting irons" ready to be picked up that night, along with the package that contained the field glasses.

The very fact that the conspirators were in possession of Spencer carbines was in itself suspicious. The first true repeating rifles, these carbines were in great demand and were reserved exclusively for the military engaged in front-line activity. They were the army's secret weapon that shortened the war by helping Sherman cut the South in two. Owning a Spencer carbine then would have been like owning a military machine gun today.

Fig. 143
page 356

Even the carbines of Booth and Oswald reveal an incidental and peculiar similarity: each was provided with wide ribbon or tape of woven cotton fabric used as an improvised sling.

Dr. Mudd's House

Fig. 48
page 109

Booth and Herold now pressed on, despite Booth's throbbing leg, until they reached Dr. Mudd's home three miles north of Bryantown, Maryland, and another ten miles down the road toward Richmond. It was now 4:00 A.M. but they pounded on Dr. Mudd's door until he answered.

Booth was able to dismount and make his way laboriously up the stairs to the doctor's settee, where Dr. Mudd inspected the broken bone. The doctor fashioned a splint out of thin wood and adapted it to minimize the motion between the two broken ends of the fibula (the smaller bone in his lower leg) in order to prevent their displacement and also to keep them from grating together, which was causing Booth so much pain. Dr. Mudd had to slit Booth's boot to get it off, and kicked it under a bed to get it out of the way. He then bedded Booth and Herold down for the night, as local hospitality would require, and sent them on their way the next afternoon. Interestingly enough, Dr. Mudd had Booth sleep in the same bed he had slept in on a previous visit some months earlier, when he was shopping for Payne's horse and familiarizing himself with the area.

After leaving Dr. Mudd's house, Booth and Herold stuck to swampy back roads, traveling from one Confederate sympathizer to the next, but had to hide out in a dense pine thicket for several days to avoid the dragnet being thrown over the area by the Yankee troops. They were forced to get rid of their horses because reward posters offering huge sums of money were now out, the countryside was now crawling with Union cavalry patrols looking for any suspects, and they were afraid the neighs of their horses would attract the enemy.

It was during these fugitive nights and days while secreted in the pine thicket that Booth probably wrote the first of the two entries in his diary.

FIG. 25
page 53

FIG. 26
page 54

Booth's Withheld Diary

April 13th, 14 Friday the Ides

Until today nothing was ever thought of sacrificing to our country's wrongs. For six months we had worked to capture. But our cause being almost lost, something decisive and great must be done. But its failure was owing to others, who did not strike for their country with a heart. I struck boldly and not as the papers say. I walked with a firm step through a thousand of his friends, was stopped, but pushed on. A Col. was at his side. I shouted sic semper before I fired. In jumping broke my leg. I passed all his pickets, rode sixty miles that night, with the bone of my leg tearing the flesh at every jump. I can never repent, though we hated to kill: our country owed all her troubles to him, and God simply made me the instrument of his punishment. The country is not what it was. This night (before the deed), I wrote a long article and left it for one of the editors of the *National Intelligencer*, in which I fully set forth our reasons for our proceedings. He or the govmt . . .

FIG. 27
page 56

Here in mid-sentence, as historian Hanchett points out, Booth stopped writing. His statement about the "long article" referred to a letter he had written the afternoon of the assassination and left with a friend and a fellow actor, John Mathews, for delivery to the Washington newspaper *National Intelligencer*, the following morning. After the assassination, Mathews opened, read, and, as he later admitted, burned the letter for fear of being incriminated in the assassination.

BOOTH'S BOOT

This is the boot which Dr. Mudd cut from Booth's fractured left leg late on the night Lincoln was shot. Inside was the name "J. Wilkes," a form Booth sometimes used in his earlier days on the stage, when he thought his acting ability was not sufficiently good and might embarrass the famous Booth name. The boot was pushed under the bed, and only when the federal authorities came in response to Dr. Mudd's summons and asked where the boot was did Mrs. Mudd remember it was under the bed. Its presence in his home nearly got Dr. Mudd hanged. Several of the commissioners voted for hanging him. It is now at the Ford's Theater Museum. *(National Park Service)*

Fig. 25

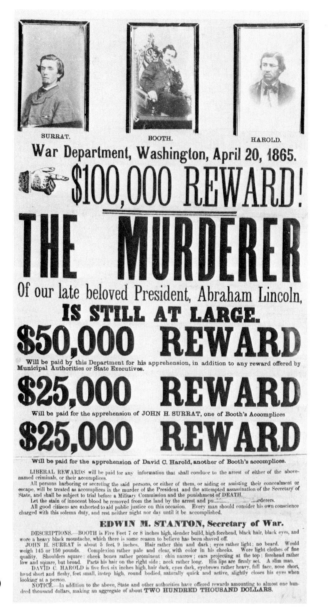

REWARD POSTER

Several different versions of the reward poster have survived. Some had misspellings. Some had no pictures of the suspects. Some had a photograph of one of Booth's brothers instead of John Wilkes. Others had a photograph of Herold added that was taken after he was captured. *(National Park Service)*

Fig. 26

On the night of his flight from Washington, Booth rode fewer than thirty miles, although it must have seemed like sixty. Because his was a simple fracture, not a compound one, the bone could not have been tearing his flesh, although it must have seemed as if it were. The man in the box at Ford's Theater with Lincoln, Henry Reed Rathbone, was a major, not a colonel.

The next entry in Booth's diary is a hand-drawn calendar, necessary because the dates already printed there were for 1864, not 1865. Booth numbered the calendar through June 18, checking off each day as it passed.

His text resumes:

Friday 21
After being hunted like a dog through swamps, woods, and last night being chased by gunboats till I was forced to return, wet cold and starving, with every man's hand against me, I am here in despair. And why, for doing what Brutus was honored for, what made Tell a hero, and yet I for striking down a greater tyrant than they ever knew, am looked upon as a common cutthroat. My action was purer than either of theirs. One hoped to be great himself. The other had not only his country's but his own wrongs to avenge. I hoped for no gain. I knew no private wrong. I struck for my country and that alone. A country groaned beneath this tyranny and prayed for this end. Yet I cannot see any wrong except in serving a degenerate people. The little, the very little I left behind to clear my name, the govmt will not allow to be printed. So ends all. For my country I have given up all that makes life sweet and holy, brought misery upon my family, and am sure there is no pardon in the heaven for me since man condemns me so. I have only heard of what has been done (except what I did myself) and it fills me with horror. God try and forgive me, and bless my mother. Tonight I will once more try the river with the intent to cross, though I have a greater desire and almost a mind to return to Washington and in a measure clear my name, which I feel I can do. I do not repent the blow I struck. I may before my God but not to man.

I think I have done well, though I am abandoned, with the curse of Cain upon me. *When if the world knew my heart, that one blow would have made me great,* though I did desire no greatness. [Italics added.]

Tonight I try to escape these bloodhounds once more. Who, who can read his fate. God's will be done.

I have too great a soul to die like a criminal. Oh may He, may He spare me that and let me die bravely.

I bless the entire world. Have never hated or wronged anyone. This last was not a wrong, unless God deems it so. And it's with Him, to damn or bless me. And for this brave boy with me, who often prays (yes before and since) with a true and sincere heart, was it crime in him, if so why can he pray the same. I do not wish to shed a drop of blood, but "I must fight the course" tis all that's left me.

Potomac Crossed on Second Attempt

Booth and Herold were finally taken by Confederate agent Thomas A. Jones down to the shores of the mile-wide Potomac River on the night of

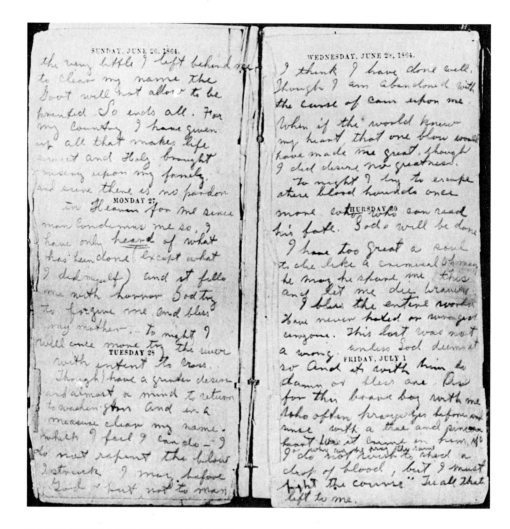

PAGE FROM BOOTH'S DIARY

In his notebook, commonly referred to as his "diary," Booth made statements like the one on the right-hand page, line five, where he said "that one blow would have made me great." On a previous page he had said, "Something decisive and great must be done." These remarks can be compared with those of Oswald, 100 years after, who said to Priscilla Johnson McMillan, in Moscow, "I want to give the people of the United States something to think about." The entire text of the two notations in Booth's diary is quoted in this chapter. (*National Park Service*)

Fig. 27

April 20. He put them in a rowboat and gave them detailed instructions for crossing the river and for obtaining help on the Virginia side. In the inky blackness they started rowing across the river, but their boat turned more to the right than they realized, and they found themselves making landfall at an unintended and unfamiliar spot. They soon discovered that they were on a long peninsula on the same (Maryland) side from which they had started out, but upriver from their expected destination. They spent an unhappy, wet, cold night in the woods on the banks of Nanjemoy Creek, thoroughly disgusted to find they were not in Virginia. The next night, they rowed successfully down the Potomac, landing on the Virginia shore near the home of Confederate sympathizer Mrs. Elizabeth Quesenberry. Later that day they made their way to the home of Dr. Richard Stuart. He, however, was already in such trouble with the authorities that he would not take them in, much to Booth's annoyance, but fed them and sent them to the cabin of a freed black, William Lucas, where they spent the night.

Rappahannock Crossed on Ferry

The next day Lucas's son Charles drove them across the neck of northern Virginia to Port Conway, on the north shore of the Rappahannock River. Here they had to wait for the ferry and with Booth on his crutch and without their horses, they were obviously now in some difficulty. But soon three Confederate soldiers appeared at the ferry, on their way home from the disbandment of Mosby's forces just south of Washington. In an effort to impress these men, Herold revealed to them that his companion and he were the "assassinators" of President Lincoln. This news was not greeted with the enthusiasm and support Herold had anticipated, but one of the troopers, by the name of Willie Jett, was sympathetic enough, in view of Booth's broken leg, to persuade his comrades to let the two strangers ride double on their horses.

They were ferried across the river to the village of Port Royal, Virginia, where Willie Jett tried to find them lodgings with two different families, but without success. The Confederate soldiers then started with them toward Bowling Green, about fourteen miles farther to the south. When the five men, mounted on the three horses, came to the Garrett farm on the right side of the road, about three miles south of Port Royal, they decided to stop there. Jett persuaded Mr. Richard Garrett to take Booth in, while the others and Herold rode on down to Bowling Green.

Unfortunate Coincidences

At this juncture, with Booth almost safely away, an event occurred back in Washington which had unhappy consequences for him. Coincidentally, two other Confederate agents, named Joseph Baden and Thomas Harbin, had been seen rowing across the Potomac River at dusk, a day or so before Booth and Herold had crossed, unseen, at approximately the same point. A telegram reporting this event was sent to Maj. Thomas Eckert in Washington, and Gen. Lafayette Baker, chief of the Secret Service, just happened to be in the office when the telegram arrived. Baker, up to this point, had been unable to contribute any leads as to the assassin's whereabouts and was embarrassed by this, so he eagerly seized upon the information in the telegram, hoping it might give him a part in the drama of the manhunt. He ordered a twenty-five-man mounted emergency patrol to be assembled from the culled-out, left-behind headquarters detail of the 16th New York Cavalry regiment, quartered nearby, whose main body had been delegated to march in the Lincoln funeral cortege. All twenty-six of the troopers present volunteered, expecting to find this duty happier than keeping house back at headquarters, and relishing the chance at the reward money. Among them was a particularly eccentric fellow, Sgt. Boston Corbett, who undoubtedly had been intentionally left behind by the officers who selected the contingent to take part in the funeral parade because of his erratic behavior and the fear that he might do something strange and spoil the formation. Corbett had a checkered past but was a man of strong convictions. He had once fancied himself a lay preacher, called by God, and while working as a hat finisher in the city from which he took his first name, he had had an encounter in 1858 with two ladies of the night which mired him in guilt and upset him considerably. As a result he went home and, "to be holy," as he put it, cut off both his testicles with a large pair of scissors. He then went to a prayer meeting, ate dinner, and noted that something was amiss, as he was swelling up with blood. The injury was attended to at the Massachusetts General Hospital, eventually healed satisfactorily, and didn't seem to bother him during his subsequent duties as a cavalryman.

FIG. 28
page 59

The Emergency Patrol

The patrol, with Corbett as the ranking sergeant, was taken down the Potomac by steamer and set out to scour the area. This group, under their commander, Lt. Edward P. Doherty, who was familiar with the countryside, interrogated William Rollins, a fisherman who lived near the ferry over the Rappahannock River. Rollins and his helper, Dick Wilson, said they had seen two men, one with a crutch, assisted across the river on the ferry, the day before, by three mounted Confederate soldiers. The troopers asked where they thought the group might be going. Rollins's new bride, Bettie, anxious to distract the reward-hungry soldiers from her husband, said she had seen Willie Jett among the group of five that included the man with a crutch. She knew Jett and knew that Jett had been keeping company with Izora Gouldman, the sixteen-year-old daughter of the operator of the hotel at Bowling Green, fourteen miles to the south. Maybe they were headed there.

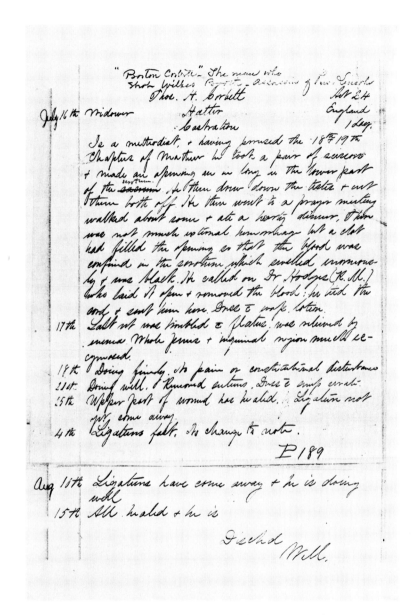

RECORD OF CORBETT'S SELF-CASTRATION

Massachusetts General Hospital notes of the care given to
"Boston" Corbett after he castrated himself in 1858 as penance
for speaking to a prostitute on the streets in Boston, where he
was practicing his trade as a hatter. (*Massachusetts General
Hospital*)

Fig. 28

With this information as their first solid clue, the troopers crossed the Rappahannock on the ferry and started down the road toward Bowling Green.

Just at that time, Herold and two of his companions were on their way back to Port Royal to see what they could do to help Booth further. After dropping Herold off at the Garrett farm, where Booth was receiving a full measure of Southern hospitality, the Confederates riding back northward toward Port Royal saw the group of Union cavalry troopers coming right at them. They turned around and raced back to the Garrett farm, telling Booth to go out into the woods and stay hidden until the cavalry had passed.

Willie Jett Talks

The cavalry patrol raced right past Garrett's farm, not suspecting that its quarry was there, and went on to find Willie Jett indeed sleeping at the hotel in Bowling Green. Awakening him, they put a pistol to his face and threatened to shoot his head off bit by bit if he did not talk; he talked. He said that the man with the crutches was back at the Garrett farm.

The troopers, who had had very little sleep for the past twenty-four hours but were now determined to get the enormous reward that had been promised for Booth's capture, turned around, even though it was past midnight, and rode as fast as they could back to Garrett's farm, with Jett as a guide.

By this time Booth and Herold had returned from the woods and had been told to sleep in the tobacco barn, a short distance from the farmhouse. Two of the Garrett boys had blocked up the barn doors and had decided to sleep in a corncrib nearby, just in case Booth and Herold might be inclined to steal any of their horses or other equipment. When the Union troopers appeared at the farmhouse and woke up the Garretts, they demanded to know where the visitors were. Mr. Richard Garrett said only that they had gone to the woods. The troopers were then about to subject him to harsh and vigorous pressure with a rope around his neck, when one of the family said, "Don't bother the old man. The men you want are in the barn."

Booth Trapped in Garrett's Barn

Lieutenant Doherty had sent out his patrol to surround the entire group of buildings and they flushed out the Garrett boys in the corncrib, nearly shooting them down with their carbines before they identified themselves. They then dismounted and surrounded the barn, pounding on the door, demanding that Booth come out, but he would not. Booth finally permitted Herold to come out, and when Herold stuck his empty hands out through the partly opened door, he was dragged bodily out by Lieutenant Doherty and handcuffed.

Booth then tried to bargain with Lt. Luther Baker, one of the two detectives with the group and a cousin of Lafayette Baker, asking him to back off and let him come out of the barn and shoot it out with them. When Baker refused, Booth made several dramatic remarks including, "Well then, my brave boys, prepare a stretcher for me."

It was by now about three o'clock in the morning, and Doherty, Baker, and the second detective, Col. Everton J. Conger, decided to set fire to the barn to flush the man out. When the brush which the troopers and a Garrett boy piled against the barn and the hay inside the barn had been set afire by Colonel Conger, at the rear corner of the structure, Booth could be seen very clearly. In the light of the burning straw, the troopers saw him going toward the fiery corner of the barn to see if he could put out the now roaring blaze. With the barn interior brilliantly illuminated, Booth was clearly visible on his crutches, immobilized and surrounded. He turned around and started toward the now open front door of the barn. Suddenly a single shot rang out, and Booth went down, fatally wounded, to die a little over two hours later.

Booth Shot

It was a frustrating, bitter moment when Lieutenant Baker and Colonel Conger, after each asking the other if he had fired the shot and receiving an answer in the negative, demanded to know who *did* fire the shot. The man who stepped forward to confess the shooting was the unstable, fanatical exhibitionist, frequently in trouble and later to be committed to an insane asylum, who had been left out of Lincoln's funeral parade because he might have disgraced his regiment. His name was Boston Corbett.

It all happened so fast that nobody could say for sure where the shot had come from. In his version of the story, Lt. Luther Baker, who had been guarding the front door of the barn, stated that, as the fire really got going, he threw open the front door to let Booth have a way out and saw Booth struggling to his feet from his position against a haymow. Booth dropped one crutch to enable him to carry his carbine at the ready while hobbling toward the side of the barn where the flames were shooting up; when he saw he could not put out the fire, he started for the open front door. Dropping his other crutch as he neared the door, he pulled out a pistol. Just then, a shot rang out and Booth jumped forward a step or two without any crutch before he crumpled to the floor, dropping the carbine from his other hand.

Lieutenant Baker then rushed to pinion him and twisted the pistol out of his hand, which (as Baker specifically stated) required some force. At this moment, Colonel Conger, the senior detective, who had heard the shot while rushing around from where he had set fire to the rear corner of the barn, arrived. His first question was, "Why did you shoot him?" When Baker said he had not fired the shot, Conger asked if Booth had shot himself. Baker, who had had a clear view of Booth, replied, "No, he did not either." Baker then asked if Conger had shot him, and Conger denied it vigorously.

FIG. 29
page 63

It was then, in answer to the question "Then who *did* shoot him?" that Sgt. Boston Corbett stepped forward.

Corbett's Testimony

The rest is legend, speculation, history, and—the most dramatic and probably the most accurate, as it turns out—the testimonies of Boston Corbett and Colonel Conger at the conspirators' trial. Corbett described the event as follows:

Lieutenant Doherty told me that Booth was in that house, saying, "I want you to deploy the men right and left around the house and see that no one escapes," which was done. After making inquiry at the house it was found that Booth was in the barn. A guard was then left upon the house and the main portion of the men were dismounted and were thrown around the barn, closely investing it, with orders to allow no one to escape. We had previously been cautioned to see that our arms were in readiness for use. After being ordered to surrender and told the barn would be fired in five minutes if he did not do so, Booth made many replies. He wanted to know who we took him for; he said that his leg was broken; and what did we want with him; and he was told that it made no difference. His name was not mentioned in the whole affair. They were told that they must surrender as prisoners. Booth wanted to know where we would take them, if they would give themselves up as prisoners. He received no satisfaction but was told that he must surrender unconditionally, or else the barn would be fired. The parley lasted much longer than the time first set; probably a full half hour, but he positively declared he would not surrender. At one time he made the remark, "Well, my brave boys, you can prepare a stretcher for me," and at another time, "Well, Captain, make quick work of it; shoot me through the heart," or words to that effect; and thereby I knew that he was perfectly desperate and did not expect that he would surrender. After a while, we heard the whispering of another person (although Booth had previously declared there was no one there but himself) who proved to be the prisoner Herold. Although we could not distinguish the words, Herold seemed to be trying to persuade Booth to surrender. After a while he sang out, "Certainly," seeming to disdain to do so himself. Said he, "Cap, there is a man in here who wants to surrender mighty bad." Then I supposed words followed inside that we could not hear, Herold perhaps thought he had better stand by him, or something to that effect. Then Booth said, "Oh, go out and save yourself, my boy, if you can" and then he said, "I declare before my maker that this man here is innocent of any crime whatever," seeming willing to take all the blame on himself and trying to clear Herold. He was told to hand out his arms. Herold declared that he had no arms, and Booth declared that all the arms belonged to him and that the other man was unarmed. He was finally taken out without arms.

Immediately after Herold was taken out, the detective, *Mr. Conger, came around to the side of the barn where I was, and passing me, set fire to the hay* through one of the cracks of the boards a little to my right. I had previously said

BOOTH'S KILLER

Boston Corbett, religious fanatic, frequently in difficulties, who had castrated himself in a moment of religious fervor, deliberately shot down Booth after easier opportunities had passed and against orders. Corbett was later declared insane, after an act of armed offense. *(National Archives)*

Fig. 29

to Mr. Conger, though, and also to my commanding officer that the position in which I stood left me in front of a large crack—you might put your hand through it. I knew that Booth could distinguish me and the others through these cracks in the barn, and could pick us off if he chose to do so. In fact, he made a remark to that effect at one time. Said he, "Cap, I would have picked off three or four of your men already if I wished to do so. Draw your men off fifty yards, and I will come out," or such words. He used such language many times. Then the fire was lit, which was almost immediately after Herold was taken out of the barn. As the flames rose, he was seen. We could then distinguish him about in the middle of the barn, turning toward the fire, either to put the fire out or else to shoot the one who started it: I did not know which, but he was then coming toward me, as it were, a little to my right—a full front breast view. I could have shot him then much easier than when I afterward did, but as long as he was there, making no demonstration to hurt anyone, I did not shoot him, but kept my eye on him steadily. Finding the fire gaining upon him, he turned to the other side of the barn and got toward where the door was. And as he got there I saw him make a movement toward the door. I supposed that he was going to fight his way out. One of the men who was watching him told me that he aimed the carbine at me. He was taking aim with the carbine, but at whom I could not say. My mind was upon him attentively to see that he did no harm, and when I became impressed that it was time, I shot him. I took steady aim on my arm, and shot him through a large crack in the barn. When he was brought out I found that the wound was made in the neck, a little back of the ear, and came out a little higher up on the other side of the head. He lived I should think, until about seven o'clock that morning, perhaps two or three hours after he was shot. I did not myself hear him speak a word after he was shot except to cry or shout as he fell. Others, who were near him and watching him constantly, said that he did utter the words which were published later.

Subsequent to his admission of the shooting, Boston Corbett was placed under technical arrest because the orders of his detail had been to capture Booth alive. He was released shortly after, however, and indeed was somewhat lionized, but was given only $1,653.85 of the reward which had been offered for Booth's capture, dead or alive. He was later made doorkeeper and sergeant-at-arms of the Kansas state legislature. One day, while he was listening to the page boys starting a mock session of the legislature, he heard one boy mock the chaplain's opening prayer. This heresy enraged him, and he suddenly leaped to his feet and pulled out his pistol, as if to shoot at the boys. As a result, he was declared insane and committed to a mental institution. Sometime later he escaped and was never heard from again. He may have died while walking across the plains in an attempt to escape to Mexico. Legends arose about his being a successful patent medicine man in the South in later years, but these were never substantiated.

Colonel Conger's Testimony

Lafayette Baker's detective, Col. Everton J. Conger, who was the senior officer present, also testified at the trial and said:

I went around to the corner of the barn, pulled some hay out, twisted up a little of it, set fire to it and stuck it back through on top of the hay. It was loose, broken up hay, and blazed very rapidly—lit right up at once. I put my eye up to the crack next to the one the fire was put through and looked in, and I heard something drop to the floor which I supposed to be Booth's crutch as he turned around toward me. When I first got a glimpse of him he stood with his back partly to me, turning toward the front door. He came back, and looked at the fire, and from the expression on his face I am satisfied he looked to see if he could put it out and was satisfied he could not do it, it was burning too much. He dropped his arm, relaxed his muscles, turned around and started for the door at the front of the barn. I ran around to the other side and when about half around I heard the report of a pistol. I went right to the door, and found Lieutenant Baker looking at Booth, holding him or raising him up, I do not know which. I said to him "He shot himself." He said, "No, he did not, either." Said I, "Whereabout is he shot—in the head or neck?" I raised him then, and looked on the right side of his neck, and saw a place where the blood was running. I said "Yes, sir, he shot himself." Lieutenant Baker replied very earnestly that he did not. I then said, "Let us carry him out of here, this will soon be burning." We took him up and carried him out on the grass, underneath the locust trees, a little way from the door. I went back into the barn immediately to see if the fire could be put out and tried somewhat myself to put it out, but I could not, it was burning so fast, and there was no water or nothing to help with. I then went back. Before this, I supposed him to be dead. He had all the appearance of a dead man, but when I got back to him his eyes and mouth were moving. I called immediately for some water, and put it on his face, and he somewhat revived, and attempted to speak. I put my ear down close to his mouth, and he made several efforts to speak, and finally I understood him to say, "Tell mother I died for my country." I said to him, "Is that what you say?" repeating it to him. He said, "Yes". They carried him from there to the porch of Mr. Garrett's house and laid him on an old straw bed or something. By that time, he revived considerably, he could then talk in a whisper. He wanted water, we gave it to him. He wanted to be turned on his side, we turned him on his side, we turned him upon his side three times, I think, but he could not lie with any comfort, and wanted to be turned immediately back. He asked me to put my hand on his throat and press down, which I did, and he said "Harder". I pressed down as hard as I felt necessary, and he made very strong exertions to cough, but was unable to do so, no muscular exertion could he make. I supposed he thought something was in his throat, and I said to him "There is no blood in your throat, it has not gone through any part of it there." He repeated two or three times, "Kill me, kill me." The reply was made to him, "We don't want to kill you, we want you to get well." I then took what things were in his pockets, and tied them up in a piece of paper. He was then not quite dead. He would once, perhaps, in five minutes, gasp, his heart would almost die out, and then it would commence again, and by a few rapid beats would make a slight motion. I left the body and the prisoner Herold in charge of Lieutenant Baker. I told him to wait an hour if Booth were not dead; if he recovered, to wait there and send over to Belle Plain for a surgeon from one of the gunships, and if he died in the space of an hour, to get the best conveyance he could and bring him on. I stayed there some ten minutes after that was said, when the doctor there said that he was dead.

I think we got to Garrett's barn about two o'clock in the morning, and it was about fifteen minutes past three that Booth was shot and carried out on the grass.

And so Lincoln's murderer himself succumbed. There followed a cumbersome, vengeful government investigation and trial of the conspirators by a military commission of seven generals and two colonels, the judge advocate general and two assistant and special judge advocates (only one of whom was a civilian) appointed by President Andrew Johnson. There has been much complaining that this military group was illegal and biased, since the war was over and civilian courts were available. No distinction was made between conspiracy to kidnap versus conspiracy to murder, and a petition sent to the President by a majority of the commission, recommending commutation of Mrs. Surratt's death sentence, was either ignored by President Johnson or withheld from him by someone. Judge Holt has been accused of withholding the petition just as he was accused of withholding Booth's diary for two years. The facts are unknown, but the commission voted to hang Mrs. Surratt, Payne, Herold, and Atzerodt, and imprison Dr. Mudd, Spangler, Arnold, and O'Laughlin.

Some thirty hours later when the boat carrying Booth's body back up the Potomac arrived, an autopsy was performed on the body on one of the monitors (warships) anchored in the Potomac near Washington.

As they are today, assassination buffs in 1865 were a perceptive, persistent, demanding lot that raised all sorts of interesting questions. Sometimes the questions dealt with medical and ballistics matters which might be clarified by doing actual experiments to reproduce the crime. Because I have both laboratory facilities and medical and ballistics training, I have always been interested in exploring these challenges. It is this "cluster of capabilities," appropriate to the problem, plus our own X-ray machines, tissue-preparing machines, farm firing ranges, and a host of friends who are top-flight pathologists, anatomists, historians, photographers, neurosurgeons, orthopedists, and arms experts, that makes it all so interesting and so easy to add useful information to this type of investigation.

For example, when I read that Corbett had been hospitalized at the Massachusetts General Hospital after he castrated himself, I wrote to my friend the director, the late Dr. John Knowles, to see if he could get me a copy of Corbett's hospital record. He replied that he heard it was in the files and, if I would supply him with the date, he would see what he could do. A week later I had a report of the handwritten admission note dated July 16, 1858, which described the incident as follows:

Is a Methodist, and having perused the eighteenth and nineteenth chapters of Matthew, he took a pair of scissors and made an opening one inch long in the lower part of the scrotum. He then drew down the testes and cut them off. He then went to a prayer meeting, walked about some, and ate a hearty dinner. There was not much external hemorrhage, but a clot had filled the opening so that the blood was confined in the scrotum, which was swelled enormously and was black. He called on Dr. R. N. Hodges, who laid it open and removed the blood; he tied the cord and sent him here.

Then followed concise progress notes indicating an uneventful course with the ligatures "coming away" in about a month.

This previous history of instability and lack of testicles did not prevent Corbett's being accepted by the army, however, and ultimately finding his way into the 16th New York Cavalry, where he fought with fanatical zeal.

At one point, he was captured, only after he had run out of ammunition, and a curious Confederate officer had the Yankee who had fought so furiously brought before him to see what manner of madman he was. Confined for a while in the infamous Andersonville Prison, Corbett was one of those lucky enough to be exchanged. During his service career, he was frequently in difficulty because of his religious fanaticism, and at the time he shot Booth, in direct disobedience to the standing order for the capture of the assassin alive, he claimed he did so on divine instruction.

The other striking feature about the murders of the assassins of both Presidents Lincoln and Kennedy is the similarities. Both Corbett and Jack Ruby stood much closer at points during the stalking of their quarries than they did when the fatal shots rang out.

The fact that Booth lived only a few hours after he was shot with a single Colt revolver bullet is, again, analogous to the interval that Oswald lived after being shot by a single bullet from another Colt revolver 100 years later.

Thus both Booth and Oswald were brilliantly illuminated when surrounded and immobilized by their captors and when shot down at the dramatic and climactic heights of an emotion-ridden moment 100 years apart. Both were forever silenced, without having been brought to trial and without having provided criminal investigators a chance to evoke from these recognition-hungry showmen information as to their motivation, assistants, or data they might have advanced in their own defense. These were two frustrating, unlawful, bitter moments, a century apart.

Exactly Where Was Corbett Standing?

While no one makes a clear statement as to exactly where Corbett was posted at the barn's periphery, it is possible to make a reasonable deduction from the testimony of those involved in setting fire to the barn. We know the barn measured fifty by forty-eight feet from the claim the family put in. The cavalry troopers had originally been dismounted and posted on three sides of the barn, at thirty-foot intervals, in order to prevent anyone from escaping.

Everyone who testified about the shooting of Booth agreed that the fatal shot was fired while Booth was making his way toward the open front door of the barn. Since the shot that killed Booth came from the side of the barn that is at the left as one faces the front door from outside the barn, and since both Corbett (who admitted shooting Booth) and Conger (whom some suspected of shooting Booth) were on the same side of the barn, according to their own testimony, it seems reasonable to assume that it was at this left rear corner of the barn that Colonel Conger and one of the Garrett boys piled brush, in preparation for setting fire to the barn. Corbett stated clearly at the trial of the conspirators that Colonel Conger had passed him, going toward the back of the barn, to set the fire. The Garrett boy who helped to pile the brush against the barn at Conger's instructions stated that he was standing within six feet of Corbett when Corbett fired the fatal shot at Booth. Corbett indicated that he crept up to the side of the barn and thrust his pistol through a wide crack between the boards of the tobacco barn, also resting his pistol on his arm to steady it as he did so.

Conger stated that after he had ignited the brush and straw at the rear corner of the barn, he then applied his eye to a nearby crack between the boards of the barn and saw Booth starting toward the fire as if to determine whether he could put it out. Conger saw him stop and turn around, to start for the front door of the barn, carrying his carbine and using his crutch. Conger then started running toward the front door of the barn. When he was halfway around, presumably at a spot near or even past the front left corner of the barn, and had passed Corbett, he heard a shot. By the time he reached the open front door, Lieutenant Baker had already rushed in to pinion Booth, whom he had seen fall.

The fact that the bullet hole was almost directly transversely through Booth's neck would favor a position for Corbett a little more toward the front of the barn rather than toward the back. It is possible, of course, that Lieutenant Baker underestimated the distance Booth actually was from the door at the moment he was shot, and Booth may actually have staggered a few more steps forward in the process of falling after he was shot. If so, Corbett's position could have been more toward the center of the barn.

The only other comments that appear in the various accounts are very loose statements such as those of Lt. Luther Baker, made at the impeachment proceedings for President Johnson, when he said, "Someone told me that if Corbett had missed Booth, he might have hit me." He did not say who said this or what the reason was for saying it. There are good reasons to doubt that this statement was accurate, because the bullet did indeed go entirely through Booth's neck and kept on going. Such a bullet would have made a loud clack if it had hit the inside of the building anywhere near Lieutenant Baker, and it did not do so. If it had struck Lieutenant Baker, we naturally would have heard a great deal more about it. Furthermore, a pistol that had been thrust through the boards of the barn at the back and fired directly at Lieutenant Baker would have made a deafening noise, leaving very little doubt that a shot had been fired in the direction of the Lieutenant. This would have sparked his wrath instantly and explosively. Combat soldiers are extremely sensitive about being exposed to fire through the carelessness of their own men.

Since Conger asked Baker whether Booth had shot himself, it is obvious that he placed the sound of the shot as inside the barn. This would be understandable, since Corbett said he had thrust his pistol muzzle through the crack into the inside of the building. With the muzzle extending even an inch or two into the building, the blast occurs inside and gives no other clue as to the position from which it is fired. Thus could Conger assume that Booth might have shot himself. It appears to us that the statements of Conger, Corbett, and the Garrett boy indicating that they were all on the same side of the barn give a reasonably clear picture of where Corbett was located along the left side of the structure.

The only contradictory statement was Corbett's remark that Colonel Conger was "a little to my right," when he set fire to the barn. I cannot explain this incongruity except to observe that a great many of the witnesses confused right with left, at various times, including Dr. Leale and Dr. Taft, as demonstrated earlier.

The questions of whether Booth shot himself and what type of weapon was used are still open to some speculation and, in an attempt to provide a few further answers, I conducted a series of studies, using the actual weapons and types of ammunition of 100 years ago, in an effort to determine if there may be any truth to the claims that contradict the testimony of witnesses, particularly the claim that Booth might have been a suicide.

Booth's autopsy report was the first document I studied, and it is reprinted here in its entirety.

Booth's Autopsy

Sunburned and haggard from twelve days of riding and rowing and hiding in the underbrush, Booth had lost his handsome theatrical appearance, but his body was identified by several persons by a permanent scar on the back of his neck. This scar has been the subject of an article by a Dr. May, the man who had originally sutured the wound and who was among those who identified it after Booth's death. Identification was further confirmed by Booth's initials, which he had tattooed on his own hand in scrawling letters as a child. His dentist, Dr. Merrill, who had filled two teeth for Booth the week before the assassination, forced Booth's mouth open and identified the fillings. Booth's family also later accepted the body as his, with no questions.

The autopsy was performed by Dr. J. Janvier Woodward of the Army Medical Museum, the same man who had performed Lincoln's autopsy twelve days before at the White House:

Case JWB: Was killed April 26, 1865, by a conoidal pistol ball, fired at the distance of a few yards, from a cavalry revolver. The missile perforated the base of the right lamina of the 4th lumbar vertebra, fracturing it longitudinally and separating it by a fissure from the spinous process, at the same time fracturing

Fig. 30
page 71

the 5th vertebra through its pedicle, and involving that transverse process. The projectile then traversed the spinal canal almost horizontally but with a slight inclination downward and backward, perforating the cord which was found much torn and discolored with blood (see Specimen 4087 Sect. I AMM). The ball then shattered the bases of the left 4th and 5th laminae, driving bony fragments among the muscles, and made its exit at the left side of the neck, nearly opposite the point of entrance. It avoided the 2nd and 3rd cervical nerves. These facts were determined at autopsy which was made on April 28. Immediately after the reception of the injury, there was very general paralysis. The phrenic nerves performed their function, but the respiration was diaphragmatic, of course, labored and slow. Deglutition was impracticable, and one or two attempts at articulation were unintelligible. Death, from asphyxia, took place about two hours after the reception of the injury.

J. J. Woodward

Booth Buried in Locked Room

Booth's body was first buried in a locked storage room in the old Capitol Prison in what is now Fort McNair, in Washington. Secretary of War Stanton kept the key. When this building was to be torn down in 1867, the bodies of all the conspirators, including Booth and Captain Wirz, the infamous commandant of the Andersonville Prison, were exhumed and reburied in a locked storeroom in Warehouse 1, at the prison.

Booth's body was released to his family in 1869 by President Johnson, after the death of Mr. Stanton, and was reburied in the family plot in Greenmount Cemetery in Baltimore, allegedly with the one boot still in place. The skull was noted to be detached from the body, and both a dentist and a brother again identified dental repairs that were definitely those of John Wilkes Booth. It is alleged that President Andrew Johnson insisted that the assassins' names must not be incised on their monuments and that no specific headstone be used to identify which was Booth's grave, for fear Southern sympathizers might make his birthday a memorial day.

During the 100 years since his death, various other people have been said to have been the "real" John Wilkes Booth and that the wrong man was shot. The proposal of a "second Booth" has been the subject of enthusiastic books, exactly as we are now hearing of books about a "second Oswald." Even a dried-up mummy exhibited at side shows was claimed to be the remains of Booth.

It has been proposed by enthusiasts, at various times, that the body buried in Greenmount Cemetery should again be exhumed and examined, to determine if a bone of one of the legs is indeed broken, if a tattoo of the initials *JWB* can still be made out on the hand, if a cicatrized scar can be seen on the back of the neck where Booth had an abscess incised, and if the head is indeed detached from the body, as would have undoubtedly occurred when the three cervical vertebrae were removed. These vertebrae are now displayed in the new museum of the

PATH OF BULLET THROUGH BOOTH'S VERTEBRAE

Photograph of John Wilkes Booth's third, fourth, and fifth cervical vertebrae (right) and spinal cord (left), with wooden probe through transverse bullet hole, going from right to left through spinal canal, penetrating the spinal cord at the level of the fourth cervical vertebra. *(Armed Forces Institute of Pathology, Washington, D.C.)*

Fig. 30

Armed Forces Institute of Pathology at Walter Reed General Hospital in Washington; the accession number is 4087, section 1, AMM. In the same way, proposals to exhume the body of Lee Harvey Oswald, to satisfy yet another author, recur periodically.

When it was mentioned that the photographic division of the old Army Institute of Pathology had reproduced the picture of John Booth for distribution on reward posters to aid in his capture after the death of President Lincoln in April 1865, Dr. Woodward's associate, E. M. Schaeffer, M.D., wrote that one of his first duties at the museum as a hospital steward of the army had been to mount on cardboard several hundred of these copies which had been made by Edward Curtis, M.D. Not long after this, Dr. Woodward received a message from the War Department directing him to take his post-mortem case and repair to the arsenal. When he returned to the museum, he said that he had made an autopsy on Booth, whom he would have recognized from the photographs, although the face was much freckled. He brought with him the cervical vertebrae and spinal cord showing the track of the bullet that had killed Booth. After further examination, these were properly prepared and placed in the museum.

The specimens had been wrapped in stout brown paper. At that time, there was a rage for relics and souvenirs of all kinds and, influenced by this feeling, Dr. Schaeffer cut off and preserved, duly labeled, a portion of the bloodstained paper as a souvenir of the tragedy. He placed it in his cabinet, forgetting it until about fifteen years later, when, while searching for some specimens of dried human blood to illustrate to his private class in microscopic techniques, he remembered the paper and submitted it to the proper treatment by macerating and teasing with needles to bring out any structure that might remain. Much to his pleasure and rather to his surprise, the red corpuscles often sought in vain in more recent cases were seen with vivid distinctness.

It was on April 29, 1865, that Surgeon General Joseph K. Barnes officially had Dr. Woodward deposit in the medical museum the portion of the spinal cord and the section of the spine consisting of the third, fourth, and fifth cervical vertebrae which were removed during the autopsy. I discovered an additional small fragment of John Wilkes Booth's body in a bottle in the Mutter Medical Museum of the College of Physicians of Philadelphia. This fragment, approximately 1½ by ¾ inches, resembled a fragment of rib cartilage and bears the following label:

PART OF THE THORAX (CAVITY OF THE CHEST) OF J. WILKES BOOTH, APRIL 14, 1865, THE ASSASSIN OF PRESIDENT LINCOLN, PROCURED AND PRESENTED BY THE MESSENGER OF THE SURGEON-GENERAL.

Corbett's Weapon

After studying the autopsy reports and the bone fragments, I turned my attention—before conducting studies of my own—to the weapon that

Corbett allegedly had used to shoot Booth and to any other weapons he might have been carrying, as well as to the weapons that Booth himself had in his possession at the time of his capture.

While the revolver mentioned by Corbett was not described in detail at the trial, there seems little reason to doubt that it was the standard .44-caliber Colt army revolver model of 1860, a percussion-cap weapon which was loaded with a substantial charge (28 grains) of black powder and fired a conoidal bullet (of 207 grains) with more than enough velocity to perforate Booth's neck and vertebrae. Corbett spoke of steadying his pistol by resting it on his arm, which was a popular way for cavalrymen to provide a rest for this otherwise heavy weapon. The fact that he hit Booth in the neck, and exactly in the spinal cord, was a sheer stroke of luck, considering the limited accuracy of pistols and his statement that he was aiming at Booth's thorax.

FIG. 134
page 336

Was It Really Corbett Who Shot Booth?

As with the assassination buffs of the Kennedy shooting, there have been a number of Lincoln assassination zealots who have raised the question of "a different shooter," other than Corbett, whose testimony that he shot Booth was accepted by the government and by the press in two different investigations.

The military commission which tried the Lincoln conspirators in 1865 accepted Sgt. Boston Corbett's statement that he shot Booth, apparently without dissent. The civil court which tried John Surratt in 1867 again accepted Corbett's statement without recorded dissension. Perhaps more significantly, the press of the day also accepted Corbett's statement. Booth's sister, Asia, is said to have been grateful to Corbett for shooting her brother and thus sparing him a public hanging.

Even the late Otto Eisenschiml, the author who delighted in posing ominous questions about the possible masterminding of roles played by others, particularly Secretary of War Stanton, in his book, *Why Was Lincoln Murdered*, concluded that the evidence favored the veracity of Sgt. Boston Corbett's claim that he shot John Wilkes Booth. In a later magazine article Eisenschiml speculated that perhaps it was Colonel Conger, after all, who might have been urged by Secretary Stanton to assassinate Booth. This speculation is actually unsupported by a reading of his text.

Several people at the scene expressed uncertainty about the shooter's identity, but such uncertainty was resolved on the spot while the events were still fresh in their minds.

Despite their hunger for reward money, none of the other troopers denied that Corbett shot him, and one of the Garrett boys (Robert) testified that he was standing only six feet from Corbett when Corbett shot Booth.

Another of the Garrett boys (William—later a minister) testified that

73

he and Lieutenant Baker were standing together at the front of the barn and that Baker definitely did *not* shoot Booth.

Lieutenant Baker later testified that he realized that he had better keep quiet about any thoughts he had had about Colonel Conger having shot Booth in case there were those who might believe that Colonel Conger had been sent out by Stanton's Secret Service men to deliberately silence Booth rather than take him alive and permit him to implicate others who might have been behind the plot. In any case, the participants appeared to have settled the question right on the spot so far as they were concerned.

Nevertheless, a century later, an enthusiastic assassination buff, the late Col. Julian Raymond, revived the question of whether John Wilkes Booth might not have shot *himself* rather than being shot by Corbett. His speculation revolved around a cluster of facts. He pointed out that Lt. Luther B. Baker, the first to reach Booth after he heard the shot, found him with revolver in one hand, his carbine fallen from his other hand, and his crutch nearby, as he collapsed.

One of Colonel Conger's first questions had been, "Did he shoot himself?" It all seemed logical enough. However, Lieutenant Baker, who had been watching him closely from only twelve or fifteen feet away, through the open door, said, "No!" He positively had not shot himself. Young Garrett confirmed this.

Colonel Raymond, furthermore, was concerned that Sergeant Corbett received only a modest (routine) portion of the $75,000 reward allotted for Booth's capture, the same $1,653.85 as each of the twenty-six enlisted men, rather than the larger portion one might have expected him to get if he were being specially rewarded or a reduced portion which he might have received if he were being punished for an illegal act in shooting Booth against orders. In rebuttal, it has been pointed out that rewards paid to military units ordinarily were apportioned according to a formula, with the commanding officer getting the largest share (Congress allotted Conger $15,000) and all others beneath him, according to their rank, receiving decreasing portions of the residue. There appears to have been some complaint that this formula was used in this instance, and a redistribution was prescribed, using a slightly more equitable formula.

To confuse matters further and to give Colonel Raymond more food for thought, while Dr. Woodward's official autopsy report on Booth's body, published in the official medical history of the Civil War, stated that his wound was caused by a conoidal pistol bullet, a description of the specimen in a folder more recently issued for the Armed Forces Institute of Pathology refers to the wounds as being from a carbine bullet. Colonel Raymond thought it possible that Sergeant Corbett might have been armed only with a powerful, large-caliber carbine, but not a revolver. Booth, on the other hand, had two large Colt revolvers, one in his hand and the other apparently in a belt holster.

Why Did Stanton Issue Corbett a New Revolver?

Fig. 31
page 76

Most interesting of all, however, was that Colonel Raymond unearthed a letter written by the inspector general, by order of Secretary of War Stanton, instructing the chief of ordnance to issue to Sgt. Boston Corbett one Colt revolver, one week after the shooting, to replace one for which he had made a satisfactory accounting. Colonel Raymond speculated that perhaps Secretary Stanton wanted to be sure that the public really believed that Corbett had shot Booth and was providing Corbett with the kind of pistol he had said he had used in doing it.

In reply to the natural question of why Booth would have shot himself in the neck rather than in the head or mouth (as most pistol suicides do), Colonel Raymond speculated that perhaps Booth was so vain he did not want his classic features marred, even in death, or that perhaps he did not wish to inflict a fatal wound.

It is true that Booth was making statements indicating that he would not be taken alive. However, people who are intent on killing themselves with a gun bring the gun around in front of themselves so they can see that it is pointed directly at their head or their heart. They do not hold it to the side where they are not sure where it is pointed. Pointing a pistol at the back part of the neck would be foolish for a suicide-prone man.

In rebuttal to Colonel Raymond's first point suggesting suicide, and remembering Colonel Conger's question, "Did he shoot himself?," it would seem a natural question for Conger to have asked, since Booth did have a revolver in his hand when he fell. However, Lieutenant Baker, the first to reach the wounded Booth, denied it without hesitation. He had been watching Booth closely through the open door, and he knew Booth had not shot himself.

As a second rebuttal to the suicide theory, I put forth the fact (based on our experiments) that if Booth had had the revolver reversed in his hand, so he could shoot himself in the neck at a downward angle, Lieutenant Baker would not have found "the pistol grasped so tightly in his hand that I had to twist it to get it out," as he so emphatically stated he did at the Johnson impeachment proceedings in 1867; it would have fallen out of his hand very readily.

When Sergeant Corbett stepped forward in answer to the question of "Who fired the shot?," none of the other troopers present scoffed or raised any objections to Corbett's statement, as they surely would have done if they had seen anything different happen. Corbett was not a popular man with the coarser of his fellow troopers, who often derided him because of his "holiness" and his eccentricities, and they would not have hesitated to ridicule any false claims he might have made, especially if it might have made Corbett's share of the reward greater, at their expense.

It is difficult to understand where Colonel Raymond got his notion that Sergeant Corbett would have been armed *only* with a carbine, since

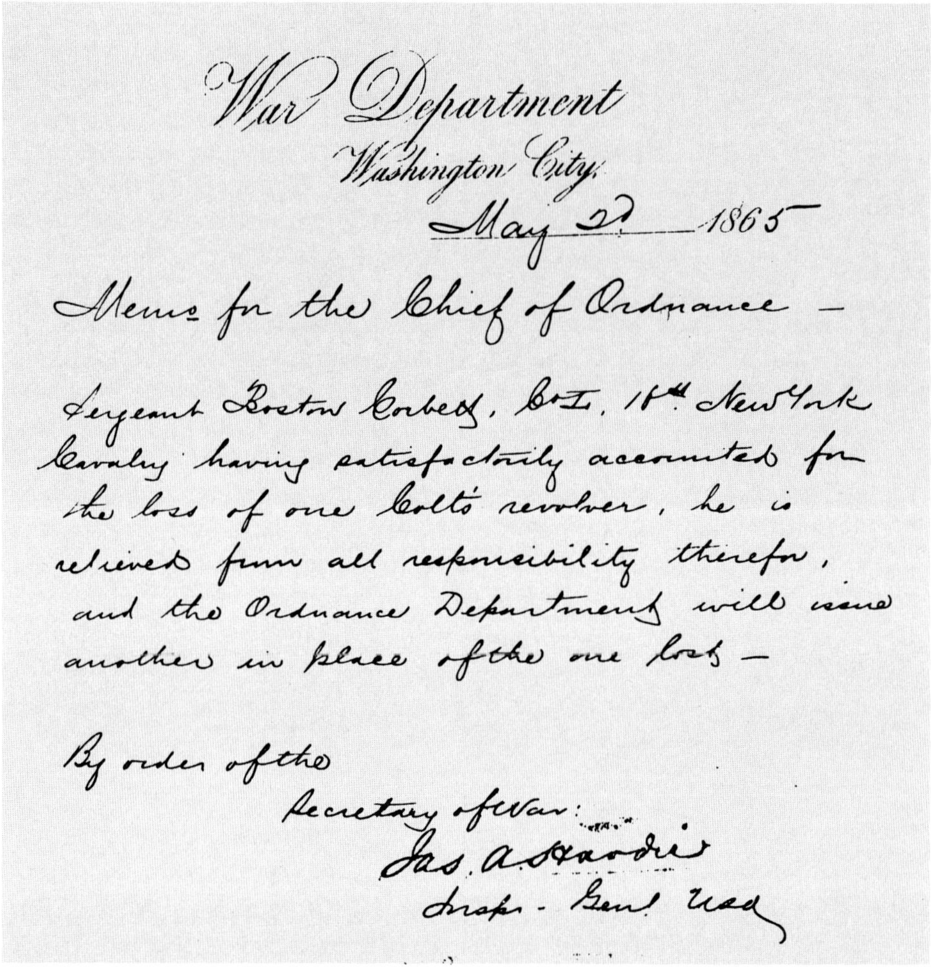

War Department
Washington City,
May 2d 1865

Memo for the Chief of Ordnance —

Sergeant Boston Corbett, Co I, 18th New York Cavalry having satisfactorily accounted for the loss of one Colts revolver, he is relieved from all responsibility therefor, and the Ordnance Department will issue another in place of the one lost —

*By order of the
Secretary of War:
Jas. A. Hardie
Insp. Genl USA*

AUTHORIZATION TO ISSUE NEW COLT REVOLVER TO SERGEANT CORBETT

This letter shows that Secretary of War Stanton ordered the Ordnance Department to supply a Colt revolver to Boston Corbett to replace one that he had lost. It does not say whether Corbett's pistol was taken from him to be used as evidence in the trial of the conspirators or whether he lost it in some other way which he explained satisfactorily. Some attach ominous significance to this letter, proposing that Corbett might not ever have had a pistol and that the Secretary of War wanted to provide him with one so that his story of shooting Booth with such a pistol would be believed. The first explanation seems much more likely. (*National Archives*)

Fig. 31

Union cavalrymen routinely carried both a revolver and a carbine; many contemporary photographs confirm this. In fact, some troopers purchased and carried a second revolver of their own in order to increase their fire power by six more rounds before having to pause to reload. By 1865 there was certainly no shortage of Colt revolvers. As the highest-ranking noncommissioned officer of the patrol sent out to capture Booth, Corbett might reasonably be expected to have been more, rather than less, well-armed than the usual trooper. Most certainly he would have carried a revolver.

With regard to the letter from Secretary Stanton ordering a new pistol to be issued to Sergeant Corbett, one might reasonably speculate that the actual pistol he used in the hunt for Booth would have been impounded by the military commission to be ready as a possible exhibit at the trial of the conspirators. Stanton's letter stated that Corbett had provided a satisfactory accounting of why he needed a revolver, even though, in the curt style of a military order, it did not provide us with any elaboration on that reason, or any details. Thus we are left with an interesting but not necessarily ominous action on the part of Stanton.

The evidence is much in favor of the historical record, but still, there is justification for further inquiry. So, I next addressed myself to the question, "*Could* Booth have shot himself?"

Could Booth Have Shot Himself?

It is true that Booth had a revolver in his hand when he was shot, that his heavy carbine had fallen between his knees, and that apparently he had dropped both his crutches some moments before. Lieutenant Baker said he staggered forward the last few steps without either crutch but carrying in his hands his heavy carbine and his very large Colt revolver.

If one actually tries to aim one of these very long revolvers into the side of one's neck, at a slightly downward angle (the direction of Booth's wound), one finds that it is necessary to reverse the pistol in the hand and press the trigger with the thumb. Because of the size and weight of the weapon, reversing the pistol requires two hands. Booth, of slight build and with a broken leg, could not possibly have held his very heavy Spencer carbine, pulled from his belt one of his pistols, reversed it in his hand, and put it up to his neck with the butt end elevated without this awkward posture being observed by some of the soldiers who were peering intently at him through the wide spaces between the boards of the tobacco barn. His figure was brightly illuminated by the burning straw inside the barn and could be clearly seen, as several of the men outside the barn stated. Lieutenant Baker in particular, who had opened the front door of the barn so that Booth could come out, had a clear view of Booth, watching him intently from a mere twelve feet. If the revolver had been fired by Booth with his index finger, with a gun so long, the track of the bullet would have been moderately, or even considerably,

FIG. 32
page 79

uphill. Furthermore, Lieutenant Baker said that it was necessary for him to twist the pistol out of Booth's hand with considerable force because of Booth's tight grip on it. This meant that Booth had to have been gripping the pistol *in the ordinary way*, expecting to use his forefinger to pull the trigger, since in the reversed position the gun can only be held very lightly and would not require any force to wrench it out of the grasp of the person holding it. One must try this for oneself to appreciate this point.

Fig. 32
page 79

When one holds this type of pistol muzzle against the side of the neck at the neck's most lateral prominence, the pistol is actually pointing at the solid portions of the front part of the spine, rather than at the spinal cord canal which lies more toward the back of the neck, where Booth was hit. Booth's vertebral wound was well toward the back of the neck, and it is hard to imagine that he would aim *that* far toward the back for fear of missing himself altogether.

Experiments to Determine Weapon Used

Fig. 33
page 81

Because of this multiplicity of suggestive materials, I thought that some experimentation was merited to compare neck wounds made by a pistol of the type carried by both Booth and Corbett, held against the skin (as it would have been if Booth shot himself) and from a pistol fired from a few yards away (as by Boston Corbett). I also felt that it would be useful to compare neck wounds made by a carbine, as proposed by Colonel Raymond and suggested in one of the modern versions of the autopsy report. I wanted to know whether or not there was a gross difference between wounds of the neck sustained under these various circumstances.

I was fortunate enough to enlist the good offices of computer specialist John W. Rountree and Mr. Val Forgett, Civil War ballistics and arms experts, and medical students Michael Macfarlane and Gary Lattimer to conduct tests using a Colt .44-caliber army pattern revolver, model of

Fig. 134
page 336

1860, of the exact type carried by both Booth and Corbett, and a Civil War .50-caliber carbine, using the same 45-grain charge of black powder (type 2 F. G.) and the same 414-grain lead bullets as those used in the Spencer (and other) Civil War carbines. The Colt revolver chambers were loaded with 28 grains of black powder and with conical lead bullets weighing 207 grains (cast from original Colt Company bullet molds by Mr. Rountree) exactly like those described in Capt. Janvier Woodward's official autopsy report. These bullets fitted so well that, when greased, no patches were needed around them to hold the powder in.

Suicide Wounds Are Different

For experimental necks I selected thighs of fresh pork, which had the same skin texture and soft tissue mass as human necks. I carefully

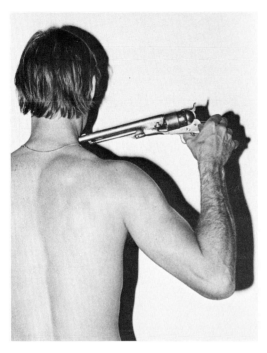

PATH OF REVOLVER BULLET

In order to make the bullet go slightly downhill, as did the wound through Booth's vertebrae, it would have been necessary for Booth to reverse the huge pistol in his small hand and to press the trigger with his thumb, as in the top picture. If this pistol is held in the ordinary manner, so that the trigger would be pulled by the finger, as in bottom picture, it is almost impossible to make the track of the ball go downhill. A Booth suicide bullet would have gone uphill. Booth was not seen to reverse the revolver, which would have taken two hands to accomplish. He was holding a pistol, his carbine and his crutch at the time. *(J. K. Lattimer)*

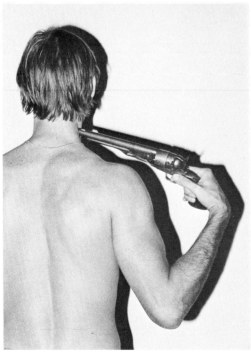

Fig. 32

dissected out all the bone, without disturbing the cylindrical configuration or integrity of the skin and muscle, so that the reaction to bullets would be similar to that in human necks. These proved to be excellent models for observing the effects of the bullet wounds on the skin. Each of the weapons was fired into them, under various test conditions. The Colt army pattern .44-caliber revolver bullets were first fired from "a few" (two) yards away, as Sergeant Corbett said he had done. These wounds of entry into the skin were half-inch punctate holes, with the usual blackened walls from the rapidly spinning greased bullets. The skin around them was otherwise clean and normal in appearance.

Fig. 33
page 81

Next, we held the muzzle of the revolver against the skin, as it would have been held if Booth had shot himself. This caused a large, smoke-blackened stain on the skin, about two inches in diameter, with much gross pitting and tattooing of the skin by embedded particles of unburned powder. In the center of this grossly blackened area was a much larger wound of entry, with some splitting of the skin, roughly twice the diameter of the wounds made from two yards away. These differences in the two types of wounds were gross and absolutely inescapable. They were consistently reproducible, as well.

Booth Did Not Shoot Himself

An experienced autopsy surgeon like Dr. Woodward would never have missed these obvious signs of a suicide wound. Dr. Woodward clearly stated that the wound was made by a conoidal revolver bullet, fired at the distance of a few yards.

Colonel Conger testified to unloading Booth's carbine and stated that both of Booth's revolvers were loaded when he retrieved them in the barn. Since he spoke in some detail of the fact that Booth's carbine had a full magazine and a live round in the chamber, one would have expected him to have been equally detailed in observing if one chamber of either revolver had been discharged. He said nothing about such a finding.

Certainly the cartridge in the chamber of Booth's carbine had *not* been fired.

Time Would Not Have Obscured the Signs of Suicide

Because the autopsy on Booth's body did not occur until some twenty-four or thirty hours after his death, and since there was no refrigeration of the body, it occurred to me that the powder burns might have faded or become less apparent after this interval. I therefore waited thirty hours before refrigerating my experimental specimens and then kept them an additional twenty-four hours in a cool refrigerator. We then rephoto-

Fig. 34
page 82

graphed them. The powder stains were still clearly visible, even though they had become a little less prominent.

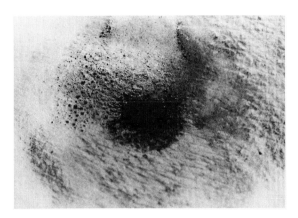

SUICIDE-TYPE
COLT REVOLVER
BULLET WOUND OF
THE SKIN OF THE NECK

Skin wound with two-inch circle of smoke staining, peppered (tattooed) with many granules of unburned powder embedded in skin, and large bullet hole of entrance, with severely blackened rim. This was caused by a Colt .44-caliber Army pattern percussion cap cavalry revolver with 207-grain conical bullet, and 28 grains of black powder, when muzzle was pressed against the skin of the neck. *(J. K. Lattimer)*

REVOLVER BULLET
WOUND FROM A
DISTANCE

Bullet wound of entrance from same Colt revolver, but fired from two yards away, showing a smaller, neater .44-caliber hole in the neck, with only a thin rim of abraded, blackened skin from the rapidly spinning bullet. There are no smoke stains and few particles of powder or debris embedded (tattooed) into the skin around the bullet hole. (The X was aiming point.) *(J. K. Lattimer)*

COLT PISTOL SETS
FIRE TO COLLAR

Booth's collar would have caught fire, as in this demonstration, if he had shot himself in the neck. The flames had to be extinguished. No such burn on his collar was noted. *(J. K. Lattimer)*

Fig. 33

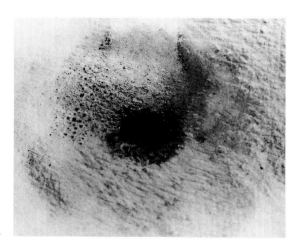

**SUICIDE WOUND ON
IMMEDIATE APPEARANCE**

**SAME WOUND
AFTER FIFTY HOURS**

Fading of powder stains was slight even after fifty hours (bottom). The Booth autopsy was done about thirty hours post-mortem. The "suicide" nature of the wound was still grossly obvious and the tattooing could not have been missed by Dr. Woodward when he did the autopsy at noon on Monday, April 28.

If Booth had shot himself, the "suicide" nature of the skin wound would still have been very obvious to Dr. Woodward, even a day later. *(J. K. Lattimer)*

Fig. 34

However, the severe pockmarking of the skin from the fragments of unburned powder and the large size of the wound entrance hole were still *very* obvious and unmistakably different from the effects of bullets fired from a distance.

These multiple factors indicate clearly that Booth did *not* shoot himself.

Could a Carbine Have Been Used?

Colonel Raymond stands alone in speculating that Booth might have been shot with a carbine. The more modern pamphlet, describing the specimen of Booth's vertebrae in the Armed Forces Institute of Pathology, does state, in direct contradiction to Dr. Woodward's original and official autopsy report, which specifies that the wounds were made by a revolver bullet, that the wound was caused by a carbine bullet.

Yet even if Raymond and the author of the pamphlet were correct, and it *was* a carbine wound, that would be still another reason to be sure that Booth had not shot himself. Nevertheless, in a search for the absolute truth, I undertook to test Raymond's carbine premise.

Booth's Vertebrae X-rayed for Us

Thanks to Dr. F. K. Mostofi and Dr. Edward R. White, Associate Director of the Armed Forces Institute of Pathology, I procured X-rays of Booth's three partially cleaned but mutually attached vertebrae (C 3, 4, and 5), which were placed in the museum by Dr. Woodward and Surgeon General Barnes, whose dissection to remove this segment of the neck almost certainly resulted in Booth's head being severed from his body.

Booth's fourth cervical vertebra had been traversed by the fatal bullet in its posterior portion. The bullet had carried away both walls of the bony canal through which the spinal cord runs along the back of the vertebral column. These are called the laminae of the vertebrae. The long slender extension (spur) of bone which extends from these laminae toward the back surface of the neck (called the spinous process) was broken off and twisted and splintered, but not pulverized, as it lay in the damaged muscles and ligaments of the neck. It was still present in the preserved specimen—an important point. This spur is visible as the slender bone lying diagonally across the center of figure 35 (X-ray of Booth's spine), the bullet having passed transversely through the spinal cord, inclining slightly downward and backward.

FIG. 35
page 85

Booth's fifth cervical vertebra, just below the main bullet track, also showed damage to the upper edge of the laminae of the spinal canal. The pedicle of the lamina on the right side of the neck (toward the gun) was also fractured fairly extensively. The direction of the hole indicated a slightly downward course of the bullet, which would certainly have required using the thumb in firing a long pistol like Booth's.

Next, I undertook to duplicate and compare these wounds of the vertebrae by infolding sets of vertebrae into the pork "necks," and firing bullets into them from a carbine, held both against the skin and from two yards away, using the same 45-grain black powder charge and 414-grain bullet weight as were used in Spencer and Maynard carbines in the Civil War. The suicide wounds from the carbine held against the skin were obviously worse than those from a distance, as with the revolver.

Booth Was Not Shot with a Carbine

FIGS. 36, 37
page 86

FIG. 38
page 87

FIG. 39
page 87

Whereas the revolver bullets had drilled a hole through the tissues and bones (laminae) over the spinal cord, leaving the fractured bone fragments in the area, the carbine bullets swept away the bones completely. The soft tissue wounds of exit were *markedly* different, with much larger quantities of fragments of vertebrae and fibrous debris carried out into each wound of exit in the skin by the carbine bullets.

The wounds of entrance from the carbine bullets were also markedly larger than those made by the pistol bullets at either close or long range.

Here again, the total effects were so much more severe from the carbine wounds that there would be little or no chance that the experienced Dr. Woodward would confuse wounds made by a .44-caliber Colt army revolver and a .50-caliber Spencer carbine.

Corbett's Version Compatible with Experimental Results

From the documentation and with the added evidence of our experiments, it seemed apparent that a self-inflicted wound would have been so grossly different from that made by a weapon fired from a distance of "a few" (two or more) yards that Dr. Woodward would have had no trouble whatsoever in distinguishing the two. Also, the severity of wounds from a carbine and from a Colt revolver were so grossly different that when Dr. Woodward said they were revolver wounds, it would seem likely that he was making an accurate diagnosis. Neither the army commission, the civil court, nor the press challenged Corbett's statement that he shot Booth with a Colt revolver. Reasonable explanations seem to me to exist for all the conjectures formed and questions asked.

Which Bone Was Broken in Booth's Leg?

When Booth leaped from Lincoln's theater box to the stage twelve feet below, his spur caught on a flag and turned him so that he landed heavily on his left foot. This fractured one of the two bones in his lower leg. Dr. Mudd, who splinted it six or seven hours later, described it as being broken squarely across, a few inches above the ankle. The motion between the two ends of the broken bone was very painful, but did not

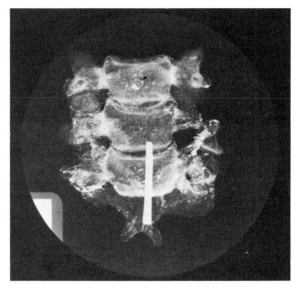

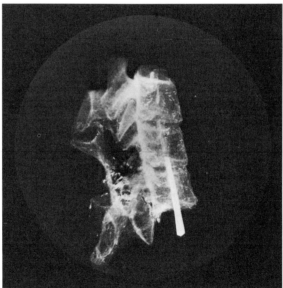

X-RAYS OF
BOOTH'S VERTEBRAE

X-rays taken in 1979 of Booth's vertebrae show tranverse bullet hole with fragments of lead in the bullet track. Bones are broken but their fragments are still
in place (not swept away) (top). The bullet was traveling a little more from
back to front and very slightly downhill, but mostly sideways through Booth's
spine, cutting his spinal cord. Note the many tiny white fragments of lead scattered along the track of the bullet (bottom). In our experiments, this was characteristic of revolver bullets. (*Armed Forces Institute of Pathology*)

Fig. 35

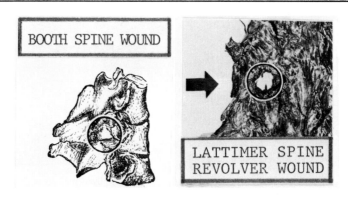

BOOTH'S WOUND AND EXPERIMENTAL WOUND

The official illustrations of the bullet wound through Booth's vertebrae (left) resembled our experimental revolver wounds (right) rather than our carbine wounds, which were much larger. (See fig. 37.) *(Left:* Medical and Surgical History of the War of the Rebellion. *Surgical Volume, Part I; right: J. K. Lattimer)*

Fig. 36

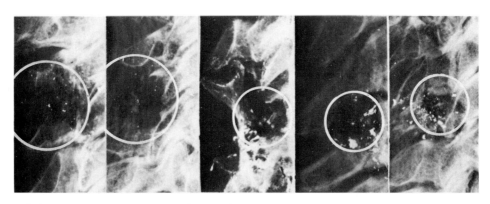

BOOTH'S SPINE X-RAYS (center) COMPARED WITH CARBINE WOUNDS (left pair) AND REVOLVER-WOUND X-RAYS (right pair)

Carbine bullets made large black holes (left) whereas revolver bullets made small round holes (right) throught the spine. The damage to Booth's vertebrae (center X-ray) matched that done to Booth-type vertebrae by CW Colt revolver bullets (X-rays at right). Revolver bullets left the broken bones still in the area, as in Booth's X-ray. Fine fragments of lead (tiny white dots) from revolver bullets were scattered in each of our revolver wounds, just as in Booth's X-ray. The damage from a CW (Spencer or Maynard) carbine bullet was much greater (X-rays at left). The carbine bullets swept away all the broken bones completely. No fine white bullet fragments were left in the wound by any of our carbine bullets. *(Center: Armed Forces Institute of Pathology: others: J. K. Lattimer)*

Fig. 37

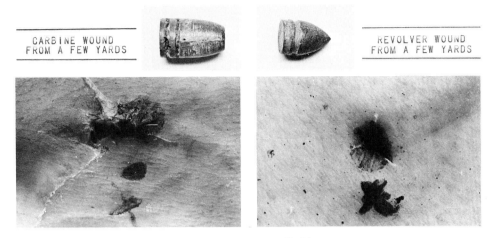

CARBINE WOUND
FROM A FEW YARDS

REVOLVER WOUND
FROM A FEW YARDS

COMPARISON OF CARBINE WOUND (left)
AND REVOLVER WOUND (right)

Experimental carbine bullet holes of entrance were larger than those made by revolver bullets, in keeping with their greater size (414 grains of lead versus the Colt revolver's 207 grains) and energy. The more massive carbine bullet was propelled by 45 grains of type 2 FG black powder; the revolver bullet by only 28 grains. Not only were these carbine wounds of entrance noticeably larger, but also the carbine bullets split the skin severely for an inch or so on each side of the bullet entry hole. Furthermore, the wounds of exit from the carbine bullets were larger and contained much more debris carried through from the vertebrae than the pistol bullets. The descriptions of Booth's wounds were in accord with experimental wounds from a revolver and not from a carbine. *(J. K. Lattimer)*

Fig. 38

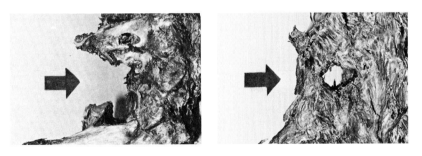

SPINE TISSUE WOUNDS, CARBINE (left) vs. PISTOL (right)

Internal neck and spine tissues (right) struck by a pistol bullet showed a round hole through the area of the spinal canal, whereas the much larger carbine bullet tended to sweep away all the structures in the area (left). Booth's vertebrae showed a hole like those made by our revolver bullets. (See fig. 36.) *(J. K. Lattimer)*

Fig. 39

prevent Booth from hobbling rapidly off across the stage, waving his dagger and shouting "*Sic semper tyrannis.*" He limped into the wings, scattering the actors before him, and then left the theater through a back door, where he was able to climb onto his horse unassisted, for the getaway ride. If he had broken the tibia (the larger bone in his lower leg) squarely across, several inches above the ankle, he would not have been able to walk on it at all, much less climb onto a horse. This clearly indicates that it was his fibula, the much smaller bone in the lower leg, that he broke. The fibula does not bear the weight as does the tibia, and could be broken squarely across above the ankle without absolutely stopping the patient from walking. The grating of the broken ends would become agonizingly painful, but he *could* hobble along. The heavy, weight-bearing tibia, broken squarely across, would have made it impossible to walk; the leg would have buckled, like a flail, and he would have fallen to the ground with severe swelling and unbearable pain.

Although it is true that several people, including Dr. Mudd, described the broken bone as the tibia, the circumstantial evidence that he was able to walk on it, climb onto his horse unassisted, tolerate the pain, and finally walk a few last steps on it twelve days later in the burning barn, without his crutch, clearly indicates that it was not his tibia that was broken squarely across; it must have been his fibula.

For those who want to know which leg was broken, there are almost unanimous references to the left leg in the testimony of those who saw him but also his left boot in the Ford's Theater Museum, cut off by Dr. Mudd so he could splint the broken bone with thin strips of wood from an old bandbox. There is little doubt that it was his left leg that was broken.

As with the Kennedy shooting, the interesting conjectures that some of the shootings might have been done by someone other than the accepted candidate are unconvincing when subjected to laboratory experimentation.

I cannot explain why whoever wrote the description of Booth's vertebral specimens in the new Armed Forces Institute of Pathology pamphlet attributed the bullet holes to a carbine, when Dr. Woodward had stated clearly they were from a revolver. This discrepancy must remain unexplained. I could find no ballistic or other evidence to negate Corbett's version of the shooting. I have every reason to believe his statement that he shot Booth with his Colt revolver from a distance of a few yards.

Finally, one must consider Corbett's fanatical devotion to religious principles. For a man of such powerful convictions to swear falsely on the Bible, under oath, would have been so contrary to his principles, so completely out of character, as to further strengthen my belief that he was telling the truth when he said he shot Booth.

Booth's demise and the circumstances of his death were only a part of the assassination drama. The tragedy of Lincoln's death and the manhunt for Booth overshadowed other events of the night of April 15, 1865.

But there were two other intended victims that night.

5.

THE STABBING OF SECRETARY OF STATE SEWARD

Fig. 40
page 90

Lincoln's secretary of state, the patrician William H. Seward, whom Lincoln had narrowly defeated for the Republican nomination in 1860, was also a target of the assassination plotters. The man assigned to kill Seward, Lewis Payne (born Lewis Thornton Powell), a Florida preacher's son, was a powerful, composed, handsome young Confederate soldier who had fought at Antietam and Chancellorsville, had been wounded at Gettysburg, and had lost two of his brothers in the war. After recovering from his wound, he had served briefly as a nurse in the Union Army Hospital where he was treated. He then escaped to join Mosby, but deserted and returned to Baltimore, where Booth recruited him. Payne was a great admirer of Booth.

Payne's Ingenious Approach to Seward's Bedroom

As the fatal hour of 10:15 approached, Payne, with the young drug clerk Herold acting as his guide, rode into Lafayette Square and up to the front of the Seward house, near the White House. Payne was not familiar enough with Washington to have located his victim's house alone, so Herold had been assigned to guide him to his target and then to join Booth on his escape route after the assassination at Ford's Theater.

Payne tied his horse to a tree, mounted the low doorstep of the massive, three-story residence, and rang the bell. When the Negro house-

coc

LEWIS PAYNE

This photograph of
Payne shows him
after his capture for
attacking Secretary
of State Seward.
(National Archives)

Fig. 40

**PAYNE'S
HANDCUFFS**

These are the handcuffs Payne wore through most of his captivity. They can be
clearly seen in the photograph of him (top) taken while he was a prisoner
on one of the monitors. Able to be released only by someone who had a socket
wrench that would fit the rather stiff bolt in the middle of the handcuffs, the
manacles (called Lilly irons by Arnold in his memoirs) were heavy and inflexible
and prevented the hands from being brought together for any purpose. In the
Philip Sang collection until 1977; now in the author's collection. *(J. K. Lattimer)*

Fig. 41

man, William Bell, opened the door, Payne indicated a small package he was carrying. He said it was medicine for Mr. Seward, and that Dr. Verdi, Seward's family physician, had sent him to direct Mr. Seward how to take the medicine. Payne insisted that the houseman lead him up the stairs to the third floor and to Mr. Seward's bedroom.

On the third-floor landing, Mr. Seward's middle son, Assistant Secretary of State Frederick Seward, intercepted Payne, saying that his father had just been composed for sleep and could not be disturbed. Insisting, Payne persuaded young Seward to look into his father's room to see if he was really asleep. This enabled Payne to make sure which room Seward was in. When the son would not permit him to enter, Payne pretended to start down the stairs but, as young Seward turned to go to his own room, Payne spun around and pointed his Whitney navy revolver at Seward's head. He pulled the trigger but the pistol failed to fire. Payne then raised the pistol and struck Seward two hard blows on the head.

FIG. 46
page 103

Despite his wounds, young Seward continued to grapple with Payne, past his sister's room, past his own room, and into the doorway of his father's room. Just at that moment, Seward's daughter, Fanny, and the male nurse, Private Robinson, opened the door to see what the commotion was about.

Seward Immobilized in Bed with Fractures

Seward was confined to his bed because he had been injured nine days previously in a carriage accident. His horses had bolted and Seward, hoping to stop them, sprang from the carriage, but his heel caught and he was thrown heavily to the ground, breaking his right arm and fracturing his jaw in two places. Attempts to immobilize his jaw by bandaging and by wiring one tooth to another had been unsuccessful, and Seward was still in great discomfort and far from well.

His son recounted that his father was lying in a recumbent position, but half-raised on one of those frameworks that are made for the accommodation of the sick and are mostly seen in hospitals. He lay at the very edge of the bed in an attempt to keep his broken right arm hanging down for traction and to keep the arm from coming in contact with the mattress. The nurses were watching continually to see that he did not fall off the bed when he dozed, since he insisted on lying just at the far edge of the bed away from the door. The gas was turned very low in the room.

Private Robinson, a convalescent wounded soldier from Maine, opened the door to see what the disturbance was and saw the flash of a knife aimed at him. He warded it off as best he could, but he was struck on the forehead and knocked to the ground. Payne then pushed the door wide open and entered the room, bounding for Mr. Seward's bed. Placing his left hand on Seward's breast, he struck straight down into his victim with the knife two or three times, with all his might.

Fanny Seward's Account

Seward's daughter, Fanny, who was in the sickroom with her father, later described the scene in her diary:

... in the hand nearest me was a pistol, in the right hand a knife. I ran beside him to the bed, imploring him to stop. I must have said, "Don't kill him." Father awakened, he says, hearing me speak the word "kill" and seeing first me speaking to someone whom he did not see, and then he raised himself and had one glimpse of the assassin's face bending over him and next felt the blows, and by their force, he being on the edge of the bed, was thrown to the floor. I have no remembrance of going around the foot of the bed to the other side but I remember standing there by the corner of the foot and thinking this must be a fearful dream. Then I looked about and saw first what I had seen before, I think, but more fully now—three men struggling beside the bed. I knew who they all were then. I could not tell the next day, that they were Fred and Robinson and the assassin. Next I saw all the familiar objects in the room, the bureau, the little stand, the book I had been reading, all looked natural. Then I knew it was not a dream. I remember pacing the room back and forth from end to end, screaming. My screams awakened Gus, but I do not remember seeing him when he came in. Some vague idea of calling for assistance carried me into the hall. I think at that time the assassin and those struggling with him were by the door in father's room and that I had passed them as I went out. I remember mother and Anna (Frederick's wife) asking me what had happened and my saying, "Is that man gone?" and they said, "What man?"

Later Fanny remembered little of what had happened, denying that she had opened a window and cried "Murder!" as Private Robinson claimed she had done. Here we encounter an interesting analogy to more recent events; both Fanny Seward and Jacqueline Kennedy were amnesic of their actions at the critical moments, when they saw their families being destroyed before their eyes. Mrs. Kennedy remembers nothing of being dumped out on the automobile trunk, just as Fanny was oblivious to her actions for a few awful moments.

Private Robinson testified at the trial that the assassin had pummeled Fanny out of the way as he came through the door, nearly punching her over him. As Private Robinson, stunned by the blow on his forehead, staggered up from the floor and caught Payne from behind, Payne had again cut Seward, this time on the left side of his neck. Then, reaching around behind him, he stabbed Robinson through the shoulder, to the bone, twice. They struggled, and Payne struck the nurse two or three times under the ear with the butt of his knife. As he reached again with his knife, Seward's oldest son, Gus, arrived on the scene and clenched Payne from behind, and the three men grappled, moving out of the room and into the brightly lit hallway.

Seward's Son's Account

Maj. Augustus H. Seward had retired to bed but had been awakened by the noise. Later, at the trial, he told his story:

I was awakened by the screams of my sister, and jumped out of bed and ran into my father's room in my shirt and drawers. The gas in the room was turned down rather low and I saw what appeared to be two men, one trying to hold the other at the foot of my father's bed. I seized by the clothes on his breast the person who was held, supposing it was my father, delirious; but immediately on taking hold of him I knew from his size and strength that it was not my father. The thought then struck me that the nurse had become delirious sitting up there and was striking about the room at random. Knowing the delicate state of my father, I shoved the person of whom I had hold to the door, with the intention of getting him out of the room. While I was pushing him, he struck me five or six times on the forehead, on top of the head, and once on the left hand with what I supposed to be a bottle or decanter that he had seized from the table. During this time, he repeated, in an intense but not strong voice, the words "I'm mad! I'm mad!" On reaching the hall he gave a sudden turn, sprang away from me and disappeared downstairs.

On his way down, on the first flight of stairs, Payne overtook Mr. Hansell, Seward's State Department messenger, who had been roused by the noise. As Payne came within reach of him, he stabbed him in the back with his knife.

Private Robinson, although wounded, managed to return to Seward's room and found him lying on the floor. He approached him, and as he pulled aside the tangled bedclothes to see if Seward's heart was beating, Seward opened his eyes, looked up, and said, "I am not dead; send for a surgeon, send for the police, close the house." Robinson found the wound and held his hand over it. Seward was bleeding profusely.

Payne fled the house, threw his knife in the gutter, jumped on his horse, and rode off, this time without Herold, who had gone to guide Booth. Payne became hopelessly lost and finally returned to Mrs. Surratt's boardinghouse just when detectives were there to arrest Mrs. Surratt. They captured him too.

The Seward family doctor, T. S. Verdi, arrived shortly and determined that Seward's wounds were not mortal.

It is amazing that the powerful ex-soldier, armed with both a revolver and a knife, failed to kill any of the five people he attacked. All three male members of the Seward family finally recovered from their wounds, as did Mr. Hansell and Private Robinson, but there were further consequences of this horrendous night. Mrs. Seward became ill with palpitations on the night of the stabbing, later suffered another heart attack, and died two months later. Fanny Seward never recovered from the horrors she went through, declined slowly, with a steadily worsening cough, and died eighteen months after the awful experience of seeing three members of her family so brutally attacked.

Vice President Johnson's Assassin

Perhaps the most fortunate victim of the assassination plot was Vice President Andrew Johnson. Booth had assigned George Atzerodt to kill the Vice President while he himself was killing Lincoln, and Payne, Seward; but Atzerodt apparently didn't have the heart for assassination.

Atzerodt took a room at the Kirkwood House, on the floor above the one on which Johnson was living, and studied the Vice President's habits. At approximately 9:30 on the evening of the assassination, Atzerodt appeared in the lobby of the hotel, presumably to try to see the Vice President at the appointed hour of 10:15. Since he was early, he went into the bar for a drink, and since it was still early when he finished that drink, he ordered another. After a third drink, he began to reflect on the fact that he had been perfectly willing to take part in the kidnapping of President Lincoln, but he really wanted no part of murder. In fact, he decided he wanted out of the murder attempt. He had one more drink and then wandered down the street without making any attempt to approach his intended victim.

And so the assassination attempt was over. Of the three intended victims, one lay dying, one was gravely wounded, and the third had escaped unscathed.

Seward's Wounds Complicated

Seward underwent a period of intense suffering as a result of his carriage accident and, just as he was beginning to recover from that, the attempt on his life. Though his wounds were not mortal, they were very complicated, and the medical problems posed by deep cuts superimposed upon the broken jaw seemed nearly insurmountable. Remarkably, Seward survived and made a complete recovery. The story of his ordeal is a fascinating one.

As with Lincoln's wound, it was difficult also in Seward's case to make a precise interpretation from the various descriptions given by doctors and witnesses of the wounds that Seward sustained in the attack. But there are, fortunately, several clues which we will piece together as accurately as possible to get a clear picture of what really happened.

Private Robinson, who was the first to attempt to stanch the blood with his hand, described cuts on the right cheek and the left side of the neck. He said he thought the right cheek was cut clear through so that one could see into Seward's mouth. In testifying at the trial of the conspirators, Private Robinson stated: "I saw him cut Mr. Seward twice that I am sure of; the first time he struck him on the right cheek and then he seemed to be cutting around his neck. I afterwards examined the wounds and found one cutting his face from the right cheek down to the neck and a cut on his neck which might have been made by the same blow, and another on the left side of the neck."

The surgeon general, Dr. Joseph K. Barnes, stated at the trial: "The Secretary was wounded in three places, by a gash in the right cheek passing around to the angle of the jaw, by a stab in the right neck and by a stab in the left side of the neck. He had recovered from the shock of the accident of ten days previous and was getting along very well. His right arm was broken close to the shoulder joint and his jaw was broken in two places; but the serious injury of the first accident had been a concussion."

From this description alone, one might even wonder if there were three separate cuts. The first physician on the scene, the family doctor, T. S. Verdi, gave this report: "The carotid artery and jugular vein had not been divided or injured; the gash was semicircular, commencing just below the high bone of the cheek and extending downward toward the mouth, and then backward over the submaxillary gland, laying open the inflamed and swollen part of the face and neck that had been injured by his previous accident. On examining further, I found another stab, under the left ear, wounding the parotid gland; but this cut, however, was not very deep. Mr. Seward had lost much blood and I immediately applied ice to arrest the bleeding temporarily."

Description of the Wounds

FIG. 42
page 96

We can deduce from these reports, and from the even more precise descriptions given by the dentist who was called in to treat Seward's jaw, that the major stab wound was a zigzag gash below the right cheekbone which went downward and forward about three inches, then backward and downward three inches, and then forward again, exposing on the right side the broken ends of the jawbone which had been incurred in the carriage accident nine days before. There were superficial cuts around the neck and a moderate cut in the left side of the neck, into the parotid gland. The right cheek hung backward and downward in a loose flap, and Stenson's (saliva) duct was severed, causing saliva to leak out through the external wound. Whether these cuts were all one long slash or the effects of several separate stabs, one on each side of the neck and one as the assassin cut around the neck, was more difficult to determine. No major vessels were cut, and the trachea was not entered. The jaw had been broken between the bicuspid teeth on each side and the arm fractured just below the shoulder, causing him to lie on the edge of the bed farthest away from the door so that his injured arm would not come in contact with the bed. His distance from the door and the darkness of the room probably saved his life.

It is apparent, from studying diagrams of the Seward house and testimony about the attack, that the door through which the would-be assassin entered must have been in the same wall against which the head of the bed rested. Seward was on the far side of the bed, dangling his right arm over the edge, so the assassin must have knelt across the bed to lean over the huddled figure propped up against a backrest. It must have

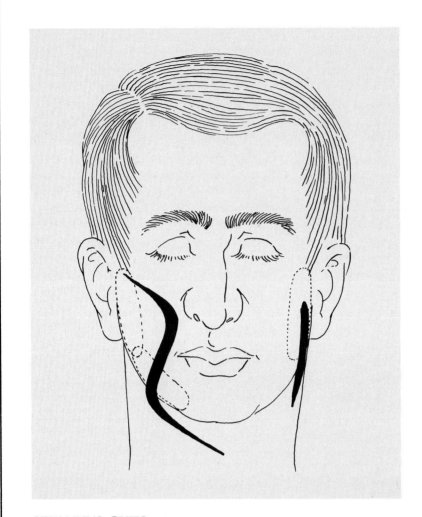

SEWARD'S CUTS

Locations of the stab wounds of Secretary Seward, from the detailed descriptions by Dr. Gunning, the dentist who fixed his jaw. The long cut on the right cheek was inflicted as he looked upward and to his left. It exposed the nine-day-old fracture of his right lower jaw. *(J. K. Lattimer)*

Fig. 42

been difficult for Payne to see clearly in the darkened room after entering from the brightly lighted hallway.

Seward must have turned his head sharply toward the left and looked upward at Payne at the same moment so that the point of the knife, striking from above, picked up the sagging flesh of the right cheek as it stretched upward, grazing and laying open the bone of his broken jaw just at the point of fracture and then coming downward and forward across his neck toward the left side—toward the assassin—as Payne pulled the knife toward himself. Payne apparently then struck him once more, making only a small second wound over the parotid gland and left side of the neck. The fact that Stenson's duct was cut by the knife is obvious, and the saliva from the cut duct appears to have discharged through the external wound, which had now compounded to outside the jaw fracture Seward had sustained in the carriage accident. The resulting scars disfigured Seward enough that he rarely permitted the right side of his face to be photographed.

FIG. 43
page 98

Seward's daughter Fanny spoke specifically of the fact that the bedclothes had been cut severely by several stabs of the knife which had missed her father. No doubt, in the dim light the assassin could not distinguish his victim clearly against the backrest on which Seward was leaning, and indeed, Private Robinson stated that Payne struck *beyond* the Secretary of State with the first blow in particular. A bed sheet, exhibiting cuts from the knife, is among the memorabilia at the Seward household museum in Auburn, New York.

Perhaps the most precise description of Seward's injuries was made by Dr. Thomas Brian Gunning, a self-made dental expert from New York who was called in later, who had become skilled in the treatment of fractures of the lower jaw by interdental splints of his own ingenious design. Dr. Gunning wrote an account in the *New York Journal of Medicine* in 1867.

Dr. Gunning's Account of New Splint for Seward's Jaw

Unsuccessful attempts had been made to hold the jaw in place by bandages and also with ligatures on the teeth, by the surgeons first called into the case. On the fourteenth, the patient was attacked by an assassin and a cut inflicted which reached from under the zygoma to the left of the trachea. Attending surgeon Basil Norris, USN [Dr. Norris was actually USA] informed me that the jaw was fractured on the right side between the bicuspid teeth and also in the ramus of the same side; that the jaw had been bandaged against the upper gum (edentulous) but this proving insupportable to the patient, the bandages were removed. On examination I found discoloration caused by the accident still remaining on the right side of the face. A cut (inflicted in the attempted assassination) commenced under the zygoma, passed forward about three inches, then downward and backward an equal distance, to the lower border of

**SEWARD'S DISFIGURED APPEARANCE AFTER
THE STABBING**

The large cuts made by the assassin on the right side of Seward's
face resulted in a distortion of his appearance. As a consequence,
he would only rarely allow photographs that would show the
scarred right side of his face. *(University of Rochester Library)*

Fig. 43

the jaw, from whence it crossed over the front of the throat to the left of the trachea. On the skin, its first direction fell somewhat from a horizontal line, the second passed down at a little less than a right angle to the first, while the third went forward and downward. These three divisions of nearly equal length, appeared to have been made by one sweep of the knife. Across the throat the wound was superficial but above the border of the jaw it grew deeper as it split the cheek—the point of the knife making no entrance into the mouth, except so far as it may be considered to have done so by laying open the right fracture externally, the gum being already lacerated internally from the great displacement of the bone following upon the original injury. The knife was evidently aimed at the throat, but the head being thrown over, the cheek and jaw received the brunt of the blow. No arteries had been ligatured. The wound was neatly sewed up, and healing by first intention, except immediately under the fracture. The swelling and stiffness made the examination difficult, but the ramus proved to be uninjured. There was, however, a second fracture, but on the other side of the mouth, the jaw fractured on both sides between the bicuspids. The (lower) jaw contained all the ten forward teeth. The right wisdom tooth and root of the left were all that remained back of the bicuspids. The part in front, containing eight teeth, was drawn down out of place, while the right back fragment with the wisdom tooth and second bicuspid was drawn up, showing its fractured end white and bare. The fracture was square across, vertical and smooth, and the parts were separated vertically over a quarter of an inch when at rest, sometimes more. On the left side, the first bicuspid fell forward and downward from the second, one quarter of an inch. This fracture passed forward somewhat in descending. Here the bone could not be seen, as the gum had separated from both teeth and lay swollen over it. Pus discharged profusely from both fractures. The gum was pale and flaccid, in keeping with the general condition of the patient. The upper jaw was entirely without teeth.

Since Seward's artificial teeth did not fit him well, Dr. Gunning decided not to try to use them as an interdental splint to which to fix the lower teeth. He proposed a new splint, but this idea was rejected by the surgeons in charge.

Twelve days later, by April 28, the jaw had become more displaced and Gunning was recalled from New York. He states:

I found the sensation of the right side of the forehead, face and lips deficient. The separation of the inferior dental nerve by the displacement of the bone and of branches of the facial nerve, by the knife, did not seem sufficient to account for it. There was also irregular motion in the right eye. The front of the jaw was lower and the right back fragment showed its alveolar to a greater extent. There were no indications of any tendency to union on either side. The fragments could be put precisely in place, no splinters or anything else intervening. There was little swelling, but great discharge of pus. Took wax impression of upper jaw and removed the tartar from the lower teeth. On April 29 I set the jaw, and held it in place by wire and silk ligatures. Took a wax impression of the teeth and gum and obtained the bite directly from the teeth. The patient felt much relieved as the ligatures held the front of the jaw well up. Tied in a gutta-percha splint, arranged the wings in it, removed it carefully from the mouth, placed the upper and lower casts and female screws in it, and set them in a vulcanizing flask.

FIG. 44
page 101

99

FIG. 44
page 101

Although the front of the jaw containing the eight forward teeth was greatly displaced (before the setting), the silk and wire ligatures held well until May 2 when they were removed and the splint applied. It was of hard vulcanized rubber, covered the roof of the mouth and adjacent gum, enclosed all the lower teeth, and went down over the gum on the outside somewhat. The opening in front was seven-eighths of an inch wide, half an inch high in the center, the wings preventing any more room sideways as they were set clear of the commissure of the lips. To have given any more room in the height, by depressing the lower jaw, would have made it very difficult to prevent the saliva from overflowing at the lips. Upon putting in the splint, the breathing was spasmodic for several minutes but this soon passed off, and I screwed it fast to the lower teeth. They held it against the upper gum for the first night, but after that a cap [on the head] with adjuncts, was worn to support the splint. The upper wings [supporting rods connected to the cap on the head] only were used, as the lower jaw was held up in the splint by screws passing into the lower canine. After giving the excellent army nurses, who were in attendance upon the patient, full directions for keeping the splint clean in the mouth and properly balanced by the cap which I had fitted to the head, I left Washington May 3. While talking was very difficult and frustrating at first, through the opening in the mouth, the patient was able to talk freely and was much encouraged when I saw him on May 8. Saliva accumulated several times in the cheek, probably from the severed steno's [Stenson's] duct, but had been let out by lancing externally. By June 11 the left side of the jaw was well united but the right still ununited, although the wound under it was nearly closed, the last of several pieces of bone having been removed around the first of June.

This splint had held the jaw firm for sixty-eight days and, while the left side was united, the right fracture was still not united. This did not surprise Dr. Gunning since the bone had been exposed to so much trauma during the twenty-four days that elapsed before he had been permitted to set it. The saliva from the right parotid gland had discharged through the fracture since the attack. Gunning felt that these unfavorable circumstances, with the enfeebled condition from loss of blood, had been followed by necrosis of the ends of the bone on that side, and, indeed, several pieces had come away externally during the first six weeks, as well as a long piece from along the inside of the jaw on the left side. Dr. Gunning removed the necrosed alveolar of the second bicuspid in June but left the tooth in as it appeared to have healthy connections with the lower parts of its socket. The other teeth had grown firm, and the external appearance indicated that the saliva followed the course taken by the point of the knife. By July 9, Stenson's duct proved to be completely closed. Gunning could not pass the smallest probe into it, and the saliva discharged entirely through the as yet ununited fracture on the right side. A second splint was inserted and worn from July 9 to August 4 and another one until October 1865.

Dr. Gunning stated: "In a letter to me of March 29, 1866, the patient says: 'The whole jaw moves quite well and firmly. Thus at last I begin to regard my cure in that respect as complete.' I have not seen him myself

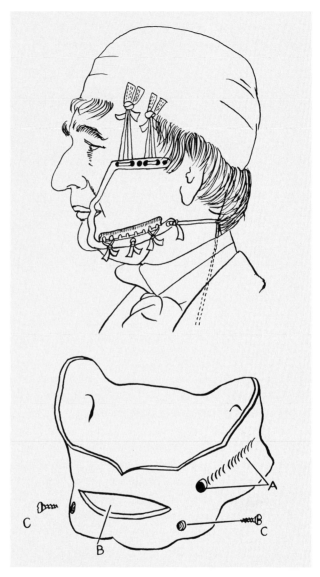

SEWARD'S
MOUTH SPLINT

Pioneer dentist Dr. Gunning had to design a special device (splint) to keep Seward's jaw fragments lined up. The lower teeth were clamped by screws (C) to a vulcanite casting (bottom) that filled his mouth, but had a narrow tunnel (B) for feeding. Saliva escaped via channels (A). Metal rods embedded in the vulcanite came out at the corners of the mouth and were fixed to a cap on his head. A sling under the chin helped by keeping the jaw pushed up into the splint. Poor Seward had to wear this for several months, but his broken jaw finally healed well. *(From Lattimer,* et al., Journal of the American Dental Association, Jan. 1968.)

Fig. 44

since October 1865, therefore cannot speak of it by personal observation."

The Protective Collar Fallacy

Much has been written about the fact that Secretary Seward was wearing some type of iron frame or collar made of leather and iron, which stopped the plunging point of the knife from entering the thorax, first on the right and then on the left. While many of Seward's biographers state that a collar was in some way connected with the apparatus to repair his broken jaw, the contemporary medical witnesses mention only bandages and wires to the teeth as being used for the jaw. None of the firsthand witnesses spoke about a collar, either in their testimony at the trial of the conspirators or at the trial of Surratt two years later.

Thus the oft-quoted legend that a collar around Seward's neck was used to hold his broken jaw in place is not borne out either by the evidence or by analysis of the reasons for such a collar. Certainly it was not the complicated apparatus which Dr. Gunning applied to Seward's head and jaw after the stabbing. It seems likely that those who saw this complicated device in place a short time after the event assumed it had been in place before the stabbing and assumed erroneously that it was the thing that was struck by Payne's knife, making sparks fly.

Quite a different explanation seems much more likely, and that is that the Secretary of State was propped up on a backrest which had metallic elements in it, whether of sheet metal or with metal pins to hold it together. The assassin's knife, in striking at the Secretary of State from above, went behind him each time because of the assassin's miscalculation of how thin the old gentleman's thorax really was. It struck the sparks from the metallic backrest behind the Secretary, which were seen in the darkened room and commented upon. It seems clear that it must have been the backrest which was struck rather than any device attached to the patient or to the patient's broken jaw as has been stated. Close examination of the record by Dr. Gunning and now ourselves shows that the devices on his broken jaw were applied only *after* the attempted assassination. Nowhere is there a description of a protective collar *before* the attempt on his life.

And so, as we see, everything possible was done for Seward to hasten his recovery, and the new interdental splint that Dr. Gunning devised actually worked. During this time, Seward's two sons were also in the process of recovering, though it was some months before Frederick's head wounds, and the resulting concussion, permitted him to leave the house.

Payne's Weapons

Again, as we did with the Lincoln and Booth killings, let us examine and

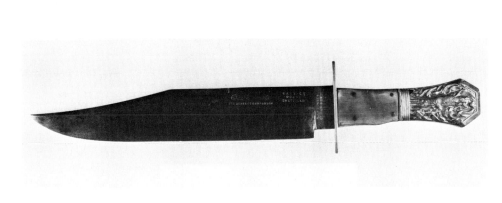

PAYNE'S KNIFE

The knife used to stab Seward on the night Booth shot Lincoln. *(J. K. Lattimer)*

Fig. 45

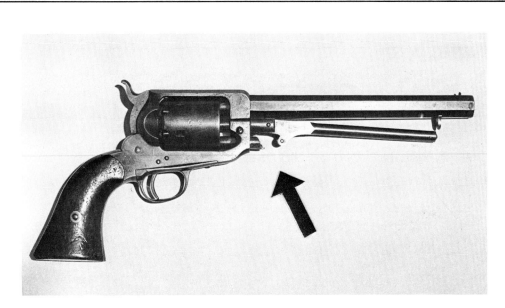

PAYNE'S WHITNEY REVOLVER

The arrow points to a break in the ramrod hinge under the barrel, caused when Payne struck Seward's son, Frederick, fracturing his skull. The ramrod then dropped into the mechanism, and the cylinder could not rotate, nor could the pistol fire. If Payne had calmly thumbed the hammer back again, he could have shot several people. Using his pistol as a club merely destroyed it. *(National Park Service)*

Fig. 46

describe the weapons that were used in Payne's attempt on the lives of the Seward family. The knife he used for the stabbing was a very large bowie knife with a straight, stiff handle and a cross guard of heavy German silver. The pommel was of silver embossed with an alligator and decorative scroll work which glittered in the light. Payne had enlisted with a Florida regiment, where the alligator motif was popular. It was made by the Garrick Works of Sheffield, England, and bears on its blade

FIG. 45
page 103

inscriptions typical of the day ("Real Life Defender" and "The Hunter's Companion"). Only faintly discernible are the words "Never Surrender." Knives of this type were popular imports from England into the South, both before and during the Civil War. A number of similar ones have been recovered from the wreck of the blockade runner *Modern Greece*, which was sunk off Port Fisher in 1862. The point is not now as sharp as the rest of the blade, which is still extremely sharp. The proximal third of the grip is covered by two pieces of horn riveted to the sides of the metal handle.

Payne's pistol was a Whitney navy revolver with a rigid frame, which made it more suitable for striking than the less rigid Colt revolvers of the day, but the blow inflicted by Payne upon the skull of young Seward broke the ramrod at its hinged joint, letting the thick portion of the ramrod enter a chamber of the cylinder. This undoubtedly prevented the cylinder from revolving, foiling further attempts to fire the pistol. During the scuffle in Seward's bedroom, the ramrod and the pin holding

FIG. 46
page 103

the cylinder in place were apparently dislodged and the cylinder fell out. Fanny Seward described Private Robinson's search on the floor for the priming because "he was afraid that if someone stepped on the percussion caps, mischief would be done." She stated that he did find the priming, indicating that some of the other chambers would have fired if Payne had continued to cock the weapon and pull the trigger, instead of using the pistol as a club after the first chamber misfired. This revolver can be seen at the Ford's Theater Museum. Payne dropped the knife as he mounted his horse, and it was found by one of the houseboys, Robert Nelson, when it became light, was brought in and given to Dr. John Wilson, M. C., U.S.A., who was one of the army doctors left to care for the three injured Seward men. The three Sewards later presented Dr. Wilson with a copy of Pitman's original official account of the trial of the conspirators, signed by all three of his patients, Secretary of State William H. Seward, Maj. Augustus H. Seward, and Assistant Secretary of State Frederick Seward.

Dr. Wilson put an identifying mark on the knife, entered it as an exhibit at the trial, and obtained a receipt for it.

At the trial Dr. Wilson identified it as the knife in question. At a later date, Sergeant Robinson requested the knife as a souvenir and it was apparently turned over to him temporarily by Secretary Stanton's office. Subsequently, Dr. Wilson appears to have been successful in reclaiming the knife, pointing out that it was legally his and that he had an official

MRS. MARY SURRATT

Mrs. Surratt ran the rooming house where the conspirators plotted, and owned the tavern at Surrattsville, Maryland (a Confederate spy house), where the carbine Herold and Booth picked up just after the assassination was stored. One of her boarders, Mr. Weichmann, may have contributed to her being hanged by indicating that she took Booth's "spy glass" to the Surrattsville tavern, and that she allegedly told the tavern keeper to have the "shooting irons" ready for the assassins, who would pick them up that night. Few people expected her to be hanged on the evidence of an unreliable witness, and it is not known whether the new President, Andrew Johnson, ever saw the commission's recommendation for mercy or was being kept in ignorance of it by others. Mrs. Surratt was hanged on July 7, 1865, along with Payne, Atzerodt, and Herold. *(National Park Service)*

Fig. 47

receipt for it that confirmed his claim. The knife was passed down through his family until it was sold in 1960 from the estate of a later Dr. Wilson of New York City. The knife and the Pitman book are now in my collection.

It was, after all, a fairly well-conceived assassination plot, considering that the idea began as a kidnapping and only haphazardly was changed to a murder, and the last-minute maneuvers were hastily planned. But, as is often the case, a few small details caused all but one of the assassinations to fail: Atzerodt never even attempted his killing job; Payne bungled his because the room was dark; even Booth, leaping to the stage, caught his spur and broke his leg, hampering his escape, thus leading to his death.

There were other deliberately cruel acts by Booth to ensure that all his associates would pay the price; once they were committed, there could be no turning back. For example, Booth left a note for Vice President Johnson on the evening of the assassination, saying, "I don't wish to disturb you; are you at home?" This raised suspicions. Possessions of Booth and Herold were left in Atzerodt's room at the Kirkwood House, and the search for Atzerodt was intensified. He was finally found at the home of a relative in Germantown on April 20, brought to trial as one of the original group of conspirators, and hung, primarily on the basis of these "plants" by Booth, which implicated him even though he had done nothing. If Booth had not given Mrs. Surratt his field glasses to deliver, she might not have been hanged. There were still other details that might have given the rest trouble but did not, luckily for them. Weichmann, the friend of John Surratt who was staying in the rooming house, was then a government employee in the office of the commissary general of prisons. He had reported his suspicions of the subversive group to an associate, who had apparently scoffed at his worries. Certainly no action was taken at the time since the plotters had not yet done anything, but the seed was planted; it was known that Booth was involved in a group whose headquarters was at Mrs. Surratt's rooming house. Later, one of the servant girls working there also went to the authorities with her suspicions. As a consequence of these leads, when Booth was seen at Ford's Theater, the authorities knew enough to go directly to Mrs. Surratt's house and search for him and his friend John Surratt.

FIG. 47
page 105

106

6.

THE FATE OF THE CONSPIRATORS

Payne Captured

The detectives returned there on April 17 to arrest Mrs. Surratt, and while they were there Lewis Payne walked in, having abandoned his horse after becoming lost. He was carrying a pickax over his shoulder. He attempted to pose as a ditch digger hired by Mrs. Surratt. Mrs. Surratt claimed she did not know him, and he was arrested. Payne was quickly identified as the person who attempted to assassinate Secretary Seward and as one of Booth's group of conspirators. It was soon established that Mrs. Surratt did indeed know him. This lie helped to hang her.

The Other Conspirators

FIG. 41
page 90

After their capture, Payne (Seward's attacker) and Atzerodt (assigned to kill Johnson) were placed with the other conspirators under the tightest of guard, manacled hand and foot. At one point, all the male conspirators, except Dr. Mudd, were kept on a monitor anchored near the navy yard and were later transferred to The Arsenal, once a prison, where a special cellblock with alternate cells vacant to prevent communication was arranged adjacent to the courtroom. The most rigid security was maintained.

Even John Surratt, despite his absence at the time of the assassination, did not escape the manhunt. His name and photograph were put on the reward posters (which have become a much sought-after collectible), and he was pursued all over the world in a dramatic chase, extending even to the Vatican, where he worked as a papal guard. He escaped from there and from several other places before extradition could be arranged. He kept up his flight for over a year before he was finally captured in Egypt and extradited to the United States to stand trial two years later. His trial brought about a reopening of the entire matter but ended with his being released, not only because he had not participated in the murder plot but also because the intense rage against the conspirators had died down. At last it was possible for the lawyers to point out that there was a difference between plotting (unsuccessfully) to kidnap and plotting to kill, as was said earlier.

Dr. Mudd's Plight

Booth ruthlessly implicated another person in the murder plot who may have been innocent or, at most, a medical member of the kidnap team. He brought him within one vote of a commission decision to hang him as well as the other four who met their death. We know that the two knew each other, but we don't know much more than that. That man was Dr. Samuel Mudd, the country doctor at Bryantown, thirty miles below Washington. Dr. Mudd had treated and set Booth's broken leg on the night of the assassination and had given Booth a place to sleep not only that night but also on a previous visit, when Booth had been shopping for the horse used by Payne and familiarizing himself with the area. In fact, it was Mudd who had introduced John Surratt to Booth, and thus got Booth in the habit of coming to Mrs. Surratt's rooming house.

Fig. 48
page 109

There is no doubt that Dr. Mudd knew Booth. On that previous visit when Booth had slept at Mudd's house, Mudd had introduced him to the man who sold Booth the very horse Payne was riding when he went to attack Seward. Mudd later admitted meeting Booth on the street in Washington sometime before the assassination. At one point during the trial, Dr. Mudd forgot to mention this particular meeting, and the omission nearly turned the commission against him.

Dr. Mudd had no way of knowing, when he attended to Booth's leg at 2:00 A.M., that the President had been murdered. In fact, both he and his wife later told federal authorities that Booth had concealed his identity from them by wearing a false beard.

On Easter Sunday, a day and a half later, after Dr. Mudd had heard of the President's murder, he asked his cousin, whom he had met at church near his home, to tell the authorities that strangers had stopped at his house on the night of the murder and that one of them had had a broken leg. The officers who came out to interrogate Dr. and Mrs. Mudd asked what had happened to the boot that had been cut off, and Mrs. Mudd remembered that it had been pushed under the bed. They found the boot, and upon opening the top of it discovered it had the name "J. Wilkes" written inside.

As previously stated, Booth had sometimes used only his first two names in his younger days so it was therefore compatible that his boot might contain only "J. Wilkes."

It was undoubtedly this disclosure to the authorities plus the production of the boot from under the bed that saved Dr. Mudd from being

DR. SAMUEL A. MUDD, WHO SPLINTED BOOTH'S LEG

Dr. Mudd was a physician in the rural town of Bryantown, Maryland, twenty miles southeast of Washington on the escape route that the kidnapping conspirators intended to take.

He knew Booth and, indeed, had introduced him to the man from whom Booth had bought the horse on which one of the conspirators (Payne) rode. Mudd was a former slaveholder and Southern sympathizer to whom Booth turned for a splint on his broken left fibula. Mudd cut the boot off Booth's broken leg and splinted it, then put him to bed until the next day. He had no way to know that the President had been murdered, but when he heard about it later, he told his cousin George, whom he met at church, to report the presence of suspicious strangers, one of whom had had a broken leg. This saved him from hanging.

It has been said that Dr. Mudd would never have been heard of if Booth's leg had not been broken. His grandson, Dr. Richard Mudd, has spent his lifetime trying to get his grandfather exonerated, but the best he has been able to do has been to get President Carter to extend his personal sympathy and to reaffirm the pardon that President Andrew Johnson afforded Dr. Mudd four years after the deed. *(National Park Service)*

Fig. 48

hanged with the four other conspirators. As it was, the vote was only five to four to spare him from hanging.

There have been those, including the late military historian Col. Julian Raymond, who had persuasive arguments and documents that led them to believe that Dr. Mudd had been recruited by Booth to be the medical officer of the kidnap team, whose duty it would have been to resuscitate or patch up Lincoln if he were accidentally injured during the kidnapping. If such were true, the doctor's role would have been to save Lincoln, not to kill him.

The fact that the doctor took in a traveler with a broken leg who arrived at his isolated home in the middle of the night, whether he knew him or not, and before he could have had any way of knowing that Lincoln had been shot, hardly seems enough grounds to incriminate him. There are, of course, some Confederate chauvinists who speculate that Dr. Mudd might have been even more proud of being a member of a successful quasi-military mission on behalf of Gen. Robert E. Lee and his armed forces, but the truth will never be known. And who is to say that justice is always done?

While Mrs. Surratt, in whose nest the plot was hatched, who transported Booth's package on the day of the murder, and who lied about knowing Payne, was hanged, there were and are many who doubt the propriety of her trial and who decry her harsh sentence. A majority of the commission signed a petition to commute her sentence, but President Johnson did not sign it. Lewis Payne, Seward's attacker, George Atzerodt, who never went near Johnson, and David Herold, the guide, were hanged at the conclusion of the trial. Dr. Mudd, Samuel Arnold, and Michael O'Laughlin, all of whom might have been willing to help with the kidnapping but certainly did not participate in the murder, were sentenced to a lifetime of hard labor in the federal prison at Fort Jefferson in the Dry Tortugas, a series of coral reefs that are barely above water even at low tide. In this island fort practically everyone died of yellow fever, including the army doctors of the garrison. It was obviously a way to get rid of the other four conspirators. O'Laughlin did die; while Dr. Mudd contracted yellow fever, he recovered. When all the army doctors had died, and nobody seemed to be able to get the epidemic under control, Dr. Mudd was asked to serve as the fort's doctor. One of his first acts was to place all the yellow-fever patients at one end of the island, ostensibly to isolate them, but unknown to him the prevailing wind then blew the disease-bearing mosquitoes out to sea. The epidemic was thus halted and gradually eliminated. Dr. Mudd was proud of his success and wrote to his wife that "for the three weeks I had the exclusive care of the sick, not one died."

In gratitude, the members of the garrison sent a petition to President Johnson, describing Dr. Mudd's heroic, lifesaving work and pleading that he be freed. This was never received, it is said, possibly due to Stanton's influence, and Dr. Mudd was returned to his cell and hard labor.

Dr. Mudd had done one unfortunate thing which undoubtedly impaired his chances for an early pardon, some time after his arrival on the island. He wrote that he was subjected to so many indignities by the Northern soldiers that he persuaded one of the sailors from a supply ship to smuggle him on board and hide him under the floorboards. He had been permitted to keep his civilian clothes, and he simply put them on and walked onto the ship. The sailor obligingly hid him, but his absence was discovered before the ship sailed, and vigorous probing of all the spaces on the ship with bayonets eventually produced him and caused him to be subjected to even more severe punishment.

Mudd's wife and family were working day and night to have him pardoned or at least brought back to the mainland where he could be visited (originally he had been assigned to a prison in Albany, New York), but their pleas were to no avail as long as Secretary of War Stanton was alive, in power, and adamant. At Fort Jefferson he was beyond the jurisdiction of the civil courts.

Stanton was a hard and vengeful man. He was determined to make examples of these criminals, and he knew he had the emotional support of the Northern populace behind him. In appointing a military commission of nine high-ranking officers to try the defendants, even though the country was no longer at war, he was on thin legal ice, but it made no difference to him.

He eventually came into conflict with the new President, Johnson (here again a similarity, in that President Kennedy was followed by a Johnson), who fired him. His friends were strong enough almost to impeach Johnson over the way he did this, but they failed. Stanton immediately resigned, and the three surviving conspirators were shortly sent home and the bodies of the others released to their families.

Harsh Treatment of the Prisoners

At the insistence of Stanton, the eight prisoners were treated with extraordinary harshness during the trial. Except for Mrs. Surratt, they were compelled to wear heavy canvas hoods over their heads so they could not communicate or be seen, which, in the heat of May, June, and July in Washington, was a cruel torture. The diet was such that severe bowel irregularities occurred, and it was said that Payne had no bowel movement for weeks at a time. They were quartered with alternate cells vacant adjacent to the prison courtroom, which was on the third floor of an old prison building—also referred to as "The Arsenal" and now Fort McNair—so that there was no chance that they could talk to each other. At the conclusion of the trial, the four who were condemned to be hanged were notified immediately, but the other four were not notified until after the first group had been hanged. They wondered what all the hammering and sawing was, as the gallows was being built in the prison yard outside their cellblock; they were allowed to go on wondering and

THE HANGING OF THE CONSPIRATORS

The gallows built by Hangman Rath in the prison yard.
(*Library of Congress*)

Fig. 49

The prisoners seated on the gallows, facing their nooses. The umbrella shields Mrs. Surratt from the broiling sun.

The soldiers below steady the poles holding up the two trap doors so they will not be accidentally knocked away before the hangman gives the signal. (*Library of Congress*)

Fig. 50

were told nothing. The officer assigned to be the hangman, Capt. Christian Rath, who had been a sheriff in civilian life, had forgotten how a gallows was built, but he sat down and drew a plan for one he felt sure would work. The basic mechanism of his gallows was like that of a hinged door mounted sideways, at the edge of a platform about ten feet from the ground, and propped up on a single pole near its outer edge.

Fig. 49
page 112

There were two such doors, one for each pair of victims. The nooses were attached to a sturdy beam that ran transversely, directly over the victims' heads, with enough slack left in the rope so that those being executed would drop approximately six feet before each noose, with its tremendous hangman's knot, would snap up like a club against the back or side of the condemned person's head. The elongated, thick knot traditionally was made from seven or eight turns of heavy rope, forming a mass about the size and shape of the head of a large baseball bat. When the supports propping up the door upon which the condemned unfortunates stood were knocked away, the victims' bodies would fall six feet and the knot, striking the back of the victims' heads, would snap the head sharply forward, causing instant unconsciousness through the crushing of the spinal cord against the spur of bone on which the topmost vertebra pivots when the head is turned. The head and the first vertebra, bent forward by the blow, cause the top vertebra to break away from the second one and crush the spinal cord against the pivot. If this part of the neck should fail to break, because of too short a drop, the victim would strangle to death in a most cruel way, writhing and "dancing" at the end of the rope. The abrupt fall, with the hangman's knot technique for breaking the neck and causing instant unconsciousness, is far more humane than the old English technique of merely lifting the victim clear off the floor to strangle slowly or the vigilante method of seating the victim on a horse or wagon with the noose attached to an overhanging tree limb and then whipping the horse away.

The weight of each victim, the sturdiness of his or her neck, and the length of the drop were all taken into consideration lest the head be jerked from the body if the drop was too long.

The Hanging

July 7 was the day selected for the hanging.

Everyone expected that Mrs. Surratt would be pardoned at the last minute by the new President because of the lesser and even questionable extent of her involvement in the plot. It was known that a majority of the commission had submitted a plea for clemency, on her behalf, to President Johnson. At one point, relays of mounted messengers were stationed at intervals between the White House and the prison to rush any message from President Johnson granting Mrs. Surratt a stay of execution, but none came. The gallows underwent its final tests, using 140-pound Parrot artillery shells at 11:30, and General Hancock waited until

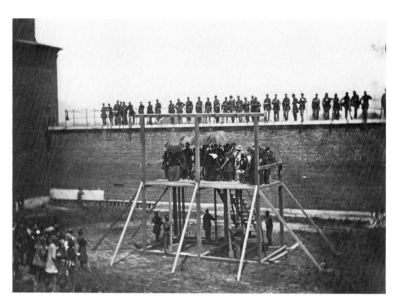

Fig. 51 General Hartranft (with book) reads the death warrants to the prisoners. *(Library of Congress)*

Fig. 52 Nooses and hoods are placed over prisoners' heads and are adjusted by hangman Rath (white hat and coat). Hands and feet are tied with strips of white cloth. *(Library of Congress)*

Fig. 53

The prisoners have dropped, bounced, and are now swinging at the ends of their ropes. (*Library of Congress*)

Fig. 54

The prisoners hung for at least twenty minutes, until well after their hearts had stopped beating. (*Library of Congress*)

FIG. 50
page 112

1:30 P.M. before proceeding. The prisoners were brought out and taken up the thirteen (some say fifteen) steps to the scaffold, and the charge and sentence read to them by General Hartranft while they sat in four chairs on the gallows platform, facing their nooses. Umbrellas were spread to shelter the hanging party from the broiling sun. Everybody waited for the reprieve to arrive. When it did not, hangman Rath finally adjusted the

FIGS. 51, 52
page 114

nooses on the victims' necks, tied their arms and legs with white strips of tent-cloth, and placed lightweight white tent-cloth bags over their heads.

After waiting as long as was reasonable, the decision was made to go ahead. As General Hartranft clapped his hands together the third time, the two soldiers underneath the gallows knocked away the supporting posts by a special mechanism and each of the two trap doors snapped

FIGS. 53, 54
page 115

downward. The bodies of the four victims dropped the requisite six feet and came up with an abrupt jerk at the end of each rope.

There are varying accounts of what happened immediately thereafter. Some reporters stated that all died quickly, others that Herold jerked and quivered, and still others that only Payne had spasmodic muscular contractions. In the official photograph taken moments after the trap was sprung, all the bodies are blurred by considerable motion and that of Herold is the most blurred of all. Mrs. Surratt's is the least so.

The Hangman's Account

Capt. Christian Rath's own account of the hanging, which he only permitted to be published thirty-three years later, is of interest.

FIG. 55
page 117

He talked to a reporter from the New York press on September 4, 1898, about the events leading to the execution, including the fact that he had never built a gallows before and was somewhat perplexed as to how to go about it. It finally came to his mind that he had once borrowed a gallows from a Virginia County sheriff at a town called Level Plains. While with General Wilcox in the field, his regiment had passed this gallows, and he was later ordered to prepare a scaffold to hang a deserter from the Forty-sixth New York Infantry.

"I remembered the Level Plains scaffold," said Colonel Rath, "and I sent for it. As I remember, the scaffold was not used after all, as the trouble was fixed up somehow.

"Well, I managed to draw plans for a scaffold guaranteed to do the work required of it and the arsenal carpenter built it. My next work was fixing nooses.

"I was determined to get rope that would not break, for you know when a rope breaks at a hanging there is a time-worn maxim that the person intended to be hanged was innocent. I wanted none of that in mine, so I got a piece of three-quarter inch, 32-strand Boston hemp. I had served in the Navy and I knew this to be a good piece of rope."

Elsewhere he wrote that he tested the ropes with bags containing 300 pounds of artillery shells to be sure they would not break.

Christian Rath late Capt 17. Mich Vol

THE EXECUTIONER

Capt. Christian Rath, of the 17th Michigan volunteers, the hangman who built the gallows and executed the four conspirators.
His graphic description of the event is detailed in the text.

Fig. 55

The night before the execution I took the rope to my room and there made the nooses. I preserved the piece of rope intended for Mrs. Surratt for the last. By the time I got at this I was tired, and I will admit that I rather slighted the job. Instead of putting seven turns to the knot—as a regulation hangman's knot has seven turns—I put only five in this one. I really did not think Mrs. Surratt would be swung from the end of it, but she was, and it was demonstrated to my satisfaction, at least, that a five-turn knot will perform as successful a job as a seven-turn knot.

I had the graves for the four persons dug just beyond the scaffolding. I found some difficulty in having the work done, as the arsenal attaches were superstitious. I finally succeeded in getting soldiers to dig the holes but they were only three feet deep.

That hanging gave me a lot of trouble. I had read somewhere that when a person was hanged his tongue would protrude from his mouth. I did not want to see four tongues sticking out before me, so I went to the storehouse, got a new white shelter tent and made four hoods out of it. The hoods were amateurish. They were different from those used nowadays, but they answered the purpose. I tore strips of the tent to bind the legs of the victims. Mrs. Surratt and Payne were hanged on one gallows and Atzerodt and Herold on the other.

The execution was successful. The four persons marched to the scaffold. They were accompanied by guards, but they required no aid. Each had a minister. After prayers I looked over the ropes and apparatus to see that everything was all right. My good-by to them was the signal for the trap to be sprung. I uttered the words and the four bodies shot downward about six feet. They bounded up again, like a ball attached to a rubber band, and then settled down. They were killed instantly.

The bodies were buried at once in the graves prepared for their reception. At the head of each coffin was a bottle containing a slip of paper on which was written the name of the victim. These bottles were placed in the graves by Capt. Richard Watts, now living at Adrian, Michigan. We did this to prevent any mistakes, if the bodies were disinterred. A few years afterward they were all taken up.

There was only one really disagreeable remembrance of the tragic event. When I took the noose from Mrs. Surratt's neck, pieces of the delicate skin came with it. The rope had cut in deeply. That rather sickened me, and I remember it to this day.

It was actually twenty or thirty minutes before the four bodies were cut down and army doctors pronounced them dead. The four shallow graves had been dug just beyond the gallows, and four navy equipment boxes were used as coffins in which the four bodies were buried in the same clothes they had on. Hangman Rath immediately started dismembering the gallows and cutting it up into segments to be sold or distributed as souvenirs. The hangman's knots were cut away and there are those who say the nooses were kept by Secretary Stanton as grim souvenirs of his campaign to punish the conspirators. Whether this is true or not remains to be seen.

Captain Rath had more to say—and an excellent memory for details:

The other prisoners held in the arsenal did not know for a certainty that there had been an execution until the following day when they went into the court-yard. The scaffold was grim evidence of the work of the preceding day. Spangler, the stage hand carpenter from Ford's Theatre, viewed the piece of death-dealing architecture scrutinizingly, then assuming a pose said:

"Captain, I've aged 10 years in the last few days. I heard the work of scaffold building. Yesterday I heard the traps fall, and then I waited my turn." He looked as if he had suffered terribly. O'Laughlin and Arnold, the two boyhood friends of Booth who were not involved in the killings, were thankful that they had escaped the noose. I cannot say as much of Mudd. A sneer always heightened his ugly countenance. Four days later these men were sent to Dry Tortugas, the islands off Florida that had attracted so much attention during the Spanish War. They were pardoned some time later. [He did not know O'Laughlin had died of yellow fever there.] Dr. Mudd seems to have worn off his bitterness, for during the yellow fever epidemic at the prison he did heroic work.

Atzerodt's body now lies in the public vault in Glenwood Cemetery in Washington in an unmarked grave, having been released in 1868 by President Johnson after being moved twice, along with the bodies of the other conspirators.

Booth, O'Laughlin, and Arnold are all buried in Greenmount Cemetery in Baltimore. Herold is buried in Congressional Cemetery in Washington, and Mrs. Surratt is in Mount Olivet Cemetery in Washington. Payne's final resting place is unknown.

When Booth's body was released to *his* family, it was picked up by undertakers named Harvey and Marr and brought to their service door. This door opens on the very same alley behind Ford's Theater out of which Booth had ridden in his vain attempt to escape, after he had shot the President. Ironically, Booth had returned to the scene of his crime.

Dr. Mudd Released

Fig. 48
page 109

Secretary Stanton was forced out of office some three years after the trial, during a conflict with President Johnson, and he died the next year. As soon as Stanton was out of office, the surviving conspirators were indeed pardoned, early in 1869, and Dr. Mudd returned to Bryantown, Maryland, where he lived out his remaining fifteen years farming, practicing medicine, and staying out of the public eye as much as possible. There were many who thought poorly of Dr. Mudd because of his possible complicity in the killing of Abraham Lincoln, and some of his hotheaded Confederate neighbors wouldn't speak to him because he had not paid the supreme price that Booth, Payne, Herold, Atzerodt, and Mrs. Surratt had paid. Spangler came to work for Dr. Mudd as a handyman and lived out his days in that capacity. Arnold and John Surratt lived past 1900 and wrote long statements about their parts in the kidnap plan, but both denied any part of the plan to kill.

And now, over 100 years later, efforts are being made to keep the memories alive and to turn some of the conspirators' homes and hiding places into monuments. Dr. Richard Mudd, Samuel's grandson, is hard at work to recover and reassemble original furnishings and memorabilia for the house and Dr. Mudd's granddaughter, Mrs. Louise Mudd Arehart, is leading a crusade to have Dr. Mudd's original house rebuilt and restored. The Maryland Historical Trust is cooperating, as is the governor.

Dr. Richard Mudd has conducted a one-man, lifelong campaign to clear his grandfather's name, but President Carter has recently stated that the conviction cannot be overturned. President Andrew Johnson had already pardoned him for anything he might have done, and that is as far as it can go. Carter has expressed sympathy and his personal belief that Dr. Mudd didn't do anything wrong, especially in the plan to murder Lincoln, and young Dr. Richard Mudd has expressed the feeling that this is the best he can hope to achieve for his grandfather's memory. And, after all, if Booth had not broken his leg we would probably have never even heard of Dr. Mudd.

Still another group of enthusiasts called the Surratt Society are hard at work restoring the Surrattsville Tavern and have done a superb job of assembling a museum and library of relics associated with Mrs. Surratt. The group conducts interesting illustrated and narrated tours of the Booth escape route, starting, of course, at Ford's Theater, where it all began.

1.

PRESIDENT KENNEDY'S ASSASSIN

Formative Years

Almost exactly 100 years after Lincoln's assassination, Lee Harvey Oswald, another Southerner and another dedicated enemy sympathizer—this time on behalf of the Russian Communists—assassinated President John F. Kennedy. Like John Wilkes Booth, he was truculent, intelligent, daring, and hungry for a shortcut to fame. Oswald shot Kennedy in the back of the neck and then in the back of the head at about 12:30 P.M. on November 22, 1963, as the President rode in a pre-election motorcade in Dallas, Texas.

Lee Harvey Oswald was born in New Orleans on October 18, 1939, some two months after his father, Robert E. Lee Oswald, died suddenly from a heart attack. His mother had to leave young Lee alone much of the time, while she went out to work, and did little to supervise his schooling or other activities during his formative years. When she did pay attention to Lee, it was to spoil him, permitting him to dominate her and even to slap her if she rebuked him.

When he was twelve years old, she brought Lee to New York and moved in with his older half brother, John, who was in the Coast Guard and who had a bride and a new baby. Lee's refractory and aggressive attitude quickly extended to include John's wife; the stress became so severe that mother Oswald finally moved out with Lee to new rooms near the Grand Concourse and then near the Bronx Zoo.

Lee did not like school, especially among the unfamiliar Yankee children, and he soon became a truant two days out of three. He enjoyed the nearby Bronx Zoo, and riding the subway down to Times Square, but he spent most of his time at home, watching television and listening to the radio.

He was particularly attracted by the all-night talk programs of the late Long John Nebel. Interestingly, in recent years, Long John was a patient of mine and told me Oswald had telephoned him from Dallas, years later, in 1962, after his return from Russia, telling of his enjoyment of Long John's shows and asking him to send him money so that Oswald could come to New York to be on Long John's show. Oswald said he wanted to "give the people of the United States something to think about." He had said this same thing to Priscilla Johnson (now McMillan) when he had defected in Moscow in November of 1959. When Nebel indicated that he could not provide money for this purpose without much justification to his network, Oswald switched from being extremely complimentary to being extremely abusive. This took Nebel aback, but caused him to remember Oswald well and to reminisce about him with some emotion.

Psychiatrist Warns of Danger

Lee stayed out of school so much that the truant officers were finally sent to find him. They took him in for evaluation and quickly realized that he had substantial psychiatric difficulties. His psychiatric social worker, Evelyn Strickman, referred his case to consulting psychiatrist Dr. Renatus Hartogs of Columbia University, who wrote up an extensive evaluation, recommending that Oswald, who badly needed a father figure, should have therapy with a male psychiatrist. If this failed to improve his situation, Dr. Hartogs recommended that Lee then be committed to an institution because of his schizoid personality disturbance with passive-aggressive features. He was described as "having a vivid fantasy life, turning around the topics of omnipotence and power." Dr. Hartogs implied that Oswald might become dangerous to society if these fantasies were allowed free rein. Lee was placed on probation.

When Mrs. Oswald learned this, she quickly, and illegally, violated the probation and moved back to New Orleans to get Lee away from the threatening situation. Lee joined the junior division of the civil air patrol and enjoyed having a uniform and the prestige of an organization in which he could take pride. He also buckled down at school, studied well, and began to spend time at the library on his own, reading about Marxism, following the publicity over the Rosenberg trial.

Six days after his seventeenth birthday, Lee joined the Marine Corps, after an unsuccessful attempt to join at sixteen, using falsified documents. In this action he was emulating his two older brothers, both of whom had left home as soon as it was possible for them to do so. By this time, his mother had moved with him to Fort Worth, Texas, and he had been attending the Arlington Heights High School. He was present while FIG. 56 candid photographs were taken for the 1957 yearbook, the *Yellow* page 125 *Jacket,* and his photograph appears in that yearbook with him laughing with a girl who is pointing a finger at him as they stand before a

124

OSWALD'S YEARBOOK PHOTOGRAPH

The 1957 yearbook, the *Yellow Jacket,* from Oswald's Arlington Heights High School in Fort Worth shows the same Oswald that we see lying on the autopsy table in 1963. In this candid photograph he is laughing as a young lady shows him animal bones. "Bing! You're hypnotized," says a classmate to Lee Oswald in the old bio lab.

Oswald was obviously still in school when the candid photographs of class activities were accumulated for the yearbook, but he left to join the Marines before graduation. Neither his formal photograph nor his name appears in the list of graduates in the yearbook.

Fig. 56

classroom case containing animal bones. The caption reads: "'Bing! You're hypnotized.'" Lee dropped out to join the Marines before graduation, however, so his picture does not appear among the formal class photos.

Marine Corps Training and Personality Difficulties

He did his basic training in California; his unit was then moved back to New Orleans for radar training. While in New Orleans on leave, he visited Fort Worth and his old high school. At this time he signed the yearbook of one of his classmates, Kleber Denny, writing: "Good luck to a good friend of mine. I hope we will meet again. Lee Oswald."

FIG. 57
page 127

Lee's IQ was 118, well above the average, and he finished his radar training seventh in a class of thirty Marines. He was given a military occupational specialty rating as an aviation electronics operator. On August 22, he was shipped to Japan, where he participated in aircraft radar-tracking activities.

Oswald's interest in the writings of Karl Marx and Marxist ideology got him into difficulties during his service in the Marines. He was fond of baiting his superiors with public interrogations on political and Marxist philosophy. It gave him great satisfaction to embarrass other people through his knowledge of this material.

One of his Marine officers, Lt. Nelson Delgado, later testified to the Warren Commission that Oswald always tried to "cut up" anyone in authority, so he would come out "top dog." Oswald would go to extraordinary lengths to challenge his superiors, especially his own sergeant. At one point, he went so far as to enter the non-coms' club and knock a can of beer into the sergeant's lap in an effort to provoke an incident. He was arrested, court-martialed, and punished with twenty-eight days of hard labor in the stockade and forfeiture of pay, plus twenty additional days of a suspended sentence he had received for an earlier violation. On that occasion, he had accidentally shot himself in the elbow with an illegal Derringer-type pocket pistol that he had left loaded in his locker —against regulations. He participated minimally in the activities of his fellow Marines, such as touch football, and they characterized him as a "loner." At one point Oswald told one of his roommates that one day he would do something "really big," something that would make him famous. Of course, he couldn't know that John Wilkes Booth had said almost the same words 100 years before.

During his Marine Corps training, Oswald was instructed in the firing of the M-1 rifle; which is a 30-06-caliber semiautomatic rifle with considerable recoil but with excellent shooting characteristics at ranges up to 200 yards. Its cartridge and bullet are roughly comparable to the cartridges and bullets of the Mannlicher-Carcano 6.5 mm carbine which he used later at Dallas. He also learned to fire the M-1 A-1 carbine. Oswald demonstrated reasonable competence with these rifles when firing them

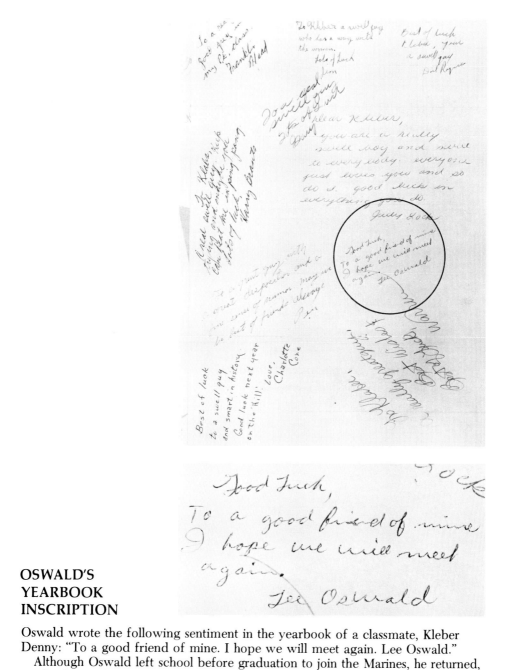

OSWALD'S YEARBOOK INSCRIPTION

Oswald wrote the following sentiment in the yearbook of a classmate, Kleber Denny: "To a good friend of mine. I hope we will meet again. Lee Oswald."

Although Oswald left school before graduation to join the Marines, he returned, resplendent in his Marine uniform, in June of 1957, on leave from radar training in Biloxi, Mississippi, and probably inscribed Denny's yearbook at that time. (J. K. Lattimer)

Fig. 57

with simple iron sights and without a telescope, at 200 yards, as we will see later. Because of the weight of this rifle, his marksmanship in the difficult offhand position was only average, but when he assumed the sitting position, where he could rest his elbows on his knees and brace himself well, as he later did at Dallas, his marksmanship greatly improved. He practiced much of his firing at a target shaped like the head and shoulders of a man as he might look seated in the rear seat of an open car. Some of the best performances in his Marine Corps rifle score book were recorded against such targets. It is probable that he learned the value of a straplike sling to steady his rifle further during his firing at these targets.

He may have developed his prowess because his older brother Robert, who later commented on the quickness of Lee's reflexes and the strength of his forearms, both of which are important for the rapid operation of a bolt-action rifle such as the Mannlicher-Carcano, taught him to shoot as a boy.

In August 1959, four months prior to his scheduled separation date, Oswald decided to terminate his Marine Corps service early and go to Russia, utilizing his accumulated Marine Corps pay. He applied for a compassionate honorable transfer to inactive reserve status, stating that his mother was disabled and he was her only support. Mrs. Oswald had sustained a minor injury to her nose while working in a candy store the previous Christmas, and, using this excuse, she supplied Lee with letters implying that he was, indeed, her sole support, even though she had resumed work.

His transfer was granted without undue delay. We were not at war, and his presence with his unit was not critical to its performance. On September 4, he applied for a passport, saying he intended to study at the Albert Schweitzer University in Switzerland and to visit several European countries—including Russia. He wrote to his mother that she would have to realize that his objectives were different from hers and his brother Robert's.

Russian Interlude; Suicide Attempt; Attempt to Renounce Citizenship

On October 17, the day after he arrived in Moscow, he told the Intourist interpreter who had been assigned to him that he wanted to renounce his American citizenship and become a Russian citizen. The Russians rejected his plea and told him to leave. That evening he locked himself in his hotel room and slashed his left wrist. He did this at a time when he knew the interpreter would be back in an hour; she returned and had him rushed to the hospital. This suicide attempt persuaded the Russians to give Oswald permission to remain in the country, where they let him be a sheet-metal worker in a radio and television factory in Minsk; but they did not grant him citizenship.

Fig. 58
page 130

Oswald was first transferred to the Hotel Metropol, and, when his official observer left him alone briefly, he took a taxi to the U.S. Embassy, where he slapped down his passport and demanded to take an oath to renounce his United States citizenship. U.S. Consul Richard Snyder, hoping to spare an earnest young American the disastrous mistake of becoming a man without a country or a Russian citizen who might never be permitted to leave, stalled Lee, writing him that, after three days, all Oswald need do was come back, and his wish would be granted. Oswald did not follow through and never gave up his American citizenship, even though he wrote to the embassy that he wished to do so. He also wrote to his brother, "I will never return to the United States, which is a country I hate."

On November 13, while waiting for the Soviets to decide whether or not he could stay, Oswald telephoned the office of United Press International and permitted one of its reporters a lengthy interview, which was subsequently widely published. His suicide attempt had apparently persuaded the Russians that he would stop at nothing to get the attention he wanted, and his willingness to talk to reporters showed that he would not hesitate to embarrass either the Americans or the Russians by a very public suicide.

A young American reporter, Priscilla Johnson (now McMillan and author of *Marina and Lee*), who had been told of Oswald's willingness to talk to female reporters, and who lived in the same building as Oswald, asked him up for an interview. To her surprise, he accepted, and they talked for some five hours, until two o'clock in the morning. Oswald, in his neat dark suit and camel's-hair vest, looked like a young college boy, but Johnson was astounded by his lack of any spirit of joy or adventure. She could only admire his willingness to take on the bureaucracy of the second most powerful nation in the world, for she knew the Soviets could be brutal. She listened while he expounded his ideology coldly and endlessly, telling her he wanted to give the American people something to think about. She felt a twinge of pity for him, but recognized that his icy dedication made him quite different from the usual escapist defectors she was so accustomed to seeing.

Meanwhile, the Marine Corps, having discovered that Oswald's plea for a compassionate release was a hoax, changed his honorable discharge to dishonorable status. He then wrote the Secretary of the Navy, John Connally, demanding that his status be reversed, but to no avail. The fact that he later shot Connally, along with President Kennedy, raised the question of whether he might have been aiming at Connally, but it seems fairly clear, in light of the evidence, that Oswald's motivation would be to kill the most prestigious person. Kennedy was obviously his target.

In Minsk, Oswald enjoyed his special status as an attractive young American curiosity, and he courted numerous young ladies before his favorite, Ella Germann, a Jewish girl, rejected his proposal of marriage. In March of 1961 he met Marina, an attractive pharmacist who was

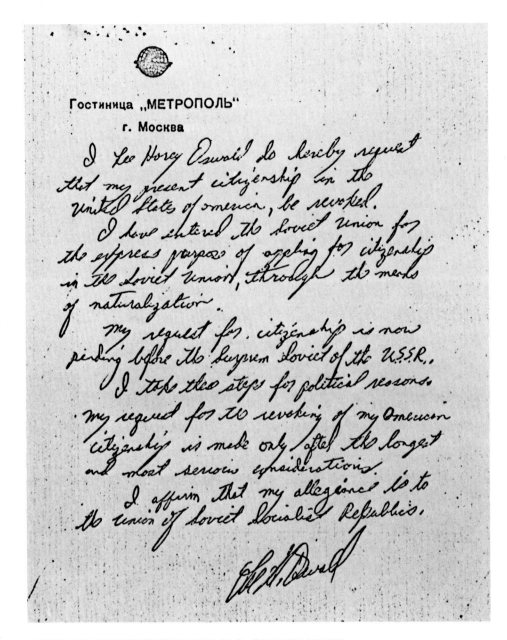

Гостиница „МЕТРОПОЛЬ"
г. Москва

I Lee Harey Oswald do hereby request that my present citizenship in the United States of america, be revoked.

I have entered the Soviet Union for the express purpose of appling for citizenship in the Soviet Union, through the meds of naturalization.

My request for citizenship is now pending before the Supreme Soviet of the U.S.S.R.

I take these steps for political reasons. My request for the revoking of my American citizenship is made only after the longest and most serious considerations.

I affirm that my allegiance is to the Union of Soviet Socialist Republics.

OSWALD RENOUNCES HIS U.S. CITIZENSHIP

In this letter to the American embassy in Moscow, Oswald requests that his citizenship be revoked and declares his allegiance to the Union of Soviet Socialist Republics. It is on the letterhead of the Hotel Metropol, where the Russians were boarding him. *(National Archives)*

Fig. 58

living with her uncle, a minor Soviet official. They were married on April 30, 1961, and on February 15 of the following year their first daughter, June Lee, was born.

Return to the U.S. with Russian Wife and Baby

By this time Oswald was thoroughly disgusted with Russian life and had decided that he would be better off in America. In Russia he was not permitted to use a rifle freely, as he had during his boyhood in America. He was compelled to join a hunting club, where he was permitted only closely supervised activity during club outings with his small sixteen-gauge shotgun. He wrote to his mother for books to read, for an American football, and for various other odds and ends to make life more pleasant for himself and Marina, but the restrictions of Russian life made him more and more unhappy.

He had applied for an exit visa for himself, and he now extended the application to include his wife and their new child. He asked his mother to appeal to various do-gooder organizations and loan programs for money to return to the United States. He told her plainly not to use her own money for this purpose, that there was plenty available from these organizations.

When the Immigration Service officers asked Oswald for addresses of relatives, and then asked his brother Robert to forward $200 for plane fare from New York to Dallas, without Oswald's knowledge, Oswald became annoyed; he was even more miffed when Robert actually sent the money. Oswald would leave Russia owing $435 to the United States and $200 more to Robert for his passage.

The necessary papers finally arrived, the passport Oswald had never really given up was reinstated, and the Oswalds left Russia on June 13, 1962. They traveled first by boat, and then by plane, arriving at Love Field in Dallas, where they were met by Robert and his family, who lived in Fort Worth. They stayed with him for a month, until mother Oswald rented an apartment for them and for herself. She drove Lee around until he found a job as a sheet-metal helper.

The local Russian émigré community adopted Marina and tolerated Lee while he tried a succession of minor jobs. He became progressively more abusive to Marina, and the loudness of their quarrels began to disturb the neighbors. At the urging of her new friends, Marina left Lee for a two-week period in November but then went back to him, much to the disgust of her friends.

The Purchase of Firearms

On January 25, 1963, Oswald was finally free of debt; he had repaid his brother and the government. Two days later he sent for a thirty-eight-caliber mail-order revolver, and on March 12 he ordered a high-powered carbine. Both arrived in Dallas on March 25. The carbine was a 6.5 mm Italian military rifle known as a Carcano, model 91-38, and was in good firing condition. It came from Kline's, the mail-order house in Chicago, to whom Oswald had sent $12.78. He had paid another $7.17 for a four-power telescope, made in Japan for the Ordnance Optics Company, which he had had Kline's attach to the carbine; for some reason, the gunsmith at Kline's used only two screws for this attachment, instead of the usual four.

The carbine arrived on March 25, 1963, at a post office box in the name of A. Hidell, which had been applied for in what was clearly Oswald's handwriting. Coincidentally perhaps, it arrived on the same day that he received his ".38 special" Smith and Wesson cutdown revolver, the barrel of which had been shortened for easier concealment.

McMillan calculated that he "sighted in" his rifle and practiced with it on April 3, 4, and 5, and possibly on April 7. On the tenth he tried to kill General Walker with it, as we shall see later.

Oswald applied a homemade sling to his carbine, fashioned from a piece of thick, flat tape. The sling bore an uncanny resemblance to the one improvised by John Wilkes Booth for *his* carbine 100 years before, which can still be seen in the Ford's Theater Museum in Washington. Oswald's sling appears in the photograph that he insisted Marina take of him in the back yard of their Dallas apartment on March 31. In the picture, he is holding his new rifle, has his new pistol on his hip, and is wearing a black shirt and black slacks. In his hand he is displaying newpapers—*The Daily Worker* and *The Militant*—which contained articles he had submitted.

Oswald was ready for a nighttime assault, and he looked it.

2.

THE ATTEMPT TO SHOOT GENERAL WALKER: A SIGNIFICANT EVENT

Ex-Maj. Gen. Edwin Walker, by far the most active, voluble, and highly visible anti-Communist living in Dallas in 1963, was the former commander of the Twenty-fourth Infantry Division in Europe, where he had served also with Special Forces units. He had been reprimanded, and had then resigned from the military, because he insisted on what the army considered to be overzealous, anti-Communist indoctrination of his troops. On the lawn of his rented house in Dallas, he maintained a large billboard displaying anti-Communist slogans. He spoke frequently and vehemently at anti-Communist rallies, and was a prime target of the Communist press, which characterized him as an aspiring Hitler.

Oswald Reconnoiters Walker's House and Plans Attack

Oswald began to compile a dossier on Walker, going to some pains to survey the area behind Walker's house, where a large yard, approximately 100 feet long, terminated at a fence that stood next to a wide, paved alley resembling a small street. Just inside the fence, General Walker usually parked his station wagon. If one continued down the alleyway behind the fence, one came to the parking lot of a church and then to the church itself, which stood adjacent to General Walker's house.

Oswald compiled a loose-leaf folder that included photographs of Walker's house and yard. The text described his plan and the philosophical justification for what he expected to accomplish by executing

Walker. Apparently, he wanted to be able to prove later that it was he who shot Walker.

Oswald Fires at Walker—and Misses

On April 10, 1963, at about 9:00 P.M., General Walker stepped into the dining room of his house, which was located opposite his station wagon parked in the back yard. No drapes, curtains, or shades hung at the windows, and the room was brightly lighted. The General sat down at his desk with his right side toward the station wagon in the yard outside. As he began to consider his income tax return, he heard a loud explosion and felt something tug at his hair. His first thought was that one of the children in the neighborhood had thrown a firecracker through the window. He glanced at the window and saw that it was closed but noted that there was a star of cracked glass just at the lower margin of the wooden sash across the middle. He also noticed that the screen was still in place. General Walker then realized that his right forearm had been struck by small fragments of something. A friend later dug those out with tweezers and found the slivers to be tiny flakes of copper-colored metal, undoubtedly fragments of bullet jacket. Unfortunately, they were discarded.

General Walker then noticed a large, oval-shaped hole in the wall to the left of his head, about six inches by three inches. He could see that this hole went through into the adjacent room. There he found plaster flung out into the room and a severely flattened, elongated bullet lying on the floor about five feet from the wall.

In passing first through the window sash and then probably sideways through the plaster and metal lath of the wall, the bullet had been deformed beyond the point where any readable grooves from the rifling of the gun could be detected on any of its surfaces. Thus it was not possible to tie it to Oswald's gun, even though this highly unusual type of bullet would not ordinarily be found in rifles in America. Neutron activation tests made by consultants for the U.S. House of Representatives Select Committee on Assassinations in 1978 showed by analysis that it matched Oswald's other Carcano bullets.

I visited General Walker in 1977 to inspect the layout and he showed me the fence and the place where his parked station wagon had been on the night of Oswald's attack. It was immediately apparent to me that Oswald must have come inside the fence, draped himself over the top of the rather low station wagon, and rested his chest and both elbows on the roof of the car while taking careful aim at Walker through the dining-room window. Oswald would have been foolish to stand outside the fence, where he would have been highly visible to anyone walking along the alley.

When I examined the window, I could see how the bullet had passed first through the screen, bending the broken ends of the wires inward toward the house, and then had struck the wooden sash across the middle of the window, where the upper and lower sashes overlap when such a window is closed. The bullet had traversed both of these wooden sashes and had made the star-shaped crack in the upper margin of the lower pane. The course of the bullet had obviously been deflected slightly upward, so that it passed through General Walker's hair instead of through his head. The bullet undoubtedly had turned sideways as a consequence of passing through the window sash and had hit the wall going sideways, accounting for the extreme sideways flattening of the

Fig. 59
page 136

bullet recovered from the next room. Because the telescope of Oswald's gun was mounted roughly two inches above the bore of the gun, at this close range Oswald was able to see the center of Walker's head clearly through his telescope as he looked just above the middle of the window. His bullet, however, still traveling two inches below the line of sight of the telescope, but climbing, hit the wooden bar and was deflected upward, thus spoiling Oswald's otherwise sure shot.

Having fired one shot at what he considered to be an easy target, and having seen Walker jump, Oswald thought his job was finished and scuttled away. At first, he was exultant to see that he had escaped without being seen, was able to hide his rifle, and was then able to return home in an attempt to retrieve the note he had left for Marina. From the content of this note, he had obviously expected he might be captured, or even killed, by General Walker's reactionary anti-Communist supporters. He was surprised and disgusted to hear on the radio, when he listened with Marina, that he had missed the General at such close range, not knowing that he had accidentally hit the window sash because of the mounting of his telescope.

Oswald learned from this experience that one does not merely fire one shot and run, but that the successful assassin must fire two or three shots. If he had fired only one shot at President Kennedy—as we shall see later—he would have missed him as he missed General Walker.

Marina Finds Oswald's Note

Since his return from Russia, Oswald had been complaining to Marina that the FBI was badgering him, and when, on the night he shot at General Walker, he did not come home for dinner, Marina felt helpless and uncertain. Despite Lee's instructions not to go into his study, she did so, and on his desk she saw a key and a note addressed to her, in Russian, that read as follows:

1. This is the key to the mailbox which is located in the main post office in the city on Ervay Street. This is the same street where the drugstore, in which you always waited is located. You will find the mailbox in the post office which is located 4 blocks from the drugstore on that street. I paid for the box last month so don't worry about it.

2. Send the information as to what has happened to me to the Embassy and

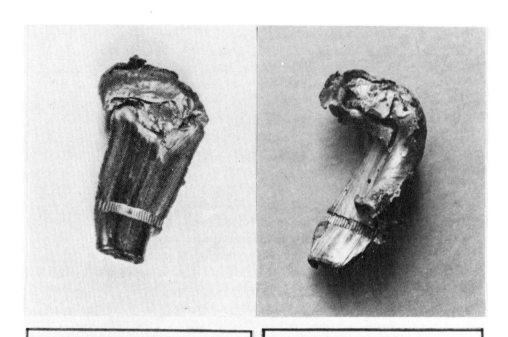

WALKER BULLET

LATTIMER
TEST BULLET

THE BULLET THAT MISSED GENERAL WALKER

The bullet recovered in General Walker's house (left) had traversed the screen, the window sash, and a wall containing metal lath or other sheet-metal elements. It was so deformed that while it looked like a flattened 6.5 mm Carcano bullet of the type used later by Oswald, the rifling scratches were too distorted to prove that it was fired from his gun. Our experimental bullet (right) fired through similar materials was similarly deformed. Neutron activation analysis also showed the Walker bullet to be of the same composition as Oswald's Carcano bullets. *(Left: National Archives; right: J. K. Lattimer)*

Fig. 59

include newspaper clippings (should there be anything about me in the newspapers). I believe that the Embassy will come quickly to your assistance on learning everything.

3. I paid the house rent on the 2d so don't worry about it.

4. Recently I also paid for water and gas.

5. The money from work will possibly be coming. The money will be sent to our post office box. Go to the bank and cash the check.

6. You can either throw out or give my clothing, etc. away. Do not keep these. However, I prefer that you hold on to my personal papers (military, civil, etc.).

7. Certain of my documents are in the small blue valise.

8. The address book can be found on my table in the study should need same.

9. We have friends here. The Red Cross also will help you. (Red Cross in English). [sic]

10. I left you as much money as I could, $60 on the second of the month. You and the baby [apparently] can live for another 2 months using $10 per week.

11. If I am alive and taken prisoner, the city jail is located at the end of the bridge through which we always passed on going to the city (right in the beginning of the city after crossing the bridge).

After reading this note, Marina was sick with worry about Lee, and about how she and the baby would survive.

At 11:30 Oswald walked in, exhilarated and tense, saying that he had just shot General Walker and had hidden his rifle. His wife was appalled; she was sure now that the FBI would come and kill them all.

Failure and Flight

When the newspapers and radio revealed that the shot had missed, Oswald, too, was appalled. He had carefully assembled proof that he had been the one American Communist who outdid all the others by killing the most outspoken enemy of Communism in this country. Now his chance to acquire heroic stature had been snatched away, just as Booth's had been when Lincoln was not in his carriage during the attempted kidnapping. Like Booth, Oswald had not been detected; he could plan to strike again.

But, for now, he had to cover his tracks. Disdainful that the police had misdiagnosed the bullet as a 30-06 rather than a 6.5 mm caliber, he had no way of knowing that the mangled bullet made this an excusable error.

Three nights later, he and Marina, preparing for bed, were awakened by pounding on their door. Marina was petrified and then greatly relieved to find that it was only their Russian-speaking neighbors, the George de Morenschildts. Morenschildt's first words to Lee were: "How come you missed Walker?" Marina thereupon observed one of her husband's icy calm performances under stress. He never wavered as he went up the stairs. He merely said: "Shh! You'll wake the baby."

A month later, he mailed Morenschildt one of his photographs holding his guns, labeled "Hunter for Fascists." Morenschildt had guessed correctly, which Oswald later told him. Still later, Morenschildt was accused of encouraging Oswald to shoot Walker, and of inspiring him to shoot Kennedy, but no evidence was ever produced to support this view. Whether Morenschildt's suicide, some years later, was related to the stresses of this phase of his variegated life is unknown.

Marina kept the incriminating note that Oswald had left for her, hiding it in her cookbooks and transferring it from place to place so he could not find it. It was her only weapon with which to blackmail him. She also cried and carried on vigorously and extracted a promise from him that he would never do any such thing again. She persuaded him to burn the notebook of his plan to kill Walker, but he insisted on saving the photographs of himself with the guns and those of the General's house, as if to be able to prove to the Communists—eventually—that it had been his doing.

In spite of his promise, less than two weeks later, on April 21, 1963, Marina found Lee putting on his best suit and preparing to depart with his pistol in his pocket. He said he was going downtown to greet a national figure who was visiting Dallas. She locked her husband in the bathroom and cried until he agreed to abandon the mission. She later hid his revolver, but gave it back to him after he promised, yet again, never to engage in murderous activities.

Worried that his cover might have been penetrated by his attempt on General Walker's life, and that his plan for greatness might be interrupted by an arrest, Oswald left once more for New Orleans, on April 24. By good luck, he was able to send Marina and the baby to Irving, a Dallas suburb, where a generous Quaker member of the community of Russophiles, Ruth Paine, agreed to provide shelter for them until they could join him in New Orleans. It is not hard to remember that Booth, too, had a supporter named Paine.

Oswald found a menial job as an oiler in a coffee-processing plant, but by July 19 he had lost it because he loitered so much with a gun enthusiast in the garage next door. Unemployment insurance tided him over while he set himself up as a one-man local "Committee for Fair Play to Cuba" and distributed leaflets. Shortly thereafter, he went to the headquarters of an anti-Castro organization and suggested that he could help them if they took him into their group. He said he had his Marine Corps manual and could be a guerrilla. He even offered to contribute money, but they rebuffed his advances. Later, these same anti-Castro men found him on the street near their headquarters giving out pro-Castro leaflets and buttonholing anyone who would listen, haranguing them about the virtues of a "hands-off Castro" policy. An altercation erupted, and both Oswald and the anti-Castro men were arrested for creating a disturbance. Oswald was jailed overnight, fined $10, and released. He carefully cut out the newspaper clipping to carry as evidence of his vigor as a Communist agitator.

Because of the publicity from this incident, Oswald was invited to appear on a radio talk show where a group debated the merits of pro- and anti-Castro viewpoints. Oswald proved to be adept at the glib generalities and counter-accusations of the professional Communist speaker. The talk show host had discovered, after inviting Oswald to defend Castro, that Oswald had a Russian background, which he had concealed, and he embarrassed Oswald by implying that Oswald was a Russian supporter and a Communist, which Oswald was trying to soft-pedal. Oswald admitted to being a Marxist but did not acknowledge that Marx was against assassination on principle.

Dry-Firing Practice

On May 11 Marina and the baby joined him in New Orleans, in a small apartment with a screened porch. During their last month there, Marina noted that Lee would sit on the porch, after dusk, pointing his rifle at nearby targets, tracking imaginary cars in the telescopic sight, and working the action of the gun over and over. He was obviously doing this to develop the familiarity and dexterity which this gun's rather stiff bolt action requires if one is to be able to fire it repeatedly and rapidly. During this period, he may also have practiced firing this gun with live ammunition, but that is less significant; dry firing of this type of rifle is far more important than the firing of live ammunition if the object is to gain speed and dexterity.

Rejection by Mexicans, Cubans, and Russians

During this discouraging period of unemployment and increasing domestic strife, Oswald proposed at various times that Marina and the baby return to Russia, or even that they *all* return. Finally, he proposed that he go to Cuba, while Marina would accept Mrs. Paine's invitation to return to Irving and stay with her while she waited for the birth of their second child. At one point Oswald even proposed that they all go to Cuba by hijacking an airplane, but Marina—pregnant, timid, and shocked by this idea—wanted no part of the proposal. Mrs. Paine drove to New Orleans and took Marina and June back to Dallas, on September 22.

Oswald finally decided that he would go to Mexico, alone, and persuade the Cuban and Russian ambassadors to let him fight in Cuba, en route to Russia. He left New Orleans by bus on September 25, for Mexico City. In Mexico City, told that the wait would be at least six months for the necessary Russian visa, he let loose a torrent of verbal abuse on the Cuban officials, which got him nowhere. The CIA noted his presence at the Cuban and Russian embassies, but, from that time on, Oswald was apparently through with Castro, too.

He returned to Dallas by bus, on October 3, 1963, tried to get work as a typesetter, but was given a negative reference by his old photo lab employer, who cautioned that he might be a Communist. He filed for the last of the unemployment checks from his old application; stayed overnight at the YMCA, saying he was a serviceman, to avoid the charge; and finally rejoined Marina and baby June at Mrs. Paine's, where Marina's new child was expected any day.

Finds Job in Dallas

Once again through the good offices of Mrs. Paine, and through her neighbor Wesley Frazier, who worked there, Lee learned about an opening at the Texas School Book Depository. He was interviewed by the manager, Roy Truly, and hired on October 16, 1963, as a temporary employee.

Lee then rented a room in Dallas under his own name, but the landlady asked him to leave. He wondered if the FBI had been asking for him, so he rented his next room under the name of O. H. Lee, at 1026 North Beckley, where he stayed during the week, asking Wesley Frazier to let him ride with him to suburban Irving on weekends.

On Friday, October 19, the Oswalds' second daughter, Audrey Marina Rachel Oswald, was born at Parkland Hospital. Oswald stayed at Mrs. Paine's and took care of the Paine children and June, while Mrs. Paine cared for Marina after the delivery. He then returned to his rented room at 1026 North Beckley, while Marina convalesced at Mrs. Paine's house. Oswald insisted that Marina tell nobody his new address or telephone number, and finally explained that he was living there under another name so he could escape the onus of any FBI contacts, which might hurt his chances for obtaining a better job.

The Dallas FBI office had indeed been notified of his appearance at the Cuban and Russian embassies in Mexico City and his file had been reopened. An FBI agent named Hosty located Marina and called on her to ask for Oswald's address and phone number. She promised she would ask him for it; she was terrified of the police. Oswald was irritated when she told him of Hosty's visit and instructed her to reveal nothing, but to copy Hosty's automobile license number when he came back. Marina followed Lee's instructions.

The Withheld Note

On November 12, 1963, Oswald apparently went to the Dallas headquarters of the FBI and asked for agent Hosty. When told he was out, Oswald left an unsealed envelope with the name Hosty on the outside, with one paragraph castigating the FBI for interrogating his wife without his permission and a second paragraph stating that, if this did not stop, he would take some unspecified action against the FBI.

The note was unsigned and had no heading, but Hosty suspected it might have come from Oswald. He put it in his file bin and forgot it.

Here, once again, is an amazing parallel with John Wilkes Booth's notebook (commonly referred to as his "diary"), in which he wrote two long philosophical and somewhat appealing discourses about his reasons for killing President Lincoln. This diary was not shown to the military commission judging the conspirators, even though the press had mentioned that it existed. Whether or not either of these documents would have influenced the fates of the participants seems unlikely, but they point up the dangers of concealing *anything* that might contain evidence.

Things have not changed much in 100 years.

3.

THE ASSASSINATION OF PRESIDENT KENNEDY

Oswald lay low for another week; then it was time for some action. His family was securely settled with the Paines in Irving. His cover at the rooming house seemed impenetrable. His paying job at the Book Depository lent him a semblance of respectability. Things might have gone on in this fashion for a long time if it had not been for a startlingly coincidental series of events.

As part of the build-up for the following year's presidential election, it was decided that President John F. Kennedy would tour several cities in Texas, attracting voters from this traditionally conservative area by exposing them to his charisma and his high competence as a speaker. There were many who were troubled by this decision to appear in a public motorcade, given the violent demonstrations by conservative groups, particularly in Dallas. Among those who advised against the trip was Evelyn Lincoln, the President's private secretary, as, a century before, it had been a Kennedy who advised Lincoln not to go to the theater. However, it was conceded that the presidential limousine did have a protective plastic bubble top, and that Mrs. Kennedy had agreed to accompany the President on one of her rare campaigning appearances. This announcement was greeted with great enthusiasm and changed a lot of minds, since Jackie's presence would add tremendously to the number of potential voters who would turn out to see her husband.

Newspapers Give Motorcade Route

The motorcade in Dallas was announced in the newspapers on Tuesday, November 19. On November 20, the papers bore diagrams of the route of the motorcade and, while earlier editions said that the motorcade might go down the center of Dealey Plaza, far away from the Texas School Book Depository, later editions indicated that it would turn down Houston Street and then left onto Elm Street, directly below the windows of the Book Depository building. From there, it would proceed slightly downhill on Elm Street, which angled away from the building toward the railroad underpass.

Thus Oswald, like Booth, learned from the newspapers that his victim would come to him, at his place of work.

Fig. 60
page 144

We can only imagine how each of these developments about the route made it easier for Oswald to plan an assassination. His conviction that destiny was forcing this role upon him must have grown with each new announcement. When he saw that the course of the automobile would be downhill away from his very place of work, making such a perfect opportunity for enfilading fire, he must have been ecstatic.

While the balance of the evidence seems to indicate that Oswald's decision to shoot at President Kennedy was made not more than two days before the actual shooting, there were various events that, previously, may have acted as a stimulus. Although he had often expressed admiration for Kennedy, he had also read Kennedy's book, *Profiles in Courage*, wherein Kennedy quoted examples of people who really believed in something and who acted on their beliefs without regard for the adverse effect of their actions on themselves or on others. Oswald, determined to influence the world by an act of heroic proportions, may have decided that he should set aside any personal admiration he might have for Kennedy in adhering to his self-ordained role to shape the destiny of the world by eliminating the number-one leader of the anti-Communist world.

Two days before the motorcade, Oswald was present in the office of Truly, the superintendent, when one of the other Texans at the Book Depository showed off two newly acquired rifles, one a 30-06 Sporter adapted from a Mauser rifle. Oswald saw the staff admiring and handling these guns, and he may have been encouraged that there already were guns in the building, reasoning that no one would think badly of him if he were to bring his own. He also may have thought that attention would be distracted from him if a search for rifles were to be made, since so many of the staff knew of the two rifles that had been displayed but did not know that he had one.

On the morning of Thursday, November 21, the day before the assassination, Oswald showed the first signs of departing from his normal routine when he spent money for an expensive breakfast, rather than preparing it in his own rooming house. Yet he left his pistol there, both then and on the twenty-second, indicating that he intended to return. He made his first definite move toward the assassination between eight and ten o'clock on the twenty-first, when he approached Wesley Frazier at work and asked if he could ride with him out to Irving that night. After he arrived, he played with the children for an unusually long time and was

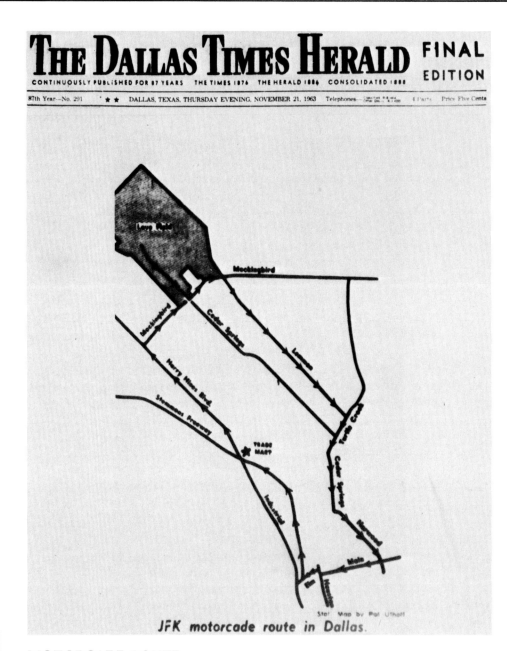

THE DALLAS TIMES HERALD FINAL EDITION

CONTINUOUSLY PUBLISHED FOR 87 YEARS   THE TIMES 1876   THE HERALD 1886   CONSOLIDATED 1888

87th Year—No. 291   ★ ★   DALLAS, TEXAS, THURSDAY EVENING, NOVEMBER 21, 1963   Telephones—   4 Parts   Price Five Cents

JFK motorcade route in Dallas.

MOTORCADE ROUTE

Oswald learned from the newspapers of November 21, the day before the shooting, that President Kennedy's motorcade route would bring him right to Oswald's working place. Booth had also learned from the newspapers of the day that President Lincoln would come to his place of work. (The Dallas Times Herald)

Fig. 60

kind to his wife, urging her to return to him and promising her a new apartment, an automobile, a washing machine, and other niceties as he had never done before. She reflected afterward that he had gone about this in a way calculated to permit her to refuse, which she did on three different occasions during the evening.

Oswald Retrieves His Rifle

He was extraordinarily tense and sleepless during the night, according to Marina, as he had been prior to his attack on Walker. He departed from his usual routine also by telling Marina not to get up and make breakfast, probably fearing that she might interrupt him in retrieving the rifle from its package in the garage. He left her practically all his money—$170—taking only about $15 with him.

He had brought from the Book Depository a long bag that he had made out of brown paper. After breaking his rifle into its two segments, so that it fit easily into the paper bag, he laid this package on the back seat of Frazier's car for the drive back into Dallas on the morning of the twenty-second. Frazier noticed that the package extended most of the way across the back seat; when he asked what the package was, Oswald said it contained curtain rods for his apartment. Upon reaching the parking lot at the Book Depository, instead of waiting for Frazier, as he usually did, Oswald hopped out, tucked the end of the bundle in his armpit, and walked into the building ahead of Frazier.

Truly and one of the other supervisors later noted that Oswald, breaking his routine that day, was already at work when they arrived.

Selects and Prepares Firing Spot

Oswald set about preparing the perfect spot from which he might do his lethal firing. He had already scouted the building to ascertain this spot. He selected a window that would be directly behind the presidential automobile as it moved slowly downhill away from him on Elm Street. By firing from behind the car he would surprise both the victim and the driver; even if, and when, the driver suspected he was being shot at and speeded up to escape, he would remain approximately in the same line of fire for several seconds. As a consequence, Oswald would have to shift his rifle very little to keep his sights on the target for additional shots. He had learned well from his failure to kill General Walker with a single bullet that one must fire multiple shots at the victim in order to insure success.

He also managed to select a window that was high enough to clear the live oak tree that was directly under the window. The sixth floor turned out to be optimum for this purpose.

First Shot Misses

Oswald waited with cold composure until the motorcade turned down Elm Street, going away from him. He identified President Kennedy's head, drew a bead on it, and fired. He worked the bolt action of his rifle firmly and quickly and fired twice more, at deliberate intervals of five seconds. Had Oswald not done this, he would again have failed to hit his man, because his first bullet hit a branch of the oak tree, which deflected it to the point of missing the President's car entirely.

One of the spectators, Mrs. Donald Baker, later testified that she saw the first bullet hit the pavement near the car.

One might ask why Oswald would fire at his victims through the branches of the oak tree. I can tell you that, sitting on the box in that window, he could see automobiles passing beneath the tree only intermittently, but fairly clearly, through the various openings between branches. Your eye synthesizes these images to give the impression that the target is more clearly in view than it really is. The President was in sight for only a fraction of a second as he passed through one large opening. Oswald, in his anxiety, yielded to the temptation of seeing his target so close, fired, and missed.

Practically everyone except Governor Connally thought it was a back-fire. He turned around, trying to look directly backward to see if the President was all right. Probably the last coherent words President Kennedy heard before his life was snuffed out were from a relieved Mrs. John Connally, the Texas governor's wife, who had turned in her seat in front of Mrs. Kennedy to say, "Mr. President, you can't say now that Dallas doesn't love you." Seconds later, he was shot through the neck and then through the brain.

Second Shot Hits Kennedy and Connally

Having missed the President with his first shot, Oswald worked the mechanism of his rifle, ejecting the empty shell case onto the floor. He now had an unobstructed shot at the back of the President as the car came clear of the oak tree approximately 190 feet from Oswald's window, an easy range for a telescope-equipped rifle, especially when the shooter is able to arrange a nearly ideal rest for his feet, elbows, and hands and has a sling to steady his rifle. It is also an easy shot even if one does not use the telescope and merely uses the conventional iron sights that are on this rifle. Oswald fired again. His second bullet hit the President just at the base of his neck on the right side, as his head was turned to the right while he waved to the people on the sidewalk. The bullet exited from the front of his neck, tumbled end over end, and struck Governor Connally in the right side of his back. The tumbling bullet tore open the Governor's chest wall, shattered his fifth rib, and exited below his right nipple, continuing to tumble as it traversed his right wrist, with which he was pressing on his left thigh to help him turn his body. The bullet then ended up going backward into his left thigh, where it was apparently stopped by the large bone of the Governor's upper leg.

Third Shot Hits Kennedy's Head

President Kennedy's elbows flew up in response to the jolt given his spine by the bullet. Exactly five seconds after he had been shot through the neck, President Kennedy received the full force of Oswald's third bullet: it hit him in the back of the head, removing practically the entire right side of the brain. He was killed instantly.

Just before the final bullet struck, Mrs. Kennedy leaned over and looked closely into the President's face. With her face just inches away from his, she was asking "What's the matter, Jack?" when the final bullet struck him, causing his head to explode with tremendous force. Mrs. Kennedy came within inches of being killed by the exiting fragments of the disrupted bullet or blinded by the flying fragments of the President's skull. Kennedy's body lurched over backward and to his left as he fell down onto the seat where Mrs. Kennedy had been sitting, while she, recoiling from the explosion and splash of his head, rose and pivoted to her right, with one knee on the seat. The car then jerked forward to begin its mad dash toward Parkland Hospital, flinging her onto the lid of the trunk. It paused momentarily, permitting Secret Service agent Clint Hill to climb up on the rear bumper of the car to try to help her as she scrambled to get down into the back seat. He then lay on top of her and the President to protect them from possible additional bullets.

But it was too late. The President's wounds were fatal.

4.

THE SCENE AT PARKLAND HOSPITAL

As soon as the driver and the Secret Service agent in the front seat of the presidential car realized that Kennedy had been shot, they sounded the alarm over their walkie-talkie radios. Word was flashed to Parkland Hospital to prepare to receive the wounded President and Governor. Parkland Hospital's trauma unit, one of the best in the country, is thoroughly familiar with gunshot wounds, encountering them almost every day. As the closest and best-prepared hospital in the vicinity, Parkland had been alerted, as usual, in advance of the presidential visit and was prepared to deal with any medical problem that might arise.

Hospital Trauma Unit Assembles

When the general alarm was sounded, indicating that someone in the presidential party had been injured and that he was on his way to Parkland Hospital, members of the various surgical and anesthesiology services were eating lunch. They headed for the trauma-room area; well prepared as they were, they were certainly not expecting anything like the horrifying scene that was spread before them. The frantic efforts to resuscitate the President are best described in the words of the official account, published in *The Texas State Journal of Medicine* in January 1964, entitled "Three Patients at Parkland."

Parkland records show that the President arrived at the emergency room sometime after 12:30 p.m. (There is conflict as to the exact moment.) At 1 p.m. Dr. William Kemp Clark, associate professor and chairman of the Division of Neurosurgery of the University of Texas Southwestern Medical School, declared him dead. During the interim of less than 30 minutes, continuous resuscitative efforts were made.

148

Later that day, several attending physicians filed reports. The following identifies these physicians and gives the gist of their reports:

Charles J. Carrico.—Dr. Carrico was the first physician to see the President. He was a resident in surgery at Parkland.

He reported that when the patient entered the emergency room on an ambulance carriage he had slow agonal respiratory efforts and occasional cardiac beats detectable by auscultation. Two external wounds were noted; one a small wound of the anterior neck in the lower one third. The other wound had caused avulsion of the occipitoparietal calvarium and shredded brain tissue was present with profuse oozing. No pulse or blood pressure were present. Pupils were bilaterally dilated and fixed. A cuffed endotracheal tube was inserted through the laryngoscope. A ragged wound of the trachea was seen immediately below the larynx. The tube was advanced past the laceration and the cuff inflated. Respiration was instituted using a respirator assistor on automatic cycling. Concurrently, an intravenous infusion of lactated Ringer's solution was begun via catheter placed in the right leg. Blood was drawn for typing and crossmatching. Type O Rh negative blood was obtained immediately.

In view of the tracheal injury and diminished breath sounds in the right chest, tracheostomy was performed by Dr. Malcolm O. Perry and bilateral chest tubes inserted. A second intravenous infusion was begun in the left arm. In addition, Dr. M. T. Jenkins began respiration with the anesthesia machine, cardiac monitor and stimulator attached. Solu-Cortef (300 mg.) was given intravenously. Despite those measures, blood pressure never returned. Only brief electrocardiographic evidence of cardiac activity was obtained.

Malcolm O. Perry.—Dr. Perry is an assistant professor of surgery at Southwestern Medical School from which he received his degree in 1955. He is 34 years old and was certified by the American Board of Surgery in 1963.

At the time of initial examination of the President, Dr. Perry has stated, the patient was noted to be nonresponsive. His eyes were deviated and the pupils dilated. A considerable quantity of blood was noted on the patient, the carriage, and the floor. A small wound was noted in the midline of the neck, in the lower third anteriorly. It was exuding blood slowly. A large wound of the right posterior cranium was noted, exposing severely lacerated brain. Brain tissue was noted in the blood at the head of the carriage.

Pulse or heart beat were not detectable, but slow spasmodic respiration was noted. An endotracheal tube was in place and respiration was being controlled. An intravenous infusion was being placed in the leg. While additional venesections were done to administer fluids and blood, a tracheostomy was effected. A right lateral injury to the trachea was noted. The cuffed tracheostomy tube was put in place as the endotracheal tube was withdrawn and respirations continued. Closed chest cardiac massage was instituted after placement of sealed-drainage chest tubes, but without benefit. When electrocardiogram evaluation revealed that no detectable electrical activity existed in the heart, resuscitative attempts were abandoned. The team of physicians determined that the patient had expired.

Charles R. Baxter.—Dr. Baxter is an assistant professor of surgery at Southwestern Medical School where he first arrived as a medical student in 1950. Except for two years away in the Army he has been at Southwestern and Parkland ever since, moving up from student to intern to resident to faculty member. He is 34 and was certified by the American Board of Surgery in 1963.

Recalling his attendance to President Kennedy, he says he learned at approximately 12:35 that the President was on his way to the emergency room and that he had been shot. When Dr. Baxter arrived in the emergency room, he found an endotracheal tube in place and respirations being assisted. A left chest tube was being inserted and cutdowns were functioning in one leg and in the left arm. The President had a wound in the midline of the neck. On first observation of the other wounds, portions of the right temporal and occipital bones were missing and some of the brain was lying on the table. The rest of the brain was extensively macerated and contused. The pupils were fixed and deviated laterally and were dilated. No pulse was detectable and ineffectual respirations were being assisted. A tracheostomy was performed by Dr. Perry and Dr. Baxter and a chest tube was inserted into the right chest (second interspace anteriorly). Meanwhile one pint of O negative blood was administered without response. When all of these measures were complete, no heart beat could be detected. Closed chest massage was performed until a cardioscope could be attached. Brief cardiac activity was obtained followed by no activity. Due to the extensive and irreparable brain damage which existed and since there were no signs of life, no further attempts were made at resuscitation.

Robert N. McClelland.—Dr. McClelland, 34, assistant professor of surgery at Southwestern Medical School, is a graduate of the University of Texas Medical Branch in Galveston. He has served with the Air Force in Germany and was certified by the American Board of Surgery in 1963.

Regarding the assassination of President Kennedy, Dr. McClelland says that at approximately 12:35 p.m. he was called from the second floor of the hospital to the emergency room. When he arrived, President Kennedy was being attended by Drs. Perry, Baxter, Carrico, and Ronald Jones, chief resident in surgery. The President was at that time comatose from a massive gunshot wound of the head with a fragment wound of the trachea. An endotracheal tube had been placed and assisted respiration started by Dr. Carrico who was on duty in the emergency room when the President arrived. Drs. Perry, Baxter, and McClelland performed a tracheostomy for respiratory distress and tracheal injury. Dr. Jones and Dr. Paul Peters, assistant professor of surgery, inserted bilateral anterior chest tubes for pneumothoraces secondary to the tracheo-mediastinal injury. Dr. Jones and assistants had started three cutdowns, giving blood and fluids immediately. In spite of this, the President was pronounced dead at 1:00 p.m. by Dr. Clark, the neurosurgeon, who arrived immediately after Dr. McClelland. The cause of death, according to Dr. McClelland was the massive head and brain injury from a gunshot wound of the right side of the head. The President was pronounced dead after external cardiac massage failed and electrocardiographic activity was gone.

Fouad A. Bashour.—Dr. Bashour received his medical education at the University of Beirut School of Medicine in Lebanon. He is 39 and an associate professor of medicine in cardiology at Southwestern Medical School.

At 12:50 p.m. Dr. Bashour was called from the first floor of the hospital and told that President Kennedy had been shot. He and Dr. Donald Seldin, professor and chairman of the Department of Internal Medicine, went to the emergency room. Upon examination, they found that the President had no pulsations, no heart beats, no blood pressure. The oscilloscope showed a complete standstill. The President was declared dead at 1:00 p.m.

William Kemp Clark.—Dr. Clark is associate professor and chairman of the

Division of Neurosurgery at Southwestern Medical School. The 38-year-old physician has done research on head injuries and has been at Southwestern since 1956.

He reports this account of the President's treatment:

The President arrived at the emergency room entrance in the back seat of his limousine. Governor Connally of Texas was also in this car. The first physician to see the President was Dr. Carrico.

Dr. Carrico noted the President to have slow, agonal respiratory efforts. He could hear a heart beat but found no pulse or blood pressure. Two external wounds, one in the lower third of the anterior neck, the other in the occipital region of the skull, were noted. Through the head wound, blood and brain were extruding. Dr. Carrico inserted a cuffed endotracheal tube and while doing so, he noted a ragged wound of the trachea immediately below the larynx.

At this time, Drs. Perry, Baxter, and Jones arrived. Immediately thereafter, Dr. Jenkins and Drs. A. H. Giesecke, Jr., and Jackie H. Hunt, two other staff anesthesiologists, arrived. The endotracheal tube had been connected to a respirator to assist the President's breathing. An anesthesia machine was substituted for this by Dr. Jenkins. Only 100 per cent oxygen was administered.

A cutdown was performed in the the right ankle, and a polyethylene catheter inserted in the vein. An infusion of lactated Ringer's solution was begun. Blood was drawn for typing and crossmatching, but unmatched type O Rh negative blood was immediately obtained and begun. Hydrocortisone (300 mg.) was added to the intravenous fluids.

Dr. McClelland arrived to help in the President's care. Drs. Perry, Baxter, and McClelland did a tracheostomy. Considerable quantities of blood were present in the President's oral pharynx. At this time, Dr. Peters and Dr. Clark arrived.

Dr. Clark noted that the President had bled profusely from the back of the head. There was a large (3 by 3 cm.) amount of cerebral tissue present on the cart. There was a smaller amount of cerebellar tissue present also.

The tracheostomy was completed and the endotracheal tube was withdrawn. Suction was used to remove blood in the oral pharynx. A nasogastric tube was passed into the stomach. Because of the likelihood of mediastinal injury, anterior chest tubes were placed in both pleural spaces. These were connected to sealed underwater drainage.

Neurological examination revealed the President's pupils to be widely dilated and fixed to light. His eyes were divergent, being deviated outward; a skew deviation from the horizontal was present. No deep tendon reflexes or spontaneous movements were found.

When Dr. Clark noted that there was no carotid pulse, he began closed chest massage. A pulse was obtained at the carotid and femoral levels.

Dr. Perry then took over the cardiac massage so that Dr. Clark could evaluate the head wound.

There was a large wound beginning in the right occiput extending into the parietal region. Much of the right posterior skull, at brief examination, appeared gone. The previously described extruding brain was present. Profuse bleeding had occurred and 1500 cc. of blood was estimated to be on the drapes and floor of the emergency operating room. Both cerebral and cerebellar tissue were extruding from the wound.

By this time an electrocardiograph was hooked up. There was brief electrical activity of the heart which soon stopped.

151

The President was pronounced dead at 1:00 p.m. by Dr. Clark.

M. T. Jenkins.—Dr. Jenkins is professor and chairman of the Department of Anesthesiology at Southwestern Medical School. He is 46, a graduate of the University of Texas Medical Branch in Galveston, and was certified by the American Board of Anesthesiology in 1952. During World War II he served in the Navy as a lieutenant commander.

When Dr. Jenkins was notified that the President was being brought to the emergency room at Parkland, he dispatched Drs. Giesecke and Hunt with an anesthesia machine and resuscitative equipment to the major surgical emergency operating room area. He ran downstairs to find upon his arrival in the emergency operating room that Dr. Carrico had begun resuscitative efforts by introducing an orotracheal tube, connecting it for controlled ventilation to a Bennett intermittent positive pressure breathing apparatus. Drs. Baxter, Perry, and McClelland arrived at the same time and began a tracheostomy and started the insertion of a right chest tube, since there was also obvious tracheal and chest damage. Drs. Peters and Clark arrived simultaneously and immediately thereafter assisted respectively with the insertion of the right chest tube and with manual closed chest cardiac compression to assure circulation. Dr. Jenkins believes it evidence of the clear thinking of the resuscitative team that the patient received 300 mg. hydrocortisone intravenously in the first few minutes.

For better control of artificial ventilation, Dr. Jenkins exchanged the intermittent positive pressure breathing apparatus for an anesthesia machine and continued artificial ventilation. Dr. Gene Akin, a resident in anesthesiology, and Dr. Giesecke connected a cardioscope to determine cardiac activity.

During the progress of these activities, the emergency room cart was elevated at the feet in order to provide a Trendelenburg position, a venous cutdown was performed on the right saphenous vein, and additional fluids were begun in a vein in the left forearm while blood was ordered from the blood bank. All of these activities were completed by approximately 12:50 at which time external cardiac massage was still being carried out effectively by Dr. Clark as judged by a palpable peripheral pulse. Despite these measures there was only brief electrocardiographic evidence of cardiac activity.

These described resuscitative activities were indicated as of first importance, and after they were carried out, attention was turned to other evidences of injury. There was a great laceration on the right side of the head (temporal and occipital), causing a great defect in the skull plate so that there was herniation and laceration of great areas of the brain, even to the extent that part of the right cerebellum had protruded from the wound. There were also fragmented sections of brain on the drapes of the emergency room cart. With the institution of adequate cardiac compression, there was a great flow of blood from the cranial cavity, indicating that there was much vascular damage as well as brain tissue damage. President Kennedy was pronounced dead at 1 p.m. by neurosurgeon William Kemp Clark.

It is Dr. Jenkins' personal feeling that all methods of resuscitation were instituted expeditiously and efficiently. However, he says, the cranial and intracranial damage was of such magnitude as to cause irreversible damage.

152

Brain Surgeon Pronounces President Dead

As soon as neurosurgeon Dr. William Kemp Clark had established that the right half of President Kennedy's brain had been shot away, that the blood which was being pumped into the veins of the body was being poured out onto the floor through the torn-open ends of the large blood vessels in the base of his skull, and that there was absolutely no hope of survival, he pronounced the President dead. The several members of the resuscitation team, who were pumping blood into various veins, oxygen into the lungs through the endotracheal tube, saline, cortisone, and other medications through still other veins, and squeezing the heart rhythmically with closed-chest cardiac massage, all gave up, reluctantly. Their apparatus was folded up and the President's clothes, which had been cut from his body in order to get at his veins and chest for the introduction of needles, tubes, and more effective cardiac massage, were balled up and prepared for sending with the body.

At this point, since there had been no reason to turn the President's body over, none of the surgeons knew that there was a bullet hole in the back of the upper part of his body about two inches below the angle between his neck and shoulder line. Certainly no one inspected it to observe whether it did or did not have the blackened rim of a wound of entrance from a spinning, high-speed bullet, in contrast to the small wound in the middle of the front of the President's neck just below the Adam's apple.

Actually, the chief anesthesiologist, Dr. M. T. Jenkins, was aware that there was a hole in the back of the President's neck, because in the process of positioning and stabilizing Kennedy's head and pushing up on his neck to straighten the airway for easier passage of the oxygen he was pumping in, his spread fingers had felt the small hole on the back of the neck. Its presence was completely overshadowed by the desperate efforts at resuscitation, and Dr. Jenkins knew that subsequently it would be inspected by experts, although he *did* mention it. He could also see a wound of exit on the front of the throat, and there was no doubt in his mind that it was the exit wound of the bullet that had entered the back.

Body Released to Dallas Medical Examiner

Dr. Jenkins saw that Dr. Earl Rose, the highly competent Dallas medical examiner, had arrived and expected to testify to him in detail about his part in the proceedings, including the bullet holes in the back and front of the neck.

After the President was declared dead, it was possible that the resuscitation team would have inspected the back of the body a bit more, as they removed their equipment, and so all would have known about the bullet hole in the back of the neck. They felt, however, that they should leave the room in order not to infringe on that poignant moment of Mrs. Kennedy's personal tragedy, when she came in to kiss her dead husband good-by and place her wedding ring on his finger. Father Huber gave the last rites.

153

As with any shooting death in any jurisdiction, the medical examiner, Dr. Rose, was preparing to do a thorough autopsy. Thus there was no reason for the trauma-team members to inspect the President's body further. Then a complication developed.

Body Removed Forcibly to Plane

Vice President Lyndon Johnson, now the President-Designate, had been taken under heavy guard to another part of the Parkland Hospital building. Remembering that the Lincoln assassination plotters had marked Lincoln's Vice President, also a Johnson, as one of the victims, there was great concern to seclude Johnson. He was moved in an armed convoy to Love Field and placed aboard Air Force One, the President's jet plane. At this point, Johnson realized that he could not leave Mrs. Kennedy behind with President Kennedy's body and requested that she too be brought to Air Force One. Mrs. Kennedy would not go without the President's body, but the medical examiner properly refused to release the body. Ignoring this legal impasse, members of the presidential party procured a hearse-ambulance and the finest bronze casket available, returned to the hospital, placed the President's body in the casket, and put the casket in the hearse. Mrs. Kennedy climbed in, and the hearse left for Love Field and the presidential airplane, over the vigorous and legitimate protests of Medical Examiner Rose.

The body was removed so unexpectedly and so abruptly from Dallas that no written report about there being a bullet wound in the front of the neck could be prepared in time to send with the body.

The small bullet hole in the front of the President's neck had been obliterated by the copious transverse tracheostomy done by Dr. Perry for the insertion of the larger endotracheal tube. There had been no time for photographs of the bullet hole during the frantic efforts at resuscitation, and the detailed medical examiner's photographs of the wound of entrance, which Dr. Rose would have taken during the autopsy, were not made because of the abrupt removal of the body. Nor was Dr. Jenkins's knowledge of the bullet holes in the back and front of the neck entered in the record before the body was carried away.

After the body had been placed on the presidential airplane, the stunned Mrs. Kennedy was asked to stand with Lyndon Johnson, and his wife, while he was sworn in as president by Judge Sarah Hughes. Then the plane left for Washington.

Navy Hospital at Bethesda Chosen for Autopsy

During the flight back to Washington, an autopsy was discussed: it could be performed either at the Walter Reed Army Medical Center, perhaps under the auspices of the Armed Forces Institute of Pathology, or at the National Naval Medical Center in Bethesda. Whether the medical

154

examiner's office in Washington or any of the medical-school departments of pathology in Washington were considered is not known. The choice was finally left to Mrs. Kennedy. Because of the President's navy connections, she chose Bethesda as the site for the autopsy.

Comdr. James J. Humes, M.C., U.S. Navy, the distinguished chief of pathology at Bethesda, was off call on this particular Friday evening and was surprised to receive an urgent demand from the hospital's telephone operator to report immediately on a matter of great importance. He was given no clue at that time that the presidential autopsy would not be done at Dallas, and much less that it would be assigned to his department.

As he neared the hospital, he ran into a monumental traffic jam; rumor was already abroad that the President was being brought there. Kennedy was very popular in the Washington area, and the intensity of the interest and the emotional reaction of the populace ran astonishingly high. Commander Humes reached the hospital with some difficulty and was informed that he, as the chief of pathology, would be in charge of the autopsy. His immediate subordinate, Comdr. J. Thornton Boswell, M.C., U.S. Navy, chief of pathology at the Navy Medical School at Bethesda, also arrived, and prepared to assist. Commanders Humes and Boswell inquired as to whether or not any of their consultants from the medical examiner's office in Washington or Baltimore should be summoned, but this action was discouraged. They did suggest, however, that a ballistics expert from the Armed Forces Institute of Pathology be asked to join them, and at some time after the autopsy had started, Lt. Col. Pierre Finck, M.C., U.S. Army, arrived to advise.

Principal Objective of Autopsy

Before the autopsy could begin, they were informed that the principal objective of the examination of the body was to retrieve a bullet or bullets that might tie the crime to the Carcano rifle discovered after the shooting on the sixth floor of the Texas Book Depository building, and thus to the assassin, if his finger or hand prints should be on the gun. They were instructed to disfigure the body as little as possible.

The Kennedy family, including Mrs. Kennedy, Attorney General Robert Kennedy, and their advisers, retired to the visitors' suite on the seventeenth floor to await the findings of the autopsy and the release of the body for embalming and preparation for a state funeral. Commander Humes was informed that speed was essential.

Before the autopsy began, at about 8:00 P.M., multiple X-rays were taken of the head, body, and limbs, down to the wrists and ankles. A quick inspection of the still-wet films, by roentgenologist Comdr. John H. Ebersole, showed that there were no bullets in the body. This was puzzling, because there appeared to be only a wound of entrance, on the back of the neck, plus the massive head wound, and the tracheostomy wound.

Permission was requested to dissect out the track of the neck bullet from its obvious hole of entry in the back of the neck, because Commanders Humes and Boswell had no clue, at this point, that there was a corresponding wound in the front of the neck, which might be the wound of exit of this bullet, since that exit hole had been obliterated by the tracheostomy tube inserted at Dallas, which had left an obvious crescentic dent in the skin of the margin of the tracheostomy hole. Their request for permission to dissect out this bullet hole, which led into the upper back and possibly into the neck, was denied, probably on the basis that it would disfigure the body.

Massive Head Wound Studied in Detail

Commander Humes then undertook a detailed study of the wound of the right side of the head, calling in the hospital's photographer, John T. Stringer, who made excellent color photographs of the scalp, the skull, and the brain from many angles. It was immediately apparent that the great majority of the right hemisphere of the brain had been gouged out by the bullet, although the cerebellum, deep down in the posterior fossa of the skull, was intact. As he proceeded, Humes looked carefully for fragments of metal or materials foreign to the brain, retrieving and labeling several bullet fragments. His work left no possibility that large curled-up structures visible in the photographs could have been anything other than natural parts of the brain, torn by the trauma. It was quite clear that the head bullet had struck the President in the back of the right side of the head and exited through the upper front portion of the skull, blasting out large fragments of the skull, that flew high into the air and were not immediately retrieved.

It was some time before the two groups of doctors, in Dallas and in Bethesda, managed via long-distance telephoning to verify what wounds actually had been made. Meanwhile, their tentative speculations were overheard and quoted, leading to many rumors, just as in the case of President Lincoln, when it was at first rumored that the bullet came from the opposite direction because the bullet hole was in the "wrong" side of the head.

Fig. 61
page 157
During the course of the autopsy, three fragments of skull that had been picked up in the street arrived from Dallas. The largest of these was triangular, approximately 6.5 by 7.5 cm. Another was about 2.5 cm square, and the third about 1.5 cm square. The largest fragment bore in one corner about a dozen minuscule metallic slivers around a semicircular, beveled defect, and the longest margin was irregular along its edge, suggesting that it was a part of a suture line where two portions of the skull had been joined. Whether this was from the sagittal suture (midline seam) or the one between the frontal and parietal bones could not be determined. The aggregate area of these fragments accounted for a major part of the missing area of the skull. These were undoubtedly the

THREE SKULL FRAGMENTS

Actual X-ray film showing the shape of the three skull fragments found in the street in Dallas following the shooting.

Note the semicircular defect with several tiny metallic fragments embedded in its rim at the lower corner of the largest fragment. This was interpreted to be the wound of exit of one of the large bullet fragments as it left the front of the skull. Their area matched the missing area fairly well. *(National Archives)*

Fig. 61

fragments that can be seen going forward and upward thirty or forty feet from Kennedy's exploding head in frames 313 to 316 of the Zapruder movie, shot during the moments just after the second bullet struck him.

Lt. Col. Pierre Finck, a consultant during the autopsy, was quoted in newspaper accounts as saying under interrogation in New Orleans that the autopsy would not qualify as a complete autopsy by the standards of the American Board of Pathology because of certain restrictions that were imposed. Here again was a similarity to Lincoln's autopsy, wherein only the head was examined. Finck alleged that one of these restrictions was a request that the doctors should not dissect out the entire bullet track through the base of the neck on the right side, presumably to avoid disfiguring the body should an open-coffin funeral be chosen.

Because there was doubt as to where the neck bullet, or possible fragments of it, might have gone inside the body, permission to open the chest was requested and granted. This revealed a bruise on the pleura. Permission to examine the abdomen was then requested, and after an unsatisfactory attempt at a transdiaphragmatic approach had been made, permission to open the abdomen was granted.

The adrenal glands were not mentioned in the autopsy report, and practically no comment had appeared about them until my report in *The Medical Times*, in 1972.

During his inspection of the body, and then the removal of the brain, Commander Humes made rough notes on pieces of paper laid on the autopsy table, where he could look directly from the head and body to the paper as he made his notes. These were not detailed drawings, nor did he intend to be dependent upon them. He had X-rays taken that would show him the *exact* location of the wound of entry into the skull and a series of photographs with the scalp intact, and others with the scalp peeled back, accurately showing the locations of the bullet holes, the cracks, and the scalloped edges of the shattered skull.

Autopsy Doctors Not Permitted to Study Photographs and X-rays

Humes did not know it at the time, but all these photographs and X-rays were commandeered during the autopsy and taken away by Treasury Department agents before the pictures could be developed. This was done to avoid the shocking effect they would have on the public if they were exploited, and particularly on members of the family if they were forced to see these photographs of the bloody remains of their relative's head displayed in lurid bookstore windows. While this quest for privacy was certainly understandable and legitimate, to deprive the autopsy team of the benefit of the photographs and particularly the X-rays on which they would depend so heavily made it impossible for Humes and Boswell to assemble the accurate report they had planned to make. This led to an avalanche of criticism of the entire post-mortem examination, which was to continue for several years, until the family finally relented and permitted the photographs to be developed and then to be inspected by a panel of experts.

Even then, the critics of the Warren Commission refused to be satisfied with the answers, since they contended that the panel of experts was sponsored by the government. The implication was inescapable: there was, in their minds, a huge government-sponsored plot.

In answer to that complaint, it was conceded that five years after the family had turned the photographs, X-rays, and clothing over to the National Archives, they might be inspected by authorized, qualified non-government investigators as well.

The investigation had begun—along with the hampered autopsy—but this was only the beginning. The controversy and the accusations and the suspicions were to rage for years, and many doctors and writers—myself among them—would enter into the search for the truth about what happened on that awful day in Dallas.

5.

THE GOVERNOR
WILL LIVE

Kennedy was dead, Johnson was the new president, and Governor
Connally lay gravely wounded in Parkland Hospital. The second bullet
shot from Oswald's rifle had crippled him—but he was going to be lucky.
He would recover. It had been a close call.

Connally's Reactions

Dazed for a moment by the shock of the bullet, Connally had revived
enough to cry out in pain and dismay as he uncoiled from trying to peer
over his shoulder, pulled his right arm up out of his lap, and clamped his
right elbow over his torn-open chest. This twisted him again to his right.
As he crumpled over backward into his wife's lap, she pulled him out of
harm's way. She did this just in time to keep him from being exposed to
fragments of the final bullet to hit President Kennedy. These largest
fragments, after the bullet was disrupted by striking the thick part of
Kennedy's skull, continued forward and struck the frame and glass of the
windshield at the front of the car.

At some point during these awful seconds, Governor Connally looked
down, saw his shirt front covered with blood, and realized that he had
been shot through and through. "My God," he said, "they're going to kill
us all." He was still dazed enough to be unaware that he had also been
shot through the wrist and in the leg. In fact, he did not notice these
wounds until the next day, when he was recovering from his reparative
surgery and asked why there was a cast on his wrist.

Also during those awful seconds, Connally was conscious enough to
hear the final bullet strike Kennedy's head and saw his own clothing
become spattered with brain tissue. He described this in his original
testimony:

160

So I merely doubled up, and then turned to my right again and began to—I just sat there, and Mrs. Connally pulled me over to her lap. She was sitting, of course, on the jump seat, so I reclined with my head in her lap, conscious all the time, and with my eyes open; and then, of course, the third shot sounded, and I heard the shot very clearly. I heard it hit him. I heard the shot hit something, and I assumed again—it never entered my mind that it ever hit anybody but the President. I heard it hit. It was a very loud noise, just that audible, very clear.

Immediately I could see on my clothes, my clothing, I could see on the interior of the car which, as I recall, was a pale blue, brain tissue, which I immediately recognized, and I recall very well, on my trousers there was one chunk of brain tissue as big as almost my thumb, thumbnail, and again I did not see the President at any time either after the first, second, or third shots, but I assumed always that it was he who was hit and no one else.

Connally further stated that he then lapsed into complete unconsciousness until the car swerved into the Parkland Hospital driveway, whereupon he regained consciousness enough to attempt to get out of the car himself before again collapsing.

His Wounds Described

Connally was cared for by the same trauma team that had worked so hard to save the fallen President. Thanks to this immediate care by a team of experts, his recovery was rapid, although the inevitable residual stiffness of his fractured arm, while moderate, will always inconvenience him slightly.

Governor Connally's wounds were also described in detail in the article "Three Patients at Parkland" in *The Texas State Journal of Medicine.* The repair of the Governor's chest wound, as described by Dr. Robert E. Shaw, professor of thoracic surgery at Southwestern Medical School, at Dallas, was as follows:

Dr. Shaw performed a thoracotomy, removed rib fragments, and debrided the chest wound. Diagnosis of the chest condition was gunshot wound of the chest with comminuted fracture of the fifth rib, laceration of the middle lobe, and hematoma of the lower lobe of the right lung.

The Governor was brought to the operating room from the emergency operating room where a sucking wound of the right chest had been partially controlled by an occlusive dressing supported by manual pressure. A tube had been placed through the second interspace of the right chest in the mid-clavicular line and connected to a waterseal bottle to evacuate the hemopneumothorax. An intravenous infusion of lactated Ringer's solution had already been started. As soon as the patient was positioned on the operating table the anesthesia was induced by Dr. Giesecke and an endotracheal tube was put in place.

As soon as it was possible to control respiration with positive pressure, the occlusive dressing was taken from the right chest and the extent of the wound more carefully determined. It was found that the bullet had made a wound of entrance just lateral to the right scapula, close to the axilla, had passed through the latissimus dorsi muscle, shattered approximately 10 cm. of the lateral and anterior portion of the right fifth rib, and emerged below the right nipple. *The wound of entrance was approximately 3 cm. in its longest diameter* and the wound of exit was a ragged wound approximately 5 cm. in its greatest diameter. [Italics added.] The skin and subcutaneous tissue over the path of the missile moved in a paradoxical manner with respiration, indicating softening of the chest.

The skin of the whole area was carefully cleansed with Phisohex and iodine. The entire area, including the wound of entrance and wound of exit, was draped partially excluding the wound of entrance for the first part of the operation.

An elliptical incision was made around the wound of exit removing the torn edges of the skin and the damaged subcutaneous tissue. The incision was then carried in a downward curve up toward the right axilla so as not to have the skin incision over the actual path of the missile through the chest wall. This incision was carried down through the subcutaneous tissue to expose the serratus anterior muscle and the anterior border of the latissimus dorsi muscle.

The fragmented and damaged portions of the serratus anterior muscle were excised. Small rib fragments that were adhering to periosteal tags were carefully removed preserving as much periosteum as possible. The fourth and fifth intercostal muscle bundles were not appreciably damaged. The ragged ends of the damaged fifth rib were cleaned with the rongeur. The pleura had been torn open by the secondary missiles created by the fragmented fifth rib.

The wound was widely opened and exposure was maintained with a self-retaining retractor. Approximately 200 cc. of clot and liquid blood was removed from the pleural cavity. The middle lobe had a linear rent starting at its peripheral edge, going down toward the hilum separating the lobe into two segments. There was an open bronchus in the depth of this laceration. Since the vascularity and the bronchial connections to the lobe were intact it was decided to repair the lobe rather than to remove it. The repair was accomplished with a running suture of #000 chromic gut on an atraumatic needle closing both pleural surfaces as well as two running sutures approximating the tissue of the central portion of the lobe. This almost completely sealed off the air leaks which were evident in the torn portion of the lobe. The lower lobe was next examined and found to be engorged with blood and at one point a laceration allowed the oozing of blood from the lobe. This laceration had undoubtedly been caused by a rib fragment. The laceration was closed with a single suture of #000 chromic gut on an atraumatic needle. The right pleural cavity was now carefully examined. Small rib fragments were removed. The diaphragm was found to be uninjured. There was no evidence of injury to the mediastinum and its contents. Hemostasis had been accomplished within the pleural cavity with the repair of the middle lobe and the suturing of the laceration in the lower lobe. The upper lobe was found to be uninjured.

Connally's wrist wounds were attended to by Dr. Charles F. Gregory, a World War II and Korean War veteran, an orthopedic surgeon certified by the American Board of Orthopedic Surgery, and professor and chairman of orthopedic surgery at Southwestern Medical School, who stated that there was a comminuted fracture of the Governor's right distal radius, which occurred when the bullet passed through the chest and struck the arm. Dr. Gregory debrided the arm wound and reduced the fracture while the patient was still under general anesthesia following the thoracotomy and repair of the chest injury by Dr. Shaw. The right upper extremity was thoroughly shaved and prepped in the routine fashion. The patient was draped in routine fashion, using stockinet. In addition, the doctors used a debridement pan.

The wound of entrance was carefully excised and developed through the muscles and tendons from the radial side of that bone to the bone itself where the fracture was encountered. It was noted that the tendon of the abductor pollicis longus was transected. Only two small fragments of bone were removed; one approximately 1 cm. in length consisted of lateral cortex which lay free in the wound and had no soft tissue connections, and another much smaller fragment 3 mm. in length. Small bits of metal were encountered at various levels throughout the wound. Wherever they were identified and could be picked up, they were submitted to the Pathology Department. Throughout the wound there were noted fine bits of cloth like mohair. Dr. Gregory was told that the patient was wearing a mohair suit at the time of the injury thus accounting for the deposition of such organic material within the wound.

After as careful and complete a debridement of the volar wound as possible and the integrity of the flexor tendons and the median nerve on the volar side established, the wound of exit on the volar surface of the wrist was closed primarily with wire sutures. The wound of entrance on the radial side of the forearm was only partially closed, being left open for the purpose of drainage. This was in deference to the presence of mohair and organic material deep in the wound.

In an additional reference to the wrist wounds (in volume 4, page 142 of hearings before the Warren Commission), Dr. Gregory described the healed wounds of Governor Connally's wrist as follows: "The upper limb of the wound on the dorsum of the wrist is about 5 cms. above the wrist joint.[This was the wound of entry of the bullet into the wrist.] The length of that excisional scar is about 4 cms. [an inch and a half]. The wound on the palmar side of the wrist [this was the wound of exit from the wrist] is now converted to a well healed linear scar approximately *one half inch in length* and located about ¾ inch above the distal flexion crease." [Italics added.]

Dr. Thomas Shires, professor and chairman of the Department of Surgery at Southwestern Medical School, operated on Governor Connally's leg wound.

Dr. Shires performed the surgery for exploration and debridement of the gunshot wound of the Governor's left thigh. The operation lasted 20 minutes. He reported that there was a 1 cm. punctate missile wound over the juncture of the middle and lower third, medial aspect, of the left thigh. X-rays of the thigh and leg revealed a bullet fragment which was imbedded in the body of the femur in the distal third. The leg was prepared with Phisohex and iodine and was draped in the usual fashion.

Following this, the missile wound was excised and the bullet tract was explored. The missile wound was seen to course through the subcutaneous fat

FIG. 62
page 164

163

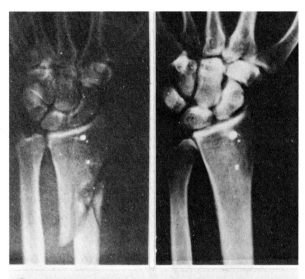

CONNALLY WRIST XRAY   TEST WRIST XRAY

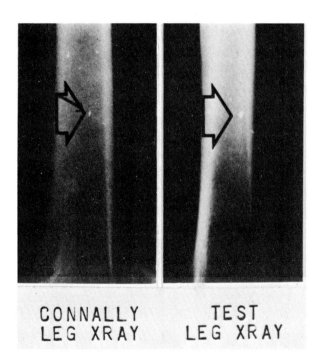

CONNALLY LEG XRAY   TEST LEG XRAY

X-RAYS OF GOVERNOR CONNALLY

The X-rays of Governor Connally showed three fragments (of soft gray lead) in his wrist (upper left) and one in his thigh (lower left). We believe these were scraped off the extruded lead core projecting from the rear end of bullet 399 (fig. 109) as it traveled almost backward through Connally's wrist bone and into his thigh, at a greatly reduced velocity. A neutron activation test revealed that the fragments in the wrist came from bullet 399. Our test wrist is at upper right and our test femur at lower right. (*Left: National Archives; right: from Gary Lattimer, J. K. Lattimer and Jon Lattimer*, Medical Times, *Nov. 1974.*)

Fig. 62

and into the vastus medialis. The necrotic fat and muscle were debrided down to the region of the femur. The direction of the missile wound was judged not to be in the course of the femoral vessels, since the wound was distal and anterior to Hunter's canal. Following complete debridement of the wound and irrigation with saline, the wound was felt to be adequately debrided enough so that three simple through-and-through, stainless steel alloy #28 wire sutures were used encompassing skin, subcutaneous tissue, and muscle fascia on both sides. Following this, a sterile dressing was applied. The dorsalis pedis and posterior tibial pulses in both legs were good.

The metallic fragment was so tiny that no attempt was made to remove it. It was located slightly distal to the wound of entry into the skin of the upper leg.

Governor Connally still bears impressive scars on his back, on the front of his chest under the nipple, on either side of his right wrist, and on top of his left thigh. He says, "The doctors tell me there is still a little metal left in me [in the wrist and leg] but they did a beautiful job. I never have any pain whatsoever, but I can't turn my right hand past a certain point. I can't even turn it palm up. It's not even a handicap, just an occasional inconvenience, but it surely is a reminder."

Considering that Governor Connally's chest wounds could have killed him had he not been given rapid surgical attention by experts, he has done well.

Despite the closeness of the flying bullet fragments, Mrs. Connally, though shocked, was uninjured. In describing the horrible moments later, she burst into tears, but made every effort to assist in reconstructing the order of events.

6.

THE SCENE OF THE CRIME; THE ZAPRUDER MOVIE

Fig. 63
page 167

It was difficult to determine exactly what had happened at the moment the shots were fired, until a spectator brought forth the most extraordinarily valuable tool of all, and put it at the disposal of the investigators into the Kennedy assassination. It was the spectacular Zapruder movie—made by an amateur camera buff, Abraham Zapruder, with an 8 mm hand-held camera.

Standing on the monument to the right of the presidential automobile and about fifty feet away Abraham Zapruder clearly documented the events in the Dallas motorcade—including the horrifying final seconds. It is worthwhile here to review that film.

The movie, which is one of the greatest of historical documents, first shows the motorcycle policemen rounding the corner from Houston Street, then turning from Houston into Elm Street. The presidential limousine comes slowly downhill toward Zapruder, with the President waving at the people on the right side of the automobile. His right elbow is up and his head is twisted to the right as he looks at the spectators. Mrs. Kennedy is waving to the people on the opposite side. The automobile disappears behind a large road sign (Stemmons Freeway) mounted at curbside, in front of and slightly to the left of Zapruder. When Governor Connally comes from behind the sign (frame 221 of the movie), his body is still twisted partly to his right; he had just given up trying to see the President over his right shoulder in response to a loud noise—undoubtedly the first shot, which missed the automobile because it struck the tree. In this frame, Governor Connally has just been struck by Oswald's second bullet, which had passed through the President's neck and, subsequently, through Connally's chest and arm, ending up in his leg. He is dazed by the stunning effect such a bullet has when it makes a major strike on the body.

DEALEY PLAZA, WHERE PRESIDENT KENNEDY WAS SHOT

Oswald chose a position high in the Texas School Book Depository building, directly behind the presidential automobile, which would roll downhill away from him, in a continuation of his line of fire, for several seconds, even if it speeded up. Oswald had to be high in the building in order to clear the oak tree, which can be seen directly beneath his window. His first bullet probably struck a branch of this tree, which had been trimmed and had rather thick branches almost to their tips. One spectator on the sidewalk reported seeing a bullet strike the pavement just behind the automobile at this point. When the car came out from under the tree, Oswald hit the President in the back of the neck (upper cross-mark) and five seconds later hit him in the back of the right side of the head (lower cross-mark).

Zapruder, from his position in the center of this scene, took a motion picture of the entire action. His movie showed Kennedy's elbows fly up in a reflex when the first bullet tipped his spine, and then showed his head explode in a splash of pink brain substance exactly five seconds later, as Mrs. Kennedy was peering intently into his face, wondering what was the matter. Zapruder continued to film the motorcade, showing Mrs. Kennedy being thrown out onto the trunk of the automobile as it lurched forward and then crawling back into the car as it disappeared rapidly under the trestle toward Parkland Hospital. The "grassy knoll" is the area immediately under Zapruder's name, with several dark patches that represent small trees and bushes set at irregular points along this little hillside. An assassin's line of fire would have been obstructed by these bushes and trees and also by the people standing at the curb between him and the presidential automobile, at unpredictable and shifting points. Furthermore, he would have had to fire across the line of travel of the automobile, which would be far more difficult than from the ideal position Oswald selected.

Guards were stationed on the trestle shown at the bottom of the picture, and a large noisy freight train was rattling its way across it at the time of the shooting.

By counting the frames in Zapruder's movie, it is possible to determine the exact intervals between each of the events shown. (*Dan Uhrbrock,* Life *Magazine,* © *1964 by Time Inc.*)

Fig. 63

167

Kennedy's Elbows Start to React

FIG. 64
page 169

As President Kennedy is seen emerging from behind the sign in frame 225, his elbows are only *beginning* to fly up, as a result of the strike on his spine. This indicates that he must have been struck only a very few frames before he emerged from behind the sign (I estimate at or just before frame 220).

FIG. 65
page 169

By frame 230, the President's hands are in front of his face as his elbows fly up. Connally's right hand has now risen out of the path of the bullet.

FIG. 66
page 169

After about one and a half seconds, in frame 236, Governor Connally's mouth can be seen to open wide, probably as he recovers from being stunned by the chest wound and attempts to take a breath. This attempt generated severe pain in the cut rib and nerve endings of his chest and the sickening feeling of not being able to draw enough air into his lungs because of his torn-open pleural cavity.

In a still photograph taken at this instant by Phil Willis, the grassy slope leading up to the higher level of the monument upon which Zapruder was standing can be clearly observed. The slope is covered with small trees in irregular positions, which would have interfered with any other gunman who might have taken a post in that place. Spectators standing along the curb—one with an umbrella extended—were also at irregular and unpredictable locations, which would have interfered with a gunman firing at the car from this site.

At the rear of this grassy knoll was a board fence about six feet tall, behind which automobiles were parked in a parking lot. The view from the top of this fence is so obstructed by the trees, the monument, the sign, and spectators on the sidewalk as to make it a highly ineffective location for a gunman to select for firing at a moving target. If, indeed, anyone *was* there, and was shooting at the presidential car, he missed completely, since the President and the car were not struck by any bullets coming from that direction.

FIG. 63
page 167

The relationships of all of these features can be seen in the aerial view of the scene.

At the moment of the shooting, a long freight train was making its way across the tracks of the triple overpass at the end of Dealey Plaza. There were guards posted on both sides of the overpass to make sure that no unauthorized persons were present there as the motorcade approached and then passed underneath. Incidentally—and incredibly—the presence of this freight train was apparently not realized by later investigators who were intent on analyzing the sounds and echoes in Dealey Plaza; their reenactments did not include the presence of the train, which was both noisy and provided an additional large surface for echoes.

KENNEDY STARTS TO REACT IN ZAPRUDER MOVIE FRAME 225

Kennedy, emerging from behind the road sign, has just been wounded. His mouth is open but his elbows are only starting to fly up. This means that he had been hit just a moment earlier, at frame 220 or just before. Connally has continued the turn toward the front he had started, and is only beginning to react to the bullet that went through his chest, right wrist, and left thigh, as well as Kennedy's neck.

Fig. 64

KENNEDY IN THORBURN'S POSITION IN FRAME 230

Kennedy's elbows are well up in Thorburn's position (see fig. 99) a half-second or so after he was hit, reflecting the strike on his lower cervical spine by the first bullet to hit him. His right elbow is slightly higher, probably reflecting the fact that he was struck on the right side of his spine. Connally is beginning to react by clamping his right elbow over his torn-open chest wall and pulling up his right wrist, which has been penetrated by the same bullet (399). His wrist is now out of the course of the bullet and will never return to it. It was obviously struck well before this frame.

Fig. 65

CONNALLY GASPS FOR BREATH IN FRAME 236

Connally's mouth flies open as he gasps, and cries out in distress. He is trying to suck air into a lung that will not fill, even as he clamps his elbow over his painful, torn-open chest.

Fig. 66

Other Book Depository Employees Hear Shots

Fig. 67
page 172

The window from which Oswald fired can be seen in photographs of the Texas Book Depository building. In a window immediately below this one, three other employees of the depository had been looking at the motorcade. They heard three shots fired from directly over their heads, followed by three empty shell cases being ejected from the rifle and striking the bare floor. There was no doubt in their minds—and, subsequently, there is no doubt in mine—as to where the shots were coming from. They ran away, for fear of being shot if discovered.

Oswald's Shooting Perch

Fig. 68
page 172

Fig. 69
page 173

Oswald had erected a wall of boxes of books between the window and the rest of the floor so that no one could see him as he prepared the position from which he planned to shoot. From a large variety of boxes, he had selected just the right ones for a seat and for a gun-rest. Two boxes were piled near the window sill so that he could rest his front hand on one of them, supporting his rifle on the back of his hand as he patiently waited for the automobile to come into the cross hairs of his telescopic sight. The fact that this window has a very low sill is another helpful feature, since it was not necessary for Oswald to reach over a high sill to point his gun down directly at the car. It seems reasonable that he could not resist the temptation to shoot at the car as he glimpsed it through the branches of the oak tree, which was directly under his window, where the car was only about 130 feet away from the muzzle of his gun. It would appear, as we have said, that his bullet struck one of the heavy branches of this much-trimmed oak tree and was either disrupted or deflected enough to miss the car completely, burying itself in the warm, soft asphalt pavement. He worked the reloading mechanism of his Mauser-type bolt action rifle quickly, just as he had practiced on the screened porch of his home, and was ready to fire a second shot when the car cleared the tree completely, giving him a clear sight of the President's back at a distance of about 190 feet. This was the famous bullet 399, which penetrated the back of the neck of the President and then went on into Governor Connally.

Kennedy's Reaction to Shots

Fig. 64
page 169

In reviewing the Zapruder film, it is apparent, as I mentioned earlier, that President Kennedy's elbows are just beginning to fly upward in frame 225, as he is emerging from behind the Stemmons Freeway sign, in front of Zapruder. It is obvious that he had been struck only a split second prior to this point, because his arms then continued their abrupt upward jerk, to assume a position with the elbows highly elevated, and with both elbows tightly flexed, by frame 230. The reaction is slightly more vigorous by the right arm than the left arm (the bullet struck him on the right), although the symmetry is impressive. His hands can be seen to fly up to the level of the lower part of his face. It is clear from this that he was *not* "reaching for his throat," as has been stated or surmised so often. This spasmodic contraction lasts for about ninety frames of the ensuing portion of the Zapruder film, or for about five seconds, although after the first second his elbows begin to sag slightly and he begins to tilt a bit to his left, with his head bowing slightly forward. The reason for this bizarre contortion of the President's arms will be explained in detail in a following chapter.

Corset and Bandages Kept President Upright

Fig. 70
page 174

He did not immediately crumple in the seat, probably because he had bound himself firmly in a rather wide corset, with metal stays and a stiff plastic pad over the sacral area, which was tightly laced to his body. The corset was then bound even more firmly to his torso and hips by a six-inch-wide knitted elastic bandage, which he had wrapped in a figure-eight between his legs and around his waist, over large thick pads, to encase himself tightly, almost like a mummy wrap. He apparently adopted this type of tight binding as a consequence of the painful loosening of his joints around the sacroiliac area, probably a result of his long-continued cortisone therapy.

Fig. 71
page 174

Because the President remained upright, with his head exposed, Oswald was able to draw a careful bead on the back of his head. The next bullet removed most of the right side of President Kennedy's brain, killing him instantly.

Arguments about Bullets

Everyone who subsequently has viewed and reported on the autopsy and X-ray evidence of President Kennedy's body now agrees that the President was hit by two bullets: 399 and the fatal one that followed five seconds later. They also agree that these were both fired from above and from the rear. There is absolutely no evidence that he was shot from the side or from the front. Even the most voluble critics of the Warren Commission report now agree that these two shots both came from the Texas Book Depository building, although some still conjecture that perhaps they came from two different windows, ignoring the fact that the rifling scratches prove that both bullets came from Oswald's gun, to the exclusion of all other guns, and that neutron activation analysis verifies that all the fragments in both victims came from only those two bullets.

A major issue upon which some critics continued to criticize the Warren Commission report is the question of whether or not one bullet (the first of the two that hit President Kennedy) could have passed

OSWALD'S FIRING WINDOW

This is the window on the sixth floor of the Texas School Book Depository building from which Oswald shot President Kennedy. The box on which he rested his rifle can be seen. The men in the window below heard the shots and heard each ejected shell hit the floor over their heads. *(Tom Dillard,* Dallas Morning News)

Fig. 67

OSWALD'S WALL OF BOXES

Inside the book depository, looking toward Oswald's window, the corner of the building just to the left of his window can be seen and the wall of boxes he arranged so that no one could see him making his preparations to fire out the open window. The boxes are arranged so that they look like the other boxes stored in this section of the building. *(National Archives)*

Fig. 68

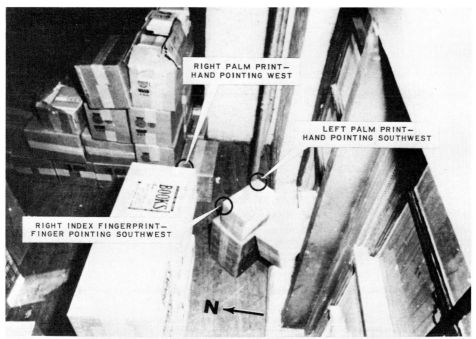

RIGHT PALM PRINT— HAND POINTING WEST

LEFT PALM PRINT— HAND POINTING SOUTHWEST

RIGHT INDEX FINGERPRINT— FINGER POINTING SOUTHWEST

BOOKS

N ←

SOUTHEAST CORNER OF SIXTH FLOOR SHOWING ARRANGEMENT OF CARTONS SHORTLY AFTER SHOTS WERE FIRED.

LOOKING DOWN INTO OSWALD'S FIRING POSITION

Oswald's firing position, behind the wall of boxes and at the sill of the open window on the sixth floor, shows the window half open and boxes piled in front of the window and on the sill in such a way that he could sit on another box (which bore his hand print) and rest his left hand, supporting the barrel of his rifle, on one of the boxes near the sill. An additional advantage, not immediately apparent unless one sits at this window, is that the sill is very low, so he did not need to raise himself over a high window sill but could sit comfortably on the box with both feet flat on the floor and rest his left hand on one of the boxes. He could then rest his rifle against the side of the window frame for lateral stability as well. It is an almost perfect position for what is called bench-rest shooting, which is by far the easiest of all forms of marksmanship. *(National Archives)*

Fig. 69

**KENNEDY'S HEAD
STILL EXPOSED
TO OSWALD IN
ZAPRUDER MOVIE
FRAME 312**

Kennedy is still sitting upright, bound by his back brace, metal stays, and body wrappings, as Oswald pulls the trigger for the fatal head wound. Kennedy's elbows and shoulders are still held high up as part of Thorburn's reflex. Mrs. Kennedy is bending over looking into his face, asking, "What's the matter, Jack?" with her head only inches away from the path of the deadly bullet. Connally has collapsed backward into the lap of his wife, out of harm's way. *(Copyright © by LMH Company. All rights reserved.)*

Fig. 70

**KENNEDY'S
HEAD EXPLODES
IN FRAME 313**

Kennedy's head explodes after being struck on the rear by Oswald's last bullet. Fragments of skull fly abruptly and very far upward and forward as the head is struck. More of the heavy wet brain substance flies out through the large wound of exit on the front right of the head, causing a jet-engine effect and helping to drive the head backward in a jet-recoil effect. This backward motion was due in even greater part to the neuromuscular reflex that stiffened Kennedy's back and neck muscles and arched his back in a final spasm caused by the bullet in the brain. *(Copyright © 1967 by LMH Company. All rights reserved.)*

Fig. 71

174

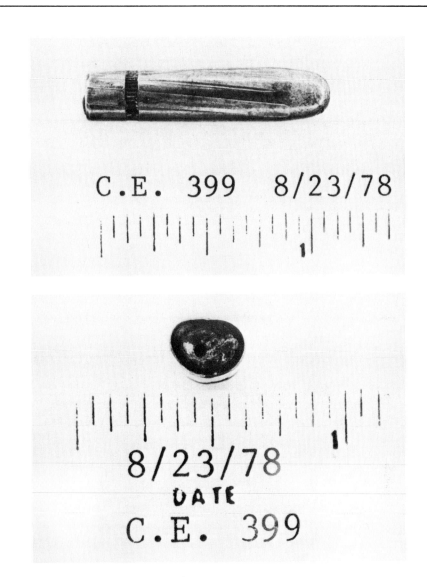

FLATTENED BASE OF BULLET 399 (THE NECK BULLET)

The photograph of the rear end of bullet 399 (bottom) shows the degree of flattening of the base segment, which I attribute to its striking Connally's rib and wrist bones while traveling mostly sideways and somewhat backward in the process of tumbling. It was this flattening that squeezed some of the soft lead out of the inside of the rear end of the jacket. A remnant of this protruding lead shows in the photograph above. Bullet 399 is also somewhat bent on its long axis, but to a degree that is so slight as to be imperceptible in these photographs, which were taken for the House Select Committee on Assassinations in 1978. *(National Archives)*

Fig. 72

through his neck and then through Governor Connally. Still skeptical, the critics argue indirectly from this that the entire twenty-seven-volume Warren Commission report is a hoax. Practically all the other doubts about shots from the side or front have been dispelled by permitting non-government analysts to review the autopsy and X-ray evidence. The 1978 House of Representatives Select Committee on Assassinations has also accepted the single-bullet conclusion.

Governor Connally's frequent statement that he believed he was hit by a bullet different from that which went through President Kennedy's neck (in spite of the circumstantial evidence, documented herein and elsewhere, that it *must* have been the same bullet that hit both him and the President) was seized upon by the critics as support for their view. They contend that it was a third bullet that hit the Governor, completely ignoring the fact that only two bullets were recovered in the car or its occupants. They also disregarded the fact that if three bullets had hit the occupants of the car, Governor Connally would have been struck by two of them, whereas he was actually hit by only one.

They argued that if three bullets hit the occupants of the car, one when Governor Connally assumes he was hit, in between the two that hit the President, the time was too short for Oswald to fire all three shots. Again, they ignore the fact that there is evidence of only two bullets hitting the occupants, five seconds apart, and that both bullets came out of Oswald's gun to the exclusion of all other guns.

Fig. 72
page 175

Some critics, who are obviously unfamiliar with high-powered military rifles and military bullets, even contend that bullet 399 could not have passed through two men and retained its so-called pristine appearance. They disregard evidence that this bullet is *not* pristine: it was flattened somewhat by hitting a glancing blow on something hard, namely Governor Connally's rib, while traveling sideways and somewhat backward. They also ignore the fact—of which infantry tacticians are well aware—that multiple soldiers are very likely to be penetrated by the same bullet if they stay close together. This is the reason for the spread formation required of all troops who are under direct fire in warfare. Numerous instances of multiple soldiers being wounded by the same bullet have been reported. In fact, the type of rifle used by Oswald has been found to be so overpowered that it has now been replaced by a lighter and less powerful rifle and cartridge as our current infantry weapon.

To go back, again: the President was dead; the Governor was maimed. How could it have happened?

7.

THE AUTOPSY RAISES QUESTIONS; WARREN COMMISSION REPORT

The nation was stunned. A beloved President was lost, and the whole country grieved for him, for his family, and for a hopeful period of history of which he had been the standard-bearer. But even in the midst of the grief and the real and poignant caring, people wondered and people asked; they speculated and imagined and argued and, finally, they began to look for answers. That's just one more way, after all, to deal with shock and grief. I was there too, and I also asked questions—though mine began somewhat later.

The plane had barely taken off for Washington with the President's body when questions began to be asked about the shooting. The medical examiner group demanded to know why all the rules of forensic procedure were broken by not having a proper medical examiner's autopsy in Dallas or in Washington. Dr. Milton Helpern, dean of American medical examiners, was embarrassed to have his foreign colleagues call up and say, essentially, "What is going on? You people do the medical examiner routine so strictly and so well that if your rules fell apart after the murder of your own President, there *must* be something peculiar afoot." Attempts to explain that the fear of a larger plot compelled the removal from Dallas, or that it was the family's right to the privacy it demanded, or that there really was no evidence of a conspiracy or a Russian connection fell on cynical ears. The anti-establishment press exploded in an ecstatic orgy of unopposed criticism.

Warren Commission Report

President Lyndon Johnson, recognizing this storm of questions and criticism, appointed a commission made up of respected citizens, and then practically forced the most impeccable jurist of them all, the Chief

Justice of the United States, Earl Warren, to be its chairman. All the facilities of the government were put at the commission's disposal, and a group of eager young staff assistants was brought to Washington with the mandate to run down every lead, test every rumor, and assemble every bit of relevant information. As always with government commissions, the young staff actually created the report that was then assembled, reviewed, and published under the names of the prestigious commissioners. Haste was demanded, and the commission staff, using the superb facilities and expert personnel of the FBI and the army weapons proving grounds at Aberdeen, Maryland, accumulated voluminous testimony, documents and evidence, which filled twenty-seven volumes and required, to store it, an extensive area on a subterranean floor of the National Archives building.

Some of the exhibits were truly fantastic. Never had the public been exposed to such a detailed and revealing look at such a complex event as the killing of President Kennedy. The Zapruder movie alone was a graphic historical document of unparalleled detail, in living color. The media and sophisticated photographic experts had an opportunity to study it in ways never before possible. The number of questions brought up for investigation was large and challenging.

Material Withheld

Unfortunately, when the massive, twenty-seven-volume Warren Commission report was finally published in 1964, it still contained some obvious flaws, many of which were related to the continued withholding of the X-rays and photographs of the body of President Kennedy. Since the X-rays were still sequestered, the true point of impact of the skull bullet was not known. The ballistic experiments by the army laboratories, meant to reproduce Kennedy's head wound, had been conducted with the misinformation that the wound of entry into the back of the President's head was at the base of the skull, rather than some four inches higher, on the upper portion of the skull. The army did not know the correct location of the wound and therefore was unable to do correct experiments until the X-rays first were officially inspected in 1966, some three years later. By that time the Warren Commission had been disbanded, and no other organization either was authorized or had the facilities or budget to repeat these experiments.

Many questions were still unanswered and many loose ends were left dangling. Critics seized upon these with enthusiasm. Cries of "whitewash" and "cover-up" (in a giant, scandalous government-media plot to fool the public) expressed the general theme of a flood of books and articles. The very repetition of these views, over the years, became so pervasive that we were all left in some doubt as to the facts.

One of the most obvious defects in the report, and the one that attracted my own attention, was the inaccuracy of the official illustrations of the President's wounds. The artist, H. A. Rydberg, had made these drawings from hearsay, in order to provide a graphic depiction of a body on which to illustrate the paths of the bullets or the effects of the bullets. They were meant to be purely schematic. Since the artist had seen neither the body nor the photographs of the body, he had no way of knowing about the large roll of soft tissue across the back of the President's neck, which made his torso a different shape from that of most persons. The artist was not aware of the steeply downward path of the bullet, at approximately a twenty-degree downward angle, which the photographs revealed it had taken through the body. The course the artist had drawn for the neck bullet was more or less parallel with the ground, not sharply downhill. It was this gross discrepancy that immediately attracted my attention. The drawing of the President's head wound was also done without the artist having viewed either the body, the photographs, or the X-rays, and showed a point of entry much too low on the skull and a wound of exit that was too small and showed too little fragmentation of the skull. My own experience with wartime head wounds from this same type of bullet convinced me that these drawings were either grossly inaccurate or that the wounds were from some different type of bullet. Because of these discrepancies, added to the storm of criticism from sharp-eyed assassination buffs, who wanted to see the photographs for themselves—and who uncovered such an interesting phenomenon as the abrupt backward jerk of the President's head after he was struck by the second bullet—I decided to look into some of these questions myself.

FIG. 73
page 180

Many of the criticisms concerned items that were still open to experimentation—such claims as that Oswald's rifle could not be used for such rapid shooting, that Oswald's ammunition was undependable, and that Oswald was an incompetent marksman, to name only a few. It occurred to me that I was uniquely positioned to be useful in testing some of these questions in the laboratory and in pursuing others with the help of the many experts in my circle of friends in the scientific and medical fields.

Questions Raised

My first task was to get my thoughts in order, organize my priorities, and plan the ways in which I might conduct the most useful inquiry I could. It seemed logical to begin with a list of questions to which I hoped to find the answers. To wit:

1. Why had the X-rays and photographs been taken away from the doctors who did the autopsy before they had a chance to use them to document their findings as they had expected to do? There was no doubt that this withholding had added to the questions and to the shortcomings of the Warren Commission report.

2. Why were the actual photographs and X-rays not included in the *final* Warren Commission report?

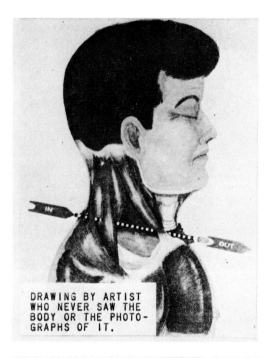

DRAWING BY ARTIST
WHO NEVER SAW THE
BODY OR THE PHOTO-
GRAPHS OF IT.

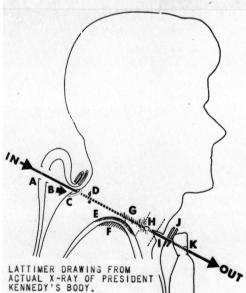

LATTIMER DRAWING FROM
ACTUAL X-RAY OF PRESIDENT
KENNEDY'S BODY.

**OFFICIAL DIAGRAM
OF THE NECK WOUND,
FROM THE WARREN
COMMISSION REPORT (above)**

Drawn from verbal descriptions only, this diagram shows the neck wound to be
less steeply downward than the actual photographs of the body showed it to be.
(National Archives)

Fig. 73

LATTIMER'S DIAGRAM OF NECK WOUND (opposite, below)

This diagram of the neck wound is based on personal observations of the photographs and X-rays. Because the National Archives requested that no tracing be made, it is not precise. Its purpose is to clarify the relative positions of the wounds in the neck and the various findings which together indicated that all were consistent with the entry of a bullet into the upper back that ranged downward and medially through the base of the neck and exited low on the trachea in the midline, just below the collar button, causing a nick in the knot of the necktie. The findings were:

A. Bullet Hole in Back of Suit Collar and Shirt. The coat and shirt were probably humped up on the back of the President's neck (see fig. 83) when the first bullet struck him. The FBI found a punched-in round hole in the back of the coat consistent with a 6.5 mm bullet, with the broken cloth fibers bent inward, indicating that this was a wound of entry. The cloth fibers of the shirt were bent inward in the same manner. Traces of copper from a bullet such as Oswald used were found on the margins of this hole in the coat by the FBI, also indicating that it was a wound of entrance.

B. Bullet Hole in Back. The bullet hole in Kennedy's upper back, about two inches below the crease of his neck, and about two inches to the right of the midline.

C. Halo around Bullet Hole. The bullet hole had around it a faint but definite halo, or circumferential bruise, typical of a wound of entry from a high-speed bullet.

D. Spine Struck by Bullet. Tiny slivers of bone could be seen in the upper (rear) area of the bullet track on the A-P X-ray film of the right shoulder and neck area. Since no lateral X-ray film was taken of this area, it was possible to determine only that they lay near the high (rear) end of the bullet track, but not the exact distance they lay from the surface. They were near the tip of the transverse process of the cervical vertebrae, which the bullet obviously grazed. They are represented diagrammatically only. (See fig. 82.)

E. & F. Pleura and Lung Bruised. The autopsy report described a 5 cm bruise on the dome of the right pleura and also on the upper tip of the right lung, but no perforation of either, compatible with the passage of a high-speed bullet close above this point.

G. Air in Tissues. There were tiny traces of air, visible in the X-rays, in the tissues along the bullet track, near the hole in the trachea.

H. Hole in Trachea. There was a ragged hole in the right side of the trachea, seen by the surgeons at Parkland.

I. Tracheostomy. There was a gaping 6.5 cm transverse tracheostomy incision low on the neck where the Dallas surgeons had enlarged the bullet hole in order to insert a tracheostomy tube. (See fig. 80.)

J. Holes in Front of Shirt. There were 1 cm vertical slits in both sides of the overlapping portion of the shirt immediately below the collar band and touching it just below the collar button. (See fig. 84.)

K. Nick in Necktie. There was a nick or crease through only the outer layer of fabric of the lower left side of the knot, compatible with the passage of a spinning 6.5 mm bullet at high speed. A bloodstain extended downward from this nick. (See fig. 85.) *(J. K. Lattimer,* Resident and Staff Physician, *May 1972)*

Fig. 73 *(continued)*

3. When it came out that Dr. Humes had tossed the original working drafts of the autopsy notes into the fire in his study, after he finished his final copies, people wanted to know why they were burned, and attached ominous implications to their being burned. If the doctor had merely thrown them in the wastebasket, no one might have thought anything of it. The act of burning them conjured up sacrilegious implications in the columns of the critics. Why were they burned?

4. Did the bullet holes in the clothing and in the body of the President actually indicate that the bullet went through the President's body from back to front?

5. Why was there a discrepancy in the level of the bullet holes in the back of the President's coat and shirt, which seemed to be considerably lower than the indicated location of the bullet hole in the skin of the back of his neck?

6. Was there actually definite evidence of a bullet track running through and through the President's body at the level of the lower neck?

7. If so, which direction was the bullet going through this track?

8. Was the angle of the bullet track through the President's body indeed downward at the required twenty-degree angle to be compatible to Oswald's firing position on the sixth floor?

9. Why did the attempts by government ballistics experts to reproduce President Kennedy's head wounds not produce skull wounds more similar to his if the last bullet did indeed enter the lower part of the back of the President's head, as indicated by the only drawing in the Warren Commission report?

10. I particularly wanted to know why there was not more evidence of shattering of the President's skull into many pieces, which, as far as the drawings showed, there was not.

11. Was there any evidence of a bullet traveling through the President's head or body from one side to the other (as from the grassy knoll), rather than exclusively from back to front?

12. Many doctors, including myself, wanted to know the state of President Kennedy's adrenal glands, in view of the rumors that he had had Addison's disease. The adrenal glands had not been mentioned in the autopsy report, even though they had been examined.

13. They wanted to know if the bullet that was alleged to have gone through both President Kennedy and Governor Connally (the famous Warren Commission bullet 399) was indeed the same bullet that went through Kennedy's neck, Connally's chest, wrist, and leg.

14. They wanted to know if this bullet was indeed pristine (completely undeformed), as alleged by some critics, or whether it was deformed, and if so, exactly how much it was deformed.

15. They wanted to know if the President might possibly have survived this first wound, as alleged, in view of the difficulties.

16. They wanted to know why the President's elbows jerked up when

he was hit in the neck, and whether he was applying his hands to the bullet hole in his throat, as some inferred.

17. They wanted to know why he did not crumple out of sight, as Connally did, if he had indeed taken a serious bullet wound through this part of his body.

18. Why was the hole in the front of the President's neck so small if it was a wound of exit?

Organizing the questions was only the first step. My next step was to apply for permission to study the restricted Kennedy autopsy photographs, X-rays, and associated materials that the newspapers said would be made available to qualified persons five years after their deposit in the National Archives by the family of the President.

I found it difficult to gain access to some of the materials, as I will discuss later, and some were even more difficult to interpret and describe.

Incomplete as it is in some details, the autopsy report from the Bethesda hospital is a valuable document, and a good place to start before going on to ask more difficult questions and before sharing the results of our own medical and ballistic studies.

Official Autopsy Report

The official autopsy report from Bethesda follows:

COMMISSION EXHIBIT NO. 387

Clinical Record		Autopsy Protocol
Date and Hour died	A.M.	Date and Hour autopsy performed
22 November 1963 1300 (CST)	P.M.	22 November 1963 (EST)
Prosector (497831)		Assistant (489878)
CDR J.J. Humes, MC. USN		CDR "J" Thornton Boswell, MC. USN
		Full Autopsy
Clinical Diagnoses		LCol Pierre A. Finck, MC, USA (04-043-322)
		Ht.—72½ inches
		Wt.—170 lbs.
		Eyes—blue
		Hair—reddish brown

Pathological Diagnoses

Cause of Death: Gunshot wounds, head.

Approved—Signature

J.J. Humes, CDR, MC. USN

Military Organization	Age	Sex	Race	Identification	Autopsy No.
President, United States	46	male	cauc.		A63-272
Patient's Identification				Register No.	Ward No.

Kennedy, John F.   Autopsy Protocol
Naval Medical School   Standard Form 503

COMMISSION EXHIBIT NO. 387

Pathological Examination Report	A63-272	Page 2

Clinical Summary:

According to available information the deceased, President John F. Kennedy, was riding in an open car in a motorcade during an official visit to Dallas, Texas on 22 November 1963. The President was sitting in the right rear seat with Mrs. Kennedy seated on the same seat to his left. Sitting directly in front of the president was Governor John B. Connally of Texas and directly in front of Mrs. Kennedy sat Mrs. Connally. The vehicle was moving at a slow rate of speed down an incline into an underpass that leads to a freeway route to the Dallas Trade Mart where the president was to deliver an address.

Three shots were heard and the president fell forward bleeding from the head. (Governor Connally was seriously wounded by the same gunfire.) According to newspaper reports ("Washington Post" November 23, 1963) Bob Jackson, a Dallas "Times Herald" photographer, said he looked around as he heard the shots and saw a rifle barrel disappearing into a window on an upper floor of the nearby Texas School Book Depository Building.

Shortly following the wounding of the two men the car was driven to Parkland Hospital in Dallas. In the emergency room of that hospital the president was attended by Dr. Malcolm Perry. Telephone communication with Dr. Perry on November 23, 1963 develops the following information relative to the observations made by Dr. Perry and procedures performed there prior to death.

Dr. Perry noted the massive wound of the head and a second much smaller wound of the low anterior neck in approximately the midline. A tracheostomy was performed by extending the latter wound. At this point bloody air was noted bubbling from the wound and injury to the right lateral wall of the trachea was observed. Incisions were made in the upper anterior chest wall bilaterally to combat possible subcutaneous emphysema. Intravenous infusions of blood and saline were begun and oxygen was administered. Despite these measures cardiac arrest occurred and closed chest cardiac massage failed to re-establish cardiac action. The president was pronounced dead approximately thirty to forty minutes after receiving his wounds.

The remains were transported via the presidential plane to Washington, D.C. and subsequently to the Naval Medical School, National Naval Medical Center, Bethesda, Maryland for postmortem examination.

General Description of Body:

The body is that of a muscular, white male measuring 72½ inches and weighing approximately 170 pounds. There is beginning rigor mortis, minimal dependent livor mortis of the dorsum, and early algor mortis. The hair is reddish brown and abundant, the eyes are blue, the right pupil measuring 8 mm. in diameter, the left 4 mm. There is edema and ecchymosis of the inner canthus region of the left eyelid measuring approximately 1.5 cm. in greatest diameter. There is edema and ecchymosis diffusely over the right supra-orbital ridge with abnormal mobility of the underlying bone. (The remainder of the scalp will be described with the skull.)

There is clotted blood on the external ears but otherwise the ears, nares, and mouth are essentially unremarkable. The teeth are in excellent repair and there is some pallor of the oral mucous membrane.

Situated on the upper right posterior thorax just above the upper border of the scapula there is a 7 x 4 millimeter oval wound. This wound is measured to be 14 cm. from the tip of the right mastoid process.

Figs. 78, 79
page 201

Fig. 80
page 201

Situated in the low anterior neck at approximately the level of the third and fourth tracheal rings is a 6.5 cm. long transverse wound with gaping irregular edges. (The depth and character of these wounds will be further described below.)

Situated on the anterior chest wall in the nipple line are bilateral 2 cm. long recent transverse surgical incisions into the subcutaneous tissue. The one on the left is situated 11 cm. cephalad to the nipple ecchymosis associated with these wounds. A similar clean wound measuring 2 cm. in length is situated on the antero-lateral aspect of the left mid arm. Situated on the antero-lateral of each ankle is a recent 2 cm. transverse incision into the subcutaneous tissue.

There is an old well healed 8 cm. McBurney abdominal incision. Over the lumbar spine in the midline is an old, well-healed 15 cm. scar. Situated on the upper-antero-lateral aspect of the right thigh is an old, well healed 8 cm. scar.

Missile Wounds:

Fig. 102
page 254

1. There is a large irregular defect of the scalp and skull on the right involving chiefly the parietal bone but extending somewhat into the temporal and occipital regions. In this region there is an actual absence of scalp and bone producing a defect which measures approximately 13 cm. in greatest diameter.

From the irregular margins of the above scalp defect tears extend in stellate fashion into the more or less intact scalp as follows:

A. From the right inferior temporo-parietal margin anterior to the right ear to a point slightly above the tragus.

B. From the anterior parietal margin anteriorly on the forehead to approximately 4 cm. above the right orbital ridge.

C. From the left margin of the main defect across the midline antero-laterally for a distance of approximately 8 cm.

D. From the same starting point as C, 10 cm. postero-laterally.

FIG. 86
page 211

Situated in the posterior scalp approximately 2.5 cm. laterally to the right and slightly above the external occipital protuberance is a lacerated wound measuring 5 x 6 mm. In the underlying bone is a corresponding wound through the skull which exhibits beveling of the margins of the bone when viewed from the inner aspect of the skull.

FIG. 102
page 254

Clearly visible in the above described large skull defect and exuding from it is lacerated brain tissue which on close inspection proves to represent the major portion of the right cerebral hemisphere. At this point it is noted that the falx cerebri is extensively lacerated with disruption of the superior saggital sinus.

Upon reflecting the scalp multiple complete fracture lines are seen to radiate from both the large defect at the vertex and the smaller wound at the occiput. These vary greatly in length and direction, the longest measuring approximately 19 cm. These result in the production of numerous fragments which vary in size from a few millimeters to 10 cm. in greatest diameter.

The complexity of these fractures and the fragments thus produced tax satisfactory verbal description and are better appreciated in photographs and roentgenograms which are prepared.

The brain is removed and preserved for further study following formalin fixation.

FIG. 61
page 157

Received as separate specimens from Dallas, Texas are three fragments of skull bone which in aggregate roughly approximate the dimensions of the large defect described above. At one angle of the largest of these fragments is a portion of the perimeter of a roughly circular wound presumably of exit which exhibits beveling of the outer aspect of the bone and is estimated to measure approximately 2.5 to 3.0 cm. in diameter. Roentgenograms of this fragment reveal minute particles of metal in the bone at this margin. Roentgenograms of the skull reveal multiple minute metallic fragments along a line corresponding with a line joining the above described small occipital wound and the right supra-orbital ridge. From the surface of the disrupted right cerebral cortex two small irregularly shaped fragments of metal are recovered. These measure 7 x 2 mm. and 3 x 1 mm. These are placed in the custody of agents Francis X. O'Neill, Jr. and James W. Sibert, of the Federal Bureau of Investigation, who executed a receipt therefore. (Attached)

2. The second wound presumably of entry is that described above in the upper posterior thorax. Beneath the skin there is ecchymosis of subcutaneous tissue and musculature. The missile path through the fascia and musculature cannot be easily probed. The wound presumably of exit was that described by Dr. Malcolm Perry of Dallas in the low anterior cervical region. When observed by Dr. Perry the wound measured "a few millimeters in diameter", however it was extended as a tracheostomy incision and thus its character is distorted at the time of autopsy. However, there is considerable ecchymosis of the strap muscles of the right side of the neck and of the fascia about the trachea adjacent to the line of the tracheostomy wound. The third point of reference in connecting these two wounds is in the apex (supra-clavicular portion) of the right pleural cavity. In this region there is contusion of the parietal pleura and of the extreme

apical portion of the right upper lobe of the lung. In both instances the diameter of contusion and ecchymosis at the point of maximal involvement measures 5 cm. Both the viceral and parietal pleura are intact overlying these areas of trauma.

Incisions:

The scalp wounds are extended in the coronal plane to examine the cranial content and the customary (Y) shaped incision is used to examine the body cavities.

Thoracic cavity:

The bony cage is unremarkable. The thoracic organs are in their normal positions and relationships and there is no increase in free pleural fluids. The above described area of contusion in the apical portion of the right pleural cavity is noted.

Lungs:

The lungs are of essentially similar appearance the right weighing 320 gm., the left 290 gm. The lungs are well aerated with smooth glistening pleural surfaces and firmness to palpation is situated in the apical portion of the right upper lobe. This corresponds to the similar area described in the overlying parietal pleura. Incision in this region reveals recent hemorrhage into pulmonary parenchyma.

Heart:

The pericardial cavity is smooth walled and contains approximately 10 cc. of straw-colored fluid. The heart is of essentially normal external contour and weighs 350 gm. Chambers contain moderate amounts of postmortem clotted blood. There are no gross abnormalities of the leaflets of any of the cardiac valves: aortic 7.5 cm., pulmonic 7 cm., tricuspid 12 cm., mitral 11 cm. The myocardium is firm and reddish brown. The left ventricular myocardium averages 1.2 cm. in thickness, the right ventricular myocardium 0.4 cm. The coronary arteries are dissected and are of normal distribution and smooth walled and elastic throughout.

Abdominal cavity:

The abdominal organs are in their normal positions and relationships and there is no increase in free peritoneal fluid. The vermiform appendix is surgically absent and there are a few adhesions joining the region of the cecum to the ventral abdominal wall at the above described old abdominal incisional scar.

Skeletal system:

Aside from the above described skull wounds there are no significant gross skeletal abnormalities.

Photography:

Black and white and color photographs depicting significant findings are exposed but not developed. These photographs were placed in the custody of agent Roy H. Kellerman of the U.S. Secret Service, who executed a receipt therefore. (Attached)

Roentgenograms:

Roentgenograms are made of the entire body and of the separately submitted three fragments of skull bone. These are developed and were placed in the custody of agent Roy H. Kellerman of the U.S. Secret Service, who executed a receipt therefore. (Attached)

Summary:

Based on the above observations it is our opinion that the deceased died as a result of two perforating gunshot wounds inflicted by high velocity projectiles fired by a person or persons unknown. The projectiles were fired from a point behind and somewhat above the level of the deceased. The observations and available information do not permit a satisfactory estimate as to the sequence of the two wounds.

The fatal missile entered the skull above and to the right of the external occipital protuberance. A portion of the projectile traversed the cranial cavity in a posterior-anterior direction (see lateral skull roentgenograms) depositing minute particles along its path. A portion of the projectile made its exit through the parietal bone on the right carrying with it portions of cerebrum, skull and scalp. The two wounds of the skull combined with the force of the missile produced extensive fragmentation of the skull. Laceration of the superior saggital sinus, and of the right cerebral hemisphere.

The other missile entered the right superior posterior thorax above the scapula and traversed the soft tissues of the supra-scapular and the supra-clavicular portions of the base of the right side of the neck. This missile produced contusions of the right apical parietal pleura and of the apical portion of the right side of the neck, damaged the trachea and made its exit through the anterior surface of the neck. As far as can be ascertained this missile struck no bony structure in its path through the body. [Note that the X-rays had now been removed by registered government agents and could not be studied for bone injury.]

In addition, it is our opinion that the wound of the skull produced such extensive damage to the brain as to preclude the possibility of the deceased surviving this injury.

A supplementary report will be submitted following more detailed examination of the brain and of microscopic sections. However, it is not anticipated that these examinations will materially alter the findings.

J.J. Humes   "J" Thornton Boswell   Pierre A. Finck
CDR, MC. USN (4978310)   CDR, MC. USN (4898780)   Lt Col. MC. USA (04-043-322)

SUPPLEMENTARY REPORT OF AUTOPSY NUMBER A63-272

Gross Description of Brain:

Following formalin fixation the brain weighs 1500 gms. The right cerebral hemisphere is found to be markedly disrupted. There is a longitudinal laceration of the right hemisphere which is para-sagittal in position approximately 2.5 cm. to the right of the midline, which extends from the tip of the occipital lobe posteriorly to the tip of the frontal lobe anteriorly. The base of the laceration is situated approximately 4.5 cm. below the vertex in the white matter. There is considerable loss of cortical substance above the base of the laceration, particularly in the parietal lobe. The margins of this laceration are at all points jagged and irregular, with additional lacerations extending in varying directions and for varying distances from the main laceration. In addition, there is a laceration of the corpus callosum extending from the genu to the tail. Exposed in this latter laceration are the interiors of the right lateral and third ventricles.

When viewed from the vertex the left cerebral hemisphere is intact. There is marked engorgement of meningeal blood vessels of the left temporal and frontal regions with considerable associated sub-arachnoid hemorrhage. The gyri and sulci over the left hemisphere are of essentially normal size and distribution. Those on the right are too fragmented and distorted for satisfactory description. When viewed from the basilar aspect the disruption of the right cortex is again obvious. There is a longitudinal laceration of the mid-brain through the floor of the third ventricle just behind the optic chiasm and the mammillary bodies. This laceration partially communicates with an oblique 1.5 cm. tear through the left cerebral peduncle. There are irregular superficial lacerations over the basilar aspects of the left temporal and frontal lobes.

In the interest of preserving the specimen coronal sections are not made. The following sections are taken for microscopic examination:
   A. From the margin of the laceration in the right parietal lobe.
   B. From the margin of the laceration in the corpus callosum.
   C. From the anterior portion of the laceration in the right frontal lobe.
   D. From the contused left fronto-parietal cortex.
   E. From the line of transection of the spinal cord.
   F. From the right cerebellar cortex.
   G. From the superficial laceration of the basilar aspect of the left temporal lobe.

Seven (7) black and white and six (6) color 4 x 5 inch negatives are exposed but not developed. (The cassettes containing these negatives have been delivered by hand to Rear Admiral George W. Burkley, MC. USN, White House physician.)

Microscopic examination:
Brain:
Multiple sections from representative areas as noted above are examined. All sections are essentially similar and show extensive disruption of brain tissue with associated hemorrhage. In none of the sections examined are there significant abnormalities other than those directly related to the recent trauma.

Heart:
Sections show a moderate amount of subepicardial fat. The coronary arteries, myocardial fibers, and endocardium are unremarkable.

Lungs:
Sections through the grossly described area of contusion in the right upper lobe exhibit disruption of alveolar walls and recent hemorrhage into alveoli. Sections are otherwise essentially unremarkable.

Liver:
Sections show the normal hepatic architecture to be well preserved. The parenchymal cells exhibit markedly granular cytoplasm indicating high gly-

189

cogen content which is characteristic of the "liver biopsy pattern" of sudden death.

Spleen:
Sections show no significant abnormalities.

Kidneys:
Sections show no significant abnormalities aside from dilatation and engorgement of blood vessels of all calibers.

Skin wounds:
Sections through the wounds in the occipital and upper right posterior thoracic regions are essentially similar. In each there is loss of continuity of the epidermis with coagulation necrosis of the tissues at the wound margins. The scalp wounds exhibit several small fragments of bone at its margins in the subcutaneous tissue.

Final summary:
This supplementary report covers in more detail the extensive degree of cerebral trauma in this case. However neither this portion of the examination nor the microscopic examinations alter the previously submitted report or add significant details to the cause of death.

J. J. Humes
CDR, MC, USN, 497831

Disposition of President Kennedy's Brain

Controversy has arisen as to the final resting place of President Kennedy's brain. Following the autopsy, excellent photographs of the brain were made, routine sections of portions of the brain were taken for microscopic study, and the entire brain was fixed in formalin inside heavy double-plastic bags, for preservation and possible further study. Secret Service agent Roy Kellerman apparently was instructed to gather up all of the materials relating to the autopsy and to transfer them to the Protective Research Division of the Department of Justice. At some point, these were kept at the White House, under security, for Dr. George Burkley, the White House physician, according to testimony in the 1978 Select Committee on Assassinations report. This report indicates that on April 22, 1965, Robert F. Kennedy, the President's brother, authorized a release of all of these materials to Mrs. Evelyn Lincoln, who then had an office in the National Archives. Mrs. Lincoln was in the process of assisting in the transfer of President Kennedy's official papers to the National Archives. In response to this order, Mr. Bouck, head of the Protective Research Division, and Dr. Burkley prepared an inventory list and transferred these materials to Mrs. Lincoln. Included in this list of materials was one stainless-steel container, seven by eight inches in size, containing what the inventory list characterized as gross material. The best speculation was that the steel container held the President's brain. On October 31, 1966, according to the testimony in the Assassinations Committee report, Burke Marshall, a representative of the Kennedy family, formally transferred the jurisdiction over the autopsy materials to the National Archives. The materials were actually in the National Archives at the time, in the custody of Mrs. Lincoln. When that transfer occurred, the stainless-steel container was not included in the list.

The Assassinations Committee indicated that it had conducted a comprehensive investigation in an attempt to locate the missing materials. Some thirty people were interviewed or deposed. Even the people associated with the interment and reinterment of the President's body were interviewed and deposed, but it could not be determined what had happened to the brain.

A Kennedy spokesman did indicate that Robert Kennedy had expressed concern that these materials could conceivably be placed on public display many years from now, and he wanted to prevent that. The chairman of the Assassinations Committee inferred from speaking to the Kennedy family spokesman that the most likely answer was that the President's brother had destroyed the documents and, presumably, the brain. This, of course, was not certain, but it was suggested.

8.

THE WITHHELD AUTOPSY MATERIALS—REVIEWED AT LAST

The Bethesda autopsy report is, of course, only the tip of the iceberg; it left many questions unanswered. Actually viewing the photographs would help. I was now ready to move on to other restricted materials, and to compare my findings, after examining those, with notes I had been making over the past several years.

I wanted to begin by reviewing the 8 x 10 color prints and 4 x 5 transparencies and the black-and-white prints of the President's head and shoulders, photographed from every angle. These were taken by navy photographer John T. Stringer just before the start of the autopsy. Commander Humes had him continue to photograph the brain and the opened brain case as the examination progressed. The pictures are technically excellent, but it was certainly understandable why they should not be exposed to the public, much less to members of the Kennedy family: they are shocking.

Restrictions on Autopsy Materials

FIG. 74
page 193

Chief Justice Earl Warren had written to me that withholding these materials from inclusion in the Warren report was his personal decision, since the testimony was clear and he wanted to spare the President's family. Secret Service agents Kellerman and Greer had taken away the photographs, X-rays, and clothing, presumably at the request of the family. Thus, these photographs were not seen, even by the men who did the autopsy and took the pictures, until three years later. Until 1966 they were kept in privacy at the Department of Justice, at the request of the

192

Supreme Court of the United States
Washington, D. C. 20543

February 3, 1972

CHAMBERS OF
CHIEF JUSTICE WARREN
RETIRED

Dr. John K. Lattimer,
Professor & Chairman,
Department of Urology,
College of Physicians & Surgeons,
Columbia University,
New York, New York 10032.

Dear Dr. Lattimer:

This is in response to your letter of January 18th which was called to my attention when I returned from extended travel over the holidays.

I believe I should assume full responsibility for not making available to the public the pictures of the wounds of the deceased President. The Commission relied upon the testimony of the doctors at the Bethesda Naval Hospital as to their findings of entrance and exit of the bullet wounds and cause of death. At my suggestion, but with the concurrence of all the members of the Commission, the photographs and X-rays themselves were not introduced into evidence because everything that was so introduced went into the twenty-six volumes of exhibits and testimony.

My reason for making this suggestion was that scavengers were trying to buy everything that pertained to the assassination for a museum which they proposed to show around the country at County Fairs, etc. in a highly emotional manner. It was my considered opinion that if the guns and the clothes of the assassin and these horrible pictures of the President were shown to the public, including the children of the country, it would merely be a horror chamber that might not only degrade our assassinated President, but might even put ideas of similar conduct into some minds, and thus endanger future Presidents.

I, therefore, suggested that these photographs and X-rays be delivered to the Department of Justice with the suggestion that they not be made public except by permission of the Kennedy family. This put their authenticity in the hands of those who would be most desirous of having the true facts of the case known.

I have not changed my mind on this subject, and I know that President Johnson did have a panel of distinguished doctors view the photographs and X-rays, and as I have been informed they agreed with the testimony upon which the Commission relied.

With best wishes, I am

Sincerely,

Earl Warren

CHIEF JUSTICE WARREN RULED ON PICTURES

In this condensation of a letter to me, the Chief Justice explained that he personally took the responsibility for making the decision not to permit the gruesome pictures of President Kennedy's head to appear in the Warren Commission report. All other members of the commission concurred in his decision. Had they been published, they would have become public property and might have been displayed where the children and family members would see them. *(J. K. Lattimer)*

Fig. 74

family. Then turned over to the National Archives, the materials were never permitted to be on public display. Only after five additional years would specified qualified medical experts be permitted to study them. Even then, additional restrictions and reservations were stipulated. No direct copies or tracings could be made of them, for example. These restrictions were relaxed slightly in 1979 for another wide-ranging review conducted by the House of Representatives Select Committee on Assassinations.

While the Warren Commission itself did not view these exhibits because of the above factors, properly authorized government officials were to be permitted to see the photos and X-rays and did so on two occasions: once in 1966, when the physicians who performed the autopsy authenticated the pictures, and once again in 1968, when a panel of three of the country's top forensic pathologists, Dr. Russell S. Fisher, Dr. William H. Carnes, and Dr. Alan Moritz, together with a top roentgenologist, Dr. Russell H. Morgan, reviewed them for the then Attorney General, Ramsey Clark, and issued a technical report about them, couched in proper medical terms and widely reproduced in the newspapers.

I journeyed to Washington several times to study the unrestricted exhibits, including the Zapruder film, Oswald's guns, and the bullet fragments. Unfortunately, no official mechanism for further investigation of all the questions existed until the House Select Committee on Assassinations review in 1978. This long period of enforced inactivity permitted critics unbridled exposure of their views. The restrictions on viewing the autopsy evidence naturally added impetus to the doubts of those people who were impressed by the intensity of some of the criticism and the lack of rebuttal, plus the lack of information about some portions of the autopsy findings. Probing into the mass of data (and rumors) about the assassination became a popular hobby of many amateur investigators.

Dr. Humes's Preliminary Autopsy Notes

An excellent—if somewhat lugubrious—example of this kind of amateur sleuthing sprang from the questions asked about the rough notes made during the Bethesda autopsy. When Dr. Humes replied to a query as to what he had done with his preliminary autopsy notes, he said he had tossed them into the fire on his hearth. A group of assassination buffs immediately seized upon this statement, reading ominous significance into the fact that the notes had been burned.

Here, again, I have deduced an interesting link between the Kennedy and Lincoln assassinations. Commander James J. Humes, the chief of pathology at the Bethesda naval hospital, was the man whom fate decreed would do the autopsy on President Kennedy. Mrs. Kennedy had chosen the Bethesda naval hospital, and Commander Humes, an experienced pathologist and, later, president of the American Society of Clinical Pathologists, was called in to be the principal prosector, although he was severely limited in what he was permitted to do by constraints imposed by the family.

During the early years of his navy career, Humes had at one point been assigned to the Detroit area and was sometimes asked to escort visiting dignitaries on sightseeing tours there, in addition to showing them the defense production lines at the factories of the major automobile makers. One of the great museums of the world, to which he sometimes took visitors, is the late Henry Ford's Greenfield Village Museum, at nearby Dearborn, Michigan, which contains Americana from the mightiest locomotive to the tiniest light bulb built by Edison, who was a great friend of Ford's. In this museum is the original rocking chair in which Lincoln was sitting when he was shot. On the upholstery of the back of the chair, at the level where a man's head might rest, is a dark area on the fabric. Humes had watched crowds of visitors persuade themselves that this stain was Lincoln's blood and then act in a morbid, sometimes joking manner about it, which Humes found disrespectful.

During the autopsy on Kennedy, for whom he had felt great admiration, he made personal notations on loose sheets of paper. These were, as is inevitable, stained with blood and fat from his surgical gloves. Normally, rough working notes such as these would be copied onto clean paper and a rough draft of the autopsy report prepared—as he later did. This draft was then checked and rechecked for clarity and accuracy with the other members of the autopsy team and then put in final form. After this, the rough drafts and soiled notes were discarded, according to normal procedure. Humes finished transcribing his notes, conferring with his colleagues, and making final revisions at about noon on Sunday, November 24. He then crumpled up the soiled notes and preliminary drafts and threw them into the fireplace in his study in the recreation room of his home where he had sequestered himself while he wrote up the report.

That Humes threw the soiled working notes into the fire, rather than in the wastebasket, was seized upon by the critics of the Warren Commission report as having great significance. They implied that he had burned them in order to destroy some unspecified evidence of some, again unspecified, irregularities.

In his defense one might speculate that if he had tried to keep papers soiled with fat and blood in his office files, they would have become rancid and objectionably malodorous.

An ironic note to this story is that the dark stain on the upholstery of the back of Lincoln's rocking chair is not blood at all, but is, in fact, Macassar, a hair pomade the men of Lincoln's day favored for keeping their hair in place. Our grandmothers, knowing that their upholstered chair backs would be stained, crocheted doilies, which they pinned on the chair backs at the heights where the men's heads would rest. They called these

Fig. 138
page 347

ANTIMACASSAR ON LINCOLN'S ROCKER

During the Civil War, men wore a pomade on their hair called Macassar, which originated on that Indonesian island. It tended to leave greasy stains on the backs of chairs, and women crocheted doilies like this to protect the upholstery. It was a dark stain of this type on the back of Lincoln's rocking chair at Ford's Theater that many guests mistook for his blood. Because of their coarse reactions, Dr. Humes moved to protect the bloodstained relics of Kennedy's autopsy. *(Chicago Historical Society)*

Fig. 75

FIG. 75
page 196

doilies antimacassars, and one can still be seen on another of Lincoln's rocking chairs.

Thus we have yet another interesting link in the chain of coincidences that bind these two martyred presidents together. Again, we see no magical significance in this association but, rather, a manifestation of the widespread interest in American history. Mrs. Kennedy remembered seeing a book in the White House library that described Lincoln's funeral. She asked that the same plan be followed. Lee Oswald was named for Robert E. Lee; and here, a museum relic of President Lincoln influenced the burning of the notes that indeed were stained with President Kennedy's blood.

List of Restricted Materials

To end the digression and return to the matter of the restricted materials, I would like to provide here a specific list of those materials, so that readers may visualize the work I was able to do and the tools that helped me do it. The first materials I viewed consisted of large color prints, plus black-and-white prints, and color transparencies thereof:

1. The head viewed from above (10 prints).
2. The head viewed from the right and above, to include part of the face, neck, and upper chest (9 prints).
3. The head and neck viewed from the left side (7 prints).
4. The head viewed from behind (4 prints).
5. The cranial cavity with brain removed (4 prints).
6. The back of the body including neck (4 prints).
7. The brain viewed from below after its removal (4 color transparencies). The brain from above (3 color transparencies). Black-and-white negatives of these same views of the brain.

The quality of almost all of these photographs was good, and in the few instances where part of one photograph was slightly out of focus, there was usually another similar view that *was* in focus. The 4 x 5 color transparencies were the sharpest of all and provided the clue as to the proper orientation of the photos of the empty brain case, which was otherwise confusing. There was also a roll of 120 Kodak film that had been spoiled by unrolling it in the light, and a notation that this had been done deliberately by one of the agents present. There was no explanation of why the agent had done this. Either he did not realize that the photographs were being taken to assist in preparing an accurate autopsy report or he thought the photographer was not authorized to take such photographs. The latter turned out to be the explanation, because an unauthorized employee had entered the room and taken pictures.

There was also one 4 x 5 transparency that had been spoiled by overexposure, with no clue as to what it was supposed to show, and one surplus color film pack, which appeared to be unexposed and unused.

In addition to the color and black-and-white prints, there were the

197

following X-rays, all of which bore the number 21296, the name of the U.S. Naval Hospital, Bethesda, Maryland, and the date 11-22-63:

Figs. 76, 77
page 199

Film 1, skull, AP view; films 2, 3, skull, left lateral view; films 7, 11, thoraco-lumbar region, AP view; film 8, right hemi-thorax, shoulder and upper arm, AP view; film 9, chest, AP view; film 10, left hemi-thorax, shoulder and upper arm, AP view; film 12, lower femurs and knees, AP view; film 13, pelvis, AP view; film 14, upper legs, AP view.

X-ray film 1 had one 13 mm and one 7 mm scorch mark on it, which did not affect its readability. X-ray film 2 had two diverging pencil lines on it, which did not affect its readability.

I was also permitted to examine the suit coat, shirt, necktie, and back brace (with its many associated paddings and bandages) that Kennedy was wearing at the time he was shot. There were also a number of very close-up, greatly enlarged photographs of the relevant segments of some of these.

I was able to check the numbers of all of the materials I inspected against the list signed by the men who did the autopsy and also against the list signed by the members of the 1968 forensic panel. I found no omissions, although there were some differences in labeling. The forensic panel had stated that their list conformed with the list in the document of transmittal from the Kennedy family in 1966, but in none of the lists were there any photographs of the bruise on the pleura and apex of the right lung, though photographs of the bruise on the lung and pleura were described by Commander Humes, in his testimony, as having been taken. There was no way to know whether the spoiled roll of 120 film or the spoiled transparency had been this exposure, or what had happened to it. Since it was the only picture attempted of an interior, superior portion of the body cavity, it may well have encountered a problem in exposure and thus have been spoiled. Later conversations I had with the photographer indicated that it might never have been taken in the uproar and distractions of the packed autopsy room. Many times previously, I had inspected the bullets and bullet fragments, the Zapruder, Nix, and Muchmore motion pictures, the rifle, and other items that are in the National Archives, but, since they were not on the restricted list, I examined them once again, in detail.

While exact measurements from a photograph or X-ray film can never be as accurate as measurements on the body itself, approximations are possible. A few of the photographs showed a ruler laid against the wound areas. But by far the greatest benefit of the photographs and X-rays was seeing the relationships of the various wounds and fragments to each other, and to other landmarks on the body.

Back Wound

On the upper back, just below the juncture of neck and back, there was an ovoid penetrating wound estimated to be approximately 6 mm x 8

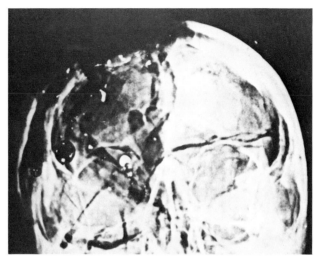

KENNEDY'S HEAD X-RAY FROM THE FRONT

Computer-enhanced X-ray of Kennedy's skull seen from the front, showing the defect in the top of the right side of his head. There are extensive fracture lines radiating from the point of entrance. The white dots are bullet fragments, the largest of which is close to the point of entry. Note that these bullet fragments are all limited to the right side of the brain case. (*National Archives*)

Fig. 76

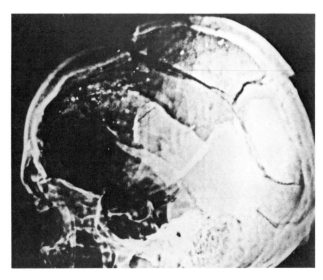

X-RAY OF PRESIDENT'S HEAD FROM THE SIDE

Computerized enhancement of Kennedy's skull X-ray, prepared for the House Assassinations Committee. It shows the type of fragmentation of the skull which reassured me that it was indeed compatible with that to be expected from the powerful type of bullet Oswald fired. The white dots in a row across the top of the skull are bullet fragments, indicating the approximate path of the bullet. (*National Archives*)

Fig. 77

Fig. 78
page 201

mm (one-fourth inch) in size, with the longer axis transverse. It was compatible with a 6.5 mm bullet wound and had a blackened rim around it, which was suggestive of a wound of entry from a high-speed bullet. This wound was estimated to lie about 5 cm to the right of the midline and approximately the same distance below the transverse double fold in the skin at the juncture of the neck and back. This fold in the skin of the neck was very prominent and may have been related to the thickening of the tissues of this area. This bullet hole was recognizable as the wound described in the autopsy report as lying 14 cm medial to the tip of the right acromion process and 14 cm below the tip of the right mastoid process.

Tracheostomy Wound

Fig. 80
page 201

There was a large transverse tracheostomy wound about 6.5 cm in length and gaping open at least 1.5 cm at its widest (mid) portion. The tracheostomy wound in the front of the neck was at a lower level than I had expected to see it. It was almost at the suprasternal notch, and its upper margin was seen to be far below the bottom of the transverse fold of skin of the back of the neck, mentioned before, indicating that the wound of exit was substantially below the wound of entry on the back of the neck. The lower lip of the tracheostomy incision had a large crescentic indentation near its center, as if from the pressure of the large cuffed tracheostomy tube inserted through it during the attempts at resuscitation. Dr. Malcolm Perry had indicated that he had created this wound by a transverse incision directly through a bullet hole in the front of the lower neck at this location.

The 1968 panel of forensic pathologists stated in their report that they could detect, among the irregularities along the upper margin of this gaping tracheostomy incision, the semicircular upper half of a wound of exit from a bullet. I did not find these photographs sharp enough or close enough to enable me to agree or disagree with this diagnosis. However, the relative heights of the two wounds did make it quite obvious in the photographs that any bullet that might have exited through this hole had had a definite downward course through Kennedy's neck, rather than the relatively horizontal course that had been depicted in the official sche-

Fig. 73
page 180

matic diagram made by medical staff artist H. A. Rydberg from verbal descriptions of the wounds and not from actual measurements, photographs, or a viewing of the body.

Another factor that made the height of the wound on the back of Kennedy's neck difficult to describe exactly was that the tissues at the back of his neck were more prominent than those of most people. This was possibly caused by his holding his shoulders high, producing a roll of tissue across the back of his neck, or his swimming, or perhaps the cortisone derivative treatments he had over the years caused a slightly

Fig. 81
page 203

greater than normal thickening of these tissues. In any case, the actual photographs showed very clearly that the course of the bullet downward

LOCATION OF BULLET HOLE IN PRESIDENT'S UPPER BACK

This is a drawing made for the House of Representatives Select Committee on Assassinations, taken from one of the photographs of the President's body made just before the autopsy started, indicating the distance of the hole from the creases at the base of the back of his neck. (*National Archives*)

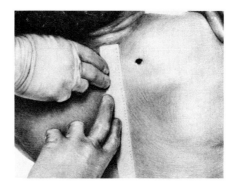

Fig. 78

BULLET HOLE IN THE BACK OF OUR KENNEDY MODEL NECK

Photograph of an actual entrance wound made by a 6.5 mm fully jacketed Carcano bullet in the skin of the back of one of our Kennedy necks. It is about one-quarter inch in diameter. Note the abraded edges with black particles on the margin. The wound on the back of Kennedy's neck looked much like this. (*J. K. Lattimer*)

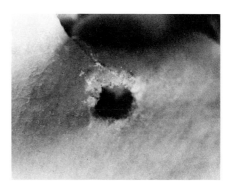

Fig. 79

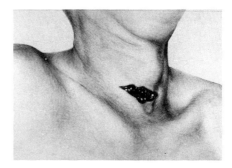

KENNEDY'S TRACHEOSTOMY WOUND

This is a drawing based on one of the autopsy photographs showing the location of the transverse tracheostomy wound in the front of the neck created by Dr. Malcolm Perry at Dallas. Dr. Perry had seen bloody air bubbles coming out of a small wound in this area, indicating that the oral-endotracheal tube which the anesthesiologist had passed down through this area might be leaking. He made this tracheostomy to insure complete and free ventilation of the President's lungs during the frantic efforts at resuscitation. The wound of exit in the front of the neck was made unrecognizable by the presence of this tracheostomy wound. (*National Archives*)

Fig. 80

through his neck was steeper than had been indicated by the schematic drawing, and that it was much more in accord with the fact that the bullet was fired downward at Kennedy, at about a twenty-degree angle, from the sixth floor of the Texas Book Depository.

The X-rays taken specifically of the area between these two bullet holes (which also include a hole in the trachea) showed tiny traces of air in the tissue planes (subcutaneous emphysema) along the line between the two holes in the back of the neck and in the trachea and also showed evidence of cracked bone, as well as two tiny slivers or fragments of bone about 4 mm and 2 mm in length, along this same track, where it came nearest to the spine, on the right side. No gross fractures were visible, although the effects of a graze of the tip of the transverse process of one of the vertebrae in the lower neck or upper thoracic region appeared obvious to me. This graze was confirmed by the 1978 Assassinations Committee review.

Fig. 82
page 203

In the autopsy report, the dome (or apex) of the right parietal pleura had been found to be ecchymotic (bloody) and bruised, even though it had not been penetrated, and while the upper tip of the right lung was also slightly bruised, there was no evidence of any actual hole, pneumothorax, or sucking wound of the chest to indicate a hole in either the pleura or lung. The apex of the pleura would have been immediately below the course of a track between the two bullet holes in the neck. The strap muscles of the neck were reported in the autopsy description to be ecchymotic even though there had been no ecchymosis or circular bruise recorded near the bullet hole on the front of the neck through which the tracheostomy wound had been made.

Holes in Coat, Shirt, and Necktie

After viewing the photographs and X-rays of the bullet holes in President Kennedy's body, I turned my attention to his suit coat and shirt. The coat was a lightweight, gray fabric which looked and felt like a tropical worsted in a sack weave. The collar, back, and upper sleeves were stiff with a substance resembling dried blood. The sleeves had been slit open and the front panels had been cut across at the nipple line, to strip off the clothing, as is commonly done during emergency efforts at resuscitation.

The coat showed a roundish punched-in 8 mm (one-fourth inch) hole in the back, compatible with the passage of a 6.5 mm bullet but with one-half of the circumference removed, along with an elongated area of the cloth, for analysis of the cloth fibers (which had shown traces of copper, and which had also revealed that the fibers had been bent inward, indicating that this was a wound of entry, according to the FBI laboratory tests). This hole was 13.3 cm below the upper edge of the collar and 4.5 cm to the right of the midline, in a position indicating that it was somewhat lower than the wound of entry into the skin on the back of the neck. The jacket had a second tiny penetrating hole, just at the lower

SHAPE OF PRESIDENT KENNEDY'S NECK

As can be seen here, Kennedy had more soft tissue across the back of his neck than most people. This may have been muscular, due to his swimming, or due, in part, to his taking of cortisone over many years for his adrenal insufficiency. It is easy to see that a bullet entering near the base of his neck at the back could pass downward at an angle of twenty degrees and exit just below his Adam's apple. (Los Angeles Times)

Fig. 81

FRACTURE OF KENNEDY'S LOWER NECK

This enlargement of one of the X-rays of Kennedy's lower neck region shows fragmentation of the tip of the transverse process of one of his lower neck vertebrae in the track of bullet 399. The fragments are not displaced, indicating a graze or brush-by type of fracture. This is compatible with the passage of a bullet such as 399 through this area. (*National Archives*)

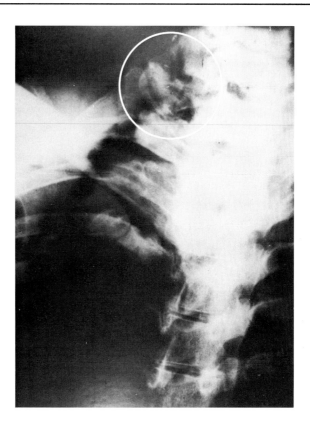

Fig. 82

edge of the collar, through both jacket and lining, directly above the hole through which the bullet obviously entered. There was no such second hole in the back of the shirt at this higher location.

The back of the shirt had a single hole, about 6 mm long and 6 mm wide, about 14.5 cm below the upper edge of the collar and about 2.8 cm to the right of the midline. While the half of this hole that remained was still roundish and appeared indented in some parts of its circumference, the other half had also been removed, along with a 1 cm strip of adjacent cloth, for analysis (as for bending of the fibers or traces of metal, as described by the FBI laboratory expert, Robert Frazier, in the Warren report).

Having seen these holes in the back of the coat and shirt, at their low locations, I returned to my file of Kennedy photographs and found several of the President, taken shortly before he was shot, with his right elbow resting on the edge of the automobile, where he could wave more easily. This position caused his suit coat to hump up at the back of his neck. It was easy to see that the bullet hole in the coat or shirt might well be at a lower point on either garment when the garment was laid out flat, in comparison to its position at the actual moment of impact, when President Kennedy was indeed waving to the crowds, with his right elbow elevated, as seen in the Zapruder movie.

FIG. 83
page 205

Whether the higher second hole at the lower margin of the coat collar was a tangential wound of the cloth, caused by a downward folding of this portion of the cloth, could not be determined, although it did seem possible. Why the shirt did not have a corresponding second hole was not clear. On further inspection, it seemed probable that the second hole in the jacket was the site from which a control sample of cloth had been removed by FBI laboratory investigator Frazier, when the margins of the bullet hole in the coat were analyzed. In any case, after seeing the actual photographs of the upward buckling of the cloth during the motorcade, it did not seem nearly so mysterious as has been implied that the bullet holes in the back of the coat and shirt were at lower positions than the bullet hole in the President's back.

The shirt was white with a thin triple gray stripe alternating with a thin triple brown stripe. The back, collar, and upper arms of the shirt were also soaked with a dark, stiff substance resembling dried blood.

FIG. 84
page 206

The shirt showed two vertical, slitlike penetrating wounds in the bloody area immediately below the collar band and touching its lowest margin. The fabric may have torn in this direction because the bullet started to turn nose downward as it left the skin of the neck at a downward angle. These vertical slits had occurred in the area of overlap just below the button joining the two sides of the collar. The shirt was new, with strong fabric and strong thread attaching the button. It was quite clear, at this examination, that no portion of these holes in the front of the shirt resembled the round, punched-in holes usually seen with wounds of entry into clothing, whereas the remaining halves of the holes

204

EXPLANATION FOR THE LOW LOCATION OF THE BULLET HOLE IN THE BACK OF THE SUIT COAT

A photograph of Kennedy taken a few minutes before he was shot, showing his suit coat humped up behind his neck. If his coat and shirt were in this configuration when he was hit, probably due to his waving, which he appears to be doing, it could account for the bullet holes in his coat and shirt being farther down from his collar than the corresponding bullet hole in his back (a point about which there has been some confusion and argument). (The Dallas Times Herald)

Fig. 83

 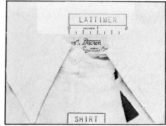

BULLET EXIT HOLES IN SHIRT

We were able to duplicate the wounds of entry and exit in models of Kennedy's neck, using the exact type of Carcano rifle and Western Cartridge Company ammunition that Oswald used, and an aiming point on the shirt that permitted the bullet to exit in the same spot at the lower edge of the collar band as in the case of Kennedy. This resulted in a vertical slit in the cloth starting at the lower edge of the collar band, exactly like that in Kennedy's shirt. The bullet then continued to tumble after it left the neck, striking our models of Connally, twenty-eight inches away, traveling almost precisely sideways, with great consistency. (*J. K. Lattimer*)

Fig. 84

BULLET GRAZED NECKTIE AFTER EXIT FROM FRONT OF NECK

KENNEDY ACTUAL   LATTIMER TEST

BULLET NICK OF NECKTIE

Our duplications of Kennedy's neck wound resulted in a duplication not only of his shirt and skin wounds but also of the nick in the left side of the knot of the necktie, exposing the lining. The necktie at left is the actual necktie worn by Kennedy and the necktie on the right is our test tie. (*Left: National Archives; right: J. K. Lattimer*)

Fig. 85

in the back of the coat and shirt still appeared punched-in, despite their partial excision.

The tails of the shirt were stained with dried brownish body fluids and substances, as is frequent with victims of gunshot wounds of the head. This was also true of Lincoln's shirt.

FIG. 85
page 206

The necktie had been nicked on its outer layer only (but not penetrated), in a manner compatible with the tangential passage of a spinning slender bullet, near the lower edge of the left side of the knot. The necktie was untied when I examined it, so I was able to see that there was a smear of some dried foreign material (resembling dried blood) extending at least 1 cm below this nick. It is possible that this stain was not readily visible when the necktie was in its original tied configuration. While it was possible that blood had merely dropped on the necktie from some other wound, the fact that the stain extended downward from the lower margin of the hole in the neck was clear and suggested that it had been carried there from the neck wound.

9.

THE HEAD WOUND, THE ADRENAL GLANDS, THE BACK PROBLEMS— NEW QUESTIONS, NEW ANSWERS, SOME SURPRISES

This examination of the restricted materials was an enlightening experience. I went back to my own files with heightened interest, perused and cross-indexed nine years of my own research against what I had just observed, and began to formulate some more questions—and even some tentative answers—based on what I had seen and thought about.

Neck Wound Compatible with Oswald's High Perch

I was satisfied that there was final and conclusive evidence supporting the assumption that there was a demonstrable bullet track through the neck, that it was back to front, and that it was at a compatible downward angle. The bone fragments, the air in the tissues, the report of a bruise on the apex of the pleura, and the hole in the trachea all lined up or fit together to indicate that a bullet had passed between the two holes in the back and front of the skin of the neck, even though any single factor might not have been conclusive. On any other course, the bullet would probably have struck some additional bones solidly, causing more gross fractures, which would also have been visible in the X-rays. It is fairly certain that the bullet grazed the tip of the transverse process of one of the vertebrae in the lower neck region without causing a severe fracture (but leaving tiny, broken-up, bony fragments behind) and without deflecting the bullet.

Although there seemed to be little reasonable doubt that the course of the bullet had indeed been from back to front, the mere fact that some critics had raised the question that it might have been going the other way led me to check the evidence carefully; again, I was satisfied. The indications were strong: all pointed to a back-to-front direction. For example, the black rim around the wound in the back of the neck strongly indicated that site as a portal of entry.

The bullet hole in the front of the neck had been cut in two by the tracheostomy incision, and so was not intact for study, but Dr. Malcolm Perry, who made that incision, had commented on the lack of distortion or discoloration around this wound. Had it been a wound of entry, it would almost surely have had a blackened rim around it, which Dr. Perry would certainly have noticed; he had had extensive experience with bullet wounds. Such a through-and-through bullet wound in the neck could not possibly have been inflicted from the front. The photographs showed that to do this the shooter would have to have been squatting down very low inside the President's automobile, as if on the floor, in front of Governor Connally's position, in order to shoot upward at the President's neck. Previous analysis of the cloth around the bullet holes in the back of the suit coat and shirt by the FBI had also indicated that the bullet had entered from the rear.

The angle of the bullet track through the neck had caused more controversy than any other element of the inquiry, so I turned my attention to this question with particular care. Again, I was satisfied once I had made a careful study of the photographs of the body: the angle of the bullet track—downward through the neck—was indeed compatible with the high perch from which Oswald shot the President.

And, finally, I satisfied myself that the locations of the bullet holes in the back of the body and in the back of the coat and shirt were not so far apart as to be irreconcilable. They were close enough so that the difference was compatible with the humping up of the jacket and shirt on the back of the President's neck when he waved. Numerous photographs were found that showed his jacket in this configuration in the period just before he was shot.

FIG. 83
page 205

Skull Wound: Official Diagrams Depicted Too Mild a Wound

I now turned my attention to the final and fatal wound—the shot that shattered President Kennedy's skull—and began to study and analyze the evidence spread before me about that massive and terrible wound.

The head wound of entry could be clearly seen in four of the color photographs to consist of an ovoid penetrating wound of the back of the head, about 7 by 15 mm in size, and about 2 cm to the right of the midline, high up above the hairline where the top of the skull was starting to curve forward, the area of the cowlick. This accounted for its ovoid shape, since it was slightly tangential to the surface of the skull. The long axis of this ovoid wound ran in a back-to-front direction. It conformed in position to the hole in the back of the skull seen in lateral X-ray film 2. This position, clearly shown in the photographs, was considerably higher than that depicted in the schematic drawings of the head wounds in the Warren report, since it lay about 10 cm higher than the occipital tuberosity of the skull, rather than just above it. It made it obvious that this bullet came within an inch or two of missing the President's head altogether.

FIG. 86
page 211

Skull Entry Wound Four Inches Higher Than On Official Diagram

The mistake in describing this hole in the skull at a lower level in the official autopsy report clearly resulted from the X-rays and photographs being taken away from the doctors who did the autopsy, and who would have depended on them for accuracy in this type of detailed measurement.

There was a large, sanguineous, everting wound of the front half of the right side of the top of the head, with a very large segment of the top of the right half of the skull and scalp missing, from about the top margin of the frontal bone, back for a distance of approximately 13 cm (five inches) along the bony seam in the midline of the head. This is the wound of exit, and one can see that the bullet must have taken away most of what is called the right parietal bone. The area of this defect would have been mostly (but not entirely) matched by the area of the bone fragments retrieved later from the street, plus an everted skull flap which had not become detached, as nearly as one could tell from the photographs, and which appeared to be everted and hanging down immediately above and in front of the right ear.

Exit Wound in Scalp

The front part of the scalp appeared to have been greatly stretched by the force of the exiting bullet and skull fragments, with a jagged tear across the top of the forehead. One long tear ran along the front side area about one inch above the frontal hairline, extending to the left of the midline. Another tear extended downward and outward to the right temple and then back above the right ear. Still other tears were described in the autopsy report in more detail.

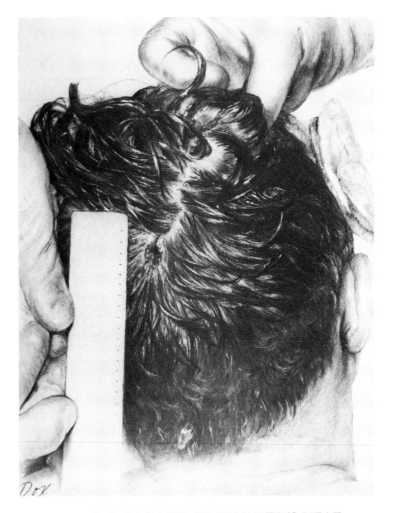

BULLET HOLE IN BACK OF KENNEDY'S HEAD

Drawing made for House of Representatives Select Committee
on Assassinations showing the general shape and location of the
bullet wound in the back of the President's head. It is fairly high
up, where the skull is beginning to curve forward, thus causing
an oval shape to the bullet hole of entry, seen near the ruler. The
bullet hole was actually slightly more toward the right side of the
head than the drawing seems to indicate. Oswald came within a
few centimeters of missing the head altogether. A turned-out flap
of skull can be seen in front of the right ear. A small tab of fat is
stuck on the outer hairs at the very bottom of the hairline in the
rear. *(National Archives)*

Fig. 86

Large Segment of Skull Gone at Right Front

Fig. 87
page 213

The front edge of the scalp defect appeared to correspond approximately with the front edge of the large bony defect in the top of the skull and probably reflected the explosive outward force as the disrupted, powerful bullet fragments exploded the three skull fragments forward and upward for a distance of thirty or forty feet, as can be clearly seen starting in frame 313 of the Zapruder motion picture. The eversion and then contraction of these flaps of expanded and everted scalp are visible for seven frames (313 through 319) of the Zapruder movie.

This is a familiar phenomenon with high-speed bullets that strike the head. The configuration and separation of these flaps of scalp could be caused only by skull fragments from the exploding head traveling upward, forward, and slightly to the right, and in no other direction. Their magnitude was decidedly in keeping with the very powerful ammunition used in Oswald's rifle.

Actual X-rays Showed More Realistic Shattering Effect

Fig. 88
page 213

Another question in my mind, as I perused the restricted materials, was why the official sketch of Kennedy's head wound, placed in the Warren Commission report, contained no suggestion of the severe skull fracture lines that such a heavy, high-speed military rifle bullet would have been expected to create, not only in the top of the skull, but also in its base. Seeing the actual X-rays convinced me that the configuration and magnitude of such cracks were indeed such as one would expect from this

Figs. 76, 77
page 199

high-energy bullet. In fairness to Dr. Humes and Dr. Boswell, who wrote up the autopsy under rushed, harassed, and restricted conditions without the help of the excellent photographs or the X-rays they had ordered taken so carefully for reference purposes, their written autopsy description does mention these cracks. In his later, more detailed testimony before the Warren Commission, Humes stated that these cracks were so numerous and so severe that the fragments of the skull came apart in his hands, so that little or no sawing of the calvarium was needed to remove the brain.

Thus, I was convinced that the extent, severity, and character of the scalp and skull wounds were compatible (severe enough) with those to be expected from a high-speed military-rifle bullet.

Artist Not Permitted to See the Body or the Photographs of It

The 1968 panel of forensic pathologists and a top roentgenologist had described the skull fractures in even more detail. Here again, one might

SECOND BULLET STRIKES PRESIDENT'S HEAD

Frame 313 of the Zapruder movie (top) shows the moment of impact of the second bullet to strike Kennedy (in the back of the head). Fragments of his skull and a cloud of brain tissue can be seen, driven forward and up, away from his head, by the impact of the bullet. The pieces of skull can be seen ten or twelve feet in the air in frame 313, but they flew thirty or forty feet in the air during our experimental replications of this event (bottom) and probably flew as high as this in Dallas. The cloud of vaporized brain tissue that occurred in our experiments was so large that it is not surprising that, in the actual event, the motorcycle police escort, just behind the car, rode forward into this cloud of exploded brain tissue, which wet their fronts as it descended. Governor and Mrs. Connally both spoke in their testimony about being spattered with Kennedy's brain tissue, in fragments as large as a fingernail. *(Top: Copyright © 1967 by LMH Company. All rights reserved. Bottom: J. K. Lattimer)*

Fig. 87

SEVERE SKULL FRAGMENTATION FROM KENNEDY-TYPE BULLETS

X-rays of the tops of several skulls show the degree of fragmentation caused in each instance by the bursting effects of the high pressures within the simulated brains caused by 6.5 mm Carcano fully jacketed military bullets. *(J. K. Lattimer)*

Fig. 88

conjecture that perhaps the diagrams in the Warren Commission report, while official, were purposely made less revealing to avoid shocking the public and, especially, the family of the President. It was apparent (and acknowledged by him) that the artist drew them from instructions and without the advantage of seeing the body, the photographs, or the X-rays.

Skull Wound of Entry Cone-shaped

Although the back of the skull retained its rounded contour, the X-rays revealed not only the multiple cracks but also a slight depression of the lower margin of the wound of entry in the skull. The wound of entry in the bone was beveled into a typical cone shape, clearly indicating that the bullet had entered from the rear of the skull. A similar, rounded nick in the upper border of the frontal bone, on the right, was also beveled in a forward direction, suggesting a wound of exit.

Radiating downward and outward from the margins of the large defect in the top portion of the skull were several enormous cracks, some of which extended to the base of the skull, plus numerous others into the floor of the anterior and middle fossa on the right, and another which extended outward into the left side of the calvarium from the margin of the major skull defect superiorly. Still other cracks extended outward from the wound of entry on the back of the head. It was undoubtedly these very large fracture lines that gave the "abnormal mobility of the underlying bones" of the frontal region, which Dr. Humes mentioned in his handwritten autopsy report (given on page 33 of volume 17 of the Warren Commission hearings). The configuration of these fracture lines supported the thesis that the President was struck by a high-powered rifle bullet (rather than some other, less powerful, type of bullet, such as from a pistol) and that the bullet entered the skull from the rear and exited from the top front.

The X-rays of the head taken before the start of the autopsy revealed at least thirty-five small metal fragments, mostly less than 1 mm in diameter, scattered throughout the right side of the top of the head. The largest was a 6.5 mm rounded fragment sheared off and stuck on the sharp margin of the bone at the wound of entry in the back of the skull. All of the metal fragments were confined to the right side of the brain area and all the fragments were above an imaginary line drawn from the wound of entry through the top of the frontal sinus. Their configuration was in keeping with the track of a bullet entering at the rear of the right side of the skull, near the midline, disrupting and exiting from the front of the head on the right. It was compatible with no other direction. There were no bullet fragments in the left side of the skull to indicate a transverse bullet wound, as from the front right.

FIG. 89
page 215

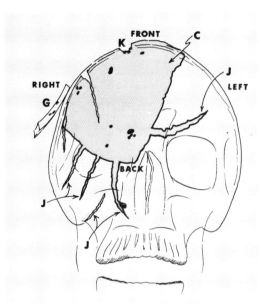

LATTIMER DRAWING FROM
ACTUAL X-RAY OF PRESIDENT
KENNEDY'S HEAD

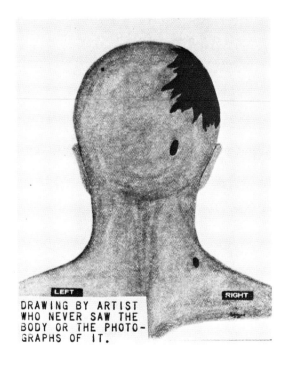

DRAWING BY ARTIST
WHO NEVER SAW THE
BODY OR THE PHOTO-
GRAPHS OF IT.

LOCATIONS OF THE BULLET FRAGMENTS IN THE PRESIDENT'S HEAD

The diagrammatic sketch (top), made from an A-P X-ray of Kennedy's head, shows that the locations of all the metallic fragments were confined to the right side of his brain case, and that there were no wounds not connected to the principal wound in the right side of the head. Letters identifying various components of the wound are correlated with the letters in figure 90. The official Warren Commission diagrammatic sketch is below. *(Top: J. K. Lattimer; bottom: National Archives)*

Fig. 89

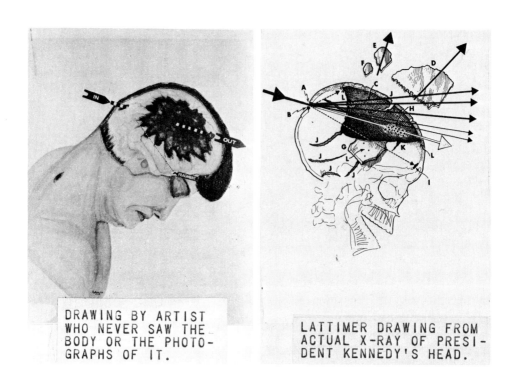

DRAWING OF KENNEDY HEAD WOUND
BASED ON THE ACTUAL X-RAYS (right)
COMPARED WITH OFFICIAL DIAGRAM IN
WARREN COMMISSION REPORT (left)

The diagrammatic drawing on the right clarifies the relative sizes and positions of the various components of the wound, the locations and approximate sizes of the bullet fragments in the tissues, and the magnitude of the damage. It shows that the extent of the damage to the head was appropriate to the great power of the weapon the Warren Commission alleged was used by Oswald. The components are:

A. Wound of Entry. The ovoid wound of entry was fairly high up on the back of the skull, well above the hairline, where the skull starts to curve forward, and about 10 cm above the occipital tuberosity. (Oswald came within a few centimeters of missing the President.) The bone at the lower margin of the hole was depressed slightly, and the wound on the inner side of the skull was characteristically larger than the wound in the outer layer (cone-shaped), as one would expect from a wound of entrance in the back of the skull. Large cracks in the skull radiated from this point.

B. Bullet Fragment Shaved Off by Skull Edge. A fragment (6.5 mm diameter) of the bullet was sheared off by the sharp edge of the thick bone of the skull

Fig. 90

216

and was embedded in the margin of the wound of entrance. Similar to the shaved-off bullet fragment in Lincoln's head (although a bit smaller), this fragment was the largest one left in Kennedy's head.

C. Large Wound of Exit in Top of Skull. A large, roughly pentangular area of the skull (about 15 cm by 13 cm) was carried away by the force of exiting fragments of the disrupted bullet.

D, E, F. Fragments of Skull (as in fig. 61). Three fragments of skull picked up in the street in Dallas accounted for a majority of the area of bone that was missing, and were probably the fragments seen leaving the head in a forward, upward direction in frame 313 of the Zapruder movie of the shooting. (See fig. 87.)

G. Everted Flap of Skull and Scalp. An additional flap of skull appeared to be turned outward and was hanging down in front of and above the right ear but had not become detached. It had three tiny bullet fragments embedded in it, each about 1 to 2 mm in size.

H. Cluster of Fragments. An elongated (4 cm) cluster of about nineteen tiny fragments of bullet in the front of the head was scattered along a line from the front edge of the large head wound of exit, back in the direction of the wound of entrance. Four or five similar tiny bullet fragments were embedded in the bone near the front edge of the wound of exit and a half-round 1 cm notch in the corner of the largest loose fragment of skull also had a crescent of tiny metallic particles surrounding it.

I. Bullet Fragments in Front of Brain. The second largest metallic fragment (7 mm by 3 mm, but crescentic) had come to rest in the front margin of the brain just above the top of the frontal sinus on the right. Neutron activation analysis revealed that this fragment came from the same bullet that struck the inside of the car's windshield and fell into the front seat. Several other tiny bullet fragments were scattered between the wound of entry and the wound of exit. There were no metallic fragments on the left side of the brain case. All the metallic fragments on the right side were above a line between the wound of entry and the top of the frontal sinus, and the majority were in the front and top of the brain case.

J. Huge Skull Fracture Lines. Multiple huge fracture lines extended from the margins of the large wound of exit, and others from the wound of entrance. These were compatible with the great force exerted by a heavy (160 grain) high-speed (2,200 feet per second) military bullet on a thick part of the skull, and to have not found them would have raised doubts that Kennedy might have been shot with some other, less powerful, type of weapon. These multiple, devastating fractures in the base of the skull were very much in keeping with the type of weapon used by Oswald.

K. Notch in Front of Skull Wound.

L. Tiny Bullet Fragments Scattered Through Head. Other fragments flew high enough to go over the windshield, while still others struck the inside of the windshield and fell into the front seat of the automobile.
(Left: National Archives; right: J. K. Lattimer)

Fig. 90 *(continued)*

Row of Metallic Fragments in Brain, between Back and Front Wounds

Fig. 90
page 216

There was one cluster of about nineteen tiny metal fragments, each about the size of a grain of sand, which, while confined to the front third of the head, were arranged roughly in a line that would pass, if extended posteriorly, through the wound of entry in the one direction and through the lower margin of the large skull defect in the anterior direction if the line were extended forward. There were about six slightly larger metal fragments measuring 1 to 3 mm in diameter in the region of the posterior margin of the large skull defect and scattered through the brain tissue. There were three more tiny fragments about 1 mm in diameter, which might have been embedded in the flap of skull that was hanging outward near the right ear. The second largest metal fragment, measuring about 7 mm in length by 3 mm in width and roughly crescentic in shape, had come to rest at the front margin of the right frontal sinus. There was an additional cluster of about a dozen very tiny (1 to 3 mm) fragments of metal embedded in one corner of the largest fragment of skull, which was picked up from the street.

Huge Skull Wound of Exit Had Cone-shaped Corner

Fig. 91
page 219

There was a rounded beveled cone-shaped defect in this same corner of this largest skull fragment, around which these dozen or so metal fragments were embedded. The margin of the frontal bone, at its right end, had a similar rounded beveled notch about 1 cm wide. Although there was no immediate way to prove an association, these rounded beveled defects or notches would have matched the approximate size of either the partial bullet jacket fragment (WCC exhibit 569) found on the floor of the presidential automobile along with some smaller particles, or the partial bullet fragment (WCC exhibit 567) found on the front seat of the presidential car. All of these fragments from the President's head and from the car came from the same bullet, as demonstrated by the 1978 activation analysis.

Fig. 92
page 221

The brain, when removed, showed a relatively intact left hemisphere, except for some surface hematoma over the frontal gyri adjacent to the main wound. From the right side of the brain, however, it appeared that approximately 70 percent of the right cerebral hemisphere was missing, with only a torn and flattened portion of the base of the right hemisphere remaining. This was compatible with the huge cavities that can be demonstrated to form in soft tissues, such as the brain, in the high-speed photographs taken of bullets passing through soft tissues by the armed forces medical research teams.

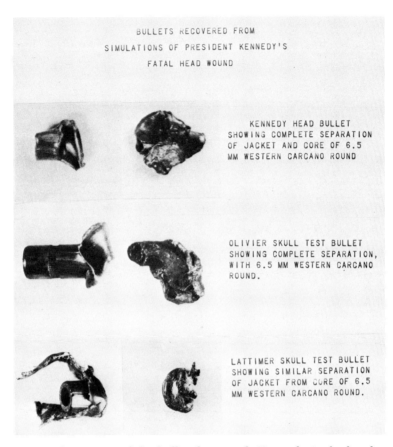

BULLETS RECOVERED FROM
SIMULATIONS OF PRESIDENT KENNEDY'S
FATAL HEAD WOUND

KENNEDY HEAD BULLET
SHOWING COMPLETE SEPARATION
OF JACKET AND CORE OF 6.5
MM WESTERN CARCANO ROUND

OLIVIER SKULL TEST BULLET
SHOWING COMPLETE SEPARATION,
WITH 6.5 MM WESTERN CARCANO
ROUND.

LATTIMER SKULL TEST BULLET
SHOWING SIMILAR SEPARATION
OF JACKET FROM CORE OF 6.5
MM WESTERN CARCANO ROUND.

SKULL BULLETS

Top: The two largest fragments of the bullet that struck Kennedy in the head and separated into an empty copper jacket, left, and the lead core, right. Both fragments bore markings from the rifling of Oswald's rifle, showing that they were fired from this rifle, to the exclusion of all other rifles. Both fragments were found in the front-seat area of the presidential automobile, apparently having struck the inside of the windshield and its frame at greatly reduced velocities before dropping. Other tiny fragments were found in the President's brain case and on the floor under the jump seats of the automobile. Neutron activation tests showed that these all came from this same bullet that struck the President's head. Still other fragments are assumed to have flown over the windshield and struck the ground or pavement ahead of the car.

Middle: Pair of fragments showing complete separation of the jacket and the lead core of one of the bullets fired by Olivier of the Aberdeen Proving Grounds into human skulls in an effort to reproduce Kennedy's wounds.

Bottom: Pair of fragments from one of our experimental shots after passing through a skull.

All three bullets were 6.5 mm Western Mannlicher-Carcano rounds.
(Bottom: J. K. Lattimer; others: National Archives)

Fig. 91

Seventy Percent of Right Side of the Brain Gone

The cerebellum appeared to be intact, despite rumors to the effect that brain fragments resembling cerebellar tissue were seen on the stretcher at Parkland Hospital. There were lacerations of the base of the brain, as confirmed by the testimony of Dr. Humes.

There was one more question—it may seem academic today—to which I felt I must address myself: Was there any sign of a bullet, a missile wound, or missile track in any part of the body other than the head and neck? Although I found none, my studies revealed some surprises, and I shall share them with you.

Examination of the X-rays of the remainder of President Kennedy's body (with the exception of the lower arms, lower legs, hands, and feet) did not reveal any traces of other bullet fragments. No suggestive wounds or deformities of the hands or feet had been recorded by the expert civilian medical teams which had inserted intravenous needles for infusions and transfusions into three of the President's four extremities during the efforts at resuscitation, nor by the surgeons who started to put in the two chest tubes, nor by the men who did the autopsy. The likelihood that an intact bullet or large bullet fragment would travel down one of the limbs into a hand or foot, from the nearest point of entry, such as that in the neck, leaving no trace, seemed unlikely, considering there were no other signs such as bloody streaks, fractures, deformities, or any other evidence to suggest this. No fracture, hole, or bullet track existed to suggest that a fragment of either bullet or bone had exited throught the floor of the brain case, in the direction of the wound low on the front of the neck, for example.

Kennedy's Adrenal Problem and Its Successful Treatment

It was interesting to be able to study the X-rays and other related materials pertaining to the rest of the President's body, considering the many rumors that swirl around such legendary figures. I was particularly interested to see his adrenal-gland areas. These were well visualized on the X-rays of the mid-portion of the body, and no abnormal calcifications could be seen to suggest tuberculosis or earlier hemorrhage of the adrenals. It is my firm belief that the President suffered from spontaneous bilateral adrenal atrophy. The available documentation of his adrenal insufficiency (Addison's disease) is described in the book *The Search for JFK* by Joan and Clay Blair. They indicate that in September of 1947, while visiting in Ireland, he was prostrated by an illness whose symptoms suggested Addison's disease. He was hospitalized in London, and brought back to New York, accompanied by a special nurse, on the *Queen Mary*, then flown by special plane to Boston and placed under the

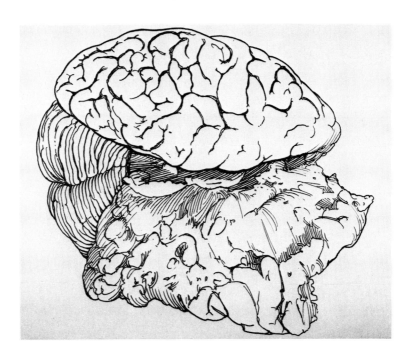

THE BRAIN WOUND

Drawing of Kennedy's brain, after removal, made for the House
of Representatives Select Committee on Assassinations, showing
that a very large portion of the right half had been shot away.
There is no possibility that the President could have survived
this extensive a wound. In effect, he was killed instantly by the
skull bullet. *(National Archives)*

Fig. 92

care of Dr. Lewis M. Hurxthal and Dr. Elmer C. Bartels, endocrinologists of the Lahey Clinic. Dr. Bartels indicated that Kennedy was indeed suffering from Addison's disease, but that he was not then in the crisis stage. The therapy given him by the British doctors had already improved the condition, and further treatment was instituted—standard for 1947—consisting of daily injections of DOCA, a newly developed adrenal hormone-like medication, for a month, followed by the implantation of DOCA pellets. New pellets had to be inserted under the skin every three or four months, but with proper attention to diet and salt and to the intake of other essential chemicals, patients usually did quite well.

When cortisone was developed in 1949, as actual replacement therapy for adrenal hormones, President Kennedy no doubt received it early on, and by 1954 he was taking 150 mg of DOCA pellets, implanted every three or four months, plus 25 mg of cortisone by mouth, every day.

President Kennedy's back had always been weak at the lumbosacral and sacroiliac joints, and with the taking of the cortisone, the ligaments undoubtedly became even more relaxed and he became even more susceptible to pain from any effort. The pain in his back was becoming so bad that he was asking for relief, even if it meant an operation, the risk of which would be considerable, because he was taking cortisone. The susceptibility to infection would be greatly increased. Dr. Hurxthal, Dr. Bartels, and the orthopedists of the Lahey Clinic were against the operation, favoring conservative treatment. Their reluctance to operate might also have been because he had had an unsuccessful attempt at a back operation in Boston in 1944 under navy auspices (although officially performed by civilian doctors). Following this unsatisfactory operation and prolonged physiotherapy, he was discharged from the navy.

Attempts to Fuse His Bad Back

The pain and disability became so severe that in October of 1954 he entered New York Hospital and underwent another attempt at fusion of both his sacroiliac and his lumbosacral joints with the implantation of metal plates. This episode is described in an article in the November 1955 issue of the American Medical Association's *Archives of Surgery*, but it does not mention the patient's name. It said in part:

A man 37 years of age had Addison's disease for seven years. He had been managed fairly successfully for several years on a program of [DOCA] desoxy-corticosterone acetate pellets of 150 mg. implanted every three months and cortisone in doses of 25 mg. daily orally. Owing to a back injury, he had a great deal of pain which interfered with his daily routine. Orthopedic consultations suggested that he might be helped by lumbosacral fusion together with a sacroiliac fusion. Because of the severe degree of trauma involved in these operations and because of the patient's adrenocortical insufficiency due to Addison's disease, it was deemed dangerous to proceed with these operations. However, since this young man would become incapacitated without surgical intervention, it was decided, reluctantly, to perform the operations by doing the two different procedures at different times if necessary and by having a team versed in endocrinology and surgical physiology helping in the management of this patient before, during, and after the operation.

Unfortunately, the wound became infected, and, in February of 1955, Kennedy underwent a second operation, for the removal of the plates; he was not out of the hospital until February 26. Although he nearly died during these two operations, he made it through successfully, thanks to replacement therapy. Such a recovery was quite in contrast to what the outcome would have been even a few years before.

Addison's disease was first described by the famous British physician Thomas Addison, in 1855, who indicated that it was usually a fatal complication. Luckily for President Kennedy, the importance of diet and electrolyte therapy had been recognized by Drs. Loeb and Atchley of New York, in the 1930s, reducing the mortality to about 80 percent. With the development of DOCA in 1947, the prognosis was changed for the better, and by 1949 the development of cortisone brought a spectacular improvement in the outlook for patients with this condition. It made the treatment somewhat akin to that of diabetes, where with adequate medication, patients could lead an almost normal life. One of the foremost authorities of our time, Dr. George W. Thorn, was fond of saying that the use of cortisone plus DOCA for Addison's disease has an almost magical effect. The patient experiences a markedly increased sense of well-being, approaching a state of euphoria, accompanied by a real increase in energy, power of concentration, muscular strength, and endurance. The treatment also causes a marked improvement in appetite and an increased feeling of warmth of the skin, and, as most patients discover, cortisone markedly increases sexual desire.

Before 1944, about half the American patients with Addison's disease had adrenal glands that had been destroyed by tuberculosis of those glands; the other half suffered from spontaneous atrophy of their adrenal glands. Since 1946, the use of new techniques to both prevent and cure tuberculosis has diminished its incidence and destructive effect in the United States. In President Kennedy's case, a careful examination of his chest X-rays showed no evidence of any tuberculous scar or focus in the lungs, and the X-rays of his adrenal-gland areas showed no calcifications or other findings that might indicate tuberculosis of his adrenal glands.

Adrenal Glands Atrophic

At the autopsy, his adrenals were found to be tiny nodules of brownish tissue, the size of a cluster of a few match heads, rather than having the general appearance, color, and dimensions of a rather large fried oyster (minus its shell) of greatly flattened pyramidal shape, which is the expected size and configuration of each normal adrenal gland. Some of this atrophy was, of course, inevitably added to by the many years of substitution therapy with the cortisone that had kept him alive. Kennedy's treatment was then managed by Dr. Ephraim Shorr, of New York Hospital, and administered under the direction of Dr. Janet Travell, who left New York Hospital and moved to Washington to become the President's official physician. In addition, her course of exercises and therapy for painful trigger spots in Kennedy's back was much appreciated by him. It kept him mobile and rehabilitated him in positively dazzling style.

This example of the conquest of a formerly fatal disease is such a superb illustration of one of the great medical triumphs of our era that it is still to be hoped that the Kennedy family will relent in its reluctance to permit the doctors involved—including Dr. Hurxthal, Dr. Bartels, and Commanders Humes and Boswell, who examined the adrenal glands in detail at the time of the autopsy—to describe officially the treatment involved.

It seems entirely probable that the severe stress under which Kennedy was placed during the weeks after the sinking of P.T. 109 may have placed such a strain on his somewhat weakened adrenals that it hastened their atrophy. That he was able to swim competitively in college and to achieve the feats of swimming and rescuing of one of his older and severely burned crewmen is a strong indication that at that time he certainly was not yet suffering from severe adrenal insufficiency.

A Plea for Release of President's Adrenal Success Story

I would like to say once again that, for the benefit of other sufferers from adrenal insufficiency, Dr. Humes and Dr. Boswell should be authorized to describe the histology and pathology of the President's adrenal glands in detail, to demonstrate that even the grinding pressures of the presidency can now be overcome by people with this formerly fatal condition. I think it should be recognized that the President's triumph over his long-term adrenal insufficiency is one of the most encouraging success stories of modern medical science, since it was only with President Kennedy's generation that competent treatment for this condition was evolved from the laboratory efforts of American medicine's golden research era. This was the time during which both government and private research money was made available to the American research establishment in a way that brought forth some of our most fabulous conquests of diseases. This occurred before excesses of government regulation brought about the current suppression of medical research initiatives here. Now it is the fashion among politicians *not* to support medical research at the level that brought about cures of polio and TB and adrenal insufficiency. That President Kennedy was not only able to carry on his duties as president but also to conduct them with verve, style, and flair unsurpassed in modern times would do much to bolster the courage of other young people with this condition. The fact that through it all, his libido and his hormones obviously continued to flow at a high level, despite the condition and thanks to its treatment, would be of great value in supporting the morale of other victims of this same disease.

No Evidence of Tuberculosis Found

Not only did I find no calcifications in the lungs or adrenals, but the kidneys, mesentery, spleen, and prostate areas were also free of any calcifications that might have indicated previous tuberculosis. The costal cartilages, however, were calcified considerably more than usual. There was an irregular, slightly globular soft-tissue density, 10 cm in diameter, overlying the left upper quadrant of the abdomen, near the midline. The nature of this was not clear, but from its location it could have been gastric or intestinal. The autopsy report described no pathology in these areas. It did not resemble an adrenal tumor. There was no abnormal density of the detrusor muscle, as from a rumored vesical neck contracture. The grinding surfaces of his molars all bore thin metal inlays, but not quite like those in people who grind their teeth while asleep. There was also an old appendectomy scar on the right lower quadrant of the abdomen and a graft donor scar on his right hip.

The front-to-back X-ray of the sacroiliac and lumbosacral areas showed that in the bodies of the last lumbar (lowest) vertebra and the first sacral segment there was some loss of bony detail, although the bony landmarks (posterior spines and transverse processes) of all the lumbar vertebrae were still visible. The joint space at L5-S1 was not visible in this projection and might have been fused during the two earlier back operations on this area.

Metallic Particle in Sacroiliac Area

There was one tiny, elongated, crescent-shaped 3 mm metallic particle over the left side of the body of the first portion of the sacrum, about an inch and a half from the midline. This was denser and more sharply defined than the irregular metallic bullet fragments in the head. It seemed likely that this represented a tiny flake of residue from the fixation devices or from the type of vitallium Wilson plate that was said to have been used during his operation for spinal fusion and then removed at a later operation. There was a second round shadow of lower density, about an eighth of an inch in diameter, whose density resembled a retained droplet of the contrast medium more than it did a nylon lock-nut insert, the two likeliest possibilities, overlying the right side of the body of the first segment of the sacral bone, about three-quarters of an inch from the midline. Comparisons with various test objects were

FIG. 93
page 227

made. Although it was the correct diameter for a lead shot, it was not dense enough for this.

Neither of these tiny items should have caused any problems, and both could have been residuals from any of the three operations he is said to have had through the same scar, the last for the removal of complex metal fixation devices from scarred or infected tissues. I am indebted to orthopedists Dr. Frank Stinchfield and Dr. Keith McElroy for their opinions on these points. The joint space between L5 and S1 was not visible on the single front-to-back X-ray of this area, and since there were no lateral, oblique, or other X-ray views of this area, it was impossible to make any further observations about Kennedy's spinal condition. Certainly none of these findings suggested a rifle, shotgun, or pistol bullet wound of the sacral area.

In addition to the X-ray findings, there were other evidences (midline lumbar scars and bone donor site on the skin of the right thigh) of the three operations that were attempts to stabilize his lower spine and his sacroiliac joints. The President was wearing a special canvas brace with metal stays to support his lumbosacral area. The brace contained, in a pocket in its back, a thick, stiff, ovoid plastic pad with laces over it, presumably to supply the added pressure over the lumbosacral area that gives relief to many sufferers from low-back pain. On this occasion, the President had bound himself even more firmly, with a six-inch Ace bandage, over abundant extra pads in addition to the usual laces and straps.

It might be conjectured, as said earlier, that this added rigidity kept his body from crumpling downward after the first wound, where he might have been out of the view of Oswald's telescopic rifle sight. Instead, the President's torso remained upright, allowing Oswald to zero in on the back of his sagging head.

Having digested and analyzed all the materials made available to me, and having perused my several years' worth of notes and study and made as many deductions as I could, I felt that I had answered many of the questions that were in my mind. My findings revealed no gross incompatibilities with the concept that two high-speed rifle bullets hit the President, both fired downward and from the rear, as from the sixth floor of the Texas Book Depository building, and that, after all, the severity of the skin, scalp, and skull wounds was indeed compatible with the type of very powerful ammunition used by Oswald. There were no signs of bullets, bullet wounds, or bullet fragment tracks through the President's body running in any other location or direction, such as transversely, or from the front, to indicate bullet hits from any of these directions upon the President's head, body, or limbs.

The arrangement of the metal fragments and wounds in the scalp and skull were all compatible with a powerful rifle bullet fired from the rear and above, and from no other direction.

These facts, as seen in the photographs and X-rays, satisfied me that

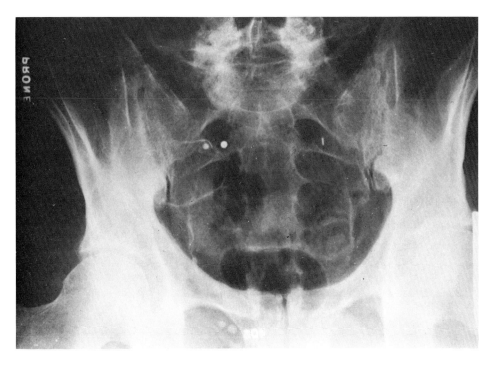

REPRODUCTION OF METAL FLAKE AND X-RAY FLUID
DROPLET IN KENNEDY'S SACRAL (Lower Back) AREA

X-ray of a test pelvis showing a tiny metallic fragment in the sacroiliac area (right) and two other dots in the other side of the sacroiliac area (left). These experiments were made to determine the nature of similar foreign bodies that could be seen in Kennedy's lower-back (sacral) X-rays. It was our conclusion that the tiny fragment of metal was left over from the removal of the metallic plates and screws used in that area (and later removed) during the attempts to fix Kennedy's lumbosacral and sacroiliac joints, some years before, and that the round dot was X-ray liquid used to make studies of the area many years previously. In any case, neither one appeared to be related to the assassination. *(J. K. Lattimer)*

Fig. 93

the alleged position of Oswald was certainly tenable. The photographs and X-rays of the head, plus the Zapruder movie film, all indicated that the President was struck in the back of the head by a second high-speed missile while his head and torso were bowing forward and his torso already tilting to the left, following the first bullet wound, through his neck. This second bullet entered the back of his skull just to the right of the midline, through a thick part of the skull, and obviously disrupted upon entry, with the edge of the skull shaving off a fragment of the bullet, which remained in or near the margin of the wound of entry, just as with President Lincoln. The disrupted bullet fragments then separated and traversed the top of the brain and exploded detached brain and skull fragments forward and upward through the top part of the right side of the front of the head. Sandlike fragments of this bullet were scattered throughout the right side of the upper and forward parts of the brain case, on the right (and only on the right) side. Another large skull fragment was turned outward to the right but did not detach. The bones of the base of the skull were severely fractured, with huge, long fracture lines extending deeply into the basilar portions of the skull, especially on the right, and causing the abnormal mobility of the bones of the skull commented upon by Drs. Humes, Boswell, and Finck, who did the autopsy. Only after the fragments of his skull flew forward and upward did the stricken President recoil backward and to his left, with a spastic lurch.

There was an unusual amount of calcification of the President's costal cartilages. On X-ray films of these areas, there were no abnormal calcifications or masses in the regions of the shrunken adrenal glands to suggest tuberculosis, hemorrhage, or tumor. Both adrenals were reduced to the size and configuration of a small cluster of match heads.

The President was wearing a special lumbosacral back brace, tightly laced over a semirigid pad and tightly bound to his body with a wide knitted elastic bandage and much padding. This extraordinary support obviously helped to keep his torso upright, rather than permitting him to crumple down out of sight, as did Governor Connally after the first bullet hit him. Kennedy remained sufficiently upright after being hit by the first bullet to enable Oswald to zero in on the back of his head for the second, and fatal, wound.

The study of the autopsy photographs and X-rays, as I have said, helped to answer most of the questions of fact that had remained in my mind about the direction and effects of the two bullets that were known to have hit President Kennedy. Relatively unhurried studies of these materials made it possible for me to take more measurements and to add a few details and reconciliations, as did the 1968 panel, but it brought to light no basic discrepancies in the concepts put forth in the Warren Commission report.

However, there were several questions still unanswered. Why, for example, was the bullet hole in the front of President Kennedy's throat so small if it was indeed a wound of exit? Why did the President's elbows fly up when he was hit in the neck? And why did his body lurch backward and to his left when he was hit in the back of the head? Could both the President and Governor Connally have been hit by the same bullet, or not? Were Oswald and his gun and ammunition incapable of doing what the Warren Commission alleged, or not?

Each of these questions was susceptible to some experimentation and the laboratory tools with which to do it were available. My two sons, who were then seventeen and fourteen, and I undertook some research into these questions, using vacation times and odd moments. Our firing experiments started in earnest about 1967, when we had finally accumulated enough of the correct type of ammunition to proceed with them in depth.

10.

WHY WAS THE WOUND IN THE PRESIDENT'S THROAT SO SMALL?

One of the earliest technical questions raised by those who first saw the President's body as he was rushed to the operating table at Parkland Hospital was "Why was the bullet hole in the front of his neck so small if it was a wound of exit?" Exit wounds are usually large and are ordinarily much larger than wounds of entry.

The size of the hole in the front of Kennedy's neck, as described by Dr. Malcolm Perry before he had to obliterate it by inserting the tracheostomy tube, was only about one-fourth inch in diameter. Some critics of the Warren Commission report seized upon this fact, indicating that it must have been a wound of entry rather than a wound of exit, as the commission had concluded. It is, of course, true that 6.5 mm fully jacketed military Carcano bullets of the type that killed Kennedy usually make a much larger wound of exit than of entrance, in unsupported skin.

The critics pointed out that if the President was shot from the front, Oswald could not have done it alone; conspirators would have been necessary. If this were so, then the Warren Commission's version of a solitary assassin would be discredited.

When newsmen interrogated Dr. Perry, they learned that the throat wound had been small and asked him point-blank if, because of its small size, it *might* have been a wound of entrance. Since Dr. Perry had no information as to the other components of the track of the bullet that caused the hole, he had to agree that it *might* have been a wound of entrance. Because air had been bubbling through the bullet hole in Kennedy's neck, suggesting that the oral endotracheal tube inserted by the anesthesiologist was not working well, Dr. Perry had cut directly across the trachea at the bullet hole to introduce a larger and more tightly fitting endotracheal tube, thus obliterating all signs of the bullet's effect. No photographs were taken of the bullet hole during this frantic attempt to save the President.

Further examination during the subsequent autopsy at Bethesda revealed compelling evidence that the hole in the front of the neck was indeed the exit wound for the bullet that had entered the back of President Kennedy's neck. As I said earlier, the fibers of the cloth of the back of his jacket and shirt were bent inward around the wound of entrance on his back. The skin around the back wound was burned with a blackened rim, in the classic effect of a spinning, high-speed bullet. There were bone fragments from where the bullet had brushed the tip of the transverse process of a vertebra in the area, and there was air in the tissues from the bullet holes through the esophagus and trachea.

The bullet left the front of the President's neck, turning slightly nose-down, as I saw it, creating half-inch-long vertical slits in this shirt immediately below and touching the collar band just to the left of the button. The collar made a strong supporting band around the front of the neck just at the bullet hole. The President's challis necktie was also in place, giving further support for the skin of the area. There was a bloodstain on the knot where blood was carried from the neck out onto the necktie. As we have seen, the bullet then continued downward and forward at about a twenty-degree angle, tumbling or yawing end over end as it traversed the thorax and wrist of Governor Connally, before ending up, now traveling completely backward, embedded in his leg. From this location it was knocked out onto the hospital stretcher.

Nonetheless, skeptics remained unconvinced that the bullet hole in Kennedy's neck could be so small if it indeed was an exit wound from such a powerful bullet. My wartime experiences with bullet wounds led me to believe that the collar band of the President's shirt had probably supported the skin of his neck sufficiently to permit a very small exit wound in the skin. This seemed so logical that I proposed in 1972, in an article in *Resident & Staff Physician*, that this was the answer to the problem of the smallness of the bullet hole. Although this was a logical assumption, I felt that I could not be absolutely sure that it was the explanation unless I reproduced a series of such wounds under controlled experimental conditions to be sure that was actually what happened. I therefore decided to set up a duplication and see what did happen when you fired such a bullet through necks that had just such a collar and necktie on each of them, under varying conditions.

It was apparent that no one else was doing, or even anticipating doing, any experiments of this type. Aware that surprises sometimes occur and that you can never be sure what is going to happen until you try it yourself, several times, very carefully, I started gathering the huge carful of gear it would take to set up the experiments under safe and unhurried conditions.

Fig. 84
page 206
I had already examined President Kennedy's shirt in detail at the National Archives and knew that the fabric and the thread holding the collar button were in new condition, or of high quality and excellent strength.

Experiments with Mock-ups of Neck and Shirt

I made appointments with Michael Macfarlane, my laboratory assistant, now a medical student, and the firing range custodians, to be sure that there would be no conflicts. I checked everything on my long list of equipment once again, to be sure that everything worked and nothing was missing. Then I consulted my friend the butcher at the Fort Lee A & P, to be sure he would have on the chosen day a large number of legs of fresh pork with the skin still on. The skin of pork legs is similar to human neck skin. I dissected out the bone, leaving the cylindrical configuration of the outer skin undisturbed, and then compressed each into a neck-like cylinder that would accommodate a size-sixteen collar and tie, like the one Kennedy had been wearing on November 22, 1963. I tried one experimental neck fashioned from a large turkey breast, with the skin still attached and the bones removed, but I found the pork legs more like human necks. A sample neck, mounted on the firing stand in front of
Fig. 94
page 233
the bullet trap is seen in figure 94. I then aligned a bullet trap on the far side of each of these necks, with its face at the same distance that Governor Connally was sitting in front of Kennedy, in order to determine the imprint of each bullet on the simulation of Connally's skin.

We set up movie and still cameras and shrugged on protective armor, since we might be exposed to a ricocheting bullet or lethal flying fragment of bone. Then the laborious process of arranging the precise angles at which the gun would be fired, to produce wounds exactly like those at Dallas, were calculated. I fired fully jacketed military bullets from sub-lots 6000 and 6001, made by the Western Cartridge Company and belonging to the same lots of ammunition used by Oswald, into the back of each of these shirted necks at an aiming point determined to be approximately at the same level as the hole in the back of Kennedy's neck. I used a 6.5 mm Mannlicher-Carcano carbine of the same model as that used by Oswald (model 91-38), with the identical type of Ordnance Optics Company telescope, sling, and steadying arrangements that he had used. Only the distance was different; ours was shorter than at Dallas, to insure that each bullet struck the exact spot we wanted to hit.

After each shot, the shedding of the armor, the rushing to see what had happened, the distant and close-up photographing, the measuring, the labeling of the specimens, the packaging of fragments for later laboratory and X-ray analysis, the recording of the data, all required a great deal of time. A new shirt and a new necktie then had to be fitted to the next "victim," and new measurements and new angles had to be established before the next shot. Sometimes we were interrupted by

TEST APPARATUS FOR REPRODUCING AND
STUDYING THE KENNEDY NECK WOUND

Pork necks or thighs with all bone removed were mounted to accommodate size-sixteen shirt collars and neckties. A bullet trap (ashcan at right) filled with mechanic's waste and fabric was placed with its entrance exactly the same distance away as Connally's back had been at Dallas. Before each shot a new disk of cardboard, with or without a mohair jacket over it, and with or without "Connally bones" behind it, was mounted at the front of the bullet trap to represent skin. Aiming points and angles at which the bullets would strike the backs of the shirts were adjusted as needed. Still and motion pictures were taken with a camera like Zapruder's. The same stand and bullet trap were used for the skull wound experiments. *(J. K. Lattimer)*

Fig. 94

thundershowers and sometimes for the spraying of all hands with mosquito repellant. We soon learned that we had to start very early in the morning to get even a few experiments done during a single day.

Collar Support of Skin

FIG. 95
page 235

FIG. 96
page 237

FIG. 97
page 238

FIG. 84
page 206

FIG. 85
page 206

FIG. 96
page 237

FIG. 97
page 238

The first neck, with shirt and tie on, was tilted so that the bullet exit hole in the front of the neck was one-fourth inch below the lower border of the band of the shirt collar. At the distance set, the collar provided only partial support to the skin. Although the exit hole in the skin was small (approximately one-fourth inch in diameter), the skin cracked open moderately for a half-inch on each side of the quarter-inch bullet hole. The bullet then passed through the center of the knot of the necktie, only slightly to the left of the midline, creating a large ragged hole, somewhat larger than the nick in the left side of President Kennedy's necktie. It should be noted that this tie was silk, whereas Kennedy's necktie was a challis by Christian Dior. The bullet then tumbled vertically as it struck the back of our Connally target, which was placed twenty-eight inches away. The bullet was traveling almost exactly sideways, nose down, by the time it reached the target, as can be seen by the imprint of the bullet left on the skin of our Connally simulation.

The second neck, also with shirt and tie on, was tilted to the exact angle President Kennedy had been in. My aiming point on the back of this shirt was at approximately the same level as the entrance hole on the back of Kennedy's body, but the tilt of this neck was adjusted one-quarter inch, so that the wound of exit of this bullet was just *at* the lower border of the band of the shirt collar. It created a vertical slit, one-half inch long, starting at the lower edge of the shirt collar band, exactly like the slit in the shirt worn by the President. At this location, the collar band provided more support for the underlying skin, and the exit wound was *very* small, measuring only one-fourth inch in diameter, without any bursting or cracking of the skin whatsoever. This bullet continued on, to brush the left side of the necktie knot, making a small nick in the left side of the knot exposing the lining. This was similar to what had happened to Kennedy's necktie, even though this again was a silk, rather than a challis, necktie. This bullet also then tumbled, nose down, and by the time it struck the face of the bullet trap, at the distance Connally was seated in front of Kennedy, it, too, was tumbling vertically and traveling almost exactly sideways.

On a third shirted neck, the collar was buttoned but the necktie was left off. My aiming point was again placed on the back of the neck, at the appropriate level where the bullet first struck Kennedy's skin. This neck was tilted so that the bullet hole of exit in the shirt was one-half inch down from the margin of the collar band (an additional quarter-inch farther away from the collar band than with the first shirt, and only slightly to the left of the midline). At this greater distance from the band

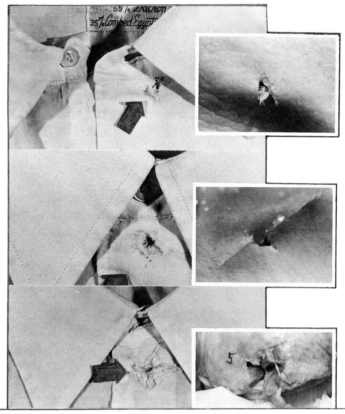

TOP EXIT HOLE IS EXACTLY LIKE THAT IN JFK'S
SHIRT, AND EXIT WOUND IN SKIN IS VERY SMALL.
AS EXIT HOLE MOVED DOWN, FARTHER AWAY FROM
SUPPORTING COLLAR BAND, THE WOUND-OF-EXIT
IN THE SKIN GREW LARGER AND LARGER.

THE SMALL NECK WOUND

The smallness of the wound in the front of Kennedy's neck has
been a point of debate from the very beginning. Critics claimed
it was so small that it must have been a wound of entrance, implying another shooter firing from the front. Experimental
studies, reported here for the first time, revealed that the support
of the President's collar band was undoubtedly the reason the
wound of exit on the front of his throat was not larger. As this
support was moved away, the exit wound became larger and
larger. *(J. K. Lattimer)*

Fig. 95

FIG. 95
page 235

FIG. 96
page 237

of the shirt collar, the collar provided little or no support to the skin, and a large funnel-shaped wound of exit occurred.

This bullet also tumbled vertically as it left the body, and it too was traveling almost sideways, nose down, when it struck our simulation of Connally's back.

I was able to deduce from these experiments that the size of the exit hole in the skin was indeed directly dependent upon the degree of support from the collar band, since the hole was very small if the exit wound was just at the collar band (as was the case with President Kennedy), but if the wound of exit was moved another quarter-inch down, away from the support of the collar band, the small wound of exit was accompanied by substantial cracks in the skin on both sides of the bullet hole.

If the wound of exit was moved down still further, to a location a full half-inch below the edge of the collar band, as in our third shirted-neck experiment, then the wound of exit became much larger. The lack of the slight support of a necktie on this preparation may have added slightly to the large size of the exit wound, but the neckties did not seem tight enough to give much support.

Between each of these experiments, we fired a control bullet from the same gun through a neck with no shirt or tie to support the skin, using cartridges from the same lot of ammunition. On the first bare neck, the wound of entry was small and punctate, with the usual blackened rim burned by the rapidly spinning bullet. The wound of exit in the unsupported skin was large and funnel-like, with jagged stellate tears, approximately one inch in diameter, in toto. This bullet also then tumbled ninety degrees and entered the back of our Connally simulation going directly sideways, but nose down. On the second unsupported neck the bullet made a punctate wound of entry and also a small wound of exit only slightly larger than the wound of entrance. This was the only bullet of the six that did not tumble, and it also made only a punctate, quarter-inch wound in the skin of our Connally target, as shown on target disk

FIG. 96
page 237

four as bullet hole 4A.

These experiments demonstrated that the reinforcement of the skin of the front of a neck by the proximity of the strong band of a shirt collar and necktie supported the skin to the extent that only a small puncture hole of exit resulted. If, however, the wound of exit was moved downward, away from the supporting collar band, one-fourth of an inch at a time, the resulting exit wound, from the same type of bullet, grew progressively larger and became progressively more funnel-shaped, stellate, and jagged. The size of the exit wound was dependent primarily on the amount of support from the collar and tie and was very sensitive to slight changes in the distance from the collar band. That the bullet was beginning to tumble or yaw when it left the neck of the President did not enlarge the size of the wound in the skin. Even when the exit hole was no larger than the diameter of the bullet used (one-quarter inch), the exit

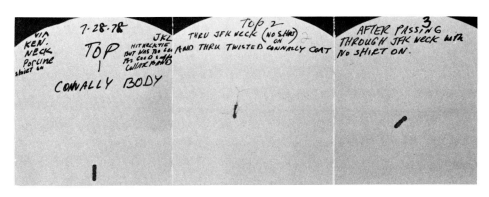

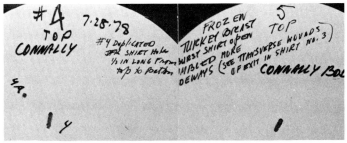

CARCANO BULLETS TUMBLED END OVER END AFTER PASSING THRU JFK NECKS AND STRUCK THE GOV. CONNALLY SIMULATIONS GOING ALMOST SIDEWAYS. 4 TUMBLED VERTICALLY, 1 HORIZONTALLY. ONLY ONE (4A) DID NOT TUMBLE. MOST OF THE BULLETS WERE DEFLECTED A BIT DOWNWARD.

TUMBLING OF CARCANO BULLETS AFTER STRIKING NECKS

Five cardboard skins simulating Connally were placed the same distance from Kennedy's neck as Connally was seated in the automobile in front of the President. The Carcano bullets that made the holes in these targets had passed through a simulation of Kennedy's neck, striking only soft tissues. Five of the six bullets tumbled end over end after leaving the neck and struck Connally's skin traveling almost sideways. Only one bullet failed to tumble (4A). The level of this bullet in Connally's skin marks the level at which all of the bullets would have struck the Governor had they not been deflected by passing through Kennedy's neck. Note that four of the six were deflected downward to a moderate degree, whereas numbers 2 and 4A were not. Four of the bullets tumbled in a vertical plane, whereas number 3 tumbled in an almost horizontal plane. The presence or absence of a shirt collar and necktie made no difference in the amount of deflection or tumbling. Bullet number 4, which caused a near duplicate of Kennedy's neck and collar wound, was deflected downward about two inches and tumbled vertically. These results confirmed our previous observations that these bullets almost always tumbled after passing through a neck. (*J. K. Lattimer*)

Fig. 96

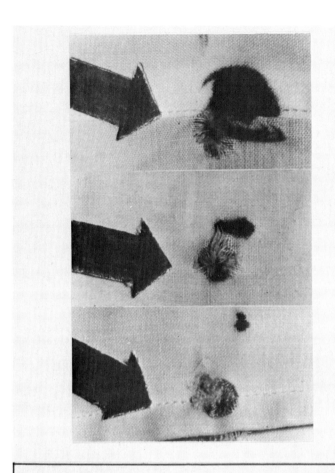

ENTRY HOLES IN BACKS OF ALL SHIRTS
WERE SAME DIAMETER AS BULLET (1/4").
BLACK DOTS ARE AIMING POINTS (WHERE
NECK BULLET STRUCK JFK SKIN).

EXPERIMENTAL BULLET HOLES IN SHIRTS

Entry holes in the back of all the shirts used in our experiments were the same diameters as the bullets (one-fourth inch). The black dots are aiming points (where the actual bullet struck Kennedy). *(J. K. Lattimer)*

Fig. 97

wound in the shirt began to show elongation from top to bottom as the bullet began to nose down when it left the neck.

If Oswald had used expanding bullets like the ammunition employed in hunting large animals, then the wounds of exit would have been *very* much larger than the wounds of entrance. Hunters use expanding bullets in an attempt to kill each animal as abruptly as possible, to end its suffering and to make it more surely recoverable for meat. The use of expanding bullets with military rifles is forbidden by the Geneva Convention. There is no evidence that Oswald used them, or that he modified his military bullets so that they might expand on contact with soft tissues. The two of his bullets that were recovered intact had not been modified or mutilated in any way. It seems unlikely that Oswald would have risked the impairment in accuracy or penetrating capability that might have resulted if he had mutilated the noses of his bullets in an effort to create an expanding (so-called dum-dum) effect.

These experiments confirmed beyond all of my doubts that the smallness of the exit hole in the front of Kennedy's neck was due to the fact that the skin was supported by a firm collar band, which restrained it from bulging and bursting open ahead of the exiting bullet. The necktie may have given added support, but it fitted so loosely that it did not appear to contribute very much support. If the bullet had not exited from the President's neck just *at* the collar band, the exit wound might have been much larger.

Fig. 95
page 235

In short, we demonstrated that the smallness of the wound in the front of the neck of President Kennedy was perfectly compatible with his being shot through the neck from the rear, by Oswald, and did not require the involvement of a second rifleman, shooting from the front.

But still more medical questions remained.

11.

WHY DID THE PRESIDENT'S ELBOWS FLY UP WHEN HE WAS HIT?

One widely held misconception about the shooting of the late President Kennedy is that the first bullet to strike him, which traversed his neck, did not cause a lethal wound. The three lengthy, careful reviews I made in 1972, 1973, and 1975 of the X-rays and photographs of Kennedy's body, which were taken at the start of the autopsy, and a detailed study of the Zapruder motion-picture film have led me to a different conclusion.

President's Spine Struck by Neck Bullet

These, plus considerations of the neurosurgical implications (by neurosurgeon Edward B. Schlesinger) and the neurological implications (by the late Houston H. Merritt) of the motions of the President's elbows, have led me to conclude that Kennedy's upper spine was hit by the first bullet that struck him. The sudden upward jerk of his flexed elbows was compatible with some degree of trauma (concussive-contusive), capable of creating an effect on his spinal cord at about the level of the sixth cervical segment, even though the bone may have been struck at a slightly lower level. This was caused by the first bullet, which entered the back of his lower neck on the right side. Five seconds later, the second bullet that struck him destroyed his brain.

Detailed inspections of the X-rays of Kennedy's body, which were taken at the Bethesda naval hospital at the beginning of the autopsy,

Fig. 82
page 203

revealed minimal fragmentation of the bone, without displacement, in the general region of the tip of the transverse processes of one of the vertebrae on the right side of the lower neck. This can be seen clearly in one of the X-rays. Another (oblique) view shows splinters lying just lateral to the spine.

In the other X-ray views of that area of the neck, in which the splinters lie superimposed over the bodies of the vertebrae, they are no longer visible. The fact that they are no longer visible led me to conclude that they are bone, rather than fragments of metal. Metal fragments might have continued to show, because their density is greater than that of bone. Admittedly it is difficult to distinguish between small fragments of metal and bone, and it was the first reaction of Dr. Russell H. Morgan, of the 1968 panel of experts, who discovered them, that they might be metal because they showed up so well. In a personal letter to me, Dr. Morgan agreed, however, that the presence of these fragments, regardless of whether they are bone or metal, indicates that the cervical spine was struck (brushed) by the neck bullet. He wrote: "Regardless of the nature of the opacities, it seems rather clear to me that the bullet that passed through President Kennedy's neck, brushed the cervical spine before emerging in front." The panel of radiologists who again examined the films for the House Select Committee on Assassinations also agreed that the spine had been grazed at least in this general area.

Model Constructed

Fig. 98
page 242

When a row of Carcano 6.5 mm fully jacketed bullets of the type used at Dallas was mounted on a rod of thin plastic and positioned across the necks of various skeletons by my younger son, Gary, now a Columbia Medical School and pathology student, in approximately the same position as the track of the bullet through Kennedy's neck, it was obvious that the course of the neck bullet lay in the vicinity of the tips of the transverse processes of the lower cervical vertebrae, or possibly the uppermost thoracic vertebra, as shown in figures 72 and 82.

Telltale Movements of Elbows

Figs. 99, 100
page 244

In the Zapruder film, it is apparent that Kennedy's elbows are just beginning to fly upward in frame 224, as he is emerging from behind the Stemmons Freeway sign, right in front of Zapruder. It is obvious that he had been struck only a split second prior to this point, because his arms then continued their abrupt upward jerk, to assume a position with the elbows highly elevated, and with both tightly flexed, by frame 235. The reaction is slightly more vigorous by the right arm than the left (the bullet struck him on the right), although the symmetry is impressive. His hands can be seen to fly up to the level of his face. It is clear from this that he was *not* reaching for his throat, as has been stated or surmised so often. This

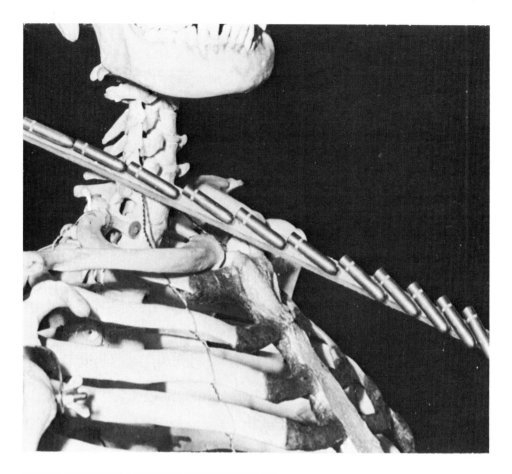

HOW THE TIP OF THE PRESIDENT'S
VERTEBRA WAS STRUCK

It seemed obvious on our first inspection in 1972 that bullet 399 hit the back of Kennedy's neck and grazed the tip of the transverse process of one of his lower cervical or, perhaps, the first upper thoracic vertebra, as in this model. (Tiny fragments of bone are visible on the X-ray of his neck, with some other areas of distortion.) It then exited with a wobble, starting to tumble end over end as a result of traversing the neck. It made holes one-half inch long, in an up-and-down direction, in the front of his shirt, just at the lower edge of his collar band, and grazed his necktie knot, leaving a bloodstained nick in the cloth of the tie. *(J. K. Lattimer)*

Fig. 98

spasmodic contraction lasts for about ninety frames of the ensuing portion of the Zapruder film, or for about five seconds, although after the first second his elbows begin to sag slightly and he begins to tilt a little to his left, with his head bowing forward a bit.

That he did not crumple down in the seat probably was because, as we said earlier, he had bound himself up firmly in a rather wide canvas corset, with metal stays and a stiff plastic pad over the sacral area, which was tightly laced to his body. The corset was then bound even more firmly to his torso and hips by a six-inch-wide knitted elastic bandage, which he had wrapped in a figure eight between his legs and around his waist, over large thick pads, to encase himself tightly, almost like a mummy wrap. He apparently adopted this type of tight binding as a consequence of the painful loosening of his joints around the sacroiliac area, probably a result of his long-continued cortisone therapy.

The effect of the bullet grazing the vertebra was undoubtedly to transmit a sharp concussive-contusive force to the spinal cord at about the level of the sixth or seventh cervical segment. As Dr. William Thorburn showed almost 100 years ago in his classic descriptions of patients with lower cervical cord lesions, trauma to the cord at this level results in the arms assuming a flexed position with the elbows raised. This can be seen in the illustration adapted here from Thorburn's book. Thorburn's patient shown in this illustration had a spinal cord lesion at the sixth cervical segment (C-6), which was clearly demonstrated at autopsy some days later. Thus, in Kennedy's case, we have an almost classic demonstration of what might be called a Thorburn position, indicating a lesion of the spinal cord in the lower neck area.

Fig. 99
page 244

Fig. 100
page 244

The question next arises as to whether the cord below this level would have been damaged so badly by even such a glancing blow on the bone (on a transverse process) that it would be physiologically unable to transmit impulses at the time of the massive brain injury caused by the second bullet, five seconds later.

Naturally we can only speculate as to whether or not the effects of the shock wave that struck the spinal cord sufficiently hard to create a sign, which can also be seen with cord transection at the level of the sixth cervical segment, would have been only transitory and therefore reversible. Nevertheless, because the wound to the cord was not direct, but, rather, an impulse transmitted from a glancing blow on the most distant part (the tip) of an adjacent vertebra, it is certainly conceivable that the spinal cord, although traumatized, might still have been able to respond to the effect on the central nervous system of the brain damage secondary to the massive penetrating, perforative brain injury five seconds later, when most of the right side of the brain was shot away by the second bullet.

The massive cerebral trauma probably was the stimulus for the stiffening of the muscles of the back and the back of the neck, which appeared to assist in pulling Kennedy's sagging torso upright and backward, about

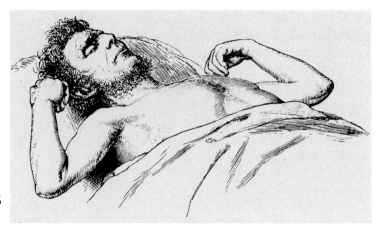

THORBURN'S POSITION

Illustration from Dr. William Thorburn's 1889 article "Cases of Injury to the Cervical Region of the Spinal Cord," showing the peculiar position assumed by the elbows immediately after an injury to the spinal cord in the lower neck region. This was confirmed at autopsy the following day.

This is the same position into which Kennedy's elbows flew after bullet 399 passed through his neck, striking the tip of the transverse process of a vertebra in the lower portion of his neck and obviously transmitting an impulse to his spinal cord to cause this reflex. (*Drawing reproduced by courtesy of Charles Griffin and Company Limited*)

Fig. 99

KENNEDY IN THORBURN'S POSITION

This drawing shows Kennedy's elbows and forearms reflexly elevated and tightly flexed after his spinal cord was jolted severely in the lower cervical region by the transmitted impulse from bullet 399. This bullet struck the tip of one of his vertebrae in the lower cervical region as it went through his neck. His hands are in front of his face. He is not reaching for the bullet hole in his neck, as has been so often alleged. His elbows remained tightly flexed and held high for the next five seconds, until his brain was shot away in frame 313. The spinal trauma probably would have left him quadriplegic, at least for a time. (*J. K. Lattimer*)

Fig. 100

fifty milliseconds after he was struck by the second bullet. This, necessarily, must be speculation, but it seems well within the range of possibility.

Air and Bacteria in Tissues of Neck a Peril

Close inspection of the X-rays of President Kennedy's neck taken at the Bethesda naval hospital at the start of the autopsy showed air in the muscle planes of his neck adjacent to the back of the esophagus and trachea. A large, ragged wound of the trachea had made it impossible for the anesthesiologist to insert a larger endotracheal tube from above, and made necessary the large tracheostomy directly across the bullet wound in the throat to get a larger tube in, during the frantic but futile efforts at resuscitation in Dallas.

The contamination of the severely devitalized tissues along the bullet track by bacteria-laden air from the wounded trachea undoubtedly would have resulted in a severe infection of the neck and mediastinum, a very vulnerable area. Any patient on long-term cortisone treatment, like the President, would have had greatly impaired resistance to infection and greatly impaired healing ability.

If such a patient also suffered even transitory trauma to the cervical portion of his spinal cord from the same bullet, his chances for survival would have been affected unfavorably by that first bullet alone. He probably would have had a period of quadriplegia, even if transitory, thus severely compromising his chances for survival.

Because, five seconds after the bullet hit his neck, a second bullet struck the back of the right side of the President's head, removing almost all of the right side of his brain, that the first bullet also might have brought about his death by infection and sepsis is academic. The atrophy of the adrenal glands and the long-term cortisone therapy, as we have said, would have made the first wound more likely to have caused his death than it would have a healthier person, because of the reduced resistance to infection and the poor healing that cortisone induces.

Fig. 82
page 203

The precision with which the signs of a spinal cord lesion fit with the other evidence (loose bone fragments) that the tip of the transverse process of one of the vertebrae of the lower neck region had been struck by the bullet that traversed the President's neck is very impressive. It makes it seem almost certain that Kennedy sustained a traumatic concussive blow to this spinal cord, which would have added monumental problems to his ability to survive, even if he had not been hit by the second bullet.

In short, the sudden upward jerk of President Kennedy's elbows just after he was shot in the back of the lower part of his neck was characteristic of a traumatic lesion of the spinal cord in the lower neck region.

Fig. 99
page 244

Fig. 82
page 203

Fig. 98
page 242

Thorburn described and illustrated this position of the elbows about 100 years ago in patients whose spinal cord lesions he later pinpointed with precision at autopsy, done a few days thereafter.

The location of the small chips of what we believe is fragmented bone, visible in the X-rays of Kennedy's neck taken just before the start of the autopsy, lies in the general area of the tips of the transverse process of the lower cervical area on the right side. They are in the expected course of the bullet that caused the President's neck wound. Their presence, along with the telltale upward, flexed movement of the President's elbows, is compelling evidence that the bullet hit (grazed or brushed) his spine in this area.

It seems possible that the traumatized spinal cord would later have become edematous at the very least, leaving the President with neurological problems of unpredictable but substantial extent.

In an embarrassed neurological condition, even if slight, it would have been still more difficult for the President to have overcome the severe infection and edema of the devitalized tissues along the bullet track in his neck and mediastinum from the holes in his esophagus and trachea, which almost certainly would have followed his wounds. His resistance to infection, of course, would have been compromised even more severely by the fact that he had adrenal insufficiency, probably some bladder outlet obstruction, and had been on long-term cortisone treatment.

Therefore, it appears all the more conceivable that the President would have died from the first bullet wound to his spine and neck, even if the second bullet had not killed him by removing most of the right side of his brain five seconds later. His adrenal insufficiency and consequent long-term cortisone treatment would certainly have been a disastrous handicap in a race for survival, compounding any possible further effects from the trauma to his spinal cord, such as quadriplegia.

Thus we see that the peculiar spastic upward jerk of the President's elbows was a diagnostic sign of a deadly shock to his spine.

But even this was not the most mysterious medical clue disclosed by the Zapruder movie.

12.

WHY DID THE PRESIDENT'S HEAD LURCH TOWARD THE GUN?

Exactly five seconds after he had shot Kennedy through the neck, Oswald fired again and hit him in the back of the right side of the head, removing practically the entire right side of his brain. The President was killed instantly.

The Second Bullet

In the Zapruder movie, just before the fatal bullet, Mrs. Kennedy can be seen to lean over and look closely into her husband's face. She explained later that she could not understand why he had such a peculiar, quizzical look on his face, or why he had his elbows up with his hands in front of his face. She was asking, "What's the matter, Jack?" with her face just inches away from his, when the second bullet struck the back of his head, causing it to explode with tremendous force. His body and head then can be seen to lurch over backward and to his left, after which he falls slowly down onto the seat where Mrs. Kennedy had been sitting. Recoiling from the explosion and splash of his head, she rose and pivoted to her right, with one knee on the seat, to permit the President to fall down onto the seat. The car jerked forward, precipitating her out onto the lid of the trunk. It then paused momentarily, permitting Secret Service agent Clint Hill to grasp the hand-grip on the left rear fender, which had been pulled away from him by the first forward lurch of the car, so he could climb onto the trunk lid to help her in her own scramble to get back into the seat. He then shielded her and the President with his body from possible additional bullets, as the car started its mad dash toward Parkland Hospital.

Mummy Wrap Keeps Kennedy Upright

The reason Kennedy did not crumple down out of sight behind the seat of the car after his first wound, as Governor Connally did, was that he was wearing a canvas corset with steel stays and a large, oval, plastic pad in a pocket over his sacrum. Like all sufferers from low-back pain, he had learned that by wrapping himself tightly he would be much more comfortable, particularly when he was faced with long periods of standing or sitting during campaign rides, motorcades, and luncheons. Because of this tight support, his body did not crumple after the first bullet struck him; he continued to sit more or less upright, tilting only slightly to his left, with his elbows flexed up, but with his head and shoulders showing over the back seat of the car. In this position, he presented a target amazingly like the head-and-shoulders targets in Oswald's rifle score book from the Marine Corps (which I own). This score book shows that Oswald had scored very well indeed in firing this general type of rifle from a sitting position.

FIG. 70
page 174

FIG. 91
page 219

The presidential car had not yet accelerated and Oswald was able to take five long seconds to draw a careful final bead on the back of Kennedy's head before he pulled the trigger. His bullet struck the President on the right side of the back of his head.

Movements of the President's Head

The five seconds that elapsed between the neck wound and the head wound can be accurately measured by counting the frames of the Zapruder movie. In frames 312 and 313, as the bullet strikes, the President's head can be seen to move very slightly forward, but starting with the next frame, his body and head lurched backward and to his left, even as his elastic scalp bulged and everted in a flash of exposed red tissue and the entire right side of his brain exploded out through the wound of exit on the upper right side of his head. Three large segments of his skull could be seen to fly upward and forward thirty to forty feet into the air.

FIGS. 70, 71
page 174

Mrs. Kennedy recoiled from the explosion, pivoting toward the back of the car and rising, with one knee on the seat, to permit the President to fall over on the seat where she had been sitting, as described above.

Questions about Backward Movement of Head

The backward movement of Kennedy's head, which then occurred, was seized upon by critics of the Warren Commission report and trumpeted with righteous indignation concurrently with the first publicly televised showings of the Zapruder motion picture, in 1975, before national audiences. The critics insisted that his backward lurch toward the left could have been caused only by a second bullet coming from the front of the presidential automobile, which drove the President's head backward and to the left.

248

This question intrigued me, and, in an effort to find out what really does happen when you duplicate the event, my sons and I undertook another series of experiments. Our aim was to discover why the President's head and body *did* move backward if, indeed, he was shot only in the back of the head.

I first undertook to reexamine any evidence that might be relevant to the possibility of a bullet having struck the President's head from the front or right front, based on my previous examinations of the autopsy photographs and X-rays. I reviewed all previous studies and experiments which had been conducted by others, and, of course, I again reviewed the Zapruder movie in great detail. Then we conducted our own experiments, and asked our own questions.

First, we asked if the backward lurch could have resulted from the abrupt acceleration of the automobile. Close scrutiny of the Zapruder movie gave us the answer: a definite no. The car did not accelerate abruptly until several frames *after* the President had lurched backward. Next, we wondered if the lurch could have been at least partly due to a jet-recoil effect from the heavy brain material leaving the front of his head with explosive force. We seemed to be on the right track.

Alvarez Experiments

Dr. Luis Alvarez, a Nobel Prize-winning physicist at the University of California at Berkeley, had been challenged to accept the backward lurch as evidence of a shot from the front. After a little calculation on the back of an envelope, however, he postulated that the explosive escape of heavy semiliquid brain material through a large wound of exit in the front of the head might have some of the propulsive or recoil effect of a jet engine, immediately driving the remainder of the head backward toward the rear of the automobile, and toward the shooter. In cooperation with three of his laboratory colleagues, Sharon Buckingham (who owned a rifle), Don Olson, and Paul Hoch, he undertook a series of experiments, using melons about the size of a human head. He wrapped these with layers of tough adhesive tape containing strong fibers to simulate the human scalp. The melons were set on stands or suspended by straps of tape and were fired into while being photographed from the side with Olson's motion-picture camera, using a remote-control apparatus. The results dramatically confirmed Dr. Alvarez's calculations.

A small jet of liquefied-melon contents escaped from a small wound of entrance; a large mass of heavy, liquefied-melon pulp jetted out the far side through a large wound of exit. This immediately drove the melons forcibly backward off the stand or caused suspended melons to revolve so violently backward and upward around the point of suspension as to tear them completely loose from the restraints. Shots through melons not wrapped with tough layers of simulated scalp did not have this effect. The results of Alvarez's experiments were published in July of 1975 in

Preprint LBL 3884 of the proceedings of the Lawrence Berkeley Radiation Laboratory at the University of California. It was these experiments —which I was permitted to study—that inspired my own.

In reviewing these experiments, it became obvious that, because of the problems in procuring and testing high-powered military ordnance, which is not readily available, there were some aspects of these tests that needed to be repeated, reexamined, and perhaps extended.

First of all, the rifle Alvarez's colleague used fired .30-caliber 30-06 cartridges with an extra charge of powder, which gave it a muzzle velocity of 3,000 feet per second, and the bullets used were the expanding, soft-nosed hunting variety. By contrast, we know that President Kennedy was hit by smaller, 6.5 mm bullets traveling at only about 2,200 feet per second (muzzle velocity) and that two of the bullets—which were recovered and presented by the Warren Commission—had intact jackets and were fully jacketed military bullets, rather than soft-nosed, expanding bullets. The theoretical possibility does exist that Oswald might have slightly mutilated the noses of the other two bullets so that their jackets would open and these bullets might then have acted as soft-nosed, expanded bullets after all. However, there is no evidence to support this theory.

It seemed worthwhile to repeat Alvarez's experiments, but to use fully jacketed 6.5 mm Mannlicher-Carcano cartridges made by the Western Cartridge Company, the same ammunition used by Oswald at Dallas. In addition, I used not just melons but skull components and combinations of melons and skull components and skull-brain simulations to find out if the reactions of these simulated heads would be the same as those demonstrated by Alvarez and his group.

Lattimer Experiments

In 1974 and 1975, my sons and I had conducted a series of experiments using a 6.5 mm Mannlicher-Carcano carbine, model 91-38, serial number C2766, equipped with an Ordnance Optics Company four-power telescope exactly like Oswald's. This was mounted exactly as on the rifle from the same lot (Warren Commission Exhibit 139) that was demonstrated unequivocally by the Warren Commission to have been used to fire both of the bullets recovered from President Kennedy's car and from his body at Parkland Hospital on the afternoon of November 22, 1963. The ammunition used in those experiments was from sub-lot 6000, manufactured by the Western Cartridge Company, of East Alton, Illinois, and verified as being one of the four sub-lots manufactured at the same time as the ammunition used in the killing of President Kennedy.

FIG. 101
page 252

When these bullets were fired into wrapped melons, the melons did indeed move backward off the stand, sometimes rocking preliminarily away. The size of the splash from our melons was not as large or as violent as in the experiments of Alvarez and his group. This may have been because our melons were greener than those of the California-based Alvarez group, which was able to pick its melons when they were riper and had more liquid content. However, it was more likely that the difference in size of splash was because Alvarez's group used soft-nosed bullets, which expanded, transferring much more energy to the inside of the melon. This caused a larger wound of exit and a larger jet of melon contents leaving the melon through the wound of exit, which then drove the melon toward the shooter with more violence.

We again arranged for the use of the range and assembled our long list of materials, including flak vests, rifles, cameras, and specimen-collecting gear for a field experiment. Combinations of human skull tops and melons were tested, and, again, all fell backward off the stand toward the shooter. No melon or skull combination ever fell *away* from the shooter.

Human skulls were then packed with solid melon contents and taped and sewed tightly together with strong tape and thread to simulate the scalp. We fired into these at the same point and at the same angle as the President was struck. The skull wounds produced were strikingly similar to Kennedy's. Again, the skulls fell or jumped off the stand toward the shooter, and large fragments of the top of the skulls flew upward and forward for distances of forty feet or more, just as fragments of Kennedy's skull can be seen to have done in frames 313 through 318 of the Zapruder movie.

FIG. 102
page 254

FIG. 87
page 213

Jet-Recoil Effect

On this occasion also, the backward lurch of our skulls was not as violent as that in the Alvarez experiments, possibly due to the less liquid consistency of the melon contents used to simulate brain tissue and to the fact that we used fully jacketed 6.5 mm non-expanding military ammunition. Alvarez noted that his melons recoiled backward faster than the President's head recoiled. When we repeated these experiments, using more accurate simulations of fresh brain tissue inside the skulls, mixed with white paint for visibility, our bullets struck the simulated heads at the same point on the right upper rear portion as with President Kennedy. The bullets always broke up on striking the skull and then diverged, making a larger wound of exit. The more liquid-like brain tissue then exited explosively, with the more massive amounts exiting through the larger wounds of exit on the front right of the heads. This caused the jet-engine, or jet-recoil, effect, to drive what was left of the heads violently off the stand, toward the shooter, in every one of twelve experiments. What remained of each head ended up on the ground to the left of its original position, in addition to being back toward the gun. A cloud of vaporized brain tissue and fragments flew up in all directions each time. I wish to reemphasize that none of our test objects in these experiments with melons and skulls ever jumped or fell off the stand *away* from the shooter.

FIG. 104
page 257

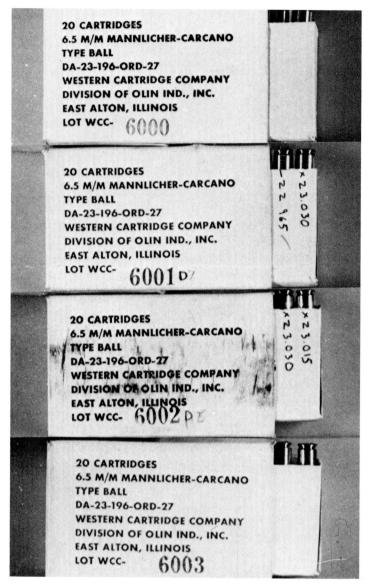

20 CARTRIDGES
6.5 M/M MANNLICHER-CARCANO
TYPE BALL
DA-23-196-ORD-27
WESTERN CARTRIDGE COMPANY
DIVISION OF OLIN IND., INC.
EAST ALTON, ILLINOIS
LOT WCC- 6000

20 CARTRIDGES
6.5 M/M MANNLICHER-CARCANO
TYPE BALL
DA-23-196-ORD-27
WESTERN CARTRIDGE COMPANY
DIVISION OF OLIN IND., INC.
EAST ALTON, ILLINOIS
LOT WCC- 6001 D

20 CARTRIDGES
6.5 M/M MANNLICHER-CARCANO
TYPE BALL
DA-23-196-ORD-27
WESTERN CARTRIDGE COMPANY
DIVISION OF OLIN IND., INC.
EAST ALTON, ILLINOIS
LOT WCC- 6002 P

20 CARTRIDGES
6.5 M/M MANNLICHER-CARCANO
TYPE BALL
DA-23-196-ORD-27
WESTERN CARTRIDGE COMPANY
DIVISION OF OLIN IND., INC.
EAST ALTON, ILLINOIS
LOT WCC- 6003

OSWALD'S AMMUNITION

The cartridges used by Oswald were an excellent American-made Western
Cartridge Company product. Four sub-lots had been manufactured, and we
tested samples from all four. They had excellent consistency of bullet weights
and powder weights. We fired about 700 rounds in our experiments, and various
government agencies fired about 200 more. We had no misfires, nor did the other
groups. They were sold in boxes of twenty, and it seems likely that Oswald was
down to his last four, since no more were found among his possessions. (J. K.
Lattimer)

Fig. 101

FIG. 103
page 256

In his book *The Shooting of John F. Kennedy*, in 1969, Col. William H. Hanson had also mentioned that the "retromovement" of the head could have been due to the jet-engine effect. However, he conjectured that the first of the three shots might have hit President Kennedy a glancing blow on the right anterior part of his skull (which was later shot away completely), thereby creating a weak spot out of which the jet of brain tissue flew more easily, creating the backward motion even more positively. Our experiments demonstrated that the jet-retro-recoil effect could be achieved even without a previous weakening of the anterior part of the head.

If a vessel filled with water is used for such experiments, a weak spot is needed to achieve such a jet-engine effect, as pointed out by Hanson. The larger wound of exit, caused by the diverging courses of the multiple fragments of disrupted bullet, probably provided this relatively weaker area, and all our bullets were either broken up or deformed enough by striking the skulls to make a much larger wound of exit than of entrance.

To catch each bullet, we arranged bullet traps made of metal barrels filled with packed mechanic's waste and layers of fabric; we covered these with cardboard screens to show the imprint of each bullet. When we mounted these traps six feet behind the target, we discovered that the bullet fragments would sometimes be deflected upward after striking some of the skulls or combinations of skulls and melons and would go completely over the bullet trap. This was similar to the change of course of the fragments of the disrupted bullet that struck the President in the back of the right side of his skull and were apparently deflected upward so as to strike the upper part of the frame and glass of the windshield of the presidential automobile. Indeed, some ninety-five grains of these fragments of the last bullet, which struck the President in the head, apparently went completely over the windshield, to strike the street farther along. The total weight of all the recovered fragments attributed to the bullet that struck the President's skull was only 65 grains, out of an expected total of 160 grains. A few tiny fragments were recovered from the President's brain, a few from the floor of the car (under the jump seats), and two large pieces from the driver's seat area. The rest flew over the windshield and down the street.

FIG. 103
page 256

FIG. 91
page 219

When we moved our bullet traps close to the skulls, we were able to recover fragments of the disrupted bullets after they had penetrated varying depths of cloth and cotton waste. The penetrating ability of these fragments was poor after disruption. The jacket of the bullet usually separated from the core, and several smaller fragments were also recovered, just as in the case of the presidential head bullet. Our trap lost twelve grains, of the original 160 grains of this bullet, for us in the form of fragments that were too small to be recovered.

In each instance in which a bullet struck one of our skulls in a slightly tangential manner, as with Kennedy's skull wound, the bullet apparently broke up or deformed enough to cause a much larger wound of

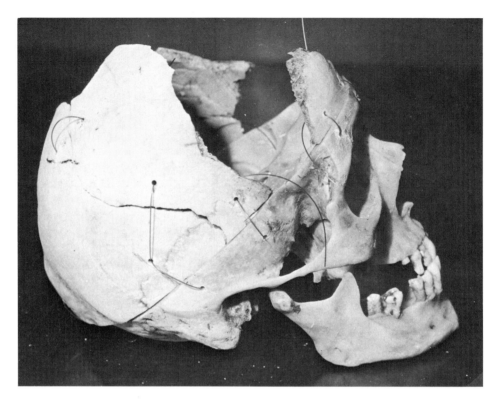

DUPLICATION OF
KENNEDY'S SKULL WOUND

Skull showing experimental duplication of Kennedy's head wound, produced by a 6.5 mm Mannlicher-Carcano fully jacketed military bullet striking at the same point and at the same angle as the one that struck the President. The wound of entry is cone-shaped, and the top of the skull has burst into many fragments, with the front segments flying so far they were not recovered. Kennedy's skull fragments were found in the street later (fig. 61). The wounds shown are very similar to those of the President. (*J. K. Lattimer*)

Fig. 102

exit. We know that each one caused a large soft-tissue cavity inside the confined brain case, with tremendous pressure, which then expanded after the bullet had left and blew the top of the calvarium into several fragments, many of which went upward and forward for great distances. X-rays of several such fragmented skulls are shown in figure 88.

These experiments recalled Commander Humes's statement that when he peeled the President's scalp back, the skull fell apart in his hands. They also matched the computer-enhanced X-rays of the President's skull, which were made available in 1978.

We were surprised to discover that the use of the more fragile dried skulls, as reported by the Warren Commission experimenters, resulted in the same marked deformation and fragmentation of the bullets as occurred with tough, fresh bone. Perhaps this was because these bullets were fired into the bases of the dried skulls, where the bone was thickest. The true location of the wound of entrance was not known because the X-rays and autopsy photos were not available for study.

In any case, our experiments verified that the backward movement of the President's head was compatible with his being struck from the rear, and that it was certainly not necessary to hit the head from the front in order to make the head move toward the gun.

One more related question remained to challenge us: Was neurologic spasm (reflex) an element in the backward lurch of the body?

The answer to this question was yes. When the brain in an intact, living, largish animal, such as a goat, is struck by a high-speed military bullet, there is a massive downward discharge of neurologic impulses from the injured brain, down the spinal cord to every muscle in the body. The body then stiffens, with the strongest muscles predominating. Since these are the back muscles and the muscles of the back of the neck, the neck arches, the back arches, and the body stiffens into an archlike configuration; the upper limbs react next.

Kennedy's head was bowed slightly forward at the moment of impact of the final bullet. Although his head was seen to move slightly forward for one frame of the Zapruder motion picture (312), in the very next frame (313), fifty milliseconds later, the contractions and dominance of his stronger back and neck muscles are beginning to pull his head and thorax abruptly backward, toward an upright or even hyperextended position. He was already leaning slightly to his left, so that the combination of the backward movement of his head from the jet-recoil effect described previously plus the stiffening and the pulling upward and backward from the predominant contractions of his neck and back muscles could understandably result in a backward lurch of his head and body, starting a frame after the bullet struck him. The torque vectors created by the forces applied to the right side of the back of his head would also tend to turn him slightly to his left, as he lurched backward. This is exactly what can be seen to happen in the Zapruder movie in frames 314 through 317.

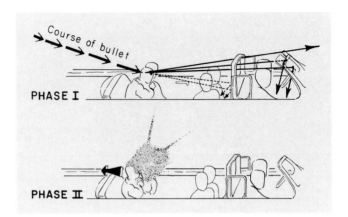

PHASE I

PHASE II

Course of bullet

RETROGRADE JET RECOIL OF HEAD

The second bullet entered the President's skull from the rear and broke up. The fragments then diverged and were deflected upward, leaving via a large wound of exit on the front right part of the head (Phase One). The brain then exploded (Phase Two), with the largest volume of vaporized, heavy brain substance leaving the skull via the easiest route, through the large wound of exit on the right temple; three additional fragments of skull were blown upward and outward. Since more of the semiliquid, heavy brain substance left the head through the anterior wound of exit on the front right portion of the skull, it created a recoil effect similar to a jet engine (arrow), which helped to drive the President's head backward toward the gun and to his left. *(J. K. Lattimer)*

Fig. 103

EXPLOSION OF BRAIN WITH RETRO-RECOIL OF HEAD (opposite)

Experimental demonstration of the backward movement of what was left of a skull after being shot by a fully jacketed Carcano bullet at the same angle as Kennedy was hit. Some of the bullet fragments were seen to be deflected upward into the bullet trap (ashcan at right, packed with cotton waste and fabric). The simulated brain (mixed with white paint to increase visibility) then exploded (Phase Two). It can be seen that more of the brain left the skull in a forward direction (to the right of the dotted line) via the larger wound of exit on the front of the skull. The impact of the bullet in Phase One sometimes moved the skull forward slightly, just before the explosion and backward recoil; however, the explosion was so violent as to dominate the scene and always filled the air with a cloud of vaporized brain substance of startling proportions. *(J. K. Lattimer, J. Lattimer and G. Lattimer,* Surgery, Gynecology & Obstetrics *142 (1976): 246-253)*

Fig. 104

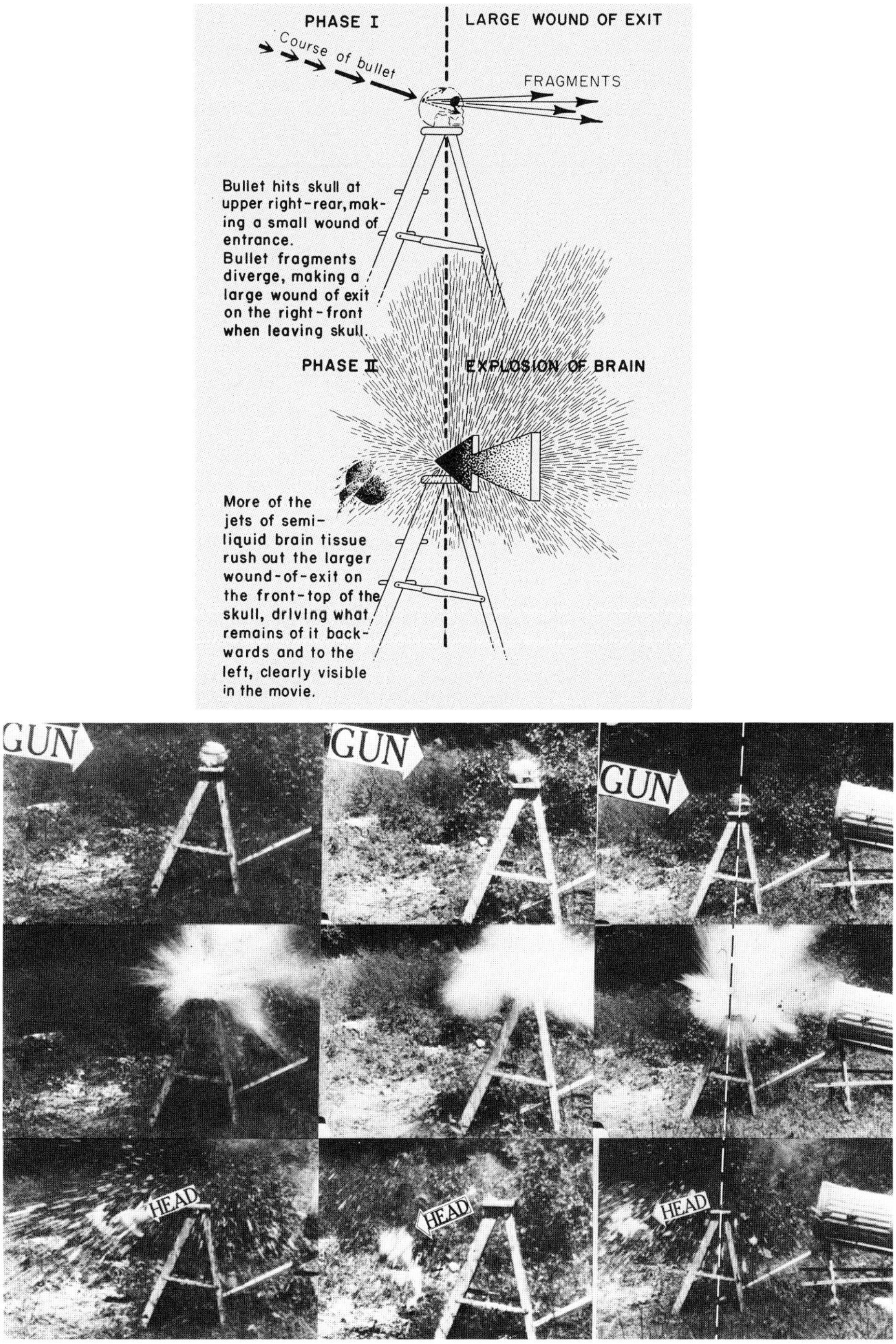
PHASE I
LARGE WOUND OF EXIT
Course of bullet
FRAGMENTS
Bullet hits skull at upper right-rear, making a small wound of entrance.
Bullet fragments diverge, making a large wound of exit on the right-front when leaving skull.
PHASE II
EXPLOSION OF BRAIN
More of the jets of semi-liquid brain tissue rush out the larger wound-of-exit on the front-top of the skull, driving what remains of it backwards and to the left, clearly visible in the movie.
GUN
GUN
GUN
HEAD
HEAD
HEAD

Fig. 104 *(continued)*

Tests done on goats, both awake and anesthetized, recorded on ultra-high-speed film at the Aberdeen Proving Grounds, demonstrated that the reactions of the goats' limbs and body began forty milliseconds after the brain was struck by a high-speed military bullet in an unanesthetized goat and fifty milliseconds after an anesthetized goat was struck in a similar manner. If we assume that neurologic conduction times would be approximately the same in humans, this would cause the reaction to start about one frame after President Kennedy's brain was struck. That is exactly what appears to happen in the Zapruder movie.

When combined with the overpowering evidence that the X-rays of his head show metallic bullet fragments arranged only from back to front in the right side of his brain case and with the skull damage all centering on the right side of his skull, we are left with absolutely no indication that he was struck from the front or right front by an additional bullet, as claimed by critics of the Warren Commission.

In fact, if his body had not lurched backward from the wound received in the back of his head, we would have been suspicious, as would Colonel Hanson have been.

It is also clear now that sudden acceleration of the automobile was *not* a factor in the backward and sideways lurch of Kennedy after he was shot. The acceleration did not occur until several frames later in the Zapruder movie.

Our experiments were successful in that they served to give us concrete evidence, rather than allow us to continue speculating and deducing. But it was not yet time to rest; still more controversy brewed. There was one slightly less successful experiment, which bears mentioning here.

We tried to fire an additional bullet from the side, into the initial wound of exit, on experimental heads that simultaneously sustained a head wound like the one Oswald inflicted. But we ran into difficulties with this. First, the air was filled with a curtain of vaporized brain substance. Second, the target jerked abruptly to the left (as toward the rear of the car), and, third, fragments would hit the simulation of Mrs. Kennedy, which we had placed directly to the left of the model of the President's head.

Most impressive, any bullets fired into the skull from the right front always caused very obvious destruction of the left side of the skull and left bullet fragments against this side of the skull. Since there was no such damage to the left side of Kennedy's head, and no bullet fragments against the left side of his skull, and since Mrs. Kennedy was not hit by any fragments and photographer Zapruder was not visibly jolted from his perch by a deafening rifle shot almost beside him, we find it very difficult to believe that another supersonic bullet was fired from the grassy knoll in the general vicinity of Zapruder. The fact that policemen could later be seen running up the grassy slope toward the railroad overpass probably merely confirms the testimony of the railroad tower employees that echoes in that location make it difficult to pinpoint the origin of any loud noise originating anywhere in Dealey Plaza.

The Secret Service chauffeur and his accompanying agent would have been acutely aware of a supersonic crack, plus a deafening explosion, if a second high-powered rifle had been fired directly at them from such close range.

Moreover, our experiments had already confirmed that it was not necessary to have a previous wound weaken the right front of Kennedy's head to achieve the jet-recoil effect, driving his head toward the back of the car. It seems probable that the neuromuscular reflex spastic stiffening, to be expected after a brain shot, was the most powerful force of all in causing the backward lurch of the President, and at just the interval seen in the Zapruder film. The jet-recoil effect of the head bullet provided a supplementary backward force.

In short, we found that the backward and sideways lurch of President Kennedy's head toward the shooter, beginning one frame after the bullet struck, was to be expected from a bullet striking his head from the rear, as it did, and did not mean he was hit by an additional bullet from the front or right front. There is absolutely no evidence that President Kennedy was struck from any direction except from the rear and above.

We believed that—on this point at least—the case could rest. It was time to move on to other questions.

13.

GOVERNOR CONNALLY'S WOUNDS: AN EXPERIMENTAL APPROACH TO QUESTIONS

Nearly all the remaining unanswered questions seemed to converge, in one way or another, on the question of bullet 399, the second of the three bullets presumed to have been fired by Oswald, and the one that had passed through President Kennedy's neck and then had gone forward to cripple Governor Connally.

So we devised another experiment to test the various theories. But before describing that experiment, let us review the events that took place when Connally was struck. Let us review those events through Connally's own testimony—his impressions of what actually happened —and through the testimony of his doctors at Parkland Hospital. Then we will review the experiments we contrived to test that evidence and the conclusions we were able to draw from those experiments and from our own deductions.

Connally Looks Back after Hearing First Shot

Governor Connally was seated in the jump seat immediately in front of President Kennedy in the open Lincoln motorcade automobile. Mrs. Connally was at his left, in front of Mrs. Kennedy. The motorcade had just made the left-hand turn into Elm Street and started down the gentle slope in front of the Texas Book Depository building when the Governor heard a loud noise. His account of what happened next is best described in his own words from the Warren Commission report:

. . . We had just made the turn, well, when I heard what I thought was a shot. I heard this noise which I immediately took to be a rifle shot. I instinctively turned

260

to my right because the sound appeared to come from over my right shoulder, so I turned to look back over my right shoulder, and I saw nothing unusual except just people in the crowd, but I did not catch the President in the corner of my eye, and I was interested, because once I heard the shot in my own mind I identified it as a rifle shot, and I immediately—the only thought that crossed my mind was that this is an assassination attempt.

So I looked, failing to see him, I was turning to look back over my left shoulder into the back seat, but I never got that far in my turn. I got about in the position I am in now facing you, looking a little bit to the left of center, and then I felt like someone had hit me in the back.

Connally Leans Back and to His Left as He Twists His Head Around

Although Connally had strained and twisted to look over his right shoulder, he did not get around far enough to see the President. In order to exert the maximum effort to look straight backward over his shoulder, a person in the right-hand jump seat of an automobile automatically leans to his left in order to get around far enough to see directly backward. This shift would have placed the Governor's body more to the left of the center of the jump seat than usual. This would account for his being hit in the right side of his back, rather than the left. Connally also stated that when he heard the first shot, he put his right hand, in which he was holding his Stetson, down on his left thigh, in order to push himself farther around toward his right. In his sworn testimony he said, "Having turned to look over my right shoulder, I threw my right wrist over on my left leg."

I postulate that neither man had been hit at this point, but that, while he was still in this position, bullet 399 passed through Kennedy's neck, hit the Governor in the back, tore open his chest, went through his right wrist, and embedded itself in his left leg.

Connally had decided, as he stated, that since he could not see Kennedy over his right shoulder, he would look over his left shoulder. And although he had begun to turn his head, he had not yet been able to unwind completely, and his body was still turned to the right, with his torso still tilted to his left. His right hand was still down in the car, where it had been pushing on his left leg just above the knee. It was at this point that he was hit. I believe that by frame 221 of the Zapruder movie (when he emerged from behind the Stemmons Freeway sign), he had already been struck by bullet 399, which had also just traversed the neck of President Kennedy.

Fig. 105
page 262

Connally Gasps for Breath after He Is Hit

Less than a second later (Zapruder frame 236), as his dazed condition wore off a bit, the Governor undoubtedly attempted to take his first

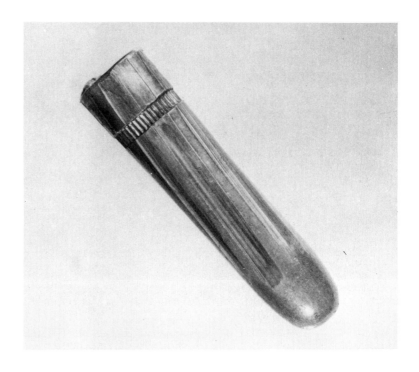

THE KENNEDY-CONNALLY
BULLET (WC Exhibit 399)

This is bullet 399, which pierced the President's neck and then tumbled so that it struck Connally's fifth rib, going somewhat sideways and a little backward, flattening the rear portion of the bullet. It then continued through his wrist and ended up going backward into his leg. This is the so-called pristine bullet, which in reality is far from pristine. Neutron activation analysis revealed that the fragments removed from Connally's wrist came from this bullet. *(National Archives)*

Fig. 105

Fig. 66
page 169

breath, with his chest torn open, his fifth rib shattered, his right lung collapsed and cut across in the middle lobe. His mouth can be seen to open (in frame 236) and his face contort, reflecting his terrible pain and the frightening sensation of trying to suck air into a damaged lung when the pleura has been torn open and the lung will not function.

Connally Clamps Right Elbow over Torn-Open Right Chest

Connally can be seen to begin to turn again toward his right, probably in a reflex move to reduce the painful motion of the shattered fifth right rib and to pull his right arm over the painful area to splint it. F. L. Mudd, a spectator at the curbside (no relation to Booth's Dr. Mudd), testified that he saw Connally "holding one arm to his side" at this point. Mrs. Connally now realized that the Governor had been horribly wounded, and pulled him over backward—he was again facing toward the right side of the car (as seen in Zapruder frame 312)—into her lap, where she could bend over him to protect him. She did this just in time to keep him from being exposed to flying fragments of the final bullet.

Connally Realizes He May Be Fatally Wounded

Connally saw blood on his shirt front and realized he had been shot through and through, perhaps fatally. He then lapsed into complete unconsciousness until the car swerved into the Parkland Hospital driveway, whereupon he regained consciousness enough to attempt to get out of the car himself, before again collapsing.

Connally Assumed Erroneously That First Shot Hit Kennedy

Connally believed that President Kennedy had been hit by the first shot, and he by the second, and he was quite adamant about this. He made the erroneous assumption, as we see it, that the first loud noise he heard was the shot that penetrated Kennedy's neck. He assumed that he himself had been hit by a second and different bullet. The circumstantial and experimental evidence clearly shows, however, that Connally was *not* hit by a bullet that came directly from a gun, but by a bullet that was tumbling, and that the most probable cause for its tumble was Kennedy's neck. In fact, if it had been an earlier bullet that traversed Kennedy's neck, Connally almost certainly would have been hit also, but in a different spot on his back. Furthermore, some sign of a third bullet would have been found in the car or its occupants (and no third bullet or bullet hole was found). The bullet that traversed Kennedy's neck was still traveling fast enough, and probably tumbling enough, to have caused very obvious damage to the interior of the car had it not hit Connally.

The Zapruder movie frame (frame 234) that Connally selected as the one at which he speculated he was hit could not possibly be the correct one, since his right hand (holding his Stetson by the brim) and wrist can be distinctly seen by this time to have risen off his left knee and they are clearly out of the line of the bullet, as in frame 230. Therefore he must have been hit well before frame 234.

FIG. 65
page 169

All Three of Connally's Wounds Were Caused by One Bullet

There is no doubt that all three of the Governor's wounds were caused by one bullet. His three surgeons all agreed on that point, which was confirmed later by neutron activation analysis. The mass of circumstantial evidence plus later research have proved beyond doubt that his assumptions were incorrect.

Entrance Wound Shown Three Cm Long in Vertical Axis

FIG. 113
page 274

In his original sworn testimony, Dr. Shaw, the chest surgeon, stated that the wound in Connally's back was not a puncture wound, but was elongated, indicating that there could have been some tumbling. His careful diagram of the wound of entry (which he revised and initialed) showed it to be elongated in its vertical (not horizontal) axis and to be at least 3 cm in length. This is important, as will be seen.

FIG. 106
page 265

FIG. 107
page 266

It would seem that all the various wounds in Governor Connally were almost undeniably made by the same tumbling bullet, which first traversed his chest, then his right wrist, and finally embedded itself in his leg, being stopped by his femur after completing a 180-degree turn, which caused it to be traveling backward as it struck his leg. Because it was a very long bullet, it was easy for it to be knocked out of Connally's leg. It was found on a stretcher in Parkland Hospital.

In an effort to determine the feasibility of the Warren Commission's proposal that a single bullet penetrated both President Kennedy's neck and Governor Connally's body, arm, and leg, my sons and I prepared a mechanical model, reconstructing the flight path of bullet 399 through the two men. This might, we hoped, make it easier to understand exactly what happened to this bullet after it hit Kennedy. We were able to prepare this model only after extensive experimentation and study of the autopsy materials.

The wounds in Kennedy's neck and in Connally's back, wrist, and leg have graduated differences in lengths, all of which fit exactly with our reconstruction of the course taken by bullet 399 in its tumbling configuration through the two men. Our reconstruction is as follows:

FIG. 108
page 268

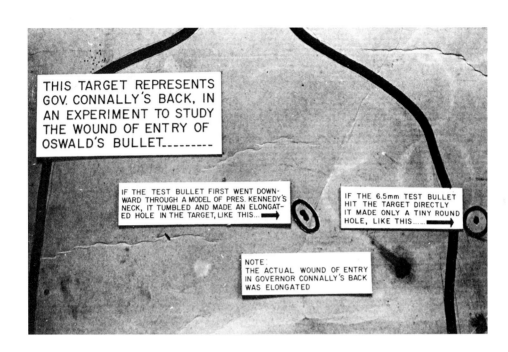

SIMULATED CONNALLY WOUND

An oval hole in our simulated back of Connally was caused by our test bullet that had first passed through a simulation of Kennedy's neck, causing that bullet to wobble and start to tumble end over end. Connally's wound of entry was elongated, like the one in the center of this target. The punctate round hole, with black margins, of the type that always occurred when our test bullets struck the Connally target without hitting something else first, can be seen to the right of Connally's outline in the photograph. These bullets never wobbled or tumbled spontaneously; they were stable in their flight to the target unless they hit something else first, such as Kennedy's neck, whereupon they turned almost completely sideways. *(J. K. Lattimer,* Medical Times, *Nov. 1974)*

Fig. 106

Mr. SPECTER. Would you draw, Dr. Shaw, right above the shoulder as best you can recollect, what that wound of entry appeared at the time you first observed it? Would you put your initials right beside that?

(The witness, Dr. Shaw, complied with the request of Counsel Specter.)

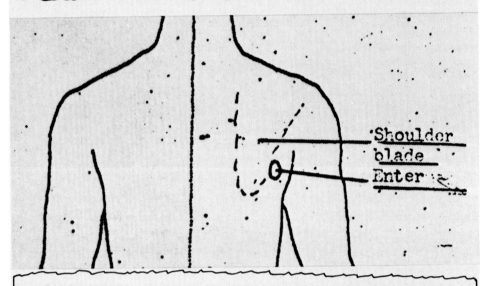

Mr. SPECTER. As to the wound on the back of Governor Connally, was there any indication that the bullet was tumbling prior to the time it struck him?

Dr. SHAW. I would only have to say that I'm not a ballistics expert, but the wound on his chest was not a single puncture wound, it was long enough so that there might have been some tumbling.

Mr. SPECTER. You mean the wound on his back?

Dr. SHAW. The wound on his back—yes, it was long enough so that there might have been some tumbling. In other words, it was not a spherical puncture wound.

Mr. SPECTER. You say the hole which appears on Governor Connally is just about the size that it would have been on his body?

Dr. SHAW. Yes; it is drawn in good scale.

Mr. SPECTER. In good scale to the body?

Dr. SHAW. Yes.

DR. SHAW'S TESTIMONY

Dr. Shaw initialed and described his careful drawing depicting the wound of entry into Connally's back, showing it as 3 cm long. He later attested to its accuracy under oath. (*Warren Commission Report, Volume Six, Pages 86 and 95 (text) and Volume Seventeen, Page 336, Exhibit 679 (drawing), National Archives*)

Fig. 107

The 6.5 mm bullet, fired from above and behind the President, entered the top of the prominent roll of soft tissue across the back of Kennedy's neck, making a wound of entry approximately 6.5 mm in diameter and bearing the typical dark circumferential rim characteristic of a wound of entry by a high-speed rifle bullet. This bullet (WC 399) grazed the margin of one of the President's vertebrae in the lower neck area, as we have said before, producing tiny fragments of bone which are visible in one of the post-mortem X-ray films of his neck.

It then traversed the soft tissues of his neck and his trachea, emerging approximately in the midline, just below his Adam's apple, and exited from his neck while traveling downward at approximately an eighteen- to twenty-degree angle. It undoubtedly began to tumble as it left the President's neck.

Models Show Neck Bullets Tumbled

FIG. 96
page 237

When our experimental bullets traversed simulations of the President's neck, as you may remember, they almost always began to tumble on their long axes.

The tumbling bullets traversed some twenty-eight inches of air space between the two men in 1/400 second, during which the bullets almost always rotated enough to assume a completely sideways position. Each bullet then entered the back of our Governor Connally, 2 cm lateral to the lateral margin of his right scapula (shoulder blade), making a wound of entrance 3 cm long (as surgeon Shaw both wrote and drew), which happens to be the exact length of this bullet. Although the question arises as to whether some of the elongation of this wound might have been attributable to a tangential course of the bullet, our experiments did not indicate this to be a factor, since any elongation caused by a tangential course would have been horizontal.

The bullet continued its rotating, end-over-end motion as it struck the Governor's fifth rib tangentially (shattered fragments of which cut the middle lobe of the right lung almost in two and also injured the lower lobe) and then exited from his body below and medial to his right nipple. Here it caused the unsupported skin to bulge and then burst open, creating the more customary large and jagged type of wound of exit, approximately 5 cm (two inches) in diameter. It should be noted that here the unsupported skin expanded ahead of the bullet and showed the characteristic large, bursting tears of a wound of exit of a tumbling high-speed bullet.

FIG. 62
page 164

After leaving Connally's chest, the bullet continued its end-over-end turn, now traveling mostly backward, and entered the dorsum of his wrist at an angle that subtended 2 cm, thus causing a 2-cm wound of entrance, and struck his radius a glancing blow while traveling at a greatly reduced speed. This softened blow shattered the radius but did not displace the fragments. Since the bullet had been traveling sideways,

THE PATH OF BULLET 399

A row of 6.5 mm Carcano bullets was glued to a strip of Lucite to show the positions of bullet 399 at various points in its flight through Kennedy and Connally, as determined by the size of the bullet holes. Visualizing the bullet's path in this way made it easier to understand why the lead fragments were found only toward the end of its rotation, when the bullet was traveling backward. These bullets almost always tumbled under these conditions.

A. The wound of entry into the back of Kennedy's neck was almost round and approximately 6.5 mm in diameter (one-fourth inch), with a black rim characteristic of a wound of entry. The bullet then grazed the tip of a vertebra in the President's neck, splintering the bone slightly.

B. The wound of exit from Kennedy's neck was destroyed by the tracheostomy incision, but was not very large (according to testimony of Dr. Perry).

C. The wounds of exit in the front of Kennedy's shirt were one-half inch long in a vertical direction, in both layers of the overlapping part of the shirt front.

D. The wound of entry into Connally's back was 3 cm long (one and one-fourth inches, the exact length of bullet 399) and was approximately twenty-eight inches away from Kennedy's neck, indicating that the bullet was tumbling end over end.

E. The wound of exit from the front of Connally's chest, below and medial to his right nipple, was large and ragged, measuring about 5 cm in diameter.

F. The wound of entrance into the top of Connally's wrist measured three-quarters of an inch in length, showing that the bullet was now turned almost entirely around, so that it was now traveling almost backward. It shattered his radius and left three fragments of lead in it, from its open rear end, where the lead was exposed.

G. The wound of exit from the underside of Connally's wrist measured only one-half inch in length. (The bullet was still turning.)

H. The wound of entrance into the top of Connally's left thigh measured about three-eighths of an inch and looked punctate, indicating that the bullet had practically completed its 180-degree tumble. One fragment of lead was left in this wound. (*J. K. Lattimer and Jamie Lattimer*)

Fig. 108

268

as well as somewhat backward, it was probably slightly flattened in its rear portion by the impact on the Governor's rib, squeezing two grains of its very soft lead core out through the rear end of the bullet, like toothpaste out of a tube. Because the bullet was now also traveling partly backward, these protruding leaden fragments were now scraped off by the arm and leg bones and remained in the wounds of Connally's radius and femur, where the bullet was finally stopped.

Fig. 109
page 270

Our experiments with a bullet that we compressed (with great difficulty, in a vise), in order to flatten it to exactly the same degree as bullet 399, showed that the unusually soft lead of the bullet's interior did indeed extrude through the rear end of the gilding-metal jacket of the bullet when it was squeezed, and that the extruded portion weighed two grains. (Bullet 399 was also missing two grains of weight.) As stated before, because the bullet was traveling mostly backward at this juncture, these protruding lead fragments were scraped off onto the bone.

Some detailed results of these experiments are given in a later chapter, devoted to the bullets.

Our reconstruction indicated that bullet 399 now emerged from the palmar side of Connally's wrist, traveling almost entirely backward as it continued its turn. I postulate that this explains why the wound of exit was smaller than the wound of entrance on the dorsal side of the wrist, since the bullet was still turning to travel almost in its long axis, albeit going backward. It was greatly slowed by its passage through Connally's thorax and partly sideways passage through his wrist.

Dr. Shires Repairs Hole in Connally's Leg

The bullet next entered the top of Connally's left thigh, about four inches above the knee. It penetrated the skin, fascia (gristle), and muscles of the leg, and then struck the bone (femur) hard enough to scrape off the fourth fragment of soft lead from the rear end of the bullet, which can be seen in the X-ray. It should be noted that surgeon Shires described this wound as "punctate" (implying that it was small, like a puncture). The bullet had been sufficiently slowed by this time so that it did not fracture the femur. The fragment in the leg was located well below the point of entry into the skin and was so tiny that it was left in place.

Fig. 62
page 164

Leg Bone Would Have Shattered if Bullet Had Not Slowed and Tumbled from Traversing President's Neck

Our experiments demonstrated that this bullet was so powerful that if it had not been slowed down by passing through President Kennedy's neck and Governor Connally's thorax and wrist, it would have shattered Connally's large leg bone.

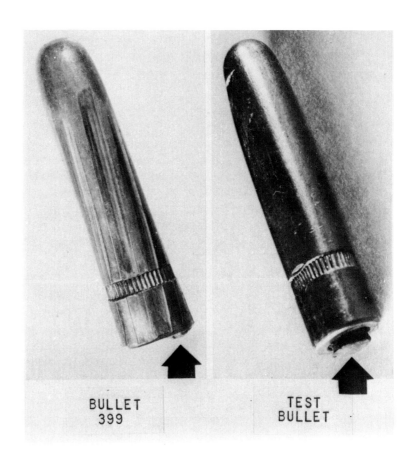

BULLET
399

TEST
BULLET

KENNEDY-CONNALLY
BULLET TESTS

Bullet 399 (left) struck Connally's fifth rib a tangential blow
while traveling backward and a little sideways, and was flattened
to the same degree as we then flattened our test bullet (right).
This flattening caused its soft lead core to extrude from the rear
end, some of which can still be seen (arrow). We believe the
remainder of the extruded lead was scraped off on the Governor's
radius and femur, since the bullet was traveling almost backward at that point. Neutron activation tests bore this out. The
extruded portions of lead from our test bullet weighed exactly
2.1 grains, the same amount as was missing from bullet 399.
(Bullet 399: National Archives; test bullet: J. K. Lattimer)

Fig. 109

We had previously found that this bullet would penetrate twenty-five inches of the toughest elm wood, or forty-seven inches of ponderosa pine, as the late Dr. John Marshall Nichols, of the University of Kansas Medical School, had previously also observed, without any deformation of the bullet. Certainly the Governor's thigh was not hit primarily by a bullet coming directly from the gun muzzle, because such bullets always shattered and displaced very large segments of the femur. Likewise, the Governor's wrist bone was not hit directly by a bullet that had not been slowed down, because our experimental bullets, coming directly from the gun, always shattered the wrist bone in an entirely different manner, causing a severe displacement and even a loss of bone, with devastating effect. The gross difference in the X-rays of the two types of wounds is clearly evident to anyone who has ever had to deal with such wounds.

Fig. 111
page 272

If, however, the experimental bullet was slowed down by making it traverse a neck, which caused it to tumble, and then a rib and an arm bone, it did not shatter the large bone of the leg (the femur).

Fig. 112
page 273

By far the most significant feature of all these wounds is the fact that the wound of entry into Connally's back is elongated in a vertical direction, and is 3 cm long, the same length as the bullet.

It should also be noted that, in testimony taken four or more months after the original operative report was written, the wound of entry, while still elongated in a vertical direction, was recollected by Dr. Shaw as being only 1.5 cm in length. Although this length is only half that described in his carefully written operative report, made on the day of the actual operation, and with the sketches of the wound drawn, corrected, and initialed by him available, it was still recorded as elongated in its vertical dimension. The vertical elongation is an important detail.

Fig. 113
page 274

In an attempt to approach these matters from every possible angle, I posed several questions to myself concerning the possibility that Governor Connally might have been hit by a bullet different from the one that exited from the front of President Kennedy's neck.

Figs. 106, 107
pages 265, 266

1. Was Governor Connally hit by a bullet that had come directly from the muzzle of a gun? The answer is clearly no. Our experiments showed that when bullets were fired directly into a target that simulated Connally, they always made a tiny round hole 6.5 mm (one-fourth inch) in diameter. The entry of the bullets into the slightly curving skin of the torso was not sufficiently tangential to elongate the wound of entry to this extent. Furthermore, any elongation caused by a tangential strike would have been in a horizontal direction, whereas the Governor's back wound was elongated in a vertical direction. During our experiments with approximately 700 rounds from all four of the sub-lots of ammunition of the type Oswald used, none of our bullets ever tumbled before they hit something, nor did they in the FBI experiments with 200 or more rounds from two of the sub-lots. Although we had to be content with four rifles of the same model as used by Oswald, the FBI used his actual rifle, and

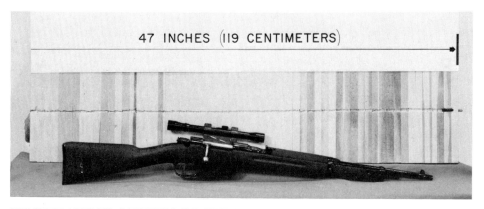

47 INCHES (119 CENTIMETERS)

PENETRATING ABILITY OF BULLETS LIKE 399

The late Dr. John Nichols demonstrated that Carcano bullets of the type used by Oswald would penetrate four feet of ponderosa pine boards and appear undamaged. *(John Nichols)*

Fig. 110

UNDEFORMED BULLET

X-ray of a bullet like 399 which has traversed 25 inches of a block of the toughest elm wood, before being stopped. The bullet is undeformed. Nichols showed that this bullet can penetrate 47 inches of ponderosa pine boards without being deformed.

The bullet is also seen to be undeformed after it was dug out of the wood. Those who thought one bullet could not go through two men and come out relatively intact never tried this kind of experiment. *(J. K. Lattimer)*

Fig. 111

OUR BULLETS THAT HIT OUR "CONNALLY"
RIBS AND ARM BONES DIRECTLY, ALWAYS
SHATTERED OUR CONNALLY LEG BONES AS
WELL.

OUR BULLET THAT WENT THROUGH A "JFK"
NECK DID NOT SHATTER OUR "CONNALLY"
LEG BONE, EVEN THOUGH IT SHATTERED
"HIS" RIB & ARM BONES.

EFFECT OF BULLETS

Above: Our experimental Connally leg bone (bottom bone in these pictures), called the femur (the largest bone in the body), was always shattered, after our Connally rib (top bone) and arm bone (middle) were traversed if the bullet had *not* been slowed down by going through a neck first. (*J. K. Lattimer*)

Below: When the bullet traversed an experimental neck, it was slowed down, tumbled, and did not shatter the leg bone. Since Connally's leg bone was *not* shattered, the bullet that hit him must have hit something else first, such as Kennedy's neck, to slow it down. (*J. K. Lattimer*)

Fig. 112

TO BE COMPLETED BY CIRCULATING NURSE

PARKLAND MEMORIAL HOSPITAL

OPERATIVE RECORD

ROOM: 220 STATUS: Pvt

NAME: John Connally

UNIT # 26 36 99

DATE: 11-22-63 Thoracic Surg AGE: RACE: W/M

PRE-OPERATIVE DIAGNOSIS: Gunshot wound of the chest with comminuted fracture of the 5th rib

POST-OPERATIVE DIAGNOSIS: Same with laceration right middle lobe, hematoma lower lobe of lung

OPERATION: Thoracotomy, removal rib fragment, debridement of wound BEGAN: 1335 ENDED: 1520

ANESTHETIC: General BEGAN: 1300 ANESTHESIOLOGIST: Giesecke

SURGEON: Robert Shaw, M.D DRAINS:

ASSISTANTS: ~~Drs. Boland and Duke~~ APPLIANCES:

SCRUB NURSE: King/Burkett CIRC. NURSE: Johnson CASTS/SPLINTS:

SPONGE COUNTS: 1ST Correct DRUGS I.V. FLUIDS AND BLOOD

2ND ~~Correct~~ 111-500 cc whole blood
11-1000cc D-5-RL

COMPLICATIONS: None

CONDITION OF PATIENT: Satisfactory

TO BE DICTATED BY SURGEON

Clinical Evaluation: Operative Findings: Description of Operation:

The patient was brought to the OR from the EOR. In the EOR a sucking wound of the right chest was partially controlled by an occlusive dressing supported by manual pressure. A tube had been placed through the second interspace in the mid-clavicular line connected to a waterseal bottle to evacuate the right pneumothorax and hemathorax. An IV infusion of RL solution had already been started. As soon as the patient was positioned on the OR table the anesthesia was induced by Dr. Giesecke and an endotracheal tube was in place. As soon as it was possible to control respiration with positive pressure the occlusive dressing was taken from the right chest and the extent of the wound more carefully determined. It was found that the wound of entrance was just lateral to the right scapula close the the axilla yet had passed through the latysmus dorsi muscle shattered approximately ten cm of the lateral and anterior portion of the right fifth rib and emerged below the right nipple. The wound of entrance was approximately three cm in its longest diameter and the wound of exit was a ragged wound approximately five cm in its greatest diameter. The skin and subcutaneous tissue over the path of the missile moved in a paradoxical manner with respiration indicating softening of the chest. The skin of the whole area was carefully cleansed with Phisohex and Iodine. The entire area including the wound of entrance and wound of exit was draped partially excluding the wound of entrance for the first part of the operation. An elliptical incision was made around the wound of exit removing the torn edges of the skin and the damaged subcutaneous tissue. The incision was then carried in a downward curve up toward the right axilla so as to not have the skin incision over the actual path of the missile ben through the chest wall. This incision was carried down through the subcutaneous tissue to expose the Serratus anterior muscle and the anterior border of the latissimus dorsi muscle. The fragmented and damaged portions of the Serratus anterior muscle were excised. Small rib fragments that were adhering to periosteal tags were carefully removed preserving as much periosteum as possible. The fourth intercostal muscle bundle and fifth intercostal muscle bundle were not appreciably damaged.

M.D.
Dr. Robert Shaw

RS:bl (continued)

OPERATIVE REPORT ON CONNALLY

This was dictated and signed by chest surgeon Dr. Robert Shaw immediately after the operation. He states, on line twelve, that the wound of entry in Connally's back was 3 cm in length. In his testimony before the Warren Commission, Dr. Shaw repeatedly reaffirmed that this operative note was accurate:

Fig. 113

DESCRIPTION OF OPERATION (Continued): The ragged ends of the damaged fifth rib were cleaned out with the rongeur. The plura had been torn open by the secondary missiles created by the fragmented fifth rib. The wound was open widely and exposure was obtained with a self retaining retractor. The right pleural cavity was then carefully inspected. Approximately 200 cc of clot and liquid blood was removed from the pleural cavity. The middle lobe had a linear rent starting at its peripheral edge going down towards its hilum separating the lobe into two segments. There was an open bronchus in the depth of this wound. Since the vascularity and the bronchial connections to the lobe were intact it was decided to repair the lobe rather then to remove it. The repair was accomplished with a running suture of #000 chromic gut on atraumatic needle closing both plural surfaces as well as two running sutures approximating the tissue of the central portion of the lobe. This almost completely sealed off the air leaks which were evident in the torn portion of the lobe. The lower lobe was next examined and found to be engorged with blood and at one point a laceration of allowed the oozing of blood. This laceration had undoubtedly been caused by a rib fragment. This laceration was closed with a single suture of #3-0 chromic gut on atraumatic needle. The right plural cavity was now carefully examined and small ribs fragments were removed, the diaphram was found to be uninjured. There was no evidence of injury of the mediastinum and its contents. Hemostasis had been accomplished within the plural cavity with the repair of the middle lobe and the suturing of the laceration in the lower lobe. The upper lobe was found to be uninjured. The drains which had previously been placed in the second interspace in the midclavicular line was found to be longer than necessary so approximately ten cm of it was cut away and the remaining portion ewas demonstrated with two additional opeings. An additional drain was placed through a stab wound in the eighth interspace in the posterior axillary line. Both these drains were then connected to a waterseal bottle. The fourth and fifth intercostal muscles were then approximated with interrupted sutures of #0 chromic gut. The remaining portion of the Serratus anterior muscle was then approximated across the closure of the intercostal muscle. The laceration of the latissimus dorsi muscle on its intermost surface was then closed with several interrupted sutures of #0 chromic gut. The subcutaneous tissue was th Before closing the subcutaneous tissue one million units of Penicillin and one gram of Streptomycin in 100 cc normal saline was instilled into the wound. The stab wound was then made in the most dependent portion of the wound coming out near the angle of the scapula. A large Penrose drain was drawn out through this stab wound to allow drainage of the wound of the chest wall. The subcutaneous tissue was then closed with interrupted #0 chromic gut inverting the knots. Skin closed with interrupted vertical sutures of black silk. Attention was next turned to the wound of entrance. It was excised with an elliptical incision. It was found that the latissimus dorsi muscle although lacerated was not badly damaged so that the opening was closed with sutures of #0 chromic gut in the fascia of the muscle. Before closing this incision the palpation with the index finger the Penrose drain could be felt immediately below in the space beneath the latissimus dorsi muscle. The skin closed with interrupted vertical mattress sutures of black silk. Drainage tubes were secured with safety pens and adhesive tape and dressings applied. As soon as the operation on the chest had been concluded Dr. Gregory and Dr. Shires started the surgery tha was necessary for the wounds of the right wrist and left thigh.

Dr. Robert Shaw

RS:bl

* There was also a comminuted fracture of the right radius secondary to the same missile and in addition a small flesh wound of the left thigh. The operative notes concerning the management of the right arm and left thigh will be dictated by Dr. Charles and Dr. Tom Shires.

Mr. Specter: Permit me to make available to you a copy of the Parkland Memorial Hospital operative record and let me ask you, first of all, if you can identify these two pages on an exhibit heretofore marked as Commission Exhibit 392 as to whether or not this constitutes your report?

Dr. Shaw: Yes, this is a transcription of my dictated report of the operation.

Mr. Specter: Are the facts set forth therein true and correct?

Dr. Shaw: Yes. . . .

(National Archives)

Fig. 113 *(continued)*

always with the same results: none of the bullets ever tumbled. They always caused only small round holes in the target.

The actual wound of entry into Connally's back was elongated to 3 cm in length, according to the original operative report. This is the exact length of the bullet (WC 399) that the Warren Commission alleges struck Connally, after passing through Kennedy's neck. It seems certain that the bullet that struck Connally was in the act of tumbling after striking something between the gun and Connally's back. Judging from the length of the wound of entry, the bullet was traveling almost completely sideways at the moment of impact on his back, and this elongation was not due to a tangential strike on his body, since its elongation was in the body's vertical axis.

Fig. 101
page 252

Our experiments with mock-ups of President Kennedy's neck showed that bullets from every one of the sub-lots of ammunition of the lot used by Oswald (Western Cartridge Company lots 6000, 6001, 6002, and 6003), ordinarily exited in a tumbling configuration and caused a similar elongated hole in a target placed to simulate Connally's back.

Although we cannot prove that it was Kennedy's neck that caused bullet 399 to be tumbling by the time it struck Connally, we can definitely say that the tumbling was compatible with the situation.

2. Were Governor Connally's wrist and leg wounds compatible with a tumbling bullet (like bullet WC 399)? Yes, both the wrist and leg wounds were compatible with a bullet of the WC 399 type (a 6.5 mm Mannlicher-Carcano fully jacketed military bullet) that had turned almost completely around in its process of tumbling. Again, as we have said before, only by traveling somewhat backward could bullet 399 leave fragments of lead in Connally's wrist wound and one embedded in his femur.

These fragments were removed later from the wrist by Dr. Gregory. The fragments can be seen at the National Archives and are clearly made of gray lead, rather than the coppery metal of a bullet jacket, which is made of tough gilding metal.

By striking Connally's rib sideways, the dense copper jacket of the bullet had undoubtedly been compressed just enough to squeeze two grains of the soft lead core of the bullet out through its open rear end. The wound of exit in his wrist measured only 1 cm after it was closed, compared to the wound of entrance, which had been more than 2 cm in length. This would appear to be further evidence that the bullet continued to turn and was still turning as it entered the upper leg, where the open rear end of the bullet, with its protruding lead core, left a fourth tiny metallic fragment, on the femur at the juncture of the middle and lower thirds of Connally's upper leg, somewhat below (distal to) the wound of entry into the skin of his leg.

3. Are the four fragments of lead seen in the Governor's X-rays too many? Some critics have contended that the four bullet fragments in Governor Connally are too many to be accounted for by the two grains of lead missing from bullet 399. In our experiments we were able to

make forty-one such fragments from the two-grain piece of lead that extruded from our test bullet. It can safely be said, therefore, that four fragments are by no means too many to be accounted for by the two grains missing from bullet 399.

4. Could Connally's wrist wound have been caused by a direct hit of a bullet like 399, which had not struck anything else first? The answer to this question is also unequivocally no. Such a direct hit would have resulted in an entirely different kind of wound of the bone. A large segment of the arm bone would have been completely displaced or destroyed, with only a gaping hole in the arm and in the X-ray. Furthermore, the bullet might have been expected to have been deformed on the nose had it hit the wrist bone directly. The nose of bullet 399 was not deformed.

The wound of exit on the palmar side of the wrist would have been far larger than the wound of entrance, whereas in Connally's case, the wound of exit was smaller than the wound of entrance, because by then, the slowed-down bullet had completed its turn and left the wrist, traveling almost completely backward, on its long axis. The wound in Connally's wrist was caused, instead, by a more or less tangential blow from a bullet traveling at a greatly reduced speed, which shattered the bone but left all the fragments in place. Dr. Gregory made this specific point when he told me about his operation on the Governor's wrist.

5. Could the leg wound have been caused by a direct hit from a bullet like WC 399 (or by a bullet that had traversed only the wrist before striking the femur)? Again the answer is no! The bullet from this cartridge is so powerful that had it not been markedly slowed down, it would have shattered Connally's femur and displaced large segments of it, as it did in our experiments.

This bullet can penetrate four feet of solid wood or three pine telephone poles side by side and come out looking completely undeformed. On the other hand, if it is fired into the thick bone of the back of a human skull, the jacket and core of the bullet will separate, releasing a myriad of additional fragments of many different sizes.

6. Was the ammunition dependable? The ammunition that was used for the shots fired at President Kennedy and Governor Connally, as well as the unfired round still in the gun, was excellent American-made ammunition. It was highly dependable.

7. Was Oswald capable with a rifle of this type? The answer is clearly yes, as will be shown in a later chapter.

To reconcile the two apparently different versions of what happened, Governor Connally's and my own, and to demonstrate that the two versions are actually perfectly compatible, I suggest that Connally heard Oswald's first shot, which missed the car completely.

Having identified this sound as a rifle shot, Connally exclaimed and twisted his body to the right to try to see Kennedy, leaning to his own left as he did so in an effort to see directly backward to where the President

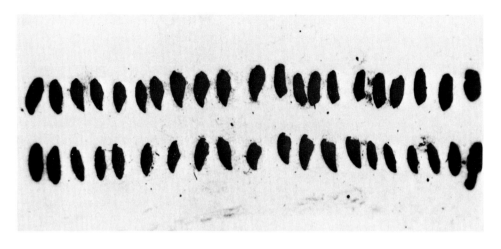

TEST
BULLET

FORTY-ONE
FRAGMENTS OF LEAD

The extruded portion of soft gray lead (arrow) from the rear end of our test bullet (below) was sliced to yield the 41 fragments seen above. Since this is the same amount of lead obviously extruded from the base of bullet 399, it means that the four fragments of lead in Connally were by no means too many for the two grains of lead missing from bullet 399, as claimed by critics of the Warren report. (*J. K. Lattimer*)

Fig. 114

was sitting. (If the reader tries this for himself, he can see that leaning to the left is a natural movement.)

FIG. 115
page 280

The Governor said that he put the heel of his right hand, in which he held his hat, on his left leg just above the knee, in an effort to push himself around further. I postulate that he remained in this position, twisted to his right, even though he had begun to turn his head back with the intention of looking over his left shoulder. While still in this twisted position, with his torso partly turned to the right and still leaning to his left, the Governor was hit in the back, wrist, and leg by bullet 399, which had first traversed Kennedy's neck at or shortly before frame 220 in Zapruder's film. This version would reconcile Connally's version of what happened with the circumstantial evidence of what actually happened. Exactly what position everyone's body was in just as the bullet struck is difficult to determine, since the car had disappeared behind the Stemmons Freeway sign at the very moment when the first bullet apparently struck Kennedy in the back of the neck. Photographs by professional cameramen Betzner and Willis at curbside, shown in *Life* for November 24, 1967, were probably taken a few tenths of a second before the first bullet hit the President. Exactly what Connally said and did, and the exact timing and order in which he did and said them, are also difficult to determine, since he himself was certainly dazed, just as my soldier patients were always dazed for a few moments after being shot through and through the chest by similar German or Italian army rifle bullets.

Everyone in the automobile was thrown into a natural panic reaction by this totally unexpected, sudden catastrophe. In such situations, circumstantial evidence is almost always more dependable and sheds more accurate light on what actually happened than the direct testimony of those who were involved or who watched the confused actions, despite their best intentions.

The elongated wound of entry into Governor Connally's back and the lack of a third bullet in the car or in its occupants, plus the experimental evidence that the wounding of both men by a bullet of the type used is perfectly feasible, are impressive support for the Warren Commission version of what actually happened.

The only apparent weakness in the theory proposed here is the failure of even one or two people visible in the photographs, in addition to Connally, to turn around and look backward after the first loud noise, which attracted the Governor's attention. Of course few looked back even after the shot that hit President Kennedy in the neck. Only two out of the dozen or so Secret Service men visible in the pictures looked back, along with photographer Willis's daughter, who can be seen to stop running and look back about the time the President was hit.

I believe that President Kennedy was hit in the neck at or shortly before Zapruder frame 220, just before he emerged from behind the Stemmons Freeway sign. My reason is that his right hand and elbow can be clearly seen to be just starting their spastic upward jerk, which carried

KENNEDY AND CONNALLY STRUCK BY SAME BULLET

The white line in the photograph shows the course of bullet 399 through the neck of President Kennedy, in the rear seat, as his head was turned to his right, while waving to the crowd. Governor Connally, seated directly ahead of him, had heard the first shot, which hit a tree and missed the automobile completely, and was trying to twist around to look directly backward to see the President. He found that in spite of leaning far over to his left, and then placing the heel of his right hand against his left thigh to push, he was still unable to twist far enough around to see back over his right shoulder. He had his broad-brimmed Stetson hat in his hand upside down, as shown. Bullet 399 then struck him in the right side of his back because he was leaning over so far to his left. It shattered his fifth rib, while going sideways and a little backward. It then exited just below his right nipple, went through his right wrist and, traveling backward, embedded itself in the skin of his left thigh. Being a long bullet, it was knocked out on his stretcher later. (Note: Connally was actually seated in a jump seat that had a lower back than the one shown above in the test vehicle.) *(J. K. Lattimer, Gary Lattimer, M. M. Macfarlane, J. T. Donovan)*

Fig. 115

his right elbow to an extremely high level. It is my belief, after consultation with neurological surgeons and neurophysiologists knowledgeable in these matters, that this was a reflex reaction to the trauma of this bullet transmitted to his spinal cord (from the hitting of the tip of the transverse process of one of his vertebrae in the lower neck region).

Photographer Willis, who took a picture from the opposite curb at about this time, said that he heard a loud noise, a noise so loud that, "in fact, the shot caused me to trip the camera shutter," even though he had not intended to do so just at that moment. This photograph was taken just prior to the time the Warren Commission believed the President was hit, and the backfire or the shot-that-missed, which the photographer heard, may have been the same sound that made the Governor try to turn to look over his right shoulder at the President. The daughter of still another photographer, Tina Towner, said that she heard the shots, thought to herself that "some dummy is lighting firecrackers," and did not bother to look further toward the source of the noise. As Mrs. Kennedy said, there is always so much backfiring and noise from a motorcycle escort that it is understandable that very little attention would be paid to a first loud noise, thus the fact that Governor Connally and Linda Willis were the only ones of whom we know who turned toward the first loud noise is not too surprising and does not necessarily weaken our reconstruction.

Some of the arguers against the claim that bullet 399 could have penetrated both men have adopted the argument of architect Robert Cutler, who postulated that the two men (President Kennedy and Governor Connally) were sitting like rigid statues in the automobile, either immobile, or rotating very slowly, as statues might be rotated, in the car. The angles of the bullet holes, which were then calculated to exit through the two statuelike bodies, were thought to be slightly out of line with Oswald's window, if one "looked back through the bullet holes, towards the window." The holes in Connally were thought to be a little too far to the right, and the angles of downward passage (declination) were thought to be slightly different. This led to the postulation that the bullet holes in Connally might have been made by a bullet fired from a different (additional) window in the same Texas Book Depository building, slightly farther to the right than Oswald's, five (or less) seconds later. Other critics have picked up this argument. They ignore the fact that both bullets recovered from the car and its passengers came from Oswald's rifle, to the exclusion of all other guns. Also that all three empty cartridge cases came out of Oswald's gun, and only his gun.

The fallacy in this argument is the fact that the exact positions of the two men at the moment they were hit are not known, because no photographs were taken just at that critical moment. Furthermore, the two men were not acting like rigid statues at the moment they were hit. Kennedy had his hand up waving and was looking to his right. Connally was trying to twist around to see the President over his right shoulder, and then to twist the other way. Unfortunately, the freeway sign blocked Zapruder's view just as Kennedy's neck was hit, so we do not have detailed views of the moment this bullet struck both men.

A most persuasive argument against the rigid-statue, third-bullet version is that it requires three bullets in the targets. Only two bullets could be accounted for in the car or in the victims, despite a detailed and vigorous search to find such a third bullet or bullet hole.

If Governor Connally had been sitting like a rigid statue, facing front, directly in front of President Kennedy, only twenty-eight inches away from him, when the first bullet to hit Kennedy traversed his neck, the bullet would have hit Connally in the left side of his back rather than the right side. Even if it missed Connally, it would have hit the back of the driver's seat and made an obvious hole. As our experiments showed, such a bullet would almost certainly have been starting to tumble after it left the President's neck and would have made a large and obvious wound in Connally or a hole in the back of the driver's seat, which would not be missed during the FBI's thorough search of the car.

The rigid-statue concept, when applied to living, moving human bodies, is not nearly as appropriate as thinking of the human torso as a soft bag full of jelly, with a few ribs and a spine on which it is suspended. The accuracy of trying to pinpoint windows 200 feet away by looking back through bullet holes in the bodies of living men who were waving or twisting around when hit does not turn out to be at all precise.

Our reconstruction, on the other hand, with an integrated mechanical model of the flight path of bullet 399, tumbling (rotating end over end) at a rate of one-half turn in five feet after it left Kennedy's neck, coincides with the Warren Commission's deduction that a single bullet (Warren Commission exhibit 399) struck both President Kennedy and Governor Connally. The nature and dimensions of the wounds, bone, and bullet fragments in the two men fit this reconstruction with reasonable certainty.

FIG. 108
page 268

The hard facts are that Connally was clearly hit by a tumbling bullet that had struck something else first, that his hand readily can be seen to have already risen out of the line of the bullet by the point when he thinks he was hit, and that there was no sign of a third bullet hitting the car. If three bullets had hit the men, Connally would have been hit twice, and he was not.

Circumstantial Evidence Overpowering Regarding Kennedy-Connally Bullet

To summarize, both of the bullets that hit the occupants of the car (five seconds apart) came out of Oswald's rifle, to the exclusion of all other guns. Oswald's hand prints were on the gun, as were fibers from the shirt he was wearing that day. Neutron activation analysis by the 1978 congressional probe showed that only two bullets created all the wounds. These facts effectively destroy the "wounds by a second rifleman" theory. Our reconstruction of the flight path of bullet 399 through both men, demonstrated as a mechanical model, reasonably fits all the wound sizes and autopsy findings. These factual, circumstantial, and experimental pieces of evidence make it impossible to refute the Warren Commission's contention that both men were hit by a single bullet.

FIG. 108
page 268

FIG. 112
page 273

If our experimental bullets struck our Connally rib, our Connally arm bone, and then our Connally leg bone (femur) without also passing through one of our Kennedy necks first, they always shattered the leg bone (femur) into multiple pieces. However, if this bullet first passed through one of our Kennedy necks, it did not shatter the femur the way it did the rib and arm bones. Governor Connally's femur was not shattered, which made us believe that the bullet that struck his leg had definitely been slowed down by passing through something else (such as Kennedy's neck). If it had not been slowed down in this way, it surely would have shattered Connally's femur.

There was speculation that Oswald might have been shooting at Governor Connally, rather than President Kennedy, but certainly Oswald's final shot was *not* directed at Connally, because by that time the wounded Connally had been pulled down out of sight by his wife, leaving only the President clearly the target for Oswald's last bullet.

There have been advocates of the idea that Oswald was shooting at Mrs. Kennedy, hitting the men by mistake. This is refuted by his failure to fire his last bullet at her when she was up on the trunk of the car, looming large in his sights.

The concept that Governor Connally was hit by an additional bullet, fired in between the two that hit President Kennedy, has been the basis of much of the confusion and complaints about the Warren Commission report, but it is clearly not true. Only two bullets hit the two men, and both came out of Oswald's gun.

14.

THE KENNEDY-CONNALLY BULLET (WARREN COMMISSION EXHIBIT 399)— COULD ONE BULLET HAVE WOUNDED BOTH MEN?

Having completed my research and experiments on the path of bullet 399, I turned my attention to the bullet itself—that small cylinder of metal which had been the subject of so much controversy, and about which there were still speculations, doubts, and unanswered questions.

Many of these doubts were over one of the specific findings of the Warren Commission; namely, that this single bullet from Oswald's rifle traversed Kennedy's neck, nicked his vertebra, turned sideways, and then pierced Connally's chest, below his right scapula. Based on a deduction by commission counsels Arlen Spector and David Belin, the commission report postulated that this same bullet then shattered the Governor's fifth rib, while turned completely sideways, emerged below his right nipple, went sideways and somewhat backward through his right wrist, tumbled still further to turn completely around, and ended up sticking backward into the skin of his left thigh. From this position the long, narrow bullet was dislodged and was found on a stretcher upon which it was deduced that Connally had lain. The rifling scratches on this bullet proved it came out of Oswald's gun.

Fig. 116
page 286

So-called Pristine Bullet Is Not Pristine; It Is Both Flattened and Bent

FIG. 105
page 262

This bullet, if seen only in a side view, which has been widely republished by critics of the Warren Commission report, appears to be deformed very little. In fact, its apparent lack of deformity permitted critics to describe it inaccurately as a pristine bullet.

Assassination buffs have tried to discredit the Warren Commission report deduction that bullet 399 could come out with so little deformity after doing all this dirty work in two victims. They have even elected to try to discredit the bullet itself, without inspecting it themselves.

FIG. 72
page 175

When I actually picked up this bullet and inspected it, I found it to be flattened on its rear end to a significant degree, as if from a severe blow on one side. (Photographs taken from the side do not show this flattening.) It is also slightly bent, on its long axis.

The soft lead at the base of bullet 399 appeared to be scooped out slightly on one side, with fine transverse scratch marks across the base in the direction of the scooping effect. Some of the soft lead of the interior of the bullet still projected slightly from the base of the bullet, at the edge toward which the scooping effect led (see arrow in figure 109, left lower end). This extruded bit of lead lay on the side of the bullet away from the flattened side.

FIG. 116
page 286

That bullet 399 was fired from Oswald's rifle has been verified by tests done by the FBI laboratory staff, who found that the rifling scratches on bullet 399 conformed exactly to the rifling scratches on the test bullets fired from the same gun. No one appears to have contested this point.

Were the Four Fragments in Connally Excessive?

FIG. 62
page 164

Critics also contended that the four fragments of bullet seen in the pre-operative X-rays of Connally's wrist and thigh were too many to be produced from the amount of lead estimated to be missing from bullet 399, that is, 2.2 grains. Again, they said this without checking for its validity. Once more it appeared to me and my sons that we could contribute answers to this question.

It would be necessary, it seemed to us at once, carefully to weigh 100 sample bullets. These would have to be identical to those fired by Oswald.

First, however, I closely examined the fragments of the bullets removed from Kennedy's head, from Connally's wrist, and from the automobile. Neutron activation analysis revealed that the wrist fragments all came from bullet 399. All the other bullet fragments, from the President's brain and from the floor of the car, came from the head bullet. No other bullets were represented in the car. The unfired cartridge found in Oswald's rifle was next examined at the National Archives.

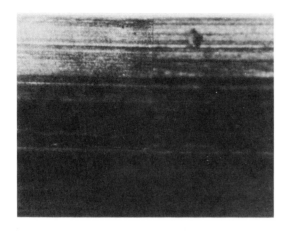

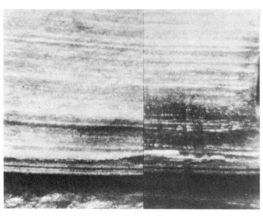

KENNEDY BULLETS BOTH FROM OSWALD'S GUN

Fragments of both bullets that struck Kennedy were recovered, and all bore the telltale scratches seen here from the rifling of Oswald's gun, which showed that they came out of Oswald's gun to the exclusion of all other guns. The comparisons are shown here for bullets 399 (top), the neck bullet, and fragments 567 (middle) and 569 (bottom) of the head bullet. (*National Archives*)

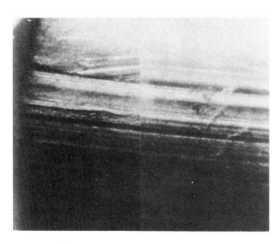

Fig. 116

After considerable difficulty, I obtained a substantial supply of exactly the same cartridges as Oswald had used. Around 1954, four lots of these cartridges had been manufactured. I was finally able to procure samples from lots 6000, 6001, 6002, and 6003, and the FBI obtained samples from lots 6000 and 6003, all of which proved consistent and reliable. One hundred of these bullets were pulled from cartridges, and my son Jon weighed them on a precision balance in the laboratories of the Englewood School for Boys. The weights ranged from 159.80 grains for the lightest bullet to 161.50 grains for the heaviest, with an average weight of 160.844 grains and a median weight of 160.80 grains.

FIG. 101
page 252

This compared fairly closely with the weight range of three sample bullets weighed by the FBI laboratory and reported by firearms expert Robert Frazier. He found them to weigh 160.85 grains, 161.1 grains, and 161.5 grains, with an average weight of 161.15 grains, whereas our larger sample yielded a mean weight of 160.84 grains.

Since bullet 399 weighed 158.6 grains when found, we have assumed that it lost between 1.2 grains and 2.9 grains, with a mean probability of 2.2 grains.

Compressing a Bullet Like 399 Squeezes Soft Gray Lead from the Rear End

Next, we compressed a bullet like Warren Commission Exhibit 399 sideways in a special vice until its configuration was as close as possible to that of bullet 399. This required great force because of the high structural density of these bullets, but it did cause the softer lead from the center of the bullet to be extruded from the open rear of the encompassing jacket (which was made of a tougher, copper-colored gilding metal) much as toothpaste is extruded from a tube.

FIG. 109
page 270

The extruded leaden metal was then sliced off flush with the base of the bullet and the cylindrical fragment weighed. It was found to weigh exactly 2.1 grains, almost precisely the same as the weight of lead estimated to be missing from the base of bullet 399.

FIG. 62
page 164

The extruded cylinder of lead weighing 2.1 grains was first placed on one of our test wrists in the same location as the large fragment seen on the X-rays of Connally's wrist. Three additional particles the same size as the other particles in Connally were then removed from the extruded cylinder and arranged in the same configuration as those seen on his X-rays of the wrist and thigh, and pictures were taken for comparison. The density of the materials was the same as from a bullet like 399.

It was seen that the largest fragment from our test bullet was slightly larger than the largest fragment in Connally.

Next, Dr. Myron Tannenbaum, our pathologist, sliced the remainder of this extruded cylinder of metal into thin fragments, each approximately the same size as those seen in Connally's X-rays, to see how many such fragments could be obtained from it.

Fragments from Our 2.1-grain Sample of Test Bullet Lead Compared with Fragments from Bullet 399

Fig. 114
page 278

Fig. 62
page 164

A grand total of forty-one such fragments (slices) were made from the extruded metal, as compared with the total of only four fragments seen in Connally's arm (three fragments) and leg (one fragment) X-rays. It should be noted that while one of the fragments in Connally's wrist was about twice the diameter of our test slices, the other three were much smaller than our slices.

For those who might argue that bullet 399 in its unfired state might have weighed only as much as our lightest sample bullet, namely 159.8 grains, we still have the fact that twenty-two such slices could have been produced from the 1.2 grains of metal that would have been involved.

At the other extreme, if it were assumed that bullet 399 happened to weigh as much as our heaviest sample bullet, 161.5 grains, then fifty-three slices might have been produced from the missing portion.

It must be pointed out that only one of the four Connally fragments was slightly thicker than those from our sample of forty-one, and that certainly the number of metallic fragments was not a valid criterion for judging how much weight was missing from bullet 399. Using the actual amount of metal (2.1 grains) extruded from our test bullet, we were able to produce forty-one fragments from it.

Next, the fragments extruded from the experimental bullet were examined as to appearance, color, and texture, and were found to be a similar lead-gray color (containing none of the copper color of the bullet jackets) and to be of the same texture as the fragment removed from Connally's wrist. In both cases the fragments appeared to be extruded soft lead like that from the centers of both the test bullet and bullet 399.

The experiment of compressing bullets to the same extent as bullet 399 was repeated ten times to rule out possible gross differences in the malleability of the materials in different bullets. The results were closely similar in every sample tested.

Ammunition Highly Dependable; 700 Rounds Without a Misfire

Our final question concerned Oswald's ammunition: Was it reliable? To test this, we fired 700 rounds of the same type of cartridge as those used by Oswald (from sub-lots 6000, 6001, 6002, 6003), manufactured by the Western Cartridge Company, a branch of the Winchester Repeating Arms Company, in the same year as those used by Oswald.

None of these rounds failed to fire, even though an additional four years had elapsed since the Kennedy shooting, making this ammunition thirteen years old at the time of testing. Dr. John Nichols had reported the same degree of dependability, and the FBI agents who fired ammunition from lots 6000 and 6003 with Oswald's rifle more than 100 times also reported no failures to fire. These various samples represented every lot manufactured, so they must have included the lot from which Oswald's ammunition came.

In all, more than 900 rounds of this Western Cartridge Company 6.5 mm ammunition have been fired in our experiments and those of others without a single failure to fire on the first attempt.

Each Lot Highly Consistent as to Bullet and Charge Weights

My son Jon weighed 180 complete, loaded cartridges of this type to see if there were gross differences in powder charges that might thus be detected, but each lot was internally consistent within 0.01 gram. Oswald's unfired round still bore the original purple lacquer placed on it by the Western Cartridge Company and bore no traces of tampering, resizing, or reloading. We also inspected the three empty rifle cartridge cases found near his firing location under magnification, and these showed no signs of reloading or resizing.

It should be pointed out that Oswald used American-made, brass-cased, Western cartridges, which should not be confused with imported cartridges with inferior powder cases and greater variance in gross weight and performance. Such imported cartridges were found to be dangerous because of a tendency of the cases to split when fired.

The answer to the question "Was Oswald's ammunition reliable?" was clearly yes. It was very reliable.

It must be remembered that bullet 399 is the one that went through President Kennedy's neck. Although it brushed a vertebra in the President's neck, it did not hit any bones solidly in the President, and indeed did not hit any vital structures. It should not be confused with the second bullet, which struck Kennedy in the right side of the back of the head, which was severely disrupted by the thick bone of the back of the skull, exactly as our test bullets were.

Could This Bullet Penetrate Two Persons?

Fig. 110
page 272

In tests conducted by Dr. Nichols, military-rifle cartridges like those used by Oswald (lot 6002) were fired into a stack of ponderosa pine boards bound tightly together and were found to have extraordinary penetrating power. Wooden blocks twenty-four and then thirty-six inches thick were completely penetrated. It was necessary to construct a wooden block forty-eight inches thick before the bullet would stop just inside the wood. These bullets were seen to be undamaged when X-rayed or recovered.

FIG. 111
page 272

Because of the great penetrating ability, it is my opinion that the bullet which struck Connally would have shattered his femur and traversed his thigh completely if it had not been slowed prior to striking him. (See the experiments described earlier.)

Passing through the soft tissues of Kennedy's neck, with its two layers of tough skin, and brushing a vertebra would have slowed the bullet slightly more than 30 percent, according to Nichols's figures.

The passage through the thorax of Governor Connally, with its two additional layers of skin, and a glancing (tangential) contact with his fifth rib would have slowed it still more, although less than the passage through Kennedy. Only the fact that it transversed the President's neck and then traveled sideways as it traversed the skin and bone of Connally's wrist could have accounted for the loss of so much energy that it did not break his leg bone.

Bullet Was Tumbling When It Hit Connally

As has often been pointed out by Dr. Milton Helpern, chief medical examiner of the City of New York (and the author's mentor), human skin is elastic and tough. It is very effective in slowing down pistol bullets, but the penetrating ability of high-speed military-rifle bullets is of quite another order of magnitude, unless these bullets begin to travel sideways (in the process of tumbling or yawing), as this one obviously did in penetrating Connally's chest and wrist. The sizes and shapes of the various bullet holes in the Governor support the view that the bullet turned as described. Our experiments have demonstrated over and over that this type of tumbling is to be expected from this bullet.

FIG. 96
page 237

Again let me say that, based on the experiments we have done, if the bullet had struck Governor Connally's back as its first point of impact without previously passing through President Kennedy, it *surely* would have shattered Connally's femur and probably would have traversed his leg completely, in addition to his thorax and wrist. It also would have made a small punctate wound of entrance on his back rather than the elongated one it did leave. The shock of being hit was so great that Connally was not even aware that his wrist and leg had also been hit, even though the large bone in his wrist had been shattered into many fragments (but not displaced) by the tangential passage of the bullet. It was only when he awoke from anesthesia and saw the cast on his wrist and the bandage on his leg that he asked what they were for. The possibility that the first bullet to strike Connally had been underpowered due to a deficient powder charge (as suggested by some) is not credible, in my opinion, because the net effect of an underpowered cartridge would have been to make the bullet drop so severely that it would have hit a portion of the automobile behind Kennedy, rather than hitting him.

FIG. 62
page 164

We did, moreover, weigh 180 of the rounds to check any sign of under-charging and found none, at least in these factory-loaded cartridges. Oswald's remaining unfired cartridge, found in his gun, was not under-charged.

Significance of This Research

In short, the so-called pristine bullet (Warren Commission Exhibit 399), which critics have been claiming could not have penetrated both President Kennedy's neck and Governor Connally's thorax and wrist and still remain undeformed, was found by us to be, in fact, deformed (flattened and bent) in a manner that required great force to duplicate on test bullets from the same lots. I think this occurred when it hit Connally's rib while traveling sideways and a little backward.

The four fragments that the Warren Commission contends bullet 399 left in Connally, while losing 2.2 grains of its weight, are by no means excessive, since we were able to slice forty-one fragments from the 2.1-grain cylinder of lead extruded from a test bullet under parallel conditions.

We found the type of Western Cartridge Company ammunition used by Oswald to be highly reliable, confirming the finding of other experimenters.

From our experiments, it appeared completely feasible that this one bullet (399) could have done all the things the Warren Commission contended it did.

With regard to the possibility that the bullet fragments in Connally could have come from a bullet deformed as was bullet 399, there was no inconsistency or incompatibility between the facts, as determined by these experiments, and the contentions of the Warren Commission.

Neutron Activation Analysis Confirmed Our Contentions

Neutron activation analysis tests done since for the 1978 House Select Committee on Assassinations did in fact prove that the lead fragments removed from Connally's wrist did come from bullet 399, and no other bullet.

15.

DID OSWALD REALLY
DO IT?

We have studied the victims and we have studied the bullet that killed one of them and maimed the other. Now, in a final investigation, let us study the assassin himself, and his weapon, and let us ask the final questions: *Could* Oswald have fired the fatal shots—and did he?

When the Warren Commission report first came out, its critics almost immediately began to claim that Oswald's Italian military Carcano rifle (caliber 6.5 mm, model 91-38) could not have been fired as rapidly and accurately as the Warren Commission investigators had proposed. These doubts were impressed upon the public by expert media techniques until a large segment of the population believed, for example, that Oswald's rifle was no good.

This was an interesting contention, and unless you have the opportunity to try if for yourself, you can have no way of knowing whether or not it holds up. It is, however, the kind of claim that is susceptible to challenge and to experimentation. It appeared to be a fine project, so my two sons, Jon and Gary, and I decided to try it as an experiment.

I had examined Oswald's rifle at the National Archives and it had seemed to me at the time that practice might have been an important factor in the operation of the rifle; perhaps Oswald had been able to familiarize himself with the rifle longer than those who later tested it. Government experts had dared to fire only a limited number of shots from it, for fear of damaging the rifle. It was obvious to me that the first thing we needed to know more about was Oswald's capability as a marksman. Had he been any good with a rifle of this type? I turned first to his Marine Corps rifle score book, which I own; it shows clearly just what sort of marksman Oswald was.

FIG. 117
page 293

I had acquired this, along with most of his letters from Russia, his court-martial papers, his applications to the Albert Schweitzer Univer-

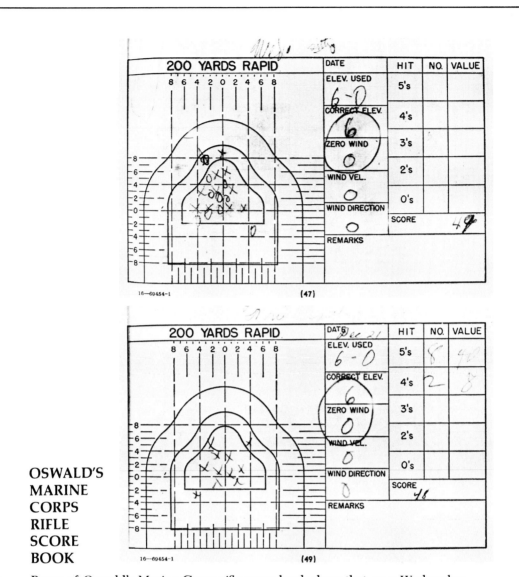

OSWALD'S MARINE CORPS RIFLE SCORE BOOK

Pages of Oswald's Marine Corps rifle score book show that on a Wednesday (above), he scored forty-nine out of a possible fifty points at rapid fire from a sitting position at 200 yards (more than twice the distance at Dallas) and did it with no telescopic sight. On the following Friday, he scored forty-eight out of a possible fifty (below). From this it is evident that Oswald was definitely marksman enough to have shot Kennedy as alleged. It should be noted that the contour of this target is remarkably similar to that of the head and shoulders of Kennedy as they projected above the back seat of the automobile in Dallas, and that the rifle used at Dallas was similar to rifles with which Oswald was trained in the Marine Corps. The author owns this rifle score book and knows it is in its original condition. (*J. K. Lattimer*)

Fig. 117

sity, and a host of documents about his childhood, when his mother and brother sold them shortly after the Warren Commission was through with them. I was curious to know more about this "modern-day John Wilkes Booth," and there is no substitute for original documents, if they are available. Many of them had been reproduced in the Warren Commission report but had been returned to their actual owners, from whom I bought them. Using these original materials, I could see just how competent Oswald was with a military rifle.

Oswald's Marine Corps Rifle Scores

Fig. 117
page 293

Firing at head-and-shoulders military targets (strikingly like the profile of President Kennedy at which he fired in Dallas), he scored forty-eight out of a possible fifty points one day and forty-nine out of a possible fifty points on another day, using a similar sitting position, at rapid fire, even without a telescope, and at more than twice the distance involved at Dallas. Thus, while he would not rate as an expert or even a highly skilled marksman in the eyes of a Marine Corps marksmanship instructor, he was a perfectly adequate marksman to do what was claimed for him by the Warren Commission.

It must be remembered that his Marine Corps rifle record, which indicated only modest scores, only a few points above the minimum requirement for sharpshooter, included firing the rifle in the standing position with nothing on which to rest the heavy gun. This so-called offhand position is much more difficult than the sitting position, where the gun can be rested by supporting the arms on the seated person's legs, much as Oswald did at Dallas. He improved on this position at Dallas by resting his forward hand on a carefully selected box of just the right height, also using a sling to steady his arm, and a telescope, which he did not have in the Marine Corps. His sitting position scores in the Marine Corps were excellent, just as they were at Dallas.

Our next step was to conduct a final series of tests in order to see for ourselves whether it was possible for ordinary civilians, after a reasonable amount of dry-firing practice, to reproduce Oswald's marksmanship. We conducted these tests by firing three shots in rapid succession at shifting targets, at ranges up to 263 feet, using equipment and positioning as similar as possible to those used by Oswald.

Simulation Arranged

Fig. 118
page 296

Since it was not practical for us to fire shots from the sixth floor of the Texas Book Depository building, as Oswald did, we arranged boxes of the same type and dimensions he used on the roof of a building that would permit a reasonable (although of course not exact) simulation of Oswald's firing position. Since, at an earlier date, I had had an opportunity to sit on the boxes in the actual window used by Oswald, I was familiar with the general configuration and characteristics of Oswald's well-arranged firing position. Photographs from the Warren Commission report, taken immediately after the shooting, also helped us to duplicate most of the conditions.

We had procured four rifles of exactly the same type used by Oswald, and four four-power telescopes made by the Ordnance Optical Company, exactly like the one he used. We positioned various types of targets at the distances at which Oswald's first shot might have been fired and at the precise distances of the two shots that struck Kennedy. We obtained a sling like the one on Oswald's gun and assembled the telescope mount with the same number of screws—two—placed in the same positions as those on Oswald's rifle.

We then selected, from our four sample rifles, the one that most closely resembled his, in both condition and ease of operation, for use in our firing tests. After much searching, we obtained several clips (cartridge holders) exactly like the ones he used, labeled SMI.

We aligned the telescopic sight by looking through the barrel at the target and then adjusting the telescope to point at the bull's eye—a technique known as bore-sighting—and then, to align the sight perfectly, we placed thin metal wafers, known as shims, under the front ring of the mount of the telescope, just as Oswald's gunsmith had done. We then conducted test firings from a fixed (bench) rest for the final adjustments of the telescope.

Mystery of Oswald's Sling Solved

Fig. 119
page 297

During the course of our experiments, a communication we received from ballistics specialist Leon Day, then of Hoboken, New Jersey, solved the mystery of the strange-looking strap Oswald had used for a rifle sling, which had been the subject of many futile questions asked by the Warren Commission investigators. The sling had been described as a strap from a camera case and even as a guitar-carrying device, but nobody could identify it with assurance. Day correctly pointed out that it was none of these, but was actually the shoulder-harness strap from a U.S. Air Force revolver holster of a now obsolete pattern. The distinctive way in which the end straps are riveted to the body of the ovoid patch, at a slight angle, plus the strange built-in curve of the patch and the additional rivets, leave no doubt as to the true identity of this strap. Where Oswald obtained it is a point still to be discovered. Perhaps he got it during his Marine Corps service in Japan, although he had used an improvised flat ropelike sling (uncannily like that of John Wilkes Booth) on his rifle shortly after he acquired it. On his mail-order form for his pistol, he had at first indicated that he wanted a holster with the pistol but had scratched out the holster request before sending in the order.

TESTING THE RIFLE

Dr. Lattimer conducted extensive tests with Mannlicher-Carcano rifles, simulating Oswald's presumed elevation, body position, and range, and has probably fired more Oswald-type cartridges and Oswald-type rifles at Oswald-type mock-ups than any other person, including Oswald. Boxes were used of the same type and dimensions as used by Oswald (some on which to sit and some on which to rest the hand) on the roof of a building that would permit a reasonable (although, of course, not exact) simulation of Oswald's firing position. Having sat on the boxes in the actual window used by Oswald in Dallas, Lattimer was familiar with the general configuration and characteristics of his well-arranged firing position with its low window sill. The advantageous nature of the arrangements made by Oswald could not be fully appreciated until this was done.
(I. E. Lattimer, J. K. Lattimer)

Fig. 118

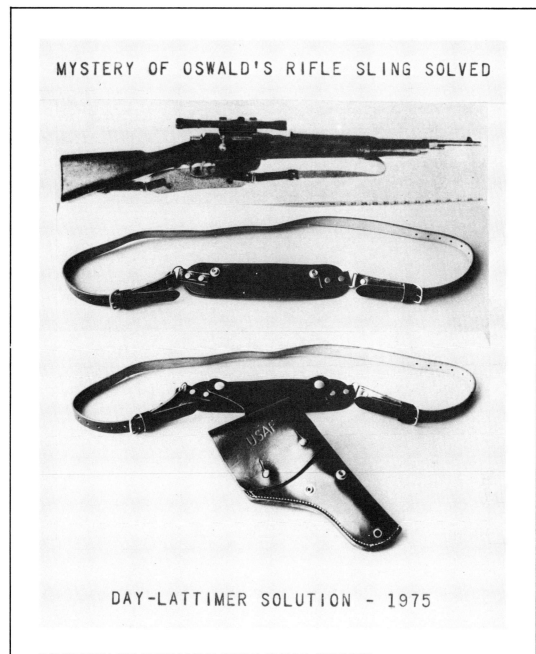

MYSTERY OF OSWALD'S RIFLE SLING SOLVED

Oswald had a peculiar sling on his rifle (top), which no one could at first identify. Twelve years later, Leon Day discovered what it was: the shoulder-harness strap of an obsolete type of United States Air Force pistol holster (middle and bottom). *(Top: National Archives; others: J. K. Lattimer)*

Fig. 119

Telescope Mounts Loosen after 111 Shots

We noted that the mount of the telescopic sight on Oswald's rifle had come loose at some unspecified point, after it was found. We knew that his (and therefore our) telescope mounts were fastened to the gun with only two short screws in shallow holes, even though there were places for four such screws. We suspected that two screws were inadequate to hold the telescope for too long, with the sharp recoil of this powerful rifle, so we watched for signs of loosening. Sure enough, after 111 shots, it became necessary to retighten the screws holding the telescope mount, because the depth of the two threaded holes was so shallow. We had watched this carefully, in view of the reported loosening of the screws of Oswald's telescope mount, either during the search for fingerprints or during the firing tests by government authorities. We had fired a large number of rounds (one hundred and eleven), and these screws did indeed tend to loosen. Yet, they did *not* loosen with the firing of only three or four shots, or even fifty or sixty.

Dry-Firing Important to Acquire Dexterity with This Rifle

We also undertook a long period of dry-firing, using dummy cartridges from our previous experiments, in order to become dexterous in the procedure of pulling back the bolt, pushing it forward quickly, aiming, pulling the trigger, and then repeating the performance as rapidly as possible, so that three simulated shots were dry-fired, as Oswald seems to have done. With the sling binding the rifle tightly to the experimenter's left arm, which rested on the box, and by resting the right elbow on the right knee (as was possible in Oswald's high perch), three cartridges could be worked through the action in six or seven seconds, still allowing a short period for aiming before each simulated shot. If the interval between each shot was increased to five seconds (ten seconds total), aiming became quite easy. We found that it was necessary not only to push this gun's stiff bolt vigorously forward but also to pull it vigorously back each time, with more force than is usually required with bolt-action rifles, keeping a firm grip on the bolt knob at all times. We acquired facility with these motions only after many, many workings of the action over a period of two weeks of both simulated and actual firing, proving that the ability to fire this rifle rapidly and dexterously requires a prolonged period of dry-firing practice.

Clip Not Always Ejected When Empty

In comparing the actions of our four rifles against each other, we found that the clip was ejected from the magazine of two of the four, but not from all of them. Two rifles would retain the clip, thus accounting for the report, which had puzzled us, that the clip was found in Oswald's rifle even though the last cartridge had been pushed into the rifle's chamber, leaving the clip empty. We had expected that all these old Carcano rifles would eject the clip when it was empty, and it was only after trying all four that we found that this was not always so. I had thought I had discovered a discrepancy in the Warren Commission report when I read that Oswald's clip was retained, but after actually trying Oswald's rifle, I discovered that the Warren Commission report had been correct on this point.

Some Carcano Actions Will Not Accept Single Cartridges

We also found that single rounds could not be inserted into some of our rifles by hand without a clip unless the bolt was dismounted and the single cartridge base inserted under the ejector. This made us think the ejector was faulty, but we soon found that many Carcano rifles of this type act this way, and that they will still accept cartridges normally if a clip is used. Thus our first impression that the ejector was defective mirrored similar hasty opinions that Oswald's rifle's firing mechanism was in some way defective. This proved to be owing to our initial lack of familiarity with these foreign rifles in their used condition, where the catch that would ordinarily hold the clip in was stuck, because of dried grease or old age.

Finally, we tested the rifle for accuracy by firing groups of three shots at a bull's-eye mounted 263 feet from the muzzle of the rifle, using a rest for the front hand as on the front box used by Oswald. Since none of us had fired this rifle, we approached it with caution, but found that it had relatively little recoil, especially considering the weight and fairly high velocity of its military-type bullet. The intensity of the recoil from the shots was similar to that of the popular 30-30 cartridge, extensively used by American riflemen.

A Very Noisy Gun

The noise from each shot, however, was very loud, and for firing a number of rounds we covered our ears with ear protectors similar to earmuffs. If one stood even a little in front of the rifle muzzle without ear coverings, the reports were so loud as to be nearly intolerable. We were impressed by the fact that if such a rifle had been discharged a few feet to the right rear of photographer Abraham Zapruder—as from the grassy knoll, which some people alleged—Zapruder would have been more than acutely aware of a deafening explosion with each shot. He surely

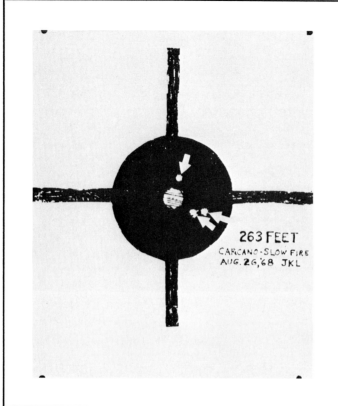

ACCURACY OF CARCANO CARBINE

Slow-fire target, showing the quite adequate accuracy of the Carcano carbine at 263 feet (the range when Kennedy was wounded in the head), using sling, rest, and sitting position, as Oswald did. *(J. K. Lattimer)*

Fig. 120

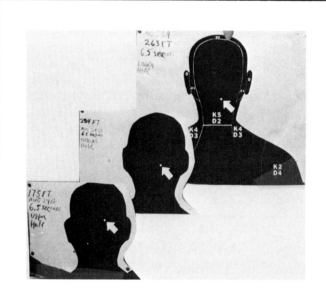

CARCANO STILL EFFECTIVE AT RAPID-FIRE

Speeding up the rate of fire so that all three shots were fired in 6.5 seconds at a shifting target caused greater spread of the pattern of bullet holes. But it was still possible to hit the head with most of the shots. *(J. K. Lattimer, Bulletin of the New York Academy of Medicine, April 1972)*

Fig. 121

would have stopped filming after the first such tremendously loud report had it been nearby.

The Secret Service agents in the presidential car would have been even more aware of such a shot fired at them from such close range, because they would also have heard a sharp supersonic crack.

The Rifle Is Accurate

FIG. 120
page 300

When we practiced slow, deliberate aiming, three shots could be clustered repeatedly in an area two inches in diameter, just to the right of the bull's-eye at 263 feet. When three shots were fired at five-second intervals, it was repeatedly possible to place them in groups measuring two to three inches in diameter at 263 feet. When the rate of fire was increased so the three shots were fired in 6.5 seconds, the spread of the bullets was greater, but all three shots landed within a circle six inches in diameter, again at 263 feet, which was the longer range of the two shots that struck President Kennedy.

FIG. 121
page 300

After two weeks of practice, it was relatively easy for each of us to place three bullets in the central area of the head (or the torso) of a military-type silhouette target if five seconds were used between shots. As the speed of shooting was increased, the spread of the bullets was still greater, but all three bullets almost always landed within the head or neck area until the telescope-mounting screws loosened.

Tracking Shifting Target Not Difficult

Judging ourselves to be as familiar with the rifle as Oswald probably was at the time of the assassination, we next arranged three silhouette targets at three different points and distances, to simulate the slight lateral and upward shift of Kennedy's car within Oswald's field of vision, and to simulate the three points at which Oswald might have fired. These were at 150, 190, and 263 feet from Oswald's perch. The torso was tilted, as was Kennedy's, for the final target (hit) at 263 feet. This arrangement required the shooter to change his point of aim between successive shots, and made it possible to study how much of a shift was required for Oswald again to zero in on the slowly moving car at the new range. It was found that this shift, while real, was small and did not prove to be any problem, since the automobile was going downhill and away from Oswald's high perch, thus shifting relatively little in his field of vision. Tracking a single target on an automobile was actually found to be easier to follow, but the dangers of making our tests in this way proved to be too great, and we went back to three static stations for our targets.

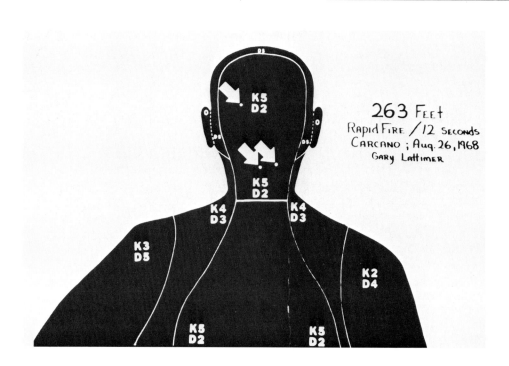

NOT A DIFFICULT SHOT

Gary Lattimer at fourteen could duplicate Oswald's marksmanship quite easily (albeit one second slower), as could his then seventeen-year-old brother, Jon. A Carcano carbine, sling, rest, telescopic sight, and ammunition exactly like those used by Oswald were employed by us in testing the contentions of the Warren Commission. *(I. E. Lattimer, J. K. Lattimer)*

Fig. 122

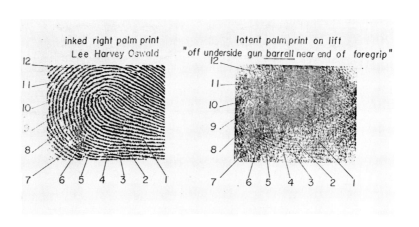

OSWALD'S PALM PRINT ON GUN

Under the protective wooden fore-end of the carbine, Oswald had touched the oily metal surface while he had it disassembled. He had wiped it clean of prints on the exposed surfaces, but this one escaped him. *(National Archives)*

Fig. 123

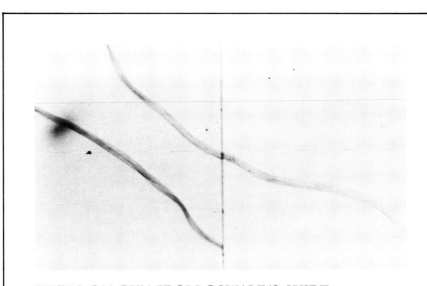

FIBERS ON GUN FROM OSWALD'S SHIRT

Micrographs like these showed that the fibers caught on the stock of Oswald's rifle, under the butt plate, matched all three types of fiber from the three-color shirt Oswald was wearing at the moment of the shooting. *(National Archives)*

Fig. 124

Rapid Firing Not Difficult

When three shots were fired within 6.5 seconds at these silhouette targets, it was found possible to hit all three targets in the head or neck area with consistency, although the spread of the bullet holes increased as rapid-fire was used. Some of the bullets landed in the neck area and others in the margins or occasionally just outside the head area. The bullets were generally clustered within an area six inches in diameter.

14-Year-Old Achieves This Easily

FIG. 122
page 302

In order to determine whether an even less experienced civilian marksman could attain this same degree of accuracy under the same conditions, we tried out my then fourteen-year-old son, Gary, a high-school student. Gary was able to duplicate the same degree of accuracy, although his rate of fire was slightly slower. His seventeen-year-old brother, Jon, a more experienced marksman, was easily able to do as well as an adult. There was no doubt, furthermore, that the strength of forearm of an adult was an advantage in operating the stiff bolt of this military-type firearm at the brisk rate required for rapid-fire. Oswald's older brother, Robert, who had taught him to shoot as a boy, had volunteered the information that Lee's arms were strong and his reflexes were quick.

It must be emphasized that a leisurely period of repeated manipulation and dry-firing (as practiced by Oswald, according to his wife's testimony) was essential for acquiring the proficiency demonstrated by the assassin. It was immediately apparent to all three of us that restriction in practice with Oswald's rifle, for fear of damaging it, would have interfered significantly with the familiarization and vigorous manipulation needed to achieve optimum proficiency in operating this unfamiliar foreign military weapon.

Interval Between Hits on Kennedy Was Five Seconds

It should also be noted that the actual interval between the two documented hits on President Kennedy was almost exactly five seconds, as measured by counting the frames of the Zapruder movie. We found no difficulty in hitting the shifting head targets twice in five seconds. We believe that the third shot had been fired *before* the other two, which hit the President. Thus the interval of five seconds between shots seemed entirely reasonable, and much easier to achieve than if *three* shots were required within the shorter interval of 5 seconds, even though this *could* be done.

We could find no evidence of a third bullet striking Governor Connally between the two bullets that hit Kennedy, despite the contentions of some critics that this happened. The findings of the expert on neutron activation analysis, Dr. Vincent P. Guinn, during the 1979 commission investigation that all of the bullets and bullet fragments in the car and in Kennedy's head and Connally's arm came from the only two bullets confirm our findings that both men were hit by one bullet (399), and Kennedy's head was hit by a second bullet, and that no third bullet was involved.

Oswald Obviously Competent to Do What Warren Commission Alleged He Did

Thus, when a rifle, telescope, and sling identical to the types used by Oswald were assembled from several such units, selecting the ones most like those used by him both as to condition and as to function, after carefully examining and measuring them, and were fired, there was no doubt Oswald could have done the lethal shooting.

Our tests left us with no reason to doubt that the type of rifle used by Oswald was accurate enough, dependable enough, and adaptable enough to be fired accurately three times in either 10 or 6.5 seconds, at a slowly moving target the size of the President's head and shoulders, even by ordinary marksmen, who had been given sufficient opportunity to practice, as contended by the Warren Commission.

Not only was Oswald's hand print on the gun, as verified by the 1978 House Assassinations Committee investigators, but also fibers with all three colors from the three-color shirt he was wearing at the time of the assassination were stuck in a crevice in the stock. When you consider that both bullets that struck the President were recovered and both came out of Oswald's gun to the exclusion of all other guns, it is difficult to deny that Oswald killed the President.

16.

THE ASSASSIN: PREPARATIONS AND FLIGHT; OFFICER TIPPIT KILLED

What a strange and horrible crime it was! Assassination is always horrifying, but when the victim is a beloved leader, it seems much more horrible. But we must, in our search for facts, pursue this crime to its conclusion and its aftermath. So let us insinuate ourselves once again into the mind and actions of Lee Harvey Oswald. Let us, in fact, backtrack to the days just preceding the assassination, when he was laying his plans.

Oswald Sees Opportunity for Fame

When Oswald discovered from the newspapers, a day or two before the event—much as had John Wilkes Booth, a century earlier—that the President was about to pass before him at his place of work, he must indeed have been electrified. Here was his chance to go down in history. Like Booth, he had had a trial session and he was now ready. His rifle was sighted in. He had learned well, from his practice session in trying to shoot General Walker, and he was eager to show the Cubans and the Russians what a hero they had lost in rejecting him the month before in Mexico City.

Early editions of the newspapers indicated that the motorcade might go down the center of Dealey Plaza, but later editions announced that it would turn and come along the north side of Dealey Plaza, on Elm Street, directly in front of the Texas School Book Depository. This would make it much easier for Oswald. It was logical that this latter route should be chosen, because of the greater numbers of potential voters who could then get a closer view of the President and his glamorous wife from the sidewalk, and because the subsequent right-hand turn onto the Stemmons Freeway could be more easily negotiated, once the motorcade had gone under the triple overpass at the far end of Dealey Plaza, en route to the Trade Mart, where the President was to give his lunchtime address.

Sets Up Ideal Position

Convinced that this was the moment he was waiting for, Oswald went around the building looking for the perfect location from which to fire a shot or shots at the presidential motorcade. He accurately deduced that a position far over at the southeast corner of the building would place him behind the motorcade as it turned and went slowly away from him, down the slope of Elm Street, toward the triple overpass. He would thus be able to get in several shots at the automobile without changing his line of fire very much, even if the car began to speed up in response to his early shots. It was also apparent that he had to seek a position on one of the upper floors in order for his bullets to clear the live oak tree just outside. The window he chose was as far over to the east as he could possibly get, was high enough so the car would clear the tree before it got too far away, and had the great extra advantage of a low window sill. This meant that the shooter would not have to reach up over a high window sill in order to point his rifle down into the automobile.

FIG. 63
page 167

By moving over a large box, on which to sit, and placing on the sill other boxes of exactly the right size on which to rest his left hand, and putting his feet flat on the floor, with his elbows resting on his thighs, he had the perfect arrangement. He also had his sling ready, to steady the rifle, and the side of the window frame for lateral stability. To have a telescopic sight, in addition, made this arrangement practically perfect to shoot at the unsuspecting President.

FIG. 69
page 173

Oswald piled up a wall of other boxes, so that no one could see what he was doing. He then pulled the elevators up and left the gates open, so that no one could use them.

FIG. 68
page 172

If one fires a high-powered rifle with the muzzle resting on a hard surface such as a window sill, the gun will jump and the bullet will be deflected from the target. It is necessary to rest the gun on something softer. One easy resting spot is the back of one's hand with the thumb muscles contracted and humped up into a soft pad that supports the barrel of the rifle. From the position of Oswald's hand prints found on the boxes sitting on the window sill, one can see that this is exactly what he did.

Oswald sat on his boxes with the icy calm he had cultivated for so long, waiting for his target to come into his cross hairs. No doubt he practiced tracing numerous unsuspecting automobiles as they drove down Elm Street below him, and no doubt he discovered he could work the bolt

307

BULLET CLIP LIKE OSWALD'S

This is the type of clip (bullet holder), containing four cartridges, Oswald used for loading his Carcano carbine on the fatal day. His clip was still in the gun, even though the last cartridge had been pushed out of the clip, into the barrel. Most of these old guns permit the clip to fall out at that point, and I was suspicious when I heard that Oswald's clip remained in the gun, even when the clip was empty. By trying Oswald's gun, however, I discovered that the clip does indeed stay in his gun when it is empty. *(J. K. Lattimer)*

Fig. 125

FIG. 125
page 308

action of his rifle at least four times before they disappeared under the overpass at the end of Dealey Plaza. He had four cartridges left, and undoubtedly hoped to use them all.

Fires Three Deliberate Shots

Resisting all impulses to fire at the front of the presidential car as it came toward him on Houston Street (the two windshield frames and the other occupants of the car would have been between him and the President), he waited calmly until the car was right below him and the President's back was in his sights. He appears to have fired once at about 150 feet, but his bullet was almost certainly deflected by the tree and missed the car. He fired again at 190 feet and hit both President Kennedy's neck and Governor Connally. He fired his third and last shot at 263 feet, hitting Kennedy in the back of the head and killing him instantly. He worked his last cartridge into the action, but the President's head had now disappeared from view, and Mrs. Kennedy was up on the lid of the trunk, blocking his view of the other occupants. He did not shoot at her, even though she made a much larger target than anyone sitting down in the car. The cross hairs of his telescopic sight must have been right on her, and he had a bullet in the chamber, but he did not fire. She was obviously *not* his target.

Oswald then hurried toward the enclosed stairway at the northwest corner of the building, laying his rifle down carefully between two boxes of books, with the fourth cartridge still in the chamber and the rifle at full cock. He had worked this fourth and last cartridge into the chamber preparatory to firing it, and left it in the gun, where it was recovered later and studied.

Intercepted by Officer Baker—and Released

Oswald hastened down the stairway, but heard the superintendent of the building, Mr. Truly, and one of the motorcycle policemen, Officer Marrion L. Baker (who had heard the shots and had seen pigeons fly up from the top of the building with each shot), starting up the stairs toward him. Baker had deduced correctly that the shots had probably come from high up in that building, if not from the roof. He rushed in, but he and Truly found the elevators pulled up and the safety gates apparently open, so that the elevators could not be used. Oswald's forethought about the elevators reminds us that Booth also took measures to ensure that no one could come to interrupt him at his critical moment, in the box at Ford's Theater, a century before.

When he heard the two men coming, Oswald ducked into a lunchroom on the second floor, near the stairway, and went to a Coke machine. Baker saw him through the glass in the door, rushed in, and stuck his drawn revolver in Oswald's abdomen, holding him until Truly appeared. (Booth too, you may remember, was trapped by an officer named Baker.) Officer Baker asked Mr. Truly if Oswald had a reason for being there, and when Truly verified that Oswald worked there, the policeman turned away and continued up the stairs toward the top of the building. Oswald thereupon strolled through the second floor of the building, drinking his Coke, speaking noncommittally to the secretaries there, and left by the front door, to walk a few blocks east on Elm Street and board a bus headed toward his rooming house. When the bus became immobilized in the monstrous traffic jam, Oswald got off and took a taxi out to his rooming house.

Goes Home and Gets Pistol

As the taxi approached 1026 North Beckley, Oswald undoubtedly looked ahead to see if he could detect police cars waiting for him. Even though he saw none, he continued a short distance past before leaving the cab, in order to have a chance to survey the area for any possible police stakeouts. When he detected none, he entered the house, where the housekeeper, Mrs. Roberts, said to him, "Oh, you are in a hurry." She was watching television and wanted to talk to him about the shooting of the President, but he would not respond. Oswald went to his room, put on a light-gray zippered jacket, and put his loaded revolver in his pocket, along with several extra .38-caliber cartridges. No additional pistol or rifle cartridges were found at his rooming house or with Marina's things.

Oswald then apparently stood at a bus stop on the street just outside his rooming house for a short time, but was obviously worried by the many police cars that rushed by with sirens shrieking and by the probability that they might be looking for someone fitting his description. He left that bus stop and walked away from the main thoroughfare down a street that angled off Beckley. He was going toward another bus line, which carried passengers across the city. The bus, which he did not wait for, would have carried him toward General Walker's house, but that bus stop was probably too exposed to the passing police cars.

Albert H. Newman, in his book *The Assassination of President Kennedy*, makes a persuasive case for the probability that Oswald was on his way to make a second attempt to kill Walker, this time with his revolver face to face at the door of the General's home.

Intercepted by Officer Tippit, He Kills Him

Police Officer J. D. Tippit, who had been ordered to cruise this area by himself, in his patrol car, and with Oswald's description blaring over his radio, happened to drive down the same street Oswald had selected. He noticed that the man walking near the bus stop was of the same height and had the same general characteristics as the one being described over the police radio as a suspect in the shooting of President Kennedy. Tippit therefore drove his police car slowly alongside Oswald and hailed him. Oswald stopped and leaned into the passenger-side window to speak to Tippit. Tippit got out of his car and walked around the front toward Oswald, starting to get his pistol out of its holster. As he got within point-blank range, Oswald suddenly pulled out his own revolver and fired four bullets into Tippit, three of which stayed within his body. Two entered his chest, and certainly would have been lethal, while the third entered his brain, and would have killed him if the others had not.

Then—in full view of several spectators—Oswald ran, discarding his empty revolver shells in a bush. These were recovered, and the scratches on them proved definitely that the revolver found on him later, at the time of his capture, was the one he used to kill Tippit.

When Oswald had got far enough away, one of the residents tried to use Tippit's police-car radio to notify police headquarters that Tippit had been shot. Although the man was not sure the radio was working, headquarters heard him and tried without success to learn more. They asked him to get off the radio so they could summon other police cars to the scene. Police cars did rush to the location, but Tippit was already dead. He could not possibly have been saved.

Tippit Autopsy

The lethal nature of three of Tippit's four bullet wounds is best appreciated by reviewing his official autopsy report, the relevant portions of which are summarized here:

Autopsy number: M63-352
Name: Tippit, J. D.   Age: 39   Race: White   Sex: Male
Admitted: 11-22-63   DOA
Autopsy date: 11-22-63, 3:15 P.M.
Autopsy by: Earl F. Rose, M.D.   Coroner: Judge Joe B. Brown, Jr.
Restrictions: None

EXTERNAL EXAMINATION:

External examination reveals a well developed white male measuring 5 foot, 11 inches in length and weighing an estimated 175 to 180 pounds. The hair is black, slightly wavy, very slight frontal balding. The irises are blue, the pupils are equal at 5 mm. Rigor is not present. Very slight posterior mottled lividity and body heat is present. Oral hygiene is good. The neck is not remarkable. Hair distribution is normal. . . . Identification bands of the left wrist, right wrist and left ankle.

There are four entrance type wounds. No. 1 is 4¾ inches from the top of the head and 3¾ inches to the right of the midline. This measures ⅜ x ¼ inch and is surrounded by a contusion ring. No powder tattooing is noted at the margins.

Wound No. 2 is 17 inches from the top of the head on the right chest. It is 4 inches to the right of the midline, above and slightly medial to the right nipple. It measures ⅜ x ¼ of an inch, surrounded by bruising. There is also a contusion ring.

Wound No. 3 is 21 inches from the top of the head, along the anterior lateral side of the right chest and is 6 inches to the right of the midline. This measures $^{5}/_{16}$ x ¼ of an inch and is surrounded by a contusion ring.

Wound No. 4 on the left chest is 20½ inches from the top of the head, 1¼ inches to the left of the midline. The wound measures ¾ x ⅜ of an inch, is transverse and surrounding this is a ¼ x ¾ inch abrasion.

There is tanning of the arms. On the left arm there is a tattoo being "Tippit". On the dorsum of the left hand there is a crusted abraded area measuring ¼ x ¼ inch. . . . The nails are quite well cared for although slightly dirty. Scar above the left knee, runs in an oblique fashion, crosses to the medial aspect of the knee, terminates on the leg measuring 7 inches. Poorly defined ¼ inch inoculation type of scar on the left deltoid region.

16½ inches from the top of the head, ¾ of an inch to the right of the midline of the back in the subcutaneous tissue a missile is recovered from this region. This is associated with the Wound No. 3.

INCISIONS: The standard "Y" thoracoabdominal and intermastoid incisions are utilized. Examination of the wound of the right temple is made. It is found to enter in the right middle cranial fossa, pursues a course which is slightly upward, backward and to the left. There is fracturing about the entrance and extensive fractures as it strikes the left occipitoparietal bone. It is recovered in this region, 3 inches to the left of the midline and approximately 1 inch from the top of the head. Examination of the brain is made. The brain weighs 1350 gm. The course of the missile through the brain is followed. It is found to enter the right temporal lobe, coursed through the brain transecting the brain stem, severing the cerebral peduncles surrounded by extensive hemorrhage, and found to exit from the brain substance in the calcarine gyrus to the left of the midline. There are penetrations of the meninges in the regions described. Examination of the brain is otherwise not remarkable.

The abdominal panniculus measures up to ⅞ of an inch. The organs are in the normal position. Examination of the serious cavities is made. There is found to be extensive peritoneal hemorrhage, approximately 300 cc. In the right pleural space there is in excess of 1000 cc. of blood.

THE COURSES OF THE MISSILES ARE FOLLOWED. The wound described as No. 2 is found to go between the second and third rib. The missile is found to penetrate the anterior edge of the right upper lobe. The bullet is found to go into the pericardial sac, there is extensive hemorrhage in the pericardial sac, approximately 4 ounces. Passes through the superior vena cava. It exits into the mediastinum, strikes the fourth thoracic vertebra to the left of the midline, courses in the substance of the vertebra and is recovered slightly to the left of the vertebra approximately 16 inches from the top of the head, having pursued a course very slightly upward, to the left, and backwards.

Wound No. 3 is found to penetrate the chest wall as externally described, is surrounded by hemorrhage, notching the dorsum of the sixth rib slightly lateral to the costochondral junction. It penetrates the anterior edge of the right lower lobe of the lung, the diaphragm, penetrates the liver, the entrance wound to the liver and laceration which is approximately 3 x 2.5 cm. It pursues a course backward, upward, and to the left and is recovered from the soft tissue of the back, 16½ inches from the top of the head and ¾ of an inch to the right of the midline. In its course it is also found to again penetrate the diaphragm after going through the liver and penetrates the posterior aspect of the right lower lobe.

Wound No. 4 is examined. It is found to be superficial and no penetration of the rib cage is noted. There is hemorrhage beneath the abraded and bruised area adjacent to the wound. No missiles are present in this area.

LUNGS: The lungs together weigh 1200 gm. The penetrations of the lung have previously been described. There are areas of atelectasis and along the courses of the bullet through the lung there is extensive hemorrhage.

LIVER: The liver weighs 1670 gm. The penetrations of the liver have previously been described. The cut surface of the liver is not remarkable. . . .

FINDINGS:

Gunshot wound to the head.
Brain parenchyma damage and hemorrhage.
Gunshot wounds of the chest.
Penetrations of the right lung, superior vena cava, and liver.
Right hemothorax.
Peritoneal hemorrhage.
Pericardial hemorrhage with cardiac tamponade.

CAUSE OF DEATH:

Gunshot wounds of the head and chest.

Oswald No Innocent Decoy

It is obvious from these autopsy findings that Oswald deliberately and systematically fired three of his four bullets into Tippit's body at close range, inflicting lethal wounds, two of which were instantly fatal, one into the brain and one into the heart. This performance reflects his iron composure under stress and indicates what a dangerous man he was. That he was captured later, with the same pistol that killed Officer Tippit on him, is further evidence that he was no innocent bystander or decoy, standing in for some other assassin. He was a self-sufficient killer.

17.

THE ASSASSIN: CAPTURE AND DEATH

Several spectators saw the shooting of Officer Tippit. They watched Oswald run, ejecting the empty shells from his revolver and replacing them with fresh ones, and they noted where the empty shells went, making it possible for them to be retrieved for analysis.

Oswald Seen as He Ducks into Theater

Oswald discarded his zippered gray jacket as he ran. Back on Jefferson Street, he ducked into the entryway of a shoe store as a police car roared by with its siren screaming and made a U-turn in the street. Johnny Brewer, the manager of the shoe store, who had heard on the radio not only that the President had been shot but also that a policeman had just been shot in his neighborhood, noticed Oswald's furtive actions and watched him dart out of the entryway and into a theater a few doors away, bypassing the ticket seller.

Brewer summoned the police, who surrounded the theater, turned up the house lights, and had Brewer go up on the stage with them to point out the man in question. They approached each of the small number of people who were watching the show, frisked them, and asked them to step outside.

Oswald Careful to Avoid a Fire Fight at His Capture

Oswald appeared to be concerned about insuring his place in history. He was careful to make no move to jump up or run, or, in fact, any move that might give the police an excuse to shoot him down. He waited until Officer McDonald walked up to him before he made any move what-

LEE HARVEY OSWALD

Here Oswald, immobilized by his captors, is giving the Communist salute and looking composed and deliberate as he contemplates playing an immortal role as the focus of attention of every television cameraman and journalist as the world's number-one Communist activist. (The Dallas Times Herald)

Fig. 126

JACK RUBY

Ruby shot Kennedy's assassin, just as Boston Corbett had shot the assassin of President Lincoln a century before. Like Corbett, he was a capricious, volatile, vigorous man who did not hesitate to resort to violence or to let his emotions run away with him. By killing Oswald, he deprived the public of any possibility of learning more about the motivation behind the assassination of the President. (*Wide World Photos, Inc.*)

Fig. 127

soever. He then got up and raised his hands, as if to be frisked, saying something like "Well, it is all over now" as he pulled out his pistol but did not fire it. The officer was able to seize his gun so that the cylinder could not revolve and no shots could be fired.

Oswald's performance suggests strongly that he did not want to initiate a fire fight in which he might be killed and thus be denied the opportunity to occupy the center of the stage of history, with all the world's television and movie cameras focused upon him, as he gloried in his position as the one Communist who actually did something really big on behalf of Communism in America. When the other officers came to McDonald's assistance, Oswald sustained a half-inch cut above his right eye, which is visible in photographs.

As with Booth, it was only a stroke of bad luck that led to his capture.

FIG. 126
page 315

Interrogations Not Recorded

He was taken to the office of Captain Fritz at Dallas police headquarters in the police and courts building, where he was interrogated intermittently on the third floor by both local and federal authorities. No detailed records or recordings of these conversations were made, unfortunately, because no recording apparatus was functioning. Oswald wanted to ask the lawyer for the Communist Party in New York, John Abt, to represent him, and he was taken through crowds several times to do this telephoning or to go to improvised press conferences. Abt's office did not answer the phone. An officer of the Dallas Bar Association visited Oswald to ask if he wanted a court-appointed legal representative to be designated to assist him, but Oswald stated that he would still like to try for the services of Mr. Abt. Oswald did ask the Bar Association representative to contact him again, later, in case he was unable to get Abt. As it turned out, he did not live long enough to achieve this objective.

Oswald was first brought to Captain Fritz's office at police headquarters at about 2:00 P.M. and was taken to the basement assembly room for police line-up procedures at 4:05 P.M., at 6:20 P.M. and again at about 7:40 P.M. He was formally arraigned, that is, advised of the charges of murdering Patrolman Tippit, at about 7:10 P.M. by a justice of the peace, David L. Johnston, who came to Fritz's office for the occasion. About eight o'clock, after further questioning, Oswald's fingerprints and palm prints were taken in Fritz's office, after which the questioning resumed. At 11:26 P.M., the Captain signed the complaint charging Oswald with the murder of President Kennedy. Shortly after midnight, the detectives took Oswald to the basement assembly room for an appearance of several minutes before members of the press. Jack Ruby was present at this press conference. At about 12:20 A.M., Oswald was delivered to the jailer, who placed him in a maximum-security cell on the fifth floor. His cell was the center one in a block of three cells that were separated from the remainder of the jail area, with extra guards nearby whenever Oswald was present. This stirred a memory that the Lincoln assassins were kept in cells with a vacant cell on either side, to minimize communications. At about 1:30 A.M., Oswald was taken to the Identification Bureau on the fourth floor and arraigned before Justice of the Peace Johnston, this time for the murder of President Kennedy.

Oswald was permitted to get eight hours of rest and sleep. Questioning resumed in Captain Fritz's office on Saturday morning, November 23, at about 10:25 A.M., lasting about an hour, and, at 12:35 P.M., he was brought back to Fritz's office for further questioning. Between 1:10 and 1:30 P.M., Oswald's wife and mother talked with him in the fourth-floor visiting area.

Oswald's Last Hours

At 1:40 P.M. Oswald again attempted to call Communist Party attorney John Abt in New York. He appeared in still another line-up at 2:15 P.M. At 2:45 P.M., with his consent, a member of the Identification Bureau obtained fingernail scrapings and specimens of hair from him. He returned to the fourth floor at 3:30 P.M. for a ten-minute visit with his brother Robert . Between 4:00 and 4:30 P.M., he made two telephone calls to Mrs. Paine at her home in Irving. It was about 5:30 P.M. when he was visited by the president of the Dallas Bar Association, H. Louis Nichols, with whom he spoke for about five minutes. From 6:00 to 7:15 P.M., Oswald was again interrogated in Captain Fritz's office, and then returned to his cell. At 8:00 P.M., he again called Mrs. Paine's residence, and asked to speak to his wife, but Mrs. Paine told him his wife was no longer there.

Oswald was signed out of the fifth floor at 9:30 A.M. on Sunday, November 24, and taken to Captain Fritz's office for a final round of questioning. The transfer party left Fritz's office at about 11:15 A.M., and at 11:21 A.M., Oswald was shot to death by Jack Ruby in the basement, as he was about to be placed in a police car for transfer to the more secure county jail.

Ruby Present at Police Headquarters on the Night of Oswald's Capture

FIG. 130
page 321

FIG. 128
page 318

Jack Ruby, the small-time night-club operator who shot Oswald, was present in the seething crowd of more than 100 reporters and cameramen in the corridor of the third floor of the Dallas police headquarters late on the night of the twenty-second, when Oswald was escorted back and forth through the crowd for various reasons. Ruby later stated to the psychiatrists who interviewed him that he was right up against Oswald several times, had his pistol in his pocket, and he could easily have shot him at close range. But he didn't.

RUBY AT POLICE HEADQUARTERS
IN DALLAS ON NOVEMBER 22

Ruby had gained access to the third floor of Dallas police headquarters, where Oswald was being held and where he was periodically dragged back and forth through the crowd to the bathroom or to press conferences. He gained this access by acting as a guide and interpreter for Israeli newspapermen and by being helpful to the radio reporters in pointing out who was who. He ingratiated himself to the journalists by bringing in hot hamburgers and cold Cokes and helping them talk to the district attorney. From this location, he could easily have shot Oswald at close range. *(National Archives)*

Fig. 128

RUBY'S DOODLES

During his imprisonment, Ruby displayed ingenuity and a surprising sense of artistic design and precision by making innumerable drawings somewhat like Navajo Indian rug designs, in shades of gray, using only a ruler and a pencil. He would make the shade darker or lighter by making his pencil lines closer or farther apart, thicker or thinner. He sharpened his pencil repeatedly by rubbing it on another piece of paper. The drawings were of great interest to the psychiatrists who were examining him.

I have a substantial collection of these drawings, which were usually given to cellmates or people in the jail who did something for Ruby. The dedication and signature on the verso were always in his surprisingly elegant Spencerian hand and usually expressed some pleasant wish for the recipient. *(J. K. Lattimer)*

Fig. 129

Ruby Waits to Shoot

Ruby waited until two days later. This deferring of the shooting from a very easy occasion to a more exciting but more difficult moment brings to mind Sgt. Boston Corbett's similar decision to defer his shooting of Booth from an easier occasion, at close range, to one that was more difficult.

My information that he had his pistol in his pocket came from the psychiatrists who were examining him to determine his state of sanity. They had learned after his jailing that Ruby was fond of making intricate Navajo Indian rug-design doodles. But the family, with the intransigence that families often display under this kind of stress, refused to let them see any of them. When the psychiatrists learned that I had several of these, they came to New York to see them, and other Ruby-related materials. It was then I learned about Ruby's revolver and that he could have shot Oswald even more easily at that time.

FIG. 129
page 319

How Ruby Got into the Police Building

Jack Ruby was an emotional, volatile, attention-seeking night-club proprietor of the world of the demimonde. On various occasions he had committed acts of violence in connection with drunken customers, but he had no substantial criminal record. Whenever he saw something exciting going on, he would join in and insist on knowing what was happening. As a consequence, he was regarded as a local "character" and was well known to many policemen, whom he welcomed to his club. Their presence afforded him a certain aura of respectability and protection. He would often pass out cards advertising his Carousel Club to the policemen of the city. He was interested in police work, occasionally hired off-duty policemen to work at his club, and at least one policeman married one of his strippers. There is no indication, however, that there was any irregularity in his relations with the police force.

When he saw the crowd gathered at police headquarters on the night the President was shot (which was two days before he shot Oswald), he became obsessed with the desire to be inside. In the crowd he discovered two reporters from an Israeli newspaper, whom he offered to guide, pointing out the personages they might want to interview. He stuck a card in his fedora band, as they had done, and accompanied them inside with the other press people, claiming to be their interpreter. He obviously knew many of the police officials, so the reporters, the radio commentators, and the television cameramen were happy to have him along to expedite their entry and to point out who was who. At times he did succeed in getting officials to speak to the reporters and commentators. After he had been upstairs a while, he realized that his presence was more or less accepted, since his face had become familiar, although he was denied access to the room where Oswald was being kept. At one

FIG. 130
page 321

RUBY AT OSWALD PRESS CONFERENCE

Jack Ruby, in dark suit and glasses, is standing on a table at the press conference in Dallas police headquarters. He later indicated to the psychiatrists that this was one of the occasions on which he could have shot Oswald at closer range than the moment he picked, two days later, just before Oswald was to disappear into a maximum-security facility. Similarly, Boston Corbett, a century before, did not shoot his victim, Booth, until the moment of maximum excitement and illumination, when he, too, fired a single fatal pistol bullet from his Colt revolver. *(National Archives)*

Fig. 130

RUBY JUST BEFORE HE SHOT OSWALD

Ruby can be seen (in hat, at right) in the basement of Dallas police headquarters. During an unexpected rearrangement of police automobiles, the officer guarding the entrance to the ramp left his post to stop the traffic so that the cars could maneuver. It was during this interval, apparently, that Ruby walked down the ramp and joined the crowd of reporters and heavily armed policemen waiting for Oswald to appear. A moment later he stepped forward and fired his fatal shot into Oswald. *(National Archives)*

Fig. 131

point, it has been said, he went across the street and brought back a large brown paper bag filled with ice-cold Coca-Colas and steaming hamburgers to distribute to the hungry media people and to some of the policemen who had been unable to leave their posts and who welcomed these refreshments. This added to his acceptability in the crowd, and also at the television station which he visited later that night.

The following day he listened to some of the heart-rending programs about the President's wife and her young children, and he became very upset. He dragged his roommate out to photograph some of the anti-Kennedy billboards in the area and he visited other club owners, expressing anger that they had not closed their clubs, as he had done.

Ruby Shoots Oswald

The following morning, November 24, Ruby rose late. At 11:17 A.M., from a building opposite the basement driveway exit of the Dallas police headquarters, he sent a telegram. Since he was carrying over $2,000 in cash in his pocket, he removed his revolver from his car trunk as a precaution. As he was leaving, he noticed activity and a crowd around the basement driveway, where the nose of an armored car was half visible, its rear end partly down in the driveway. He asked what was happening and was told that Oswald was being moved.

Ruby, by that time known to the crowd and the reporters in the area, calmly walked down the ramp while the policeman at the street entrance was busy stopping traffic to let the police transfer car drive out and turn around. He took his place in the circle of newsmen forming the walls of a chute down which Oswald would have to walk en route to the unmarked police car. The armored car was to go first, as a decoy. A large number of heavily armed Texas Rangers had been brought into the basement to insure against any armed attempt to kidnap or lynch Oswald, since, as expected, threats against his life had been received.

FIG. 131
page 321

When Oswald arrived in the basement, the brilliant lights for the motion-picture and television cameras went on and bathed him in a blazing glare of light. Surrounded and nearly immobilized by his captors, he approached the police transfer car. Ruby suddenly stepped forward out of the crowd, pointed his pistol at Oswald's lower chest, and fired a single round of .38 special ammunition from his Colt Cobra revolver.

FIG. 132
page 323

Policemen immediately jumped on Ruby, grabbing his revolver so that the cylinder could not turn, and wrestled him to the ground. He was cursing and mumbling, indicating that he had wished to fire more shots into Oswald, had he been given a chance. From his mutterings, there was no doubt that he was attempting to kill Oswald.

FIG. 127
page 315

322

RUBY SHOOTS OSWALD

Here Ruby can be seen pressing in on Oswald with his pistol held low, fairly close to his body, in approved police fashion, so that it cannot easily be knocked aside. He appears to be pulling his trigger with his middle finger, a possible evidence of unusual expertise. Certain pistols balance better when the middle finger is used to fire them, and this may have been true of Ruby's. Oswald can be seen to grimace as the bullet pierces every important structure in his body at this level, in a way that brought about his death within two hours despite the efforts of one of the best trauma teams in the country at Parkland Hospital. (*Bob Jackson*, The Dallas Times Herald)

Fig. 132

Oswald and Booth, Ruby and Corbett

There are interesting similarities with the fatal wounding of John Wilkes Booth, a century before. Here again an accused presidential assassin, surrounded and restricted by his captors but truculent and defiant, shuffled forward into a blazing glare of light, and onto the stage of history. This time the light was from the blazing floodlights in the basement garage of the Dallas police headquarters, rather than from the blazing barn in which Booth was surrounded and trapped. Here again a single pistol shot rang out, and Lee Harvey Oswald crumpled to the floor, ashen, with his limbs flopping. A little over two hours later he was dead, despite the vigorous efforts of a skilled trauma team. Here again an attention-hungry fanatic, accused of having slain the President, was silenced before society had a chance to draw from him any information concerning his motives, any possible implication of others, or any explanation of his own actions. This time the shooting was seen by millions, on television, and a nation's outrage and frustration was compounded a thousand times more than in the case of Booth, where the circumstances of the shooting were not known to the public immediately after the event.

Jack Ruby (born Jacob Rubenstein), like Boston Corbett, was an unstable person, craving recognition, given to outbursts of emotion, temper, and actual violence, intermittently in minor trouble with the authorities. He gained access to Oswald by energetically ingratiating himself with the crowd of newsmen, radio interviewers, and policemen who surrounded Oswald following the arrest. Photographs in the Warren Commission report show Ruby in the press conference crowd before whom Oswald was interrogated two days prior to the shooting.

Parkland Hospital's Operative Findings

Oswald was rushed to the Parkland Hospital, over the same route the President had taken two days earlier. Although he was on the operating table approximately twenty minutes after the shooting, he was already in deep shock, obviously because of massive internal blood loss. Drs. Thomas Shires, Malcolm O. Perry, Robert N. McClelland, and Ronald C. Jones (who had also worked on Kennedy and Connally) opened his abdomen through a xyphoid-to-pubis midline incision at 11:44 A.M., in the same emergency suite where his victims had lain two days before, and in the same hospital where his second child had recently been born.

The account of the operation follows:

Operative Record. Date: 11/24/63. Parkland Memorial Hospital.
Name. Oswald, Lee Harvey
Age. Twenty-four years
Pt. No. 25260

Clinical Evaluation. Previous inspection had revealed an entrance wound over the left lower lateral chest edge and an exit was identified by subcutaneous palpation of the bullet over the right lower lateral chest cage. At the time he was seen preoperatively, he was without blood pressure, heart was heard infrequently at 130 beats per minute, and preoperatively had an endotracheal tube placed and was receiving oxygen by anesthesia at the time he was moved to the operating room. Measured blood loss: 8, 376 cc. [This obviously included some of the huge amount of transfused blood that was being pumped into his vessels.]

Description of Operation. Under endotracheal oxygen inhalation, a long midline abdominal incision was made. Bleeders were not apparent and none were clamped or tied. On opening the peritoneal cavity, approximately 2 to 3 liters of blood, both liquid and in clots, were encountered. These were removed. The bullet pathway was then identified as having shattered the upper medial surface of the spleen, then entered the retroperitoneal area, where there was a large retroperitoneal hematoma in the area of the pancreas. Following this, bleeding was seen to be coming from the right side, and on inspection, there was seen to be an exit to the right through the inferior vena cava, thence through the superior pole of the right kidney, the lower portion of the right lobe of the liver, and to the right lateral body wall. First the right kidney, which was bleeding, was identified, a pacemaker was then inserted into the wall of the right ventricle and grounded on the skin, and pacemaking was started. A very feeble, small, localized, muscular response was obtained with the pacemaker but still no effective beat. At this time we were informed by Marion T. Jenkins, M.D., the anesthetist, that there was no sign of life in that the pupils were fixed and dilated, there was no retinal blood flow, no respiratory effort and no effective pulse could be maintained even with cardiac massage. The patient was pronounced dead at 1:07 P.M. The anesthetic agent consisted entirely of oxygen. No anesthetics as such were administered. The patient was never conscious from the time of his arrival in the emergency room until his death at 1:07 P.M. [He had struggled briefly in the ambulance, en route to the hospital.] The subcutaneous bullet was extracted from the right side during the attempts at defibrillation, which were rotated among the surgeons. The cardiac massage and defibrillation attempts were carried out by Dr. McClelland, Dr. Perry, and Dr. Jones. Assistance was obtained from the cardiologist, Fouad Bashour, M.D.—[Signed] Tom Shires.

In preparation for the operation, the superbly organized trauma group of Parkland Hospital, which had been informed that Oswald was on his way after having been shot, had assembled a resuscitative team in the emergency operating room. On Oswald's arrival, Dr. Akin introduced a number thirty-six cuffed, endotracheal tube and had connected it to the anesthesia machine for assisted ventilation and oxygen. It was obvious that the patient was in extremis, as judged by his general pallor, dusky or ashen gray nail beds, cold extremities, gasping respirations, dilated pupils, and dry conjunctiva. Three members of the staff, Drs. Charles D. Coln, Charles A. Crenshaw, and Gerald E. Gustafson, were performing venous cutdowns, one in each of the lower extremities, and one in the left forearm. Because of the obvious chest wound and the appearance of pneumothorax on the left, Dr. Jones inserted the chest tube and connected it to a closed, water-sealed drainage bottle, as had been at-

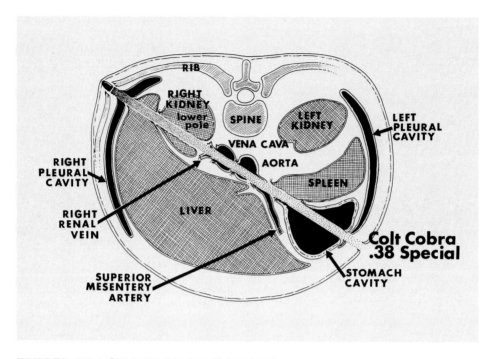

BULLET TRACK THROUGH OSWALD

A .38 special bullet from Ruby's Colt Cobra revolver entered Oswald's lower thorax on the left front, perforated the lower end of the chest cavity, which filled with blood even though the lung was not struck. It then went through the diaphragm, into and out of the stomach, and along the top of the spleen. It cut off the main intestinal artery (superior mesenteric) at its origin on the main artery of the body (the aorta), traversed the aorta and the main vein of the body (the vena cava), and cut the right kidney vein. It then broke up the right kidney before traversing the tail of the liver and the right diaphragm. It continued through the right chest cavity, again without striking the lung, broke the eleventh rib and was caught by the skin, which is very thick at that point and retained the bullet. No one treated at Parkland Hospital had survived this multiplicity of wounds, and even if the patient did survive the initial wound, he might well have died from deterioration of the damaged liver or other later consequences. It is most unusual for a single bullet to strike all these structures, but, since it did, it made a wound that was uncontrollably fatal. (*J. K. Lattimer*)

Fig. 133

tempted in the case of President Kennedy. The head of the emergency-room cart was lowered into a Trendelenburg (head-down) position. There was no perceptible peripheral arterial pulsation. However, the cardioscope tracing showed an electrical cardiac activity with a heart rate of approximately 130 per minute. Blood was sent to the blood bank for immediate typing and crossmatch, and two units of uncrossmatched, Type O, Rh negative blood were started by pressure infusions from plastic blood containers. William Risk, M.D., the urology resident, had inserted a Foley catheter into the bladder, obtaining only a scanty quantity of urine, which was not blood-tinged, despite the massive wound of the right kidney. The abdominal incision was made exactly twelve minutes after the patient first entered the emergency operating room. A vein in the right forearm was also cannulated to aid in attempts at fluid replacement. The abdominal incision was made at 11:44 A.M., and by 12:15 P.M., he had received 3,000 ml of blood and 800 ml of 5 percent dextrose in lactated Ringer's solution. By 12:30 P.M., he had received 6,000 ml of blood, and his measured blood loss was 5,000 ml at that time, except that it was obvious that there was additional loss in the tissues. Five percent dextrose in lactated Ringer's solution was again started, and the patient's pulmonary status seemed satisfactory. At 12:37 P.M., the heart sound became weaker and the pulse rate slowed from eighty to sixty, forty, and then became imperceptible, confirmed by the cardioscope. By this time, the patient had received 15½ units of blood and 4,200 ml of 5 percent dextrose in lactated Ringer's solution. It was judged that the period of cerebral hypoxia in the time between the gunshot wound and the beginning of effective ventilation had caused irreparable damage to the cardiovascular center of the brain, introducing the final cardiac asystole, despite all resuscitative measures.

It is well known to military and trauma surgeons that bullets that perforate both the aorta and the vena cava are almost uniformly fatal, especially if other organs are injured. A review of the records of Parkland Hospital, the trauma center for the Dallas area, revealed that this was true in its experience also, in a long list of gunshot wounds treated over the years.

Oswald's Autopsy Report

Drs. Earl F. Rose and Sidney C. Stewart, of the Dallas County Medical Examiner's Office, performed the autopsy on Oswald on November 24, 1963, at 2:45 P.M. Relevant portions follow:

External examination reveals a 5 foot, 9 inch white male, the estimated weight is 150 pounds. Rigor is not present, slight cooling of the body. There is faint posterior mottling and lividity. . . . The hair is brown, slightly wavy. Small amount of dried blood in the hair which has run from the hairline to the right and backward. . . . There is a left periorbital hematoma which is purple in the central portion, fading at the margins to a faint lemon-yellow. Total diameter of this is

1¾ x 1¼ inch. The irides are grey-blue, the pupils are equal at 8 mm. The sclera and conjunctiva are not remarkable.

Various scratches and abrasions of a minor type are described in detail, including a one-centimeter cut above and lateral to the right eye. The incisions for the insertion of the chest tube on the left, the thoracotomy for the cardiac massage, the midline laparotomy incision, and the various cutdown incisions on the limbs are then described in detail.

23 inches from the top of the head and 3⅜ inches to the left of the midline anteriorly and 10¾ inches to the left of the midline posteriorly, over the lower aspect of the left chest there is an entrance type of wound which measures ¼ x ⁵⁄₁₆ inch in diameter. This is surrounded by a contusion ring, the total diameters of the contusion ring are ⅜ of an inch. 22 inches from the top of the head and 9¼ inches to the right of the midline anteriorly and 8¼ inches to the right of the midline of the back there is a vertical 2 x 1 inch gaping wound. [Bullet was removed via this incision.] Posterior to this by ½ inch there is a ¾ x ⅜ inch irregular contused area. [This appears to be the place where the bullet had come to rest after perforating the fractured eleventh rib.]

INCISIONS: The standard "Y" thoracoabdominal and intermastoid incisions are utilized. Reflecting the skin there is found to be a wound between the fourth and fifth ribs which extends through the soft tissue and measures 6 inches in length. This conforms to the wound on the left chest. The incision is continued through the abdominal wall as well as the thoracotomy wound to the left of the midline of the chest.

SEROUS CAVITIES: Examination of the serous cavities is made. In the left pleural space approximately 175 cc. of blood. In the right pleural space there is in excess of 600 cc. blood. In the peritoneal cavity there is in excess of 1000 cc. of blood with clot formation. In addition, there is massive retroperitoneal hemorrhage. The omentum adjacent to the transverse colon and stomach is hemorrhagic and irregularly torn. . . .

FIG. 133
page 326
COURSE OF WOUND IS FOLLOWED: It is found to notch the undersurface of the seventh rib at the costochondral junction, this is surrounded by hemorrhage. In its course it notches the diaphragmatic attachment in this region, however, the left lung is not penetrated. The course is found to go from left to right and backward. In its course it is found to strike the anterior edge of the spleen and there is a cruciate laceration of the spleen measuring approximately 1.5 x 2 cm. The missile is found to penetrate the stomach along the greater curvature of the body of the stomach, the penetration measuring 9 mm. It exits from the stomach along the posterior wall, lesser curvature, 2 cm. distal to the cardioesophageal junction. The penetration measures 8 mm. It pursues a course backwards and to the right slightly caudal to the celiac axis and there is extensive hemorrhage in this area. The anterior and right anterio-lateral aspect of the aorta is torn with the superior mesenteric artery being severed. The right renal artery shows destruction and hemorrhage along the cephalad portion. The right renal vein is torn and the tear involves the inferior vena cava, the dorsal surface. It courses through the upper pole of the right kidney along the anterior surface causing a jagged and irregular laceration covering a distance of 5 x 2 cm. with penetration into the calyces. It becomes peritonealized in the hepatorenal pouch

and there is a jagged and irregular laceration of the liver covering a distance of 9.5 x 2 x 2 cm. From the liver it penetrates the diaphragm posteriorly on the right side. It then passes adjacent to the lung in the pleural space and the right lung is not penetrated. The eleventh rib to the right of the midline is irregularly fractured and an exit type of wound in this region and in the soft tissue along the posterior axillary line right side there is an incised wound and fragmentation of the rib.

The remainder of the autopsy account describes no other abnormalities, and the microscopic findings are only those of disruption and fresh hemorrhage in the areas mentioned. The pancreas apparently was not penetrated after all, but was surrounded by hemorrhage. Its ductal system was not remarkable. The adrenal glands were both surrounded by hemorrhage, but both were intact. The brain weighed 1,450 gm and showed no gross abnormalities. Further sections and special studies were to be done on it.

Oswald was gone—but not forgotten. He was, in addition, certainly not understood. Why had he killed the President? Who—if anyone—had persuaded or influenced him to do it? Or had he worked alone?

18.

DID OSWALD ACT ALONE?

There was no doubt that Oswald had killed the President; the facts speak for themselves.

But, still, many people contended—and contend to this day—that there must have been certain other factors, which the authorities have either overlooked or chosen to ignore or to deny. The strongest suspicion is that Kennedy's assassination must have been a plot, and that Oswald had not acted alone but was, rather, a pawn in a larger operation. This is an attractive concept, and in the beginning I myself suspected it might be so. Certainly this book would be incomplete without a discussion of this theory and a comment on the claims that have been put forward and that might give it credibility.

Concerning the issue of whether or not Oswald had accomplices, there are no data and, since the question is not open to experimentation, there is no way to contribute any new test results on this matter. Yet it is crystal clear that no one met Oswald outside the Texas Book Depository building, handed him tickets or money, or helped him get across town. He had to do this by himself, and in the process he was captured. The last thing a fleeing person would do would be to divest himself of his money (Oswald left almost all of his with his wife) and then go back to his rooming house (the address of which would quickly become known) if he were trying to make an escape aided by accomplices.

As far as other shooters participating in the firing at President Kennedy, it is also crystal clear that no other shooter hit the President, since both bullets that struck him were recovered, showing scratches that proved they both came out of Oswald's gun to the exclusion of all other guns. Oswald's palm print was on the gun, fibers from all three colors of the three-color shirt he was wearing that day were present, clinging to the gunstock, and there are no disparities to indicate that he could not have done it.

But those who disagreed with the Warren Commission report, and with

Figs. 123, 124
page 303

the obvious facts, were persistent. They have paraded before the public the list of unanswered questions we have been considering in this book, especially the question of why the President's head went backward toward the gun.

New Investigation Authorized

The critics were so vigorous and so skillful that they eventually persuaded Congress to appropriate more than $4.5 million to reopen the investigation of the assassination and also of the killing of Martin Luther King, Jr. This had also happened with the assassination of Lincoln.

No government group had done any medical or anatomical ballistic experiments, since the true impact point had been revealed by the partial release of the sequestered X-rays and autopsy photographs. Incredibly, the new Assassinations Committee elected to do no such experiments either. It reviewed several articles in medical journals that I had written between 1966 and 1979, and adopted many of the conclusions I had proposed several years earlier to account for some of the puzzling findings. For example, it agreed that the President's spine had been hit sufficiently hard that he might have been paralyzed by the neck bullet. It adopted my explanation for the smallness of the bullet wound in the front of the President's neck. It published references to my work on the jet recoil of the President's head toward the gun.

It firmly concluded that Lee Harvey Oswald and only Lee Harvey Oswald had killed the President.

Questionable Interpretation of Police Sound Tape

Late in 1978, at the very end of the proceedings, the chairman of this Select Committee suddenly reversed his conclusion and declared that perhaps a fourth shot *had* been fired in Dealey Plaza, after all, on the afternoon of the assassination. No explanation was offered as to who might have fired the shot, or why, and all the members of the committee did not agree with him.

This last-minute change of opinion was based on an analysis of a police sound tape, which was said to reveal sounds recorded by the open radio microphone of a police motorcycle that might have been in Dealey Plaza at the time of the shooting. To accept this interpretation requires the acceptance of a long list of coincidences. It is necessary to believe that the motorcycle policeman, H. B. McLain, accidentally switched his motorcycle radio to transmit, though he had been ordered to keep it on receive, to get orders from the motorcade commander. It is necessary to believe that this policeman also accidentally switched his radio set to channel one, instead of channel two, even though he had been ordered to keep it on channel two, the channel specifically set aside for the motorcade. It is necessary to believe that the radio orders he was hearing and obeying were actually coming from someone else's motorcycle radio, some distance away, and that he could hear them despite the engine noise of several other motorcade motorcycles and the cheers and applause of the people on the sidewalk. It is necessary to believe that, coincidentally, a second traffic controller's motorcycle radio set was also accidentally left on, and was turned accidentally to the send position and stuck open on the same channel (one) and that the sound of the church bells that can be heard on the tape (there are no churches in Dealey Plaza) was captured by this police receiver and superimposed on the tape of McLain's accidental broadcast. It is necessary to believe that the pops and crackles interpreted as a fourth gunshot on the tape are not just more of the frequent pops and crackles that occur on these tapes at other points. Furthermore, it is necessary to believe that the agents in the presidential car and the people standing on the grass of Dealey Plaza, toward whom this rifle shot would have been fired, were aware of neither a supersonic crack plus the excessively loud noise of a high-powered rifle shot fired directly toward them from only fifty feet away nor the impact of a bullet near them.

Hardest of all for me to believe, however, based on my experience with this type of high-powered rifle, is that photographer Zapruder, who was only a few feet away from the alleged origin of this rifle shot, would not have jumped "right out of his skin," as they say, from the loudness of this truly deafening explosion right beside him. The wobbles of his camera following each of Oswald's shots from roughly 300 feet away are clearly detectable, yet his film shows no trace of the staggering impact of what would have been a shattering explosion immediately beside and slightly behind him. Here again, people unfamiliar with firing this very loud type of high-powered rifle are not aware of how startling it is.

Thus I am distressed that the 1979 House of Representatives Select Committee on Assassinations seems to have based its pronouncement that there might have been a fourth shot fired (and therefore more shooters) entirely on an analysis of this sound tape. Moreover, the fact that they did not have a freight train (as was present in 1963) going across the noisy cross-over of the triple overpass at the time of their reenactment of the shooting, providing an additional large surface for reflections, plus its inherent noises, may be irrelevant but was a surprising omission.

Oswald's Solitariness

A strong indication of Oswald's solitariness as a killer—as he was solitary in life—is the insightful description of him made by his wife, Marina, who talked at length with Priscilla McMillan. McMillan was the reporter and author who interviewed Oswald in Russia, and who later actually lived with Marina, had her confidence, and was able to converse with her in both English and Russian, at great length, while preparing her excellent book, *Marina and Lee*. She often asked Marina whether Lee might have been capable of joining with an accomplice to kill the President. "Never," Marina said. "Lee was too secretive ever to have told anyone his plans. Nor could he have acted in concert, accepted orders, or obeyed any orders or plans by anybody else." The reason that Marina gave was that "Lee had no use for the opinions of anybody but himself. He had only contempt for other people. He was a lonely person, he trusted no one and he had the fantasies of a sick person; to get attention only for himself."

The people who knew Lee in Dallas agreed with her. "I'd have thought it was a conspiracy," one of the Russian friends said, "if only I hadn't known Lee." Another one said, "Lee could not have been bought, not for love, not for money and not for the sake of a political plot." These people think, as Marina does, that Lee acted on impulse and first thought seriously about killing the President only a day or two before he did it. McMillan also quotes Marina as dismissing any notion that Lee knew his killer, Jack Ruby. "How could Lee have known Ruby?" she asked. "He didn't drink, he didn't smoke, he didn't go to night clubs."

Oswald's older brother Robert's perception of Lee was that his becoming a truant from school marked his first open rejection of the rules by which other people live. As he grew up, Lee became increasingly contemptuous of rules, in school, in the Marine Corps, and in Russia, becoming more and more unfriendly and a loner, and indicating to the psychiatrists even as a boy that he "did not need any help from anybody." That kind of rebellion against authority would make it difficult for him to be a member of a highly organized, highly disciplined assassination team. They would not be able to trust him or depend on him to do what he was told.

The single most persuasive indication that Oswald was *not* a member of a group assigned to kill President Kennedy, as I see it, was the fact, pointed out earlier, that he shot at General Walker. In doing this he risked capture, which would have destroyed his usefulness in any future attempt on the President. He was so aware of the possibility of capture or even that he might be killed, in shooting at Walker, that he left a note with his wife telling her where to dispose of his clothing and his personal effects if this happened. If he had been a member of a group, the entire group would have been exposed to the possibility of detection if he had been captured after shooting at the General.

Significance of the Lack of a High-Quality Rifle

A professional killer financed by a government agency, whether Russian or any other, would have been equipped with a very high-quality rifle and a very high-quality telescopic rifle sight. Even his pistol would have been of high quality. Although such equipment would have been more expensive than Oswald's, the total cost would not have been really great.

Oswald's guns were so cheap it seems obvious he bought them himself, with his own money. The guns and the telescopic sight he bought proved to be adequate for killing both President Kennedy and Officer Tippit, but they were not nearly as foolproof as they could have been for a few more dollars. As one example, the fact that the mount of Oswald's telescopic sight was held on the rifle by only two screws in very shallow holes, in an improvised manner, would have been unacceptable to a KGB or CIA agent. If such a person had been successful in locating and motivating a skilled human being, like Oswald, willing to give up his life if necessary, he would have been incompetent if he had not provided him with a superb rifle and a superb telescopic sight. In point of fact, such agents are highly competent at that sort of thing. Oswald would have had no trouble purchasing an expensive rifle, telescopic sight, and pistol. All he would have needed was a modest amount of additional money. Good equipment is the best investment you can make for a technical project. No Russian marksman would be so poorly equipped.

Even the ammunition Oswald used was not the high-quality expanding-bullet type a professional killer would have used. At one point, Dr. Olivier, of the Aberdeen Proving Grounds, and I speculated on whether Oswald might have actually selected the bullets he used because they could penetrate so far into a block of wood, reasoning that they might therefore penetrate the protective plastic "bubble-top" that would shield the President if it rained. But after seeing how the back of a skull caused these bullets to shatter, I am sure the extremely strong plastic of the bubble-top would also have shattered them in exactly the same way. If Oswald had wanted to be able to pierce the bubble-top, he would have needed armor-piercing bullets, and he had none. Furthermore, it is impossible to purchase armor-piercing ammunition for his rifle, at least in this country. It would have to be made up specially, and there is no indication that Oswald either had any or had ordered any.

In fact, he had no more bullets at all for his rifle when he was captured. He was apparently down to his last four carbine cartridges, since none were found in his room or in the baggage he had left with his wife. To be out of ammunition is a sin no professional gunman would have committed. Moreover, the last type of bullet a professional killer would select is the more humane "ball" type of fully jacketed military bullets that Oswald used.

That Oswald used weapons of such low cost, and therefore of marginal dependability, was impressive additional evidence to me that he was not in the pay of anyone else. He clearly financed his own weapons out of his own pocket with his own meager funds. He was independent in this, as in everything else he did.

In brief, the evidence seems to me to be persuasive that Oswald acted alone in shooting President Kennedy.

19.

THE KILLER'S KILLER: JACK RUBY

The victim is dead, the assassin is dead, but there remains one more character in this tragic series of events, one more person to explore and attempt to understand: Jack Ruby, the man who shot Lee Harvey Oswald.

As we attempt to understand this man and what he did, the eerie similarities between this presidential assassination and the one a century before seem to assault us at every turn. The uncanny network of coincidence is never stronger than with Jack Ruby.

FIG. 134
page 336
The pistol Ruby used to shoot Oswald was a Colt revolver, a .38 Special, of the model known as the Cobra. It had a two-inch barrel, was of blued steel with brown plastic grips, and its serial number was 2744-LW. This pistol was equipped with a special shield, called a shroud, covering the hammer so that it could be fired from inside a pocket, if necessary, with the shroud protecting the hammer from catching in the cloth lining of the pocket. A "piece"—gangland parlance for a firearm—with such a short barrel is notoriously inaccurate, except at point-blank range.

As Boston Corbett did a hundred years ago, using the same type of weapon, Ruby employed a somewhat sophisticated technique. Ruby's gun fired a fairly advanced type of cartridge, called a .38 Special, now the standard police cartridge in the United States. He did not extend his arm at full length and attempt to aim his shot from a distance, as an amateur might, but bent his body slightly forward and advanced his shooting hand only partway, in approved close-combat fashion, so that the pistol would be less obvious, would be firmly held, and would be better protected from any blow by an onlooker or protector of Oswald. He then advanced quickly, until the tip of his gun practically touched his victim, and fired his single bullet into Oswald's midsection.

That Ruby was able to kill his man with a single bullet from his Colt

BOTH ASSASSINS KILLED
WITH COLT REVOLVERS

Colt revolvers were used to shoot both of the presidential assassins, killing each victim with one bullet, 100 years apart. On the left is the Colt "army" or "cavalry" type .44-caliber percussion-cap revolver, model of 1860, used by Corbett to shoot Booth. On the right is the Colt Cobra revolver used by Ruby to shoot Oswald. Note the shroud over the hammer of the Cobra, to permit it to be fired from within a pocket without the fabric of the pocket catching on the hammer. (*Left: National Archives; right: Colt Firearms Company*)

Fig. 134

revolver was surprisingly analogous to the success of his predecessor Boston Corbett, who slew Booth with a single shot, also from a Colt revolver. That Ruby's bullet struck both vena cava and aorta; detached the superior mesenteric artery; perforated the right renal artery and vein as well as the spleen, the stomach, the right kidney, and the liver; and holed the pleura in the costophrenic angle both anteriorly and posteriorly, is nothing short of remarkable. It was probably even more lethal than if he had struck Oswald directly in the heart. That the bullet struck a rib and cartilage anteriorly and the eleventh rib posteriorly was probably the only reason that it did not exit from the body and strike some of the police officers standing directly behind and to the right of Oswald. It was equally remarkable, of course, that Corbett's one bullet hit Booth exactly in the spinal cord. That Ruby did not get off additional shots resulted from the alacrity and vigor with which policemen seized his gun and gun hand and wrestled him to the floor. Their grip on the gun undoubtedly immobilized the cylinder so that it could not turn again, and the weight of the several men, who could be clearly seen to jump on Ruby in the television films, probably prevented him from firing more shots.

Ruby later reported that he had purchased the gun about three years earlier to protect himself when he was carrying considerable amounts of cash for the transaction of his night club's business. He ordinarily transported the gun in his car trunk, which he also used as his temporary bank. Ruby is quoted by Police Officer McMillan, who helped subdue him, as saying to Oswald: "You rat, son of a bitch, you shot the President," and then firing his shot. He quoted Ruby as saying repeatedly during the scuffle to subdue him, "I hope I killed the son of a bitch." When Ruby was told Oswald would probably die, Ruby said, "I meant to shoot him three times but you police moved too fast and prevented me from doing so."

In retrospect, it is interesting that John Wilkes Booth and Lee Harvey Oswald were both shot down deliberately, while confined, in the glare of blazing lights provided by their captors. Both were shot by persons acting against orders or against the law. Booth was restricted by his broken leg and Oswald by his handcuffs. Both of the men who admitted shooting them were later characterized as insane and were remarkably similar in many ways. Each man bided his time before firing his shot, and the technique of both appeared to reveal a certain degree of expertise in the way in which they handled their weapons. Although both shootings may well have been the actions of excited men in attacking what they considered to be a national enemy, there are many sophisticated observers who regard this point of view as unduly naive. They believe that since both accused presidential assassins were active enemy sympathizers (Booth of the Confederacy and Oswald of the Communists), and since both shootings took place during an era of large-scale undercover operations, psychological persuasion, philosophic rivalry, and intelligence activity, both men may have been silenced as part of a larger design.

THE PRESIDENTIAL ASSASSINS LIE DYING

Booth (top), paralyzed by Corbett's bullet, dying on the porch of Garrett's farmhouse. Oswald (bottom) en route to the hospital after being shot by Ruby, unconscious most of the time and bleeding to death internally.

Both assassins took about two hours to die after they were shot with one bullet from a Colt revolver. *(Top: National Archives; bottom: Wide World Photos, Inc.)*

Fig. 135

It is also interesting that information has recently been put forth which suggests that Booth was on the payroll of a dummy company in New York City that was a front for the undercover operations of Gen. Lafayette C. Baker, chief of the National Police Detectives, which was Secretary of War Stanton's "secret-police" operation during the Civil War. Furthermore, the compendium of suggestive circumstantial evidence accumulated by the late Otto Eisenschiml makes wonderful reading and implies (but never actually states) that Stanton encouraged the plot to assassinate Lincoln.

In any case, against this background of similar features, it is nothing less than amazing that each of the accused presidential assassins, Booth and Oswald, was killed by a single bullet fired from a Colt revolver. Both men lingered for a little over two hours before dying. As most military and accident-room surgeons know, a great many pistol bullets are fired into people without hitting any structure that would bring about such a rapid death.

Fig. 135
page 338

Unlike Corbett, Ruby was neither released from his imprisonment nor rewarded. No time had elapsed for a reward to be offered because of the alertness of the late police officer Tippit, of the Dallas police force, in locating Oswald, on an inconspicuous street near Oswald's rooming house, within forty-five minutes of the assassination of President Kennedy.

Booth, in contrast to Oswald, had made good his escape for a somewhat longer period, with a well-trained helper, and he was armed. He remained at large for some twelve days before he was captured, during which time a large reward was offered for his apprehension and during which time the temper of the nation to see him brought in, dead or alive, grew to furious intensity. The fact that Corbett had caused him to be brought in dead probably made Corbett's crime seem somewhat less heinous than that of Ruby, whose victim was thoroughly enmeshed in the due processes of law at the time he was shot.

Following Ruby's unbelievable shooting of Oswald, the police jailed him in the very cell block on the fifth floor of the police headquarters building where Oswald had been held only moments before. Ruby was never released except to attend his own trial.

Ruby was convicted and sentenced to death on March 14, 1965, after a confusing period during which his defense lawyers argued about who was truly his representative. Ruby was defended by Melvin Belli, a flamboyant attorney from California, but the case was lost at trial.

During his imprisonment Ruby spent countless hours making strangely attractive doodles resembling Navaho Indian rug designs, as mentioned earlier. These he bestowed on those who did things for him. The psychiatrists were bemused by them, and several are shown in figure 129. Different lawyers were arguing over who should be engaged to prepare an appeal, late in 1966, when Ruby developed a cough. The cough worsened, and X-rays were taken. These revealed widespread cancerous areas in his lungs. A biopsy indicated that this was an extremely malignant cancer of the lung itself. Ruby developed phlebitis, as many cancer victims do, and this gave off an enormous blood clot (embolus), which lodged in his lungs and killed him on January 3, 1967.

The question was raised as to whether he might have known he had cancer at the time he shot Oswald, three years previously. When tiny traces of the cancer were found to have spread to his brain, it was asked if they might have upset his judgment.

The question of whether or not one forefinger was missing also needed answering. It was raised because he used his middle finger to pull the trigger.

The precise nature of Ruby's cause of death and the extent of his brain involvement are best appreciated by reviewing the data from his official autopsy report. Relevant portions follow:

Autopsy Number: M67-007   Unit No.: 31 88 01
Name: Ruby, Jack   Age: 55   Race: White   Sex: Male
Date of Death: January 3, 1967,   Autopsy Date: Tuesday,
          10:30 A.M.   January 3, 1967, 11:26 A.M.
Autopsy by: Earl F. Rose, M.D.   Coroner: Judge W. E. Richburg
Place of Autopsy: Morgue, Parkland Memorial Hospital, Dallas, Texas.

External examination revealed a 5 foot, 8½ inch white male. Estimated weight of 145-150 pounds. No rigor is present. There is very minimal mottled posterior lividity. Body heat is present. The hair is brunette and there is greying. . . . It is thinning, more marked over the crown of the head but also bilaterally of the frontal regions. . . . The head in its entirety is free of injury. The back of the ears are not remarkable. . . . The irides are brown. The sclera and conjuctiva are not remarkable, free of any injury of hemorrhages. The pupils are equal, they measure 6 mm. . . .

The right wrist is examined. This is not remarkable. In the mid-portion of the volar radial aspect of the right arm there is a vertical 1½ inch hairline white scar. The dorsum of the hand is examined. It is not remarkable. The nails are clean and well cared for. No foreign type of material is noted beneath these. There is no callusing of the palms. No jewelry is present on the right hand. . . . To the distal portion of the proximal phalanx of the index finger of the left hand there is a remote amputation associated with a ⅝ inch scar. This is well healed. The nails are clean and well cared for. No jewelry is present. No burns are encountered. No callusing of the palms. . . .

LIVER: The weight of the liver is 1800 grams. The surface of the diaphragm associated with the liver is free of metastases. There are a number of tumor nodules in the liver. In the left lobe measuring 8 mm., in the right lobe the size varies from 4 mm. up to the largest which is 1.4 cm. in greatest diameter. More pronounced over the superior surface of the liver. The edges of the liver are very slightly rounded. The capsule is smooth aside from the nodules as noted. The number of metastases is limited, 14 are counted. The cut surface of the liver is predominantly uninvolved by tumor. . . .

LUNGS: The lungs together weigh 1700 grams. The pleural surface on the left is quite smooth although in the interlobar fissure there are some nodular projections. The visceral pleura is intact throughout . . . tumor nodules are palpable and they are numerous thorughout the parenchyma. There is tumor involvement peribronchially more marked on the right side and there is a projecting tumor mass of the right mainstem bronchus from the middle lobe bronchus and sclerosis of the surrounding tissue with lymph node tumor involvement grossly. There is also anthracosis of the lymph nodes. The sections of the iungs show marked nodular tumor involvement peripherally. The nodules, sizes of 2 to 4 mm., are distinct, firm, flat and slightly raised. No caseation. In the right lower lobe there is one area that is confluent of approximately 2 cm. The peribronchial lymph nodes along the right side are extensively involved. There is little aeration of the left lung, the right shows minimal aeration with some focal areas of atelectasis. The lung tissue of the left lung between the tumor is pink to grey and exudes some fluid when compressed. There is a distention of both pulmonary arteries with non-adherent ante mortem emboli. These measure up to 1.5 cm. in diameter, several show branching, these are twisted and firmly impacted. There are emboli in the smaller arteries bilaterally. No pulmonary infarcts. . . .

PORTACAVAL SYSTEM is examined. The portal system is not remarkable. The caval system is examined and there is found to be a thrombosis the tail of which is somewhat tortuous and irregular extending to 3 cm. above the bifurcation. Examination of the iliac vein is made. The thrombosis is found to extend down the right leg, into the femoral vein and this is traced to below the right popliteal fossa. Approximately 5 cm. above the popliteal fossa the thrombosis is adherent to the wall of the vein. This continues for some distance and there are small projections of this into the smaller radicles. This is pursued through the proximal third of the back of the calf at which area the thrombosis continues to be somewhat adherent with a very slight brownish color. The superficial veins are not remarkable. Re-examination of the legs are made and they are found to be symmetrical. The pelvic-periprostatic vessels are grossly not remarkable.

MUSCULO-SKELETAL SYSTEM: In addition to what has been described there is nodularity of the rib on the left side and of the eighth rib on the right side. . . .

BRAIN: The external configuration of the brain is normal. The weight of the brain is 1330 grams before fixation. It is symmetrical. No evidence of increased intracranial pressure. The cerebral vessels are quite thin and delicate. . . .

It has a normal size and shape, and external examination reveals no abnormalities. The arteries at the base of the brain show minimal atherosclerosis with no significant luminal narrowing. No aneurysms are present. The leptomeninges are thin and delicate with no evidence of acute or chronic inflammation. The pattern of the gyri and sulci is normal, and there are no congenital malformations. Careful inspection of the uncal gyri and cerebellum reveals no evidence of herniation in either area.

Multiple coronal sections of the cerebral hemispheres reveal multiple nodules of metastatic tumor, all located within the right hemisphere. The largest nodule of tumor is located within the right thalamus and measures 15 x 10 x 10 mm. The nodule of tumor is well circumscribed but unencapsulated, and its cut surface is translucent and gelatinous with slightly projecting opaque greyish-white granules, measuring up to 1 mm. in greatest dimension. No glial capsule can be detected at the margins of this nodule. The nodule is ellipsoidal in shape and lies at the superior and lateral extremity of the thalamus, just below the body of the right caudate nucleus. The metastatic nodule, however, is restricted to the lateral lobe of the thalamus and does not involve the caudate. There are seven additional nodules of metastatic carcinoma. All are located within the right hemisphere, along the junction of grey and white matter. Most are located in the lower parts of sulci, and none is visible from the external surface. In the right parietal lobe there are two metastatic nodules. The larger is located supero-laterally and measure 7 mm. in diameter, and the smaller is located superiorly, near the midline, and measure 5 mm. in diameter. A 4 mm. diameter nodule is located in the right temporal lobe at its lower and lateral edge, distant from and not involving the hippocampus. Near the junction of the occipital and parietal lobes there is a single nodule of tumor, 3 mm. in diameter, located near the midline superiorly. In the right occipital lobe there are three nodules of tumor, each measuring 2 mm. in diameter. Two are located on the mid-lateral part of the occipital lobe, and one on the inferior surface of the right occipital lobe. On cut surface each of the seven cortical nodules is well circumscribed but unencapsulated, greyish-white, soft, and granular. Except for these seven nodules and the large metastatic nodule in the right thalamus, no other metastatic tumor is discovered within the cerebral hemispheres. Careful study of the cerebral cortex reveals no abnormalities other than the metastatic tumor. The basal ganglia are intact except for the thalamic metastasis. Careful gross inspection of the hippocampus on each side reveals no abnormalities, and there is no evidence of sclerosis of the hippocampus. The amygdaloid nuclei are normal.

Sections of the brain stem are normal. No metastatic tumor is present within the midbrain, pons or medulla. Sections of the cerebellum reveal a single nodule of metastatic tumor, 4 mm. in diameter, located within the upper part of the inferior cerebellar vermis. This nodule presents a granular greyish-white cut surface, identical with the nodules of metastatic tumor seen in the right cerebral hemisphere. No other abnormalities are noted in the cerebellar tissue. . . .

Microscopically the metastatic tumor nodules within the brain consist of papillary adenocarcinoma with a histologic structure identical with the tumor seen in other parts of the body. The metastatic nodules are moderately well circumscribed but unencapsulated. . . .

Careful study of the various parts of the brain in sites uninvolved by tumor reveals no abnormalities. . . .

Lung: Multiple sections of the lung are examined. The peripheral lung sections show small rounded masses of tumor with slightly irregular edges of tumor which are attached to and advancing on the surrounding alveolar walls. There are areas of tumor coalescence with a single microscopic foci of necrosis with marginal angiofibroblastic invasion and a paucity of inflammatory cells. There is minimal compression of the lung tissue surrounding the tumor masses, however, there are small fragments of tumor attached to alveolar walls before the advancing edges of the tumor and small clumps of viable tumor free in the alveolar spaces. In areas the tumor masses are geographically related and merge with normal bronchioles and there are vessels throughout tumor masses, these are not invaded by the tumor, nor are other vessels invaded. The tumor stroma has the appearance of thickened and edematous preexisting lung stroma with modest focal lymphocytic infiltrates. The tumor cells follow the alveolar walls with occasional papillary projections and infolding of tumor cells. . . .

Lung sections to show emboli demonstrate laminated emboli within several smaller dilated arteries and there is marginal angiofibroblastic invasion and proliferation with some hematoidin pigment. There is minimal inflammatory cell infiltration associated with the vessel wall-clot interface.

Lymph Nodes: The mediastinal nodes examined show tumor involvement which is similar to that of the lung, however, some areas show more mucin production and there is marked fibrosis. There is also dense hyaline tissue with anthracotic pigment. . . .

Substernal Fat: Tumor of the type found in the lungs.

Pancreas: Multiple sections of the pancreas are examined. There is tumor involvement of the head of the pancreas as grossly noted. The tumor involves the muscular layer of the duodenum as well as the pancreas adjacent. The tumor is in areas similar to [or] identical in appearance to that of the lung. . . .

Sections of the prostate show several small areas of disorganized glandular proliferation, the glands are small, there is varying amounts of fibrosis associated, many of the cells are cuboidal, no perineural invasion demonstrable.

Femoral vessels: Sections taken from the level of the knee show laminated clot in the lumen with early angiofibroblastic invasion of the clot-wall interface. There is some edema of the wall with a few mononuclear cells infiltrating. Smaller veins show organization which is more advanced, other small veins are normal in appearance. . . .

Adrenals: Two sections of each adrenal are examined. There is lipid depletion, a few of the periadrenal arterioles show hyalinization of the wall. The adrenal artery section is not remarkable. There is no tumor involvement. . . .

Kidney: The pelvis and hilar vessels are not remarkable. There is a fibrous walled cyst lined by cuboidal epithelium with the fibrous wall compressing the adjacent parenchyma where there are a few hyalinized glomeruli. . . .

Bone: Rib sections show healing fracture with callus formation and there is tumor metastasis of the type previously described.

From these autopsy findings, it can be seen that Ruby was suffering from a highly malignant cancer of the lung, which had spread widely throughout his body, with tiny deposits of tumor in many vital organs, including the liver and even the brain. These tumor deposits, called metastases, would eventually have killed him. They were, however, *not* the cause of his death. In fact, they were all quite tiny at the time he died, and even though several of these tiny tumors had started to grow in the brain, none of them was large enough to have been present at the time he shot Oswald. It is unlikely that they would have disturbed the function of the brain even at the time of his death, because of their as yet small size. Even though they were all in the right side of his brain, his pupils had not yet become unequal in response to their presence.

The condition that killed Ruby was a cluster of large blood clots originating in the vein from his right leg. These clots (emboli) had broken loose and had been carried by his bloodstream into the heart and then out into the main arteries of both his lungs. They were packed so tightly within these blood vessels that it was difficult to dislodge them, even on the autopsy table. Emboli are a frequent complication in patients with cancer, the reason for which is not known. In Ruby's case, they were large and they were lethal.

I have given the finding of an amputated left index finger only to show that the missing finger was *not* on his gun hand, and did *not* account for his using his middle finger of his right hand to pull the trigger of his revolver. When I first heard that he was missing one index finger, I suspected that was the reason he fired his pistol with his middle finger, but it did not turn out to be so.

The only other unusual findings were a one-inch innocent cyst of the right kidney and a beginning cancerous change in the prostate gland. Both of these findings were purely incidental and did not contribute in any way to his death.

No, Ruby's cancer did *not* affect his judgment at the time he shot Oswald. And no, again, he did not even suspect that he was ill in any way, much less that he had cancer. His illness was in a very early stage in 1963 (if present, at all)—too early for symptoms.

Now the participants are gone. The drama is played out; now it is history.

Yet this drama has one final twist. The assassination of President John F. Kennedy has turned out to be almost a "replay" of the assassination of President Abraham Lincoln, point by point. The similarities, coincidences, and associations are so striking as to be worthy of assembling in the epilogue that follows.

20.

SIMILARITIES AND COINCIDENCES IN THE LIVES OF PRESIDENTS LINCOLN AND KENNEDY

For two Presidents who lived 100 years apart, there was a fascinating cluster of coincidences and associations, not only in the events surrounding their assassinations, but also in the events and in the lives of the people surrounding them.

To begin with the most obvious: both Presidents were shot in the back of the head, on a Friday, while seated beside their wives. Both were in the presence of another couple, and in each case that man was also wounded by the assassin. Governor Connally was struck, almost fatally, by the same bullet that had gone through President Kennedy's neck. Major Rathbone was stabbed by Booth when he tried to grapple with him.

FIG. 136
page 346

Rathbone later married the girl who was with him on that dismal night, Senator Harris's daughter, Clara, but their lives came to an equally dismal conclusion. Rathbone obtained a post in the foreign service and was stationed with his family in Germany. There he became progressively more depressed and finally murdered Clara. He was committed to a German insane asylum and eventually died there.

Governor Connally and his wife have gone through some unhappy, although not disastrous, experiences since the assassination. Connally became disenchanted with the Democratic Party and switched to the Republican side, just as the Republican standard-bearers suffered a crushing blow from the Watergate fiasco. Connally himself was harried, but was exonerated.

THE MEN WHO WERE WITH THE TWO PRESIDENTS

Maj. Henry Reed Rathbone (top) and Gov. John Connally were both seated with their Presidents at the time of the assassinations. Both men were wounded by the assassin but did not die. Rathbone was stabbed by Booth with his razor-sharp hunting knife when he tried to grapple with him after Booth had shot Lincoln. He sustained an eight-inch cut on his upper arm, which bled profusely and hampered his removing the bar Booth had used to wedge the door shut. Connally was struck by bullet 399, which had first gone through Kennedy's neck. He probably would have died if he had not had prompt surgical treatment. *(Top: National Archives; bottom: Bill Gardner Collection, Texas State Archives)*

Fig. 136

BULLETS THAT KILLED LINCOLN AND KENNEDY

The round ball (top) is of the type that killed President Lincoln. It was .44 caliber, weighed 146 grains and was made of Britannia metal. The elongated 6.5 mm Carcano-type bullet (bottom) that killed President Kennedy was about .26 caliber and weighed little more: 160 grains. Both of them effectively destroyed the brain, even though the Kennedy bullet was traveling at a much higher speed: 2,200 feet per second, versus about 500 feet per second for the pistol ball. Despite this difference, there was no hope that either Lincoln or Kennedy could have been saved even by modern neurosurgical and support methods. *(J. K. Lattimer)*

Fig. 137

ROCKING CHAIRS OF LINCOLN AND KENNEDY

President Kennedy's bad back was relieved by the motion of the rocking chair, and Lincoln liked the motion of the chair even when he went to the theater after long tense days at the office. He was seated in this chair (left) when he was shot. Note the dark stain on the cushioned back, where his head rested. For more on this see fig. 75. *(Left: National Archives; right: John F. Kennedy Library)*

Fig. 138

THE TWO FIRST LADIES

The two first ladies had a great deal in common. Mary Todd Lincoln (top) and Jacqueline Bouvier Kennedy were both twenty-four years old when they married. Both were socially prominent women who spoke French fluently; both lost a child while in the White House; both were seated beside their husbands when they were shot; and both were subjected to a period of intense agonizing waiting while frantic but vain attempts at resuscitation of their husbands went on in the next room. Both had held the bullet-torn heads of their husbands immediately after they were shot, until a doctor took over. *(Top: National Archives; bottom: John F. Kennedy Library)*

Fig. 139

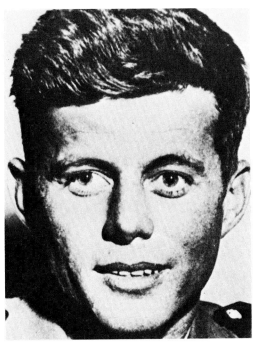

THE WANDERING EYE

Both Presidents had an eye that appeared to deviate from their line of sight in some portraits. This did not interfere with the eyesight of either man and certainly was not due to a dislocated lens or other severe ocular disorder of the type associated with Marfan's Syndrome, which Lincoln is sometimes, erroneously, said to have had. *(Top: National Archives; bottom: U.S. Navy Photo)*

Fig. 140

Neither President's wife was injured by the assassin, although each was very close to the President.

Both Presidents were given closed-chest cardiac massage and artificial respiration, among other measures, to no avail.

In each case it was possible to rush topflight medical personnel to the side of the dying President, but in each case nothing could be done, because one side of the brain had been hopelessly and irretrievably damaged by the assassin's bullet.

Fig. 137
page 347

Both President's wives held their husbands's bullet-torn heads in their hands, and were thereafter subjected to a harrowing, agonizing wait, while desperate but futile efforts were made to save their husbands' lives.

Only partial autopsies were done on each man. Both Presidents lay in state in the East Room of the White House, and on the same catafalque base. Mrs. Kennedy remembered that she had read about the funeral of Lincoln and asked that the same type of bier be used for her husband. She had apparently seen a book describing Lincoln's funeral in the White House library and asked that "the arrangements be as similar as possible" to those of President Lincoln. She knew exactly where to locate the book that gave this information. She also asked that the same funeral parade arrangements be used as for President Lincoln, with some regiments marching in massed "regimental front" and some in "company front," with a row of muffled drums across the front of each large unit.

Not only were both Presidents shot on a Friday, but in each case it was the Friday before a major holiday! Lincoln on Good Friday, before Easter, and Kennedy on the Friday before Thanksgiving.

Fig. 138
page 347

Both Presidents were rocking-chair enthusiasts: Kennedy used one to soothe his bad back; Lincoln was shot while sitting in a rocking chair.

After both assassinations there were loud and insistent claims that the fatal shot must have come from a different direction. In each instance, when all of the evidence was in, these claims were discredited. In each case, press photographs of the body were forbidden by a Cabinet member.

Both Presidents were fatalistic and disdained bodyguards; they exposed themselves freely to the public. Both had remarked on how easy it would be to shoot a president. Kennedy had even specified the high-powered rifle and telescopic-sight combination as recently as the day before he was shot.

Fig. 139
page 348

Each President in his thirties married a socially prominent twenty-four-year-old girl who spoke French fluently. While in the White House, each President had a family of three children, and some of both Presidents' children rode ponies on the White House grounds. Both Presidents' wives lost a child through death while they were in the White House, Patrick Kennedy and William Lincoln.

Fig. 140
page 349

Both Lincoln and Kennedy were tall, lean, athletic men. Lincoln was six feet four inches, and Kennedy, a little over six feet. Kennedy had a lazy muscle in one eye which would sometimes permit it to deviate, and one of Lincoln's portraits suggests a possible similar lazy muscle. Both Lincoln and Kennedy were second children and both grew into men who expressed themselves exceptionally well in both writing and speaking. Lincoln's addresses became literary classics, and Kennedy won a Pulitzer Prize for one of his several books. Both men had been boat captains: Lincoln, the co-captain of a Mississippi river boat, and Kennedy of torpedo boat 109. Both served in the military: Lincoln as a captain in the Black Hawk Indian War and Kennedy as a navy lieutenant in the South Pacific in World War II.

Biographer David Keiser has pointed out a wealth of family facts about the two men.

Before each was elected president, a sister died.

Each President also was related to a U.S. Senator: Lincoln to General Isaac Barnard, who became a senator from Pennsylvania in 1827, and Kennedy to his younger brother Edward (Ted), who was elected from Massachusetts in 1962. Both Lincoln and Kennedy were elected to Congress in the year '47 and were runners-up for the vice-presidential nominations of their parties in the year '56. Both men served in the House of Representatives before becoming president.

In running for national office, each man had a series of historic debates with better-known opponents: Senator Stephen A. Douglas and Vice-President Richard Nixon. Lincoln and Kennedy were both famous for their wit, and both were fond of quoting the Bible and Shakespeare.

Each man was elected president of the United States in '60, and each of their opponents was present at their inauguration. Douglas kindly held the new President's hat.

Both men had relatives who had been mayors of Boston for an extraordinary number of terms. F. W. Lincoln, a cousin of Abe's, was mayor for seven terms and was characterized as the "most-elected" mayor ever. J. F. Fitzgerald, Jack's grandfather, was elected mayor of Boston for five terms.

Both Lincoln and Kennedy had a relative who graduated from Harvard and became U.S. Attorney General in a Democratic administration: Levi Lincoln, Sr., in the Cabinet of President Thomas Jefferson and Robert F. Kennedy in his brother John's Cabinet.

Each President had a next of kin who was an ambassador to Great Britain. Robert Todd Lincoln, the oldest son of the President, was U.S. Ambassador from 1889 to 1893. The father of President Kennedy, Joseph P. Kennedy, was U.S. Ambassador from 1938 to 1940.

Both Presidents had the legality of their elections contested but won anyway. Lincoln fought against slavery and kept the United States from being split apart. Kennedy fought against Communist aggression, especially in Cuba, and kept the very world from being split apart.

Both Presidents were deeply concerned with the problems of American blacks and each made his views known in '63. Kennedy delivered his civil-rights message to Congress in 1963 and Lincoln presented his

VICE PRESIDENT ANDREW JOHNSON

Vice Presidents named Johnson succeeded both Lincoln and Kennedy. Andrew Johnson succeeded President Lincoln and Lyndon Johnson succeeded President Kennedy. Both were Southerners and both were large men. *(National Archives)*

Fig. 141

PRESIDENT JOHNSON'S URETERAL STONES

Lyndon Johnson shows the scar through which his ureteral stones and gall bladder were removed in 1965. He and Andrew Johnson were the only two Vice Presidents to have ureteral stones. *(United Press International)*

Fig. 142

Emancipation Proclamation, freeing all slaves, in 1863. In 1964, two authors, William O. Douglas and Harry Goldin, published books with surprisingly similar titles: *Mr. Lincoln and the Negroes* and *Mr. Kennedy and the Negroes.*

Both Presidents had a friend and consultant named Billy Graham. Lincoln's Billy Graham was William Mentor Graham, a New Salem, Illinois, schoolmaster, who helped Lincoln with his studies. Kennedy's Billy Graham was the Reverend Billy Graham, the evangelist, with whom he often talked.

Both Presidents knew a prominent Illinois Democrat named Adlai Stevenson. Lincoln's Stevenson was the grandfather of the U.S. representative to the United Nations, who was well known to President Kennedy.

Both Lincoln and Kennedy were famous for words that ring out for sacrifice and liberty. In his Gettysburg Address, Lincoln said, "It is rather for us to be here dedicated to the great task remaining before us . . . that this nation, under God, shall have a new birth of freedom—and that government of the people, by the people, for the people, shall not perish from the earth."

Kennedy, in his Inaugural Address, declared, "Let every nation know, whether it wishes us well or ill, that we shall pay any price, bear any burden, meet any hardship, support any friend, oppose any foe to assure the survival and the success of liberty . . . ask not what your country can do for you—ask what you can do for your country."

Figs. 141, 142
page 352

The names Lincoln and Kennedy each contain seven letters.

Both Lincoln and Kennedy were succeeded by Vice-Presidents named Johnson. They were our only two Vice-Presidents who had ureteral stones. Both Vice-Presidents were Southern Democrats and both had been in the Senate. Andrew Johnson had been born in 1808 and Lyndon Johnson in 1908. The names Andrew Johnson and Lyndon Johnson each contain thirteen letters. Both Johnsons had been the only Vice-Presidents from the South in the last hundred years. Both entered their presidency in their mid-fifties and both were the fathers of two daughters. Each Johnson was opposed for reelection by a man whose name started with *G*; Grant, in the case of Andrew Johnson, and Goldwater, in the case of Lyndon Johnson.

The assassins, themselves, shared many similarities. Both were dedicated enemy sympathizers. Oswald was a Marxist, striving to strike a heroic blow that would show Russia and Cuba just how outstanding *he* was. Booth was dedicated to striking a heroic blow for the Confederacy. Each man was obviously willing to put his life on the line, but craved and expected world recognition as a reward.

Both assassins were in their twenties. John Wilkes Booth was born in 1838, and Lee Harvey Oswald in 1939.

Both were Southerners. Oswald's father was Robert E. Lee Oswald, and Oswald's first name (Lee) was handed down from that of the

Confederate general who was the "commander" of John Wilkes Booth.

The names John Wilkes Booth and Lee Harvey Oswald each contain fifteen letters.

Other coincidences surround the circumstances of Oswald's and Booth's escapades. A man called Oswald (but properly named Oswell) Swan helped Booth in his escape. A woman named Paine got Oswald his job at the Texas School Book Depository building. Lewis Paine (also Payne and Powell) assisted Booth.

Both Oswald and Booth learned that their victims were about to come before their places of employment by reading about it in the newspapers a day or two before. As a result of this knowledge, both men selected their place of work for their assassination attempt, and prepared the site with great care. Booth secreted a bar of wood behind the door so that he could prevent anyone from following him into the theater box and dug a hole in the plaster so that he could fit the bar into its place without any delay. Booth also drilled a peephole through the second door, inside the box, so he could look through and find out exactly where his victim was seated before he exposed himself in the theater box to fire the fatal shot.

Oswald, 100 years later, erected a wall of boxes of books between his firing position and the floor of the warehouse. In this protected position he could raise the window and stack his boxes in precisely the best positions for his enfilading line of fire, down onto the route the presidential limousine would follow.

Both men saw assassination as a route to glory, fame, and the accolades of their group, but both were cut down before they could receive any reaction—notoriety or censure—from the public.

Booth asked his captors to move back so that he could put on more of a display in fighting them all. He probably dreamed of playing an even more dramatic role on the stage of a courtroom, with the eyes of every newspaper editor in the world focused upon him and his every word and gesture. The fact that he was robbed of this opportunity, by being shot down by Corbett even before he could make an entrance for his final scene, was an unhappy surprise.

Much the same thing happened to Oswald, who was clearly *not* trying to escape, but in all probability was heading across town to add the assassination of General Walker, who had eluded him on his first attempt, to his list of newsworthy achievements on behalf of world Communism.

When he was trapped by police in the theater, Oswald was careful not to jump up, or run, or pull out his gun and thus risk being shot down. Instead, he sat waiting quietly until the policeman arrived at his seat. It seemed obvious that he too wanted to play out a grander role on the stage of a courtroom, with television and newsreel cameras focused on him and the world hanging on his every word. There he could demonstrate that he alone was the one Communist advocate who was willing to go all the way and actually *do* something on behalf of Communism in America.

Both assassins were trapped by officers named Baker. Lt. Luther B. Baker, a member of the cavalry patrol that located Booth, was standing in the opened front door of the barn ready to seize Booth as he came out. This happened after the barn had begun to burn fiercely, and even as he watched Booth closely, he heard the shot and saw Booth fall.

Dallas motorcycle patrolman Officer Marrion L. Baker, having seen pigeons fly up from the top of the Texas Book Depository building as Oswald fired at Kennedy, rushed into the building, revolver drawn. With Superintendent Truly he rushed to the elevators, only to find that Oswald had pulled them up and left them out of operation. Rushing up the stairway, Baker saw Oswald in the lunchroom and held him at pistol point until Truly verified that Oswald worked there. Officer Baker then released him and continued up to the roof.

Both Booth and Oswald were halted by diligent officers, but then released because no alarm was out for them as yet. Booth was halted at the Navy Yard Bridge, but then released.

It seems apparent that Oswald's shooting of Kennedy was a crime of opportunity, made possible only when the planners of the motorcade unsuspectingly elected to run the route underneath his window.

The personalities of the two assassins were also somewhat similar.

Both Booth and Oswald had been deprived of a father figure to guide them. Both assassins had two older brothers who overshadowed them in their careers. Booth's older brothers, Junius Brutus, Jr., and Edwin were already experienced, highly successful dramatic actors, whereas the young John Wilkes, though dashing and handsome, did not have the same training, example, and psychological support from the famous and talented father, Junius Brutus Booth, who had died when John Wilkes was only thirteen. Neither did he have the same degree of preparation for his career on the stage. In fact, he was worrying about difficulties with his voice becoming rough. He sometimes felt compelled to go so far as to use the name "J. Wilkes" instead of J. Wilkes Booth, in some of his earlier roles, so the family name would not be disgraced if he gave a poor performance. All of this aggravated Booth's need for a short cut to greatness, and was impressively similar to the situation of Oswald, 100 years later, who also had two older brothers, John and Robert, both of whom had more successful careers in the field he admired the most: the military. Robert had been in the Marine Corps and John in the Coast Guard, where they did well. He had kept close track of Robert's career in the Marines, trying to keep up with Robert's accomplishments.

In July 1952, three months after his eighteenth birthday, Robert enlisted in the Marines. Lee was full of questions. What would he be doing? Would he go overseas? He told Lee he wouldn't know where he was going until after boot camp. Soon after he left, Lee bought a copy of the Marine Corps handbook. He said he was going to keep up with Robert, learn everything he was learning. Lee was only twelve, but he planned to enlist in the Marines as soon as he was old enough. He saw in the Marines

BOOTH'S SLING
ON HIS SPENCER
CARBINE (ABOVE)
IS SAME AS
OSWALD'S SLING
(RIGHT)

**CARBINE
SLINGS LOOK
IDENTICAL**

The first carbine slings adopted by both Booth and Oswald, 100 years apart, look almost identical. Both are made of a flat strip of fabric resembling heavy cloth tape or flattened rope. Not only did each man have a carbine, but each man's attention was attracted by this peculiar flat type of material, which he adapted for the purpose of making a sling. Their similarity is striking. Booth's sling is shown (left) attached to his Spencer carbine, and Oswald's is shown attached to his Carcano carbine.

Oswald was dressed completely in black, apparently for the nighttime attempt on General Walker's life. The carbine and the revolver for which he had sent away had been delivered to him on the same day. He insisted that his wife, Marina, take his photograph holding them, and he inscribed one copy to his baby daughter to remember him by and later sent another copy to George de Morenschildt, inscribed, "Oswald the fascist hunter," after De Morenschildt had guessed correctly that it was Oswald who had shot at Walker and missed. (*Left: National Archives; right:* Detroit Free Press)

Fig. 143

an escape from the drabness of school, a chance to lead his own life, away from his mother, and an opportunity to impress the world. Oswald's relationship with his hard-pressed mother undoubtedly had a great deal to do with the molding of his personality and his rebelliousness in his search for a quick way to fame. This was a desire shared by his mother, who felt frustrated at every turn in her search for recognition. Psychiatrist D. A. Rothstein speculated that, despite Lee's hostility to his mother, he may have revealed an attachment to her by acting out through the assassination his conception of her wish to become famous.

Oswald did enlist as soon as he was seventeen. At first he made good progress as a Marine, good enough at least to win him the promotion to private first class after about six months in the service. Because of his personality difficulties and his rejection of any authority, however, his military career was blighted. His promotion did not last and he was reduced to private. He was also fined and placed in the brig. The final disaster of his brief military career was the changing of his discharge to dishonorable status, which the navy, through the then Navy Secretary, John Connally, refused to revise to honorable status. These disappointments and frustrations rankled deeply.

Fig. 143
page 356

Booth and Oswald both made a habit of writing down their thoughts, their plans, and their beliefs—Booth in his diary, Oswald in his journal and in his many letters. And in both cases some of these writings were withheld in the investigations that took place after their deaths.

Booth's notebook, usually referred to as his diary, with its two long, philosophical entries, was not shown to the commission trying the other conspirators because the Attorney General did not regard its contents as being of sufficient importance to the case. The diary had been mentioned by the press, but the members of the commission and their advisers did not realize this, and never asked for it. It came to light two years later, during hearings concerning the possible impeachment of President Johnson. There was a question whether some pages of notes had been torn out after it was removed from Booth's body, although the evidence for this is slim. Some suspected that Secretary of War Stanton had proposed that it be withheld because it might attract sympathy for Booth.

Similarly, in the case of Oswald, his unsigned note to Agent Hosty of the Dallas office of the FBI, a few days before the assassination, was not shown or mentioned to the Warren Commission. It came to light only much later.

Even though the contents of both of these documents might have been correctly judged to be unimportant, or even uncertain as to their origin, the fact that *any* document would be withheld from highest authority is disturbing in itself. It shows that human nature does not change readily, even in 100 years.

It is interesting that the Lincoln assassination inquiry was reopened in

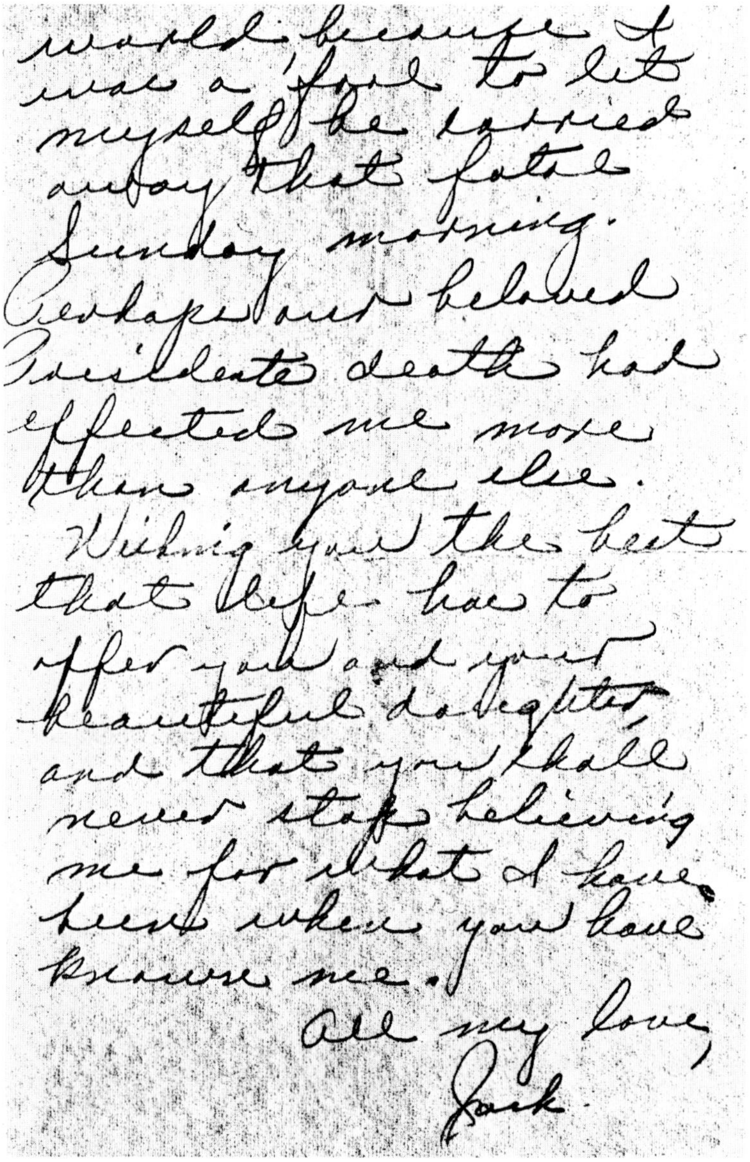
world because I
was a 'fool' to let
myself be carried
away that fatal
Sunday morning.
Perhaps our beloved
Presidents death had
effected me more
than anyone else.
Wishing you the best
that life has to
offer you and your
beautiful daughter,
and that you shall
never stop believing
me for what I have
been when you have
known me.
All my love,
Jack.

RUBY'S SUPERIOR PENMANSHIP

The last page of a letter from Jack Ruby to a friend, which shows the attractiveness of his script as well as the generally pleasant philosophy expressed in most of his post-trial letters. Earlier letters dealt with his wish to demonstrate that Jewish people are willing to fight for the right, as they see it, but tend to be persecuted. He was preoccupied with demonstrating that Jews could indeed do brave and vigorous things. *(J. K. Lattimer)*

Fig. 144

THE ASSASSINS ABOUT TO BE ASSASSINATED

The assassins of both Lincoln (Booth, top) and Kennedy (Oswald, bottom) are shown here just before the fatal bullets, from Boston Corbett and Jack Ruby respectively, struck them. Each man was bathed in a brilliant glare of light, Booth from the burning barn and Oswald from the television and movie camera lights. Each man was immobilized by captors who surrounded him and each man received a fatal wound from a single bullet of a Colt revolver. Each lived for about two hours and died denying the world any further word from them. (*Top: National Archives; bottom:* Dallas Morning News)

Fig. 145

1867 for the trial of John H. Surratt, and again in 1868 during the attempt to impeach Andrew Johnson over his firing of Stanton.

Similarly, the Kennedy assassination inquiry was reopened in 1975 as part of an investigation of the CIA by a commission headed by Vice-President Nelson Rockefeller, and again in 1978, by a House of Representatives select committee to investigate the assassinations of Kennedy and Martin Luther King, Jr.

FIG. 145
page 359

The fate of the two assassins was certainly similar. Both Oswald and Booth were in their turn assassinated; shot down while trapped in a blaze of brilliant light surrounded and immobilized by their captors. Booth was in the burning tobacco barn with the guns of the cavalry patrol trained on him through the wide cracks between the boards. Oswald, a century later, was brilliantly illuminated by the blazing television and newsreel lights, immobilized and surrounded by heavily armed Texas policemen in the basement of the Dallas police headquarters. Each assassin had been exposed to his target earlier, but it was only at the crescendo of the drama, when the brilliant illumination flared up, that the violent action was triggered.

There are similarities to be found between the two men who killed these two assassins also.

Jack Ruby and Boston Corbett were volatile, unstable men, who would readily resort to violence. Both were later characterized as insane. Both were unmarried at the time they did the shooting. Ruby demonstrated his tendency to violence by throwing drunken customers down the stairs of his night club on occasion, and Corbett did not hesitate to try to shoot down some of the page boys of the Kansas state legislative chamber when they appeared to be mocking the chaplain's opening blessing. Both Ruby and Corbett were preoccupied with at least lip service to their religious beliefs. Corbett castrated himself as penance for exchanging words with a prostitute while in his favorite role as a roving

FIG. 144
page 358

lay preacher; and Ruby wrote wildly in letters about his Jewishness and his desire to demonstrate that Jewish boys actually had "guts" after all. He mentioned this to the Dallas police sergeant who was guarding him, as well. At the same time, he was agitated over the thought that Jews might be blamed for the assassination of the President.

Each assassin shot his man down illegally, thus denying society any information they might have given about motives or about the implication of others.

Each assassin's assassin had had an opportunity to shoot his man down at closer range, Ruby having been right up against Oswald as they pushed him through the crowd on the third floor of the Dallas police headquarters at a press conference two days before he shot him. It was only at the last and most dramatic moment that Ruby elected to step forward and kill his man. Similarly, Corbett had said that he had had earlier opportunities to shoot Booth at closer range, as he came around the barn looking through the various cracks, but did not elect to shoot

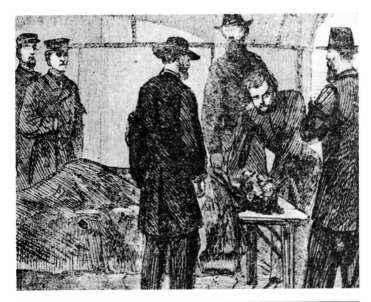

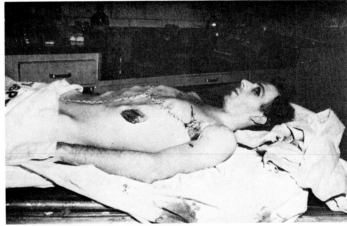

THE AUTOPSIES OF BOOTH AND OSWALD

Autopsies were done on both Booth (top) and Oswald, and care was taken to identify the bodies without any doubt. Booth's body was identified by the dental work, by a scar on the back of his neck, and by his name tattooed on his hand. Oswald had been in close contact with both his mother and his wife and was identified by his fingerprints, taken on his enlistment in the Marines and again during his arraignment after the shooting of Kennedy and Tippit. On the autopsy table his facial characteristics are easily recognizable as the man in the multiple photographs available, including the one in his high-school yearbook. Minor discrepancies in estimations of his height and weight, during his autopsy, appear to us to be within the expected variations of the method of comparing measurements of living and dead people. *(Top: National Archives; bottom: from Chief Jesse Curry's J.F.K. Assassination File, 1969)*

Fig. 146

ACUTE AMNESIA AFTER EXTREME STRESS

These two young women, Fanny Seward (top) and Jacqueline Kennedy, living a century apart, suffered acute amnesia of the events immediately following the horrifying scene of a loved one being destroyed before their eyes. Fanny Seward had no memory of raising the window and screaming for help, or shouting "Murder," in the moments after she saw the assassin Payne butchering her father with an enormous knife. She was sure he had been killed.

Similarly, 100 years later, Jacqueline Kennedy had no memory of the events taking place for several seconds immediately after her husband's head exploded in her face as she was peering intently into his face, only inches away, asking, "What's the matter, Jack?" She does not remember rising to let him fall down on the seat where she had been sitting, or being precipitated onto the rear of the automobile, as it jerked forward, or scrambling back into the seat. She does remember holding her husband's shattered head together during the frantic ride to the hospital. *(Top: National Archives; bottom: John F. Kennedy Library)*

Fig. 147

Figs. 134, 135
pages 336, 338

him down until the flames leaped up and Booth made a move for the door. Ruby and Corbett each used a Colt revolver and fired only one, lethal, bullet. Each victim survived a little over two hours without having a chance to utter any further significant words. This is extraordinary in itself, since single pistol bullets rarely kill their victims.

An autopsy was done on each man, but persistent and recurring suggestions were made, in each case, that the body should be exhumed to satisfy some new group of inquirers. In Booth's case they still want to

Fig. 146
page 361

see if the body really has a broken leg, and in Oswald's case whether there is evidence of a childhood mastoid infection, and a scar from an accidentally inflicted pistol bullet wound, incurred while he was in Japan, in the Marines. Critics ignore the fact that Oswald's pre- and post-Russia chirography match precisely.

There were also many odd associations and opposites which are of interest. President Kennedy's secretary, whose name was Mrs. Lincoln, had a husband known as Abe. President Lincoln had a secretary named John Kennedy, a former police chief from New York City, who was acting as his adviser and who had warned him not to go to the theater than night. Mrs. Lincoln had told President Kennedy not to make the trip to Dallas.

President Kennedy was shot in a Ford product—a Lincoln automobile —and Lincoln was shot in Ford's Theater.

Oswald fired from a warehouse and ran to a theater, while Booth fired in a theater and fled to a warehouse—a tobacco barn.

President Kennedy knew a Dr. Charles Taft (the son of President Taft), and President Lincoln knew a Dr. Charles Taft, who, in fact, was the second doctor to reach him at Ford's Theater, in the vain attempt to save his life.

On the day each President was assassinated, two young women, both

Fig. 147
page 362

raised in New York State, but in different centuries, developed amnesia from witnessing the bloody attack. Miss Fanny Seward, daughter of Secretary of State Seward, had no memory of many of the things she was observed to say and do during the excitement of seeing her father and brother attacked before her eyes. A century later, Mrs. Jacqueline Kennedy remembered absolutely nothing about being precipitated out onto the lid of the trunk of the car after her husband was shot.

We must be careful, of course, not to attach more than the proper amount of significance to these similarities; we must, in effect, know how to recognize simple coincidence when we see it.

Many of the Kennedy and Lincoln similarities and associations had to do with the fact that the two Presidents were shot almost exactly 100 years apart (ninety-eight and a half years), and have no magical significance beyond that fact. Our presidential terms are still four years in length, and our traditional paths to the presidency wind through similar congressional routes, particularly in families with political backgrounds. The similarities in the numbers of letters of various names is not surprising considering that it is the same civilization and the same country and that our language and name lengths fall into certain patterns of convenience, habit, and custom that are slow to change. The similarities in names may reflect the static quality of names in the United States, now that immigration has slowed.

The similar personal characteristics of these two distinguished families, the Lincolns and the Kennedys, probably reflect only the traditional directions in which politically oriented, well-motivated, highly successful young Americans went to fulfill their traditional roles in a society that obviously has not changed all that much in 100 years. The similarity in numbers of births and deaths of the various children was a little surprising, considering the advances in living conditions in the interim, but there would not appear to be any magical influence at work.

Successful assassins usually prepare the site for their deed very carefully, and try hard to surprise their victims, shooting them in the head if at all possible, and practicing their act ahead of time. That firearms were used as the instruments of all four of these killings merely reflects that this is the traditional way assassins act in the United States. It confirms that we Americans have been a gun-oriented society ever since the Colt and the Winchester became instruments of conquest of our wilderness. That the techniques of assassins have not changed much in a century may also reflect the fact that our Western books, motion pictures, and television films still heavily extol the Colt revolver.

Both Ruby and Corbett demonstrated a little more than conventional technique in shooting their men. Ruby kept his pistol arm low and protected by his body, in approved police-combat style, as he leaned forward in his lunge at Oswald. He did not extend his arm at full length, as an amateur might, where it could have been seen and knocked aside. Furthermore, he appears in the photographs to be using his middle finger to pull the trigger. This maneuver is sometimes used by sophisticated pistol shooters, if they find that a particular pistol balances better when fired with the middle finger.

Corbett, likewise, showed the expert technique of an accomplished cavalryman by using his left forearm, held transversely, on which to steady the barrel of his pistol, as he aimed through the crack in the side of the barn.

Other societies use their own traditional weapons. In Japan, for example, even recently, we have seen razor-sharp traditional samurai swords thrust into the abdomens of politicians who were making statements before the television cameras. In Beirut and Tel Aviv, submachine guns are preferred. In Lucrezia Borgia's day, it was poison. But in America, it has always been the revolver or the carbine. There was a popular saying in the old American West that while it was God who created all men equal, it was Samuel Colt who kept them that way.

The worrisome question that remains, after all our investigations, all our observations, all our musings, is this: What *causes* this recurring illness of the mind that we have seen surface in these two impressively similar demonstrations, 100 years apart? Certainly the loss of a father's guidance and the envy of the two older siblings are suggestively similar factors focusing our attention on the importance of family guidance and affection. The stresses of our increasingly competitive society, staggering now under a stifling mantle of government overregulation, will continue to create the kind of stresses that exploded in these two dramatic examples of what dedicated men can do to others.

The actions of the assassins and the assassins' assassins seem to reflect primarily the pathological compulsions of this type of person. People of this type are striving to demonstrate that they deserve more recognition than their peers and hope that through one extravagant, devastating act, aided by the media, they can become world-renowned. They can demonstrate that they, above all others, were the ones who were the ultimate achievers in the sense that they had really *done* something for their cause, by killing the leading opponent. The fact that these opponents represented the political system made these assassinations a politically oriented matter; but it appears that it was primarily the quest for recognition that motivated these killers, far more than any personal animosity they felt toward the victims. It takes a certain type of personality to accomplish a violent, morbid act, intelligent enough and cool enough to circumvent the protective screen, and willing to give up his life, if necessary, to become famous.

My Final Impressions

The discovery that impressed me the most was how easy these assassinations were to commit. It quickly became apparent to me that if our American presidential candidates and Presidents are to avoid being assassinated by fanatics or disgruntled persons seeking instant deification by the media, and who have free access in our open society, they will have to change the degree to which they expose themselves to the possibilities of direct gunfire. If amateurs can do it this easily, professionals would find it very easy indeed.

I hope that this book, if it has done nothing else, has provided some hard facts, based on actual experiments, illustrated with photographs, showing what happened when Oswald's two bullets struck the occupants of the presidential car. I have tried to strip away the smoke screen of speculations and unproved theories, and to show that the apparent disparities are easily reconciled with the experimental findings when the experiments are done in depth.

It appeared to me that there was a need for this work. The ballistic experiments done for the Warren Commission were conducted with the faulty information that the bullet hole in the back of President Kennedy's head was four inches lower than it actually was. Neither the investigators for the Rockefeller (CIA) Commission nor the more recent investigators for the House of Representatives Select Committee on Assassinations attempted to do any medical or anatomical ballistic experiments to test the effects of these bullets on bones or tissues. This area has been neglected.

The efforts of the assassination-buff critics to jostle the public into suspecting a larger plot were the same a century ago as they are now. Artful innuendo to suggest the involvement of other, unspecified, plotters has been used to intrigue Kennedy assassination buffs, but to date it has not even approached the high art to which writer Otto Eisenschiml raised it in intriguing us about the Lincoln affair.

When some enthusiastic critic tells you even such simple things as that Oswald's rifle was no good or that the ammunition could not possibly fire that well, you are helpless. If you have no way to try it for yourself, then you have no way to know what is the truth. I have tried with these pages to demonstrate what happens when you bring to bear the laboratory and X-ray facilities of a large, modern medical center on the points of confusion that are still susceptible to laboratory testing. By doing this, it is possible, with reasonable certainty, to determine what the facts really were. I hope this has been of some help.

In retrospect, the events at Dallas were such an impressive replay of the same events, bringing up the same questions that occurred after the assassination of President Lincoln, that it is almost startling. The similarities are worth this second look.

This book provides some additional facts, filling in some of the gaps left by the Warren Commission. It tells why I switched from wondering if there might be a wider plot, to having no doubt that Oswald did it by himself.

It points out the many similarities between the two assassinations, but particularly the similarities on points of medical interest.

It is a replay of history.

SELECT BIBLIOGRAPHY

LINCOLN

BRENNAN, JOHN C. *Pictorial Primer Having to Do with the Assassination of Abraham Lincoln.* Laurel, Md.: Minuteman Press, 1979.

BRYAN, GEORGE S. *The Great American Myth.* New York: Carrick & Evans, 1940.

CHACONAS, JOAN L. *The Search for J. Wilkes Booth (April 14-26, 1865).* Clinton, Md.: The Surratt Society, 1980.

Criminal Court of the District of Columbia. *The Trial of John Surratt.* Washington, D.C.: U.S. Government Printing Office, 1867.

EISENSCHIML, OTTO. *In the Shadow of Lincoln's Death.* New York: Wilfred Funk, 1940.

———. *Why Was Lincoln Murdered?* Boston: Little, Brown & Company, 1937.

GUNNING, T. B. "Fracture of the Jaw." *Independent Practitioner* 1 (1880): 568.

HALL, JAMES O. *Notes on the John Wilkes Booth Escape Route.* Clinton, Md.: The Surratt Society, 1980.

HANCHETT, WILLIAM. "Booth's Diary." *Journal of the Illinois State Historical Society,* February 1979.

———. "The Eisenschiml Thesis." *Civil War History* 25 (1979).

KAUFFMAN, MIKE. "Fort Lesley McNair and the Lincoln Conspirators." *The Lincoln Herald* 80 (1979).

KEISER, DAVID S. "Presidential Parallels," Greensboro, N.C.: unpublished.

KIMMEL, STANLEY. *The Mad Booths of Maryland.* Indianapolis: Bobbs-Merrill, 1940.

KUNHARDT, DOROTHY and PHILIP B. *Twenty Days.* New York: Harper & Row, 1965.

LATTIMER, JOHN K. "Similarities in Fatal Woundings of John Wilkes Booth and Lee Harvey Oswald." *New York State Journal of Medicine* 66 (1966): 1782-1794.

———. "The Stabbing of Lincoln's Secretary of State on the Night the President Was Shot." *Journal of the American Medical Association* 192 (1965): 99-106.

———. "The Wound That Killed Lincoln." *Journal of the American Medical Association* 187 (1964): 480-489.

LATTIMER, JOHN K., BARTLETT, CHARLES E., HUMPHREY, W. MERRILL. "An Historic Case of Jaw Fracture." *Journal of the American Dental Association* 76 (1968): 102-106.

MOORE, GUY W. *The Case of Mrs. Surratt: Her Controversial Trial and Execution for Conspiracy in the Lincoln Assassination.* Norman, Okla.: University of Oklahoma Press, 1954.

OLDROYD, OSBORN H. *The Assassination of Abraham Lincoln.* Washington, D.C.: privately printed, 1901.

OSTENDORF, L., and KEISER, D. S., "Presidential Parallels in Pictures," *The Treasure Chest*, 1964.

PITMAN, BENN. *The Assassination of Abraham Lincoln and the Trial of the Conspirators.* Facsimile Edition. New York: Funk & Wagnalls, 1954.

ROSCOE, THEODORE. *The Web of Conspiracy.* Englewood Cliffs, N.J.: Prentice-Hall, 1959.

KENNEDY

ALVAREZ, LUIS W. *A Physicist Examines the Kennedy Assassination Film.* Lawrence Berkeley Laboratory, University of California, preprint LBL-3884, July 1975.

BLAIR, JOAN, and BLAIR, CLAY. *The Search for JFK.* New York: Berkley Publishing, 1976.

BLOOMGARDEN, HENRY S. *The Gun: A Biography of the Gun That Killed John F. Kennedy.* New York: Grossman Publishers, 1975.

BROMBERG, WALTER. *Crime and the Mind.* Rev. ed. New York: The Macmillan Co., 1965.

CARNES, DR. WILLIAM H., FISHER, DR. RUSSELL S., MORGAN, DR. RUSSELL H., MORITZ, DR. ALLEN R. "Report of the Panel of Forensic Pathologists on the Autopsy Findings, Photographs and X-rays [of President Kennedy]." *The New York Times*, January 17, 1969.

CURRY, JESSE. JFK Assassination File, Dallas, 1969.

HANSON, WILLIAM H. *The Shooting of John F. Kennedy.* San Antonio: The Naylor Company, 1969.

KAPLAN, JOHN, and WALTZ, J. R. *The Trial of Jack Ruby.* New York: The Macmillan Co., 1965.

LATTIMER, GARY, LATTIMER, J. K., LATTIMER, JON. "The Kennedy-Connally One Bullet Theory: Further Circumstantial and Experimental Evidence." *Medical Times*, November 1974, 33-56.

LATTIMER, J. K. "Factors in the Death of President Kennedy." *Journal of the American Medical Association* 198 (1966): 327-333.

———. "Observations Based on a Review of the Autopsy Photographs, X-rays and Related Materials of the Late President John F. Kennedy." *Resident and Staff Physician*, May 1972.

LATTIMER, J. K., and LATTIMER, JON. "The Kennedy-Connally Single Bullet Theory: A Feasibility Study." *International Surgery* 50 (1968): 524-532.

LATTIMER, J. K. LATTIMER, J., LATTIMER, G. "Further Information about the Autopsy of President Kennedy." *The Forensic Science Gazette* (Dallas). 4 (1973): 3-9

LATTIMER, J. K., LATTIMER, JON, LATTIMER, GARY. "Could Oswald Have Shot President Kennedy: Further Ballistic Studies." *Bulletin of the New York Academy of Medicine* 48 (1972): 513-524.

————. "An Experimental Study of the Backward Movement of President Kennedy's Head." *Surgery, Gynecology and Obstetrics* 142 (1976): 246-254.

McMILLAN, PRISCILLA JOHNSON. *Marina and Lee*. New York: Harper & Row, Publishers, 1977.

NEWMAN, ALBERT H. *The Assassination of John F. Kennedy: The Reasons Why*. New York: Clarkson N. Potter, 1970.

NICHOLS, J. M. "President Kennedy's Adrenals." *Journal of the American Medical Association* 201 (1967): 129-130.

OSWALD, ROBERT and others. *Lee: A Portrait of Lee Harvey Oswald by His Brother*. New York: Coward-McCann, 1967.

"Three Patients at Parkland." *Texas State Journal of Medicine* 60 (1964): 60-74.

U.S. House of Representatives. *Investigation of the Assassination of President John F. Kennedy*. Hearings before the Select Committee on Assassinations. Washington, D.C.: U.S. Government Printing Office, 1979.

Warren Commission. *Hearings and Reports of the President's Commission on the Assassination of President Kennedy*. Washington, D.C.: U.S. Government Printing Office, 1964.

INDEX

(The figures in italics refer to illustrations and captions.)

61, *63*, 64, 66-67, 88, 324, 337, 360
Crenshaw, Dr. Charles A., 325
Cuba: Oswald's interest in, 138-39, 306, 353
Curtis, Dr. Edward, 34, 36, *37*, 38, *39*, 72
Cutler, Robert, 281

Daily Worker, The, 132
Dallas, Tex., 140; Kennedy motorcade in, *14*, 123, 142-43, 146, 166, *167*, 184, 281-82, 306-07, 309, 331-32, 355
Dallas Bar Association, 316, 317
Dallas police headquarters, 316-17, *318*, 320, *321*, 322, 324, 360
Day, Leon, 295, *297*
Dealey Plaza, Dallas, *167*, 168, 259, 306-07, 309, 331-32
Delgado, Lt. Nelson, 126
de Morenschildt, George, 137-38, 356
Denny, Kleber, 126, *127*
Deringer, Henry, 48, *49*
derringer pistol. *See* pistols, derringer
Doherty, Lt. Edward P., 58, 60-61, 62
Douglas, Stephen A., 351
Douglas, William O., 353

Ebersole, Comdr. John H., xx, 155
Eckert, Maj. Thomas T., 19, 21, 58
Egypt, 107
Eisenschiml, Otto, 21, 339, 366; *Why Was Lincoln Murdered,* 73

face wounds of Seward, 94-95, *96*, 97, *98*, 99
Federal Bureau of Investigation (FBI): and Kennedy assassination, 178, 186, 202, 204, 209, 271, 282, 285, 287, 289, 357; and Oswald, 135, 137, 140
Ferguson, James P., 46
Ferree, Pvt. Sheridan, 48, *49*
Finck, Lt. Col. Pierre, 155, 158, 183-88, 228
Fisher, Dr. Russell S., 194
Fitzgerald, J. F., 351
Forbes, Charles, 19
Ford's Theater, *20*, 119, 120; Booth's familiarity with, 6, 10, 13, *14*, 15, *18*, 19; Lincoln's assassination at, *20*, 21, *23*, 24,

25, *26-27*, *196*, 363; Lincoln theater party at, 13, *14*, 15, *16*, 17, *18*, 19
Ford's Theater Museum: Booth's left boot in, *53*, 84; Booth's pistols and knife in, 48, 132; Payne's revolver in, 104
forensic panel (1968): review of Kennedy autopsy material by, 194, 198, 200, 212, 228, 241
Forgett, Val, 78
Fort Jefferson: federal prison at, 110-11, 119
Fort Worth, Tex., 124, 126
Frazier, Robert, 204, 287
Frazier, Wesley, 140, 143, 145
Fritz, Captain, 316-17

Gardner, Alexander, 7
Garrett, Richard, 57, 60, 65
Garrett boys (Robert and William), 60, 61, 68-69, 73, 74
Garrett farm: Booth's hideout and assassination at, 57, 60-62, 64-66, 67-69
Garrick Works, 104
Gautier's Restaurant, 10
Giesecke, Dr. A. H., Jr., 151, 152, 161
Glenwood Cemetary, Washington, 119
Goldin, Harry, 353
Gouldman, Izora, 58
Graham, Billy, 353
Graham, William Mentor, 353
Grant, Gen. Ulysses S.: in Civil War, 5, 7, 12-13; planned to attend Lincoln theater party, 13, *14*, 15, *16*, 17, *18*, 19, 27, 46
Grant, Mrs. Ulysses S., 13, 15
Great Britain, 3
Greenfield Village Museum, 195
Greenmount Cemetery, Baltimore, 70, 119
Greer, Bill, 192
Gregory, Dr. Charles F., 162-63, 276, 277
Guinn, Dr. Vincent P., 305
Gunning, Dr. Thomas Brian, *96*, 97; interdental splint of, 97, 99-100, *101*, 102
Gurley, Rev. Dr. Phineas, 32
Gustafson, Dr. Gerald E., 325

Hall, Dr. James C., 34
Hall, James O., 19
Hanchett, Dr. William, 21, 52
Hancock, Gen. Winfield Scott, 113

hanging of Lincoln conspirators, 8, 10, *105*, 106, 110, 113, *114*, *115*, 116, *117*, 118-19; gallows, 111, *112*, 113, 116, 118-19; graves, 118; noose, 113, 116, 118
Hansell (State Dept. messenger), 93
Hanson, Col. William H.: *Shooting of John F. Kennedy, The,* 253, 258
Harbin, Thomas, 57-58
Harris, Clara, 17, *18*, *20*, 21, 345
Harris, Senator and Mrs. Ira, 17
Hartogs, Dr. Renatus, 124
Hartranft, Gen. John F., 10, *114*, 116
Harvey and Marr (undertakers), 119
Hawk, Harry, 21, *23*
Hay, John, 6
head wounds, 42, 43-44, *45*, 207; from high-speed bullets, 212, 214, 218, 226, 255. *See also* Kennedy head wound; Lincoln head wound
Helpern, Dr. Milton, 43-44, *45*, 177, 290
Herndon, William, 40
Herold, David, 119; accompanied Booth on escape route, 8, 13, 50-52, *54*, 55, 57, 60, 93; as conspirator of Booth, 8, 10-11, 13, 89, *105*, 106; surrender of, 60, 62, 64, 65; trial and hanging of, 66, *105*, 110, 111, *112*, *114*, *115*, 116, *117*, 118
Hill, Clint, 147, 247
Hoch, Paul, xx, 249
Hodges, Dr. R. N., 67
Holt, Judge Joseph, 66
Hosty, James, Jr., 140, 357
Hotel Metropol, 128, *130*
House Select Committee on Assassinations, xx, 360, 366; and Kennedy autopsy materials, 190-91, 194, *199*, *201*, 202, *212*, *221*, 241; and Mannlicher-Carcano bullets, 134, *175*, 176, 282-83, 291; and possibility of fourth shot, 331-32; and rifle, 305
Huber, Father Oscar, 153
Hughes, Sarah, 154
Humes, Comdr. James J., xx, 155-56, 158, 182, 183-90, 192, 194-95, *196*, 198, 212, 214, 220, 224, 228, 255
Hunt, Dr. Jackie H., 151, 152

221; entry, 156, 158, *167,* 178, 179, 182, 188, 209-10, *211,* 214, *216,* 218, 228, *254;* exit, 156, *157,* 179, 186, 188, 210, 214, *216,* 249-51, 253, 255, *256;* extruding and fragmented brain tissue from, 149, 150, 151, 152, 160-61, *167, 174,* 186, *213,* 220, 248, 249-51, 253, *256;* jet-recoil effect from, xx, *174,* 179, 228, 229, 253, 255, *256, 257,* 258-59, 331; neurological reflex from, xx, *174,* 243, 255, 258-59; path of bullet, 188, *199,* 214, 218; photographs of, 197, 210, 228; skull fractures, flap, and fragments from, 147, 156, *157,* 158, *174,* 179, 182, 185-86, 188, 190, *199,* 210, 212, *213,* 214, *216,* 218, 228, 248, 251, *254,* 255, 256, 258; X-rays of, 198, *199,* 210, 212, 214, *215, 216,* 228, 255, 258. *See also* Lattimer studies of Kennedy assassination, head wound
Kennedy neck wound, 149, 150, 151, 166, *169,* 184, 207, 290; drawings of, 200, *201,* 202; entry, xx, 146, 153, 154, 155-56, *167,* 185, 186-87, 188, 200, 202, 209, 267, *268;* exit, 146, 153, 154, 156, 183, 185, 186-87, 188, 200, 228-31, *235,* 239, 267, *268,* 331; path of bullet, xvii, 156, 179, *180,* 182, 186, 200, 202, *203,* 208-09, 231, 241; photographs of, 197, 200, *201;* reaction of elbows to (Thorburn's position), xx, 147, *167,* 168, *169,* 170, *174,* 182-83, 229, 240, 241, 243, *244,* 245-46, 247, 279, 281; and roll of soft tissue, 179, 200, *203,* 267; spinal cord damage from, xx, 240-41, 243, *244,* 245-46, 281, 331; X-rays of, 202, *203,* 245-46, 267. *See also* Lattimer studies of Kennedy assassination, neck wound
Kent, William T., 28, 48, *49*
King, Dr. Africanus, 30
King, Martin Luther, Jr., 331, 360
Kirkwood House, 94, 106
Kline's mail-order house, 132
knife: bowie, used by Payne, xx, 91, *103,* 104, 106; used by Booth, *20,* 21, *24,* 26, 48
Knowles, Dr. John, 66

Lahey Clinic, 222
Lattimer, Gary, xvii, xviii, 78, 241, 292, 294-95, 298-99, 301, *302,* 304-05. *See also* individual Lattimer studies
Lattimer, Dr. J. K., xvii-xxi, 158, 331; collection of, xviii-xix, *22,* 40, *90,* 106, 248, 292, *293,* 294, *319,* 320. *See also* individual Lattimer studies
Lattimer, Jon, xvii, 287, 289, 292, 294-95, 298-99, 301, *302,* 304-05. *See also* individual Lattimer studies
Lattimer studies on Booth assassination, 66-67, 72-75, 77-78, *79,* 80, *81, 82,* 83-84, *85, 86, 87,* 88
Lattimer studies on Kennedy assassination, xvii, 179, 182-83, 194, 198, *227,* 365-66; bullet holes in clothes, 198, 202, 204, *205, 206,* 207, 209, 231-32, *233, 234, 235, 236, 237, 238, 239, 242, 268;* Carcano rifle, xix, 292, 294-95, *296,* 298-99, *300,* 301, *302,* 304-05, *308;* Connally wounds, xx, *164, 206,* 232, 233, 234, 236, 237, 261, *265,* 267, 269, 271, 273, 276-77, 283, 287; firing experiments, *136, 201, 206, 213, 219,* 235, *238,* 239, 241, 250-51, *252,* 253, *257;* firing experiments on bullet 399, xx, *164,* 229-32, 233, 234, 236, 237, 264, *265,* 267, *268,* 269, *270,* 271, *273,* 276-77, *278,* 282-85, 287-91, 305; head wound, xx, 209-10, *211,* 212, *213,* 214, *215, 216,* 218, *219,* 220, *221,* 249-51, *252,* 253, *254,* 255, *256, 257,* 258-59, 331; neck (back) wound, 198, 200, *201, 206,* 208-09, 229-32, *233, 234, 235, 236, 237, 238,* 239-41, *242,* 243, *244,* 245-46, 267, *268,* 276, 331; on restricted material, xvii-xx, 197-98; tracheostomy wound, 200, 202
Lattimer studies on Lincoln assassination, 40, 42-44, *45*
Leale, Dr. Charles: treated Lincoln, *24,* 27-28, *29,* 30, 32-34, *39,* 40, *41,* 48, *49,* 69
Lee, Robert E., 5, 6, *7, 9,* 12-13, 110, 197, 354
leg fracture. *See* Booth leg fracture
leg wound. *See* Connally leg wound

Level Plains scaffold, 116
Liebermann, Dr., 34
Life magazine, 279
Lincoln, Abraham, *7, 23;* Booth's plan to kidnap, 6, 8, *9,* 10-12, 51, 110; and Civil War, 5, 7, 47; enjoyment of theater of, 6, 12, 21, 27; eye muscle problem of, *349, 350;* fatalistic attitude of, 19, 47, *350;* mementos of, *37, 38, 49,* 195, *196,* 197, *347;* physique of, 38, 40, *350;* similarities to Kennedy of, *347, 349,* 350-51, 353
Lincoln, Evelyn, 142, 190-91, 363
Lincoln, F. W., 351
Lincoln, Levi, Sr., 351
Lincoln, Mary Todd, 13, 15, 17, 19, *20,* 21, *22,* 26, 345, *348,* 350; reaction to assassination of, 27, 28, 32, *41, 348,* 350
Lincoln, Robert Todd, 351
Lincoln, Tad, 32, 40
Lincoln assassination: actual shooting, *20,* 21, 26-27; Booth's plan and preparations for, 7, 8, *9,* 10, 12-13, *14,* 15, 17, 19, *20,* 21, 354, *358;* conspiracy theory of, 21, 73-74, 75, *76,* 77, 339, 360, 366; funeral of, 58, 197; mortal wounding of, 27, 28, *29,* 30, 46-47, *347;* moved to Petersen's rooming house, 27-28, *29,* 30, *31;* and presidential guard, 19; pronounced dead, 28, 32, 33-34; questions about, 44, 46; reopening of inquiry about, 10, 331, 357, 360; similarities to Kennedy assassination, xxi, 5, 13, 15, *37,* 111, 142, 154, 194-95, *196,* 197, 207, 344-45, *346,* 350, 363-64, 366; survived for nine hours, 28, *29,* 32, 33, 47; suspicions of plot reported, 8, 106; theater party, 13, *14,* 15, *16,* 17, *18,* 19. *See also* Lattimer studies on Lincoln assassination; Lincoln autopsy
Lincoln autopsy, 34-36, 38; ball recovered, 27, 33, 36; conflicting statements about, xxi, 35-36, 38, *39,* 40, 42-43; partial nature of, 34-35, 158, 350; similarities to Kennedy autopsy, 35, 156, 158. *See also* Lincoln head wound
Lincoln conspirators trial (1865), 19, 51, 68, 102, 106, 108, 110-

11, 357; harsh treatment of prisoners, 111, 317; by military commission, 10, 15, 66, 73, *105*, 111, 113; Pitman's account of, 104, 106; testimony at, 36, 62, 64-66. *See also* hanging of Lincoln conspirators

Lincoln head wound: brain damage from, 27, 28, 30, 32, 33, 40, 42-43, 46-47, *49*, *347*; bullet fragment in, 34, 36, *37*, 42, 47, *216*, 228; discharge of brain tissue from, 33, 42; entry, 27, 28, 34, 36, *37*, 38, 42, 44, 46; examination and treatment of, *24*, 27-28, *29*, 30, *31*, 32-34, 40, 47, *350*; Lattimer's studies on, 40, 42-44, *45*; path of ball, 32, 33, 34-36, 38, *39*, 42, 46-47; position of ball, 32, 33, 35-36, 38, *39*, 40, *41*, 42; roofs of eye sockets fractured, 43-44, *45*

Lloyd, John M., 8, 11, 51
Loeb, Dr. Robert, 223
Lucas, Charles, 57
Lucas, William, 57

Macfarlane, Michael, 78, 232
Mannlicher-Carcano rifle. *See* Carcano 6.5 mm carbine
Marine Corps, U.S., 355; Oswald in, 124, 126, 128, 129, 292, *293*, 294, 333, 355, *357*; Oswald's fingerprints from enlistment in, 361
Marshall, Burke, xix, 191
Marx, Karl, 126, 139
Marxism. *See* Communism
Maryland Historical Trust, 120
Massachusetts General Hospital, 58, *59*, 66
Mathews, John, 52
May, Dr. J. F., 34, 69
McClelland, Dr. Robert N., 150, 151, 152, 324-25
McDonald, M. N., 314, 316
McElroy, Dr. Keith, 226
McLain, H. B., 331-32
McMillan, Officer, 337
McMillan, Priscilla Johnson, *56*, 124, 129, 132; *Marina and Lee*, xx, 332-33
Medical Times, The, 158
Merrill, Dr. (Booth's dentist), 69
Merritt, Dr. Houston H., 240
Mexico City, Mex.: Oswald's trip to, 139, 140, 306
Militant, The, 132

Minsk, USSR, 129
Morgan, Dr. Russell H., 194, 241
Moritz, Dr. Alan, 194
Mosby, John Singleton, 6, 57, 89
Mostofi, Dr. F. K., 83
Mount Olivet Cemetery, Washington, D.C., 119
Mudd, F. L., 263
Mudd, Dr. Richard, *109*, 120
Mudd, Dr. Samuel A., 6, 10, 119-20; treated Booth, 51-52, *53*, 84, 108, *109*, 110; trial and imprisonment of, *53*, 66, 108, *109*, 110-11, 119
Mudd, Mrs. Samuel, *53*, 108, 110-11
Murray, Martha, 13
Mutter Medical Museum (Philadelphia), 72

Nanjemoy Creek, 57
National Archives: Kennedy assassination material in, 178, 190-91, 194, 198, 232, 276, 285, 292; restrictions on Kennedy material, xvii-xx, 159, 183, 194
National Intelligencer, Washington, 52
National Park Service, *31*, 38
Navy Yard Bridge, 8, 26, 50, 355
Nebel, Long John, 124
neck wounds, gun: entry, 80, *81*, 83-84, *87*; exit, 84, *87*; from high-speed bullets, 230-31, 267; in suicides, 78, 80, 83-84. *See also* Booth neck wound; Kennedy neck wound
neck wounds, knife: of Seward, 94-95, 97, 99
Nelaton probe: used to examine Lincoln, 30, 32, 33, 36, 47
Nelson, Robert, 104
Newman, Albert H.: *Assassination of President Kennedy, The*, 310
New Orleans, La.: Oswald in, 124, 126, 138-39
New York City, N.Y.: Oswalds in, 123-24
New York Herald, 9
New York Hospital, 222, 224
New York Journal of Medicine, 97
New York Times, xviii, xx
Nichols, H. Louis, 317
Nichols, Dr. John Marshall, 271, 272, 289-90
Nixon, Richard, 351
Norris, Dr. Basil, 97

O'Laughlin, Michael, 119; as conspirator of Booth, 10-11; trial and imprisonment of, 66, 110, 111, 119
Olivier, Dr. Alfred J., *219*, 334
Olson, Don, xx, 249
O'Neill, Francis X., 186
Ordnance Optics Company, 132, 232, 250, 295
Oswald, Audrey Marina Rachel, 140
Oswald, John, 123, 355
Oswald, June Lee, 131, 139, 140
Oswald, Lee Harvey: assassination plan and preparations of, 15, 129, 143, 145, 170, *172*, 307, 354, *358*; attempted escape and capture of, 309-14, *315*, 316, 330, 339, 354-55, 363; attempted to shoot Walker, 132, 133-35, *136*, 137-38, 145, 306, 333, *356*; autopsy of, 327-29, *361*, 363; character and personality of, 5, 123, 126, 137, 313, 332-33, 355, 357; as Communist sympathizer, 123, 124, 126, 132, 137-39, 143, 306, *315*, 316-17, 337, 353, 354; craving for fame of, 5, *56*, 67, 123, 126, 137-38, 143, 306, 314, *315*, 316, 324, 353, 354, 357; at Dallas police headquarters, 316-17, *318*, 320, *321*, 322, 324; detainment of, 50, 309-10, 355; employed at Texas School Book Depository, *14*, 140, 142, 143, 145; firing position of, xvii, 128, 145-46, *167*, 170, *172*, *173*, 182, 209, 228, 248, *293*, 294-95, *296*, 298-99, 307; firing practice and marksmanship of, 126, 128, 132, 139, 248, 277, 292, *293*, 294, 298, 304, 307; hand prints and shirt fibers on rifle, 282, *303*, 305, 330; identification of body of, *361*; interest in Cuba of, 138-39, 306, 353; journal of, 357; learned necessity of firing multiple shots, 135, 145; Mannlicher-Carcano rifle of, 126, 128, 131-32, 145-47, 155, 170, 171, 176, 198, *216*, 239, 250, 271, 281-82, 285, *286*, 289, 291, 292, *293*, 294-95, *296*, 297, 298-99, *300*, 301, *302*, *303*, 304-05, 307, *308*, 309, 330, 334, *356*; in Marine Corps, 124, 126, 128, 129, 292, *293*, 294, 333, 355, 357; marriage and

family of, 129, 131, 132, 134, 138, 139, 140, 143-44, 317, 330, *356, 361;* moved to Soviet Union, 128-29, *130,* 131, 333; note to Marina of, 135, 137, 138, 333; plan to kill Walker of, 133-34, 138; proposals to exhume body of, 70-71, 363; psychiatric problems of, 124, 333; purchase of rifle by, 131-32; Ruby's assassination of, *4,* 67, *315,* 317, *321, 322, 323,* 324, *326,* 335, *336,* 337, *338,* 339, *358, 359,* 360, 363, 364; shooting of Kennedy by, 123, 146-47, 166, *167,* 168, *169,* 170-71, *174,* 184, *211,* 226, 247, 260-61, 279, *280,* 281-83, 309, 365; shooting of Tippit by, 310-13, 316, 334; similarities to Booth of, *4,* 5, 13, *14,* 15, 50, 51, *56,* 67, 123, 132, 137, 138, 141, *144,* 295, 306, 309-10, 316, 324, *338,* 339, 353-55, 357, *358, 359,* 360, 363; sling for rifle of, 51, 128, 132, 146, 294, 295, 297, 298, 307, *356;* suicide attempt of, 128-29; treated at Parkland Hospital, *323,* 324-25, *326,* 327; tried to renounce citizenship, 128-29, *130;* trip to Mexico of, 139, 140, 306; weapons of, 126, 128, 131-32, 143, 194, 295, 310-11, 313-14, 316, 333-34, *356;* youth of, 123-24, *125, 127,* 197, 333
Oswald, Marina: Lee's note to in case of capture or death, 135, 137, 138, 333; marriage and family of, 129, 131, 132, 134, 138, 139, 140, 143-44, 317, 330, *356, 361;* on Oswald, 332-33; testimony of, 304
Oswald, Robert, 128, 131, 294, 304, 317, 333, 355
Oswald, Robert E. Lee, 123, 353
Oswald, Mrs. Robert E. Lee, 123-24, 128, 131, 294, 317, 357, *361*
Our American Cousin, 13, *14, 16, 18,* 21, *23*

Paine, Ruth, 138, 139, 140, 142, 317, 354
Parker, John, 19
Parkland Hospital, 147, 154; Audrey Marina Rachel Oswald born at, 140; Connally treated at, 161-64, 260, 263,

346; Kennedy treated at, 148-53, 184, 230-31; Oswald treated at, *323,* 324-25, *326,* 327
Payne, Lewis, 6, 8, 89, 108, *109,* 119, 354; arrest of, 8, 93; attempt to assassinate Seward, 8, 13, 89, 91-95, 97, 102, *103,* 104, 106-07, *362;* hanging of, 8, *105,* 110, *112, 114, 115,* 116, *117,* 118; and plan to kidnap Lincoln, 6, 10-11; trial and imprisonment of, 66, *90,* 93, 95, 107, 111
Perry, Dr. Malcolm O., 149, 150, 151, 152, 154, 184, 186, 200, *201,* 209, 230, *268,* 324-25
Peters, Dr. Paul, xvi, 150, 151, 152
Petersen's rooming house, 27-28, *29,* 30, *31*
Peterson, Dr. Harold, xxi
Philadelphia Medical and Surgical Reporter, 32-33
pistols, derringer: Lincoln assassination weapon, *20,* 21, 36, 48, 49; type of Oswald's, 126. *See also* Colt revolvers; revolvers
Pitman account of conspirators' trial, 104, 106
Port Conway, Va., 57
Port Royal, Va., 57, 60
Potomac River: Booth's escape across, 55, 57
powder. *See* carbines, experiments with; Colt revolvers, experiments with
Powell, Lewis Thornton. *See* Payne, Lewis
Preprint LBL 3884, 250
press, 73, 177; announcement of Kennedy motorcade route in, 13, *14,* 142-43, *144,* 306-07, 354, *358;* announcement of Lincoln theater party in, 13, *14, 144,* 354, *358*

Quesenberry, Elizabeth, 57

Rappahannock River: Booth's escape across, 57, 58
Rath, Capt. Christian (hangman), 10, *112,* 113, *114,* 116, *117,* 118, 119
Rathbone, Maj. Henry R., 17, 21, *29,* 55, 345; knifed by Booth, *20, 24, 26,* 27, 28, *346*
Raymond, Col. Julian, 74-75, 78, 83, 110

Resident & Staff Physician, 231
revolvers: Smith & Wesson of Oswald, 131-32, 295, 310-11, 313-14, 316, 334, *356;* Whitney navy of Payne, 90, 91, *103,* 104. *See also* Colt revolvers
Richards, A. C., 19
rifles, 51; M-1, 126. *See also* carbines
Risk, Dr. William, 327
Roberts, Mrs. (Oswald's landlady), 310
Robinson, Private (Seward's nurse), 91-93, 94, 97, 104
Rockefeller Commission, xx, 360, 365-66
rocking chair: of Kennedy, *347,* 350; of Lincoln, 15, 21, *22,* 195, *196, 347,* 350
Rollins, William and Bette, 58
Rose, Dr. Earl F., 153-54, 311-13, 327-29, 340-43
Rosenberg trial, 124
Rothstein, Dr. D. A., 357
Rountree, John W., 78
Ruby, Jack, 332; assassination of Oswald by, 67, *315,* 317, *321,* 322, *323,* 324, *326,* 335, *338,* 339, *359,* 360, 363, 364; autopsy report of, 340-43; at Dallas police headquarters, 316, 317, *318,* 320, *321,* 322, 324; doodles of, *319,* 320, 339; illness and death of, 339-40, 343-44; imprisonment and trial of, 339; revolver of, 335; similarities to Corbett of, *315,* 320, *321,* 324, 335, *336,* 337, *359,* 360; unstable character of, *315,* 320, 324, 337, 360
Rydberg, H. A., xx, 179, 200

Saucerote, Dr., 43, 44
Schaeffer, Dr. E. M., 72
Schlesinger, Dr. Edward B., xx, 240
Secret Service, 6, 11; and Kennedy assassination, 147-48, 187-88, 190, 192, 247, 259, 279, 301; and Lincoln assassination, 58, 74
Seldin, Dr. Donald, 150
Seward, Anna, 92
Seward, Maj. Augustus H., 92-93, 102, 104
Seward, Fanny, 91, 92-93, 97, 104, *362,* 363
Seward, Frederick, 91-92, 102, *103,* 104, 363
Seward, William H: jaw and